The Great Divestiture

The Great Divestiture

Evaluating the Welfare
Impact of the British
Privatizations 1979–1997

Massimo Florio

The MIT Press
Cambridge, Massachusetts
London, England

Massimo Florio is Professor of Public Economics and Jean Monnet Chair of Economics of European Integration, University of Milan. He has been a Visiting Scholar at the London School of Economics and in other British Universities. As an advisor to the European Commission, he has authored the EC "Guide to Cost-Benefit Analysis of Investment Projects" on behalf of the Regional Policy Evaluation Unit, and he has been involved as an independent expert in the economic evaluation of public policies and projects.

© 2004 Massachusetts Institute of Technology

This book was set in Palatino on 3B2 by Asco Typesetters, Hong Kong.

Printed and bound in the United States of America.

Library of Congress Cataloging-in-Publication Data

Florio, Massimo.
  The great divestiture : evaluating the welfare impact of the British privatizations,
  1979–1997 / Massimo Florio.
     p.   cm.
  Includes bibliographical references and index.
  ISBN 0-262-06240-2 (alk. paper)
    1. Public welfare—Great Britain. 2. Privatization—Great Britain. 3. Great Britain—
  Social policy—1979– 4. Public welfare. 5. Privatization. I. Title.

HV248.F59   2004
362.941′09′048—dc22   2003068893

To Antonella

Contents

Acknowledgments

I started to read and to think about British privatization more than ten years ago, when I was at the London School of Economics (LSE) as a visiting scholar in the Department of Economics. I enjoyed the atmosphere, a wonderful library, many seminars, and lively informal discussions with brilliant colleagues. In my LSE years, I had been working on research on public-investment appraisal in the United Kingdom under the Thatcher government. I discussed several times with Nicholas Stern the idea of applying social cost-benefit analysis to public divestitures. I started writing the book several years later, in 1998. The research was made possible by generous funds awarded to the Department of Economics, University of Milan, by the Italian Ministry of University. I am particularly grateful for the friendly encouragement and support of Giuseppe Bognetti (Head, Department of Economics, University of Milan) and Luigi Bernardi (University of Pavia).

A research draft was circulated in 2002 and tested against the comments of a number of experts. Papers related to the project were presented on several occasions, including the European Economic Association conference in Stockholm, the International Institute for Public Finance conferences in Helsinki and Prague, the Public Economics Theory conference in Paris, several annual meetings of the Italian Society for Public Economics in Pavia, and in many informal meetings, including one at the Department of Applied Economics at Cambridge University. Particularly helpful was the Milan European Economy Workshop, entirely devoted to a lively discussion of the research draft with British and Italian experts. Among those who were so generous as to invest some of their time in commenting on aspects of the research and the project, I wish to gratefully mention four anonymous referees by the MIT Press, who provided extremely competent advice, as well as Alan Bell (OFTEL), Elisabetta Bertero (LSE), Remi

Boelart (Limburg), Dieter Bös (Bonn), Bruno Bosco (Milan), Martin
Cave (Warwick), Daniele Checchi (Milan), Jonathan Leape (LSE), Rob-
ert Millward (Manchester), David Newbery (Cambridge), Roberto
Pedersini (Milan), Diego Piacentino (Macerata), Michael Pollitt (Cam-
bridge), Pippo Ranci (Italian Authority for Electricity and Gas), Mal-
colm Sawyer (Leeds), Robin Simpson (National Consumer Council,
UK), Jeremy Turk (BT), and Catherine Waddams Price (East Anglia).
Their comments and their criticism were really helpful in the process of
writing the final text. I am also grateful to Chris Austin and Agnes
Bonnet (Rail Strategic Authority), Richard Budd (Regulatory Economics, BT), Robin Cohen (formerly with London Economics), Michael
Jones (Union Energy, Trade Union Congress), Nicola Shaw (ORR), Pe-
ter Wantoch (Competition Commission), and Chris Webb (OFGEM)
for information and personal comments on earlier stages of the research. Nothing I have written, however, can be attributed to them or
their organizations, and the usual disclaimer applies.

In London I enjoyed over the years the warm hospitality of two
friends, Simonetta Agnello-Hornby and Dario Castiglione (the latter
now at Exeter University), and I was helped in bibliographical and
data research by an informal network of capable young collaborators:
Katiuscia Manzoni (City University), Barbara Marchitto (Birkbeck
College), and Riccardo Puglisi (LSE). Their efforts were all the more
valuable because at the same time they were working hard on their
Ph.D. theses. Coauthors of related working papers include Katiuscia
Manzoni on financial returns of privatized companies, Riccardo Brau
(Cagliari) on price trends, Mara Grasseni (Nottingham and Milan) on
macroeconomic trends, and Orietta Dessy (Southampton and Milan)
on labor issues. Research assistance in Milan, particularly with data
elaboration, was provided by Sara Colautti (long-term data on the U.K.
economy), Carla Ferlenghi (British Telecom case history), Cristian
Rigamonti (macroeconomic and industry time series), and Elena Dug-
nani (electricity prices).

Susan Boyle translated most of a previous draft. She had to deal with
rather technical jargon, very long sentences, and very short deadlines.
Any remaining errors in the final text, however, are my own. Jone
Cocco-Ordini helped with the lengthy editing process, with the arrangements for visits and interviews in London, and with the excellent
organization of the Milan European Economy Workshop. Alessandra
Cavada edited graphs, tables, and texts of the research draft. All did
their best to keep me producing draft after draft until the final version.

I am also very grateful to senior editor John Covell, editor Kathy Caruso, the MIT Press staff, and particularly to Michael Harrup for an admirably efficient and careful editing process. I am grateful as well to the editors and publishers of, respectively, *Fiscal Studies, Annals of Economics and Statistics*, and *Applied Economics* for granting permission to utilize material from the following articles: M. Florio (2003b), "Does Privatization Matter? The Long-Term Performance of British Telecom over 40 Years," *Fiscal Studies* 24, no. 2:197–234; R. Brau and M. Florio (2002), "Privatisations as Price Reforms: Evaluating Consumers' Welfare Changes in the UK," forthcoming in *Annals of Economics and Statistics*, 2004; and M. Florio and K. Manzoni (2004), "Abnormal Returns of UK Privatizations: From Underpricing to Outperformance," *Applied Economics* 36, no. 2:119–136.

Introduction

Privatization policies may induce significant changes in the state of a country's economy, with direct and indirect effects on various markets. Numerous subjects come into play: consumers, shareholders, foreign financial investors, company managers and workers, taxpayers, politicians, and regulators. The effects on the welfare of the various agents should be considered simultaneously. In this perspective, the evaluation of these policies should be carried out to consider the costs and benefits in terms of social welfare.

Having said this, the most logical route, although beset with difficulties, is to study the effects of privatization policies on the different economic agents and then aggregate the results. This implies explicitly discussing various methods for carrying out this aggregation, starting from the macroeconomic perspective, which is a crude approximation method to measure collective welfare, but easy to implement. Then one can resort to the tool kit of welfare economics, which is more precise from a theoretical viewpoint, but more difficult to use practically.

This book tries to use the British experience, by far the most important privatization case history available, as an illustration of a systematic method of investigation. This entails an exposition that runs in parallel on various levels. In each chapter some research topics are first introduced briefly, then the available evidence from the U.K. experience is presented, and finally the results are discussed.

What I believe an economist can say to evaluate the welfare effects of British privatization is much less than was purported by the rhetoric that accompanied and followed this policy. Many questions are still unanswered, many conjectures not proven. I am not able to propose a precise quantification of the aggregate welfare effects, just some conjectures. Nevertheless, the reconsideration of the studies carried out by other scholars and the additional empirical evidence presented here suggest that the great British privatization was not the unconditional success it is commonly thought to have been. The increases in productivity attributable to the changes in ownership of the privatized firms (and not to the change of regulatory regime, to the increase in demand, or to exogenous technical progress) were on the whole smaller than is often believed. The regressive distribution effects, some of which are clearly attributable mainly to privatization, were on the other hand not negligible. The joint consideration of the two effects does not appear to lead to an indisputable Paretian improvement (for what this criterion is worth).

Chapter 1 offers a broad historical overview of the origins of public intervention in the economy and in the nationalized sector in the United Kingdom. The starting point is the establishment of forms of public ownership of enterprises or of regulation of the private sector dating back to the nineteenth century, up to the Labour government nationalization in postwar years. The last section of the chapter is a reconstruction of the large-scale privatization of the Thatcher-Major period. This chapter lays no claims to originality, and anyone who knows the economic history of the United Kingdom will probably find it superfluous. However, some less expert readers may find it useful as background information to place British denationalizations in a broad historical perspective.

Chapter 2 concerns privatization theories. Although the approach of this work is mainly empirical, it seems appropriate to clarify from the beginning which conceptual framework was behind the collection and discussion of the data. I consider some of the propositions of the theory of property rights, of public choice, of the Austrian school, and of the principal-agent approach. I then present a framework of applied welfare economics. This is my preferred approach for the research, but I do not confine myself to a rigid model.

Chapter 3 is a selective presentation of some macroeconomic trends during the period of the Thatcher-Major governments. I am especially interested in the variables that in principle are correlated to a policy of large-scale privatization: output, investments, employment, prices, distribution of income, and public finance. The causal relationships between privatization and each of these trends are difficult to identify. The discussion appears, however, to be useful. It allows me to examine a large-scale policy in the broader context of the development path of an economy. The chapter does not allow for a univocal diagnosis, but it raises a number of questions that may find an interpretation in subsequent chapters.

Whereas the first three chapters deal with general issues, the next five chapters examine specific microeconomic impacts. Each of these chapters is organized as follows: a short presentation of the topics for analysis, empirical evidence, a discussion, and usually some suggestions for further reading.

Chapter 4 focuses on firms and examines productivity changes, finding that evidence of a structural break of labor productivity growth caused by privatization is weak.

Chapter 5 examines shareholders, with particular reference to the return on capital invested by savers, the relationship between shareholders and managers, and the ownership pattern of privatized companies. My main finding is that although public offerings are usually underpriced but subsequently underperform, for the British privatized companies there is evidence of both underpricing and outperformance (at least until 1997, the end of the Conservative government years). This is perhaps an indication of persistent excess profits.

In chapter 6, on workers and managers, I discuss changes in industrial relations, wages, and employment, and I find weak evidence that workers lost much more through privatization than they would have lost under continued public ownership.

In chapter 7, on consumers, I discuss price trends as well as the quantity and quality of goods after the change of ownership. The longest chapter in the book, it offers a review of evidence for each sector and an attempt, albeit very crude and tentative, to measure the welfare impact of price changes with and without privatization in a simple counterfactual scenario of public ownership.

The discussion in chapter 8, on taxpayers, involves the interplay between privatization and tax reform, and the long-term net wealth and financial position of the state after divestiture. The chapter displays evidence of a dramatic fall in public-sector net worth and some evidence that privatization contributed to that trend.

Finally, based on the issues raised in all of the previous chapters, chapter 9 studies the effects on the aggregate welfare of the largest of the British divestitures, that of British Telecom (BT). The reasons for this choice, in addition to BT's important size from a number of viewpoints (capital, turnover, employment, etc.), are as follows: The privatization of telecommunications is universally considered the most successful example of the policy of the Thatcher government. Widely imitated in all countries, this case now has nearly twenty years of history behind it and thus allows me to adopt a long-term perspective, which is of particular interest here. Other cases, like railways and electricity, have a shorter history. Sectors such as steel and coal are less interesting because they were industries in structural decline when they were privatized. But telecommunications is a dynamic sector that is central to the scenario of the coming decades. Finally, the privatization of telecommunications apparently has less social impact than that of industries such as water and gas. It follows that if a series of problems occurs in the case most favorable to privatization, it is likely that these will manifest themselves to a greater degree in more controversial cases.

Based on my own reading of more than forty years of BT data, I conclude that virtually any benefit to the consumer from BT's privatization was generated by a combination of long-term technological change, strict regulation, and allowed competition in the 1990s. Privatization per se contributed little or nothing to consumers' welfare.

The principal results of my overall interpretation of British privatization in the time period 1979–1997, the uninterrupted Conservative government years, are presented in the epilogue (chapter 10). Readers who want to get an idea of what is in store for him or her can obviously start reading from the end. Those interested in more detailed statistical material, in related research papers, and in reading comments on the book or offering their own may visit the author's Web site at the Department of Economics at Milan University: www.economia. unimi.it/florio/index.html.

1   Historical Background

1.1   A Double Track

Many years ago, at the beginning of *Industry and the State*, Philip Sargant Florence, a British economist, proposed a double chronology, one institutional and one cultural, to show the progressive shift in opinions and in the economic organization of the United Kingdom from laissez-faire to socialism. His long list of cultural and political events that contributed to the change starts with Adam Smith's *Wealth of Nations*, followed by major books by Jeremy Bentham and David Ricardo. Then there are the socialists and reformers—Robert Owen, John Stuart Mill—the Fabian Essays, and the new policy mood in Victorian times: the Reform Acts (1832, 1862, 1885). In the new century, among the contributory events, there are the influences of the Labour party and the Liberal government, John Maynard Keynes's *General Theory*, and the Beveridge Report (1942). On the other column of the chronology, which lists the main industrial legislation, there is an impressive array of acts starting with the 1801 Health and Morals Act (pauper apprentices in the textiles) and concluded by iron and steel nationalization by Labour (1949) and denationalization by Conservatives (1953), which was an exception to the prevailing trend of the times. When the book was published in 1957, the great postwar nationalization, promoted by Labour, and including the Bank of England and the electricity, coal, gas, transport, and telecommunications sectors, appeared to be irreversible. The public corporation was considered a pillar of British industry. For decades, no government really questioned this, in spite of occasional oscillations, until the arrival of Margaret Thatcher's government in May 1979.

If, today, we were to update the chronology of Sargant Florence in light of subsequent events, we would have to ask ourselves where we would place privatization. Was it a major divide in British economic evolution, as, for example, Karl Polanyi ([1944] 2001) described the Poor Law reform in his own celebrated book, *The Great Transformation*? Or, was it just a partial reshuffling of governance structures, with a limited impact on economic performance? To answer these questions we must go beyond a short-term reading.

The parallel growth of capitalism and public intervention in Great Britain is a subject that defies simplistic interpretative models. The two decades of the great divestiture (1979–1997) cannot be fully understood unless we begin with the five years of great Labour nationalization (1945–1951), which in turn were the result of a long evolution.

Many of the themes that came back into fashion with privatization were anything but new. The policy of comprehensive regulation in some sectors, the attempt to limit the field of action of the trade unions, the active attitude of public institutions toward unemployment, the encouraging of the middle class's participation in the stock market, the question of the corporate governance of large firms, the concern for the decline of national industry in international competition—these issues have been features of British economic history for over a century. We need to remember some of these past experiences to understand the last twenty years.

The organization of this chapter is as follows. First, I start from a discussion of the traditional view that associates Victorian times with the "golden age" of economic individualism, followed by the rise of socialism at the end of the nineteenth century. I review, against the interpretations proposed by such early scholars as Dicey (1907) and Sargant Florence (1957), the alternative view proposed more recently by Tomlinson (1994) and Millward (2000), of a more gradual shift of the boundaries of public intervention. I cite selected evidence that may support the view that a Victorian welfare state and a large vintage of municipal public firms were established well before the foundation of the British Labour Party (1900) or David Lloyd George's liberal government (1906).

Second, I review how World War I marked a transition from the Victorian welfare state to a large-scale public intervention, and how the years following the great slump of 1929 reinforced an economic trend that culminated in the public procurement planning arrangements during World War II. Thus, I show the increasingly pervasive role of the state in the management of many industries as an evolution of economic governance structures. This process only partially correlates with the diffusion of socialist ideas and of working-class organizations. Other factors also played a major role in the shift toward big government.

Third, I depict Clement Attlee's nationalization (1946–1951), from this angle, as the result of a long-term convergence of an ideology (Clause IV of the Labour Party constitution, approved in 1918) and of a response to structural change in the British economy. This response had a dimension of rationalization and amalgamation of some industries (e.g., coal, electricity, railways) that were already very far from the free-market paradigm. At the same time, I discuss, as a parallel process, the gradual transformation of large British firms into economic structures dominated by a bureaucracy of top managers and by financial institutions, a far cry from the entrepreneurial firm model.

Fourth, my reading of the performance of the nationalized industries between Attlee and Thatcher is one of technocratic drift: a process of waning of ideological motivations, of loss of a clear social mission, and of increasing stress on the managerial-financial targets. This, combined with occasional short-termism in price control for anti-inflationary objectives, in the context of more general income policies, destabilized the finances of nationalized industries and eventually destroyed the rationale for public ownership of those industries. The long-term performance of the nationalized industries, however, was not so disappointing.

Fifth, I discuss the advent of a neoliberal ideology with Thatcher, an ideology that apparently involved a commitment to entrepreneurship and free markets. I suggest, however, that this return to laissez-faire was very weakly rooted in past British experience. It assumed that socialism was responsible for the stagnation of the British economy, something that probably had other explanations more related to structural aspects of British industry. In fact, the Conservative governments in the 1980s and in the 1990s tried to reverse a secular coevolution of markets and the state that was the core of British capitalism. Although highly successful in the implementation of the Conservative agenda, the privatization policy was probably a failure in terms of a social pedagogy of entrepreneurialism. The firms privatized under this policy were established as oligopolistic or monopolistic firms, under the control of different bureaucratic layers: top managers, regulators, and financial institutions. From this perspective, the policy outcome should be assessed in terms of its objective impact on various social agents.

Sixth, I discuss some of the legacies of the Conservative years (1979–1997), particularly in regard to public spending and taxation, distribution of incomes, productivity, and regulatory arrangements. I identify some of the issues that I shall discuss in detail in the following chapters. Suggestions for further reading and a statistical appendix complete the chapter.

1.1.1   The Myth of an Individualism Era

All exercises in periodization run the risk of being too rigid. A traditional view associates the economic supremacy of Britain with a golden age of individualism in the nineteenth century and the country's economic decline with extensive public intervention after 1890.

Classical economists had won their intellectual battle for free trade together with or immediately after the British victory in the Napoleonic wars. As Bairoch (1989) observed, however, it would be some time before the intellectual supremacy of laissez-faire was reflected in policy (see also Payne 1978; Checkland 1989; Schremmer 1989; and Landes 1965). The free-traders, economists, and industrialists of the Anti-Corn League advocated for many years the repeal of the Corn Laws, which protected inefficient British agriculture through import duties. The abolition finally took place in 1846 and was perceived as a major change in political and social equilibria, shifting power from the rural landlords toward the urban industrial classes. Three years later, protectionism in the shipping laws came to an end. The Bank Charter Act of 1844 institutionalized monetary discipline and granted the Bank of England a monopoly on issuing money, a system that was to stay in operation until 1931.

In 1825, Parliament repealed the Bubble Act (1720), a law that, in the wake of the speculative events of the South Sea bubble (an early example of large-scale financial fraud), had laid down strict constraints on public limited companies. Under the Bubble Act, establishment of any new public limited company required an act of Parliament. It was another thirty years before limited liability of registered companies was fully recognized (in the Joint Stock Company Acts of 1856 and 1862).

In 1834, the reform of the Poor Law only accentuated the moralistic approach to poverty relief that had prevailed for centuries in the parish councils (the bodies in charge of Poor Law administration). In principle, under the revised law, assistance was denied to able-bodied people who refused to work in the workhouses, where wages were lower than the market minimum level. Polanyi, in *The Great Transformation* ([1944] 2001), stresses the role of this policy in creating labor conditions more favorable to industrialization and capitalism than those that had existed prior to the reform. Around 1840 the electoral roll listed just five hundred thousand people out of a population of fourteen million (Checkland 1989), and the House of Lords maintained strong power as compared with the House of Commons.

On the other hand, as Sargant Florence conceded, one must not exaggerate the consistency of these public policies with classical economic thought. Early economists did not view at all favorably the legislation that liberalized the creation of joint-stock companies, the institution in regard to which advocates of the recent privatization most exercised free-market rhetoric. The personal responsibility of the entrepreneur is in fact an essential ingredient of the line of reasoning that, from Adam Smith onward, sees free individual economic action as a requirement of social order—free, but also *individual*. If economic action is no longer attributable to individuals, but to "anonymous" companies, and if the shareholders in such companies are not fully answerable for the credit granted to them with their own personal estate, then the moral and practical requirement of classical liberalism becomes rather obscured. The role of top management appears to be particularly problematic, in many ways detracting from the orthodox principle of individual responsibility.

At the culmination of the Victorian era, around 1885, joint-stock companies accounted for 5–10 percent of the major firms in Britain and were concentrated in a few sectors such as steel, shipbuilding, and cotton (Payne 1978). Many "public" companies were in fact private companies in disguise. Private ownership in the larger firms no longer bore any resemblance to that of the individual entrepreneur. Investors could divide their capital among dozens of different companies, and the firms' management could silence any dissent that arose about corporate governance or the firm's performance by guaranteeing a satisfactory moderate dividend, achievable without risks or an excessive managerial effort. Payne says that the small shareholders in these firms were, for the most part widows, orphans, clergymen, and the like—people whose wish for information about the companies in which it had been suggested they invest quite often did not go much farther than the mere names of the companies. These savers were perhaps not that much different from those who, under the generic name of "the public," were to have their praises sung a century later with the rhetoric of "popular capitalism" under Thatcher.

Against a precocious trend toward large monopolistic companies, in laissez-faire Great Britain, Parliament never passed an antitrust law. Monopolies acts were passed later, in 1948 and 1973, but the subject of competition was not yet central to the privatization policies of the governments of Thatcher and John Major. Paradoxically, it was New Labour that brought the subject up again (following a European Union directive) with the Competition Act of 1998.

The golden age of laissez-faire consequently does not correspond to the classical vision, given that alongside the Lancashire entrepreneur, the manager of the anonymous monopoly companies soon emerged, together with his complement, the uninformed, passive private shareholder. It is true that the clearest signs of the "collectivist" tendency became evident only after about 1870 (confirming the chronology of Dicey, but not his interpretation). We can trace back to the previous era, however, many premonitory signs of this second phase of British capitalism.

1.1.2   The Victorian Welfare State

The neoliberal views that offered an intellectual justification for privatization at the end of the twentieth century were probably more influenced by some strands of North American contemporary thinking than by Adam Smith or by classical British economists. I discuss some of these ideas in chapter 2. In fact, the Victorian state was not "minimal," as was implied by the neoliberal nostalgia for a lost paradise before "socialism." The British ruling class at the time was ready to delegate to public agencies important social and economic functions. I review here four well-known issues: municipal corporations, public works, labor protection, and taxation.

1. Municipal Corporations. Local governments in the Victorian period were very active in establishing early examples of public utilities or of other forms of public provision of services. This was in general a response to the huge structural problems created by the industrial revolution and urbanization. Industrial entrepreneurs often favored municipal corporations for the provision of transport, water, and energy over the old, inefficient system of licenses to private monopolists. Parliament passed a Municipal Corporation Act as early as 1836. In 1848, as a result of pressure from reformists such as Edwin Chadwick, Par-

liament made municipalities responsible for sanitation, which led to public intervention at a local level in areas such as sewers, water supply, cemeteries, and public housing. Thanks to Lord Shaftesbury, as of 1851, municipalities were able to build dwellings for the poor, and subsequently they could oblige owners to redevelop unhealthy property they leased. In 1869, Glasgow municipalized the production and distribution of gas; Birmingham took over the existing private firm for the distribution of gas in 1874. Hundreds of local councils had to follow their example.

2. Public Works. Adam Smith explicitly mentioned public works as an appropriate area for government spending. As of about 1830, private local consortia managed the British road network. Prior to this, rural roads had been managed by landlords—the major ones by the Crown with the involvement of the Post Office—whereas most of the new "macadamized" roads were financed by capitalist companies through user tolls. The network extended for 21,000 miles, as much as in France, which had a territory three and a half times larger (Girard 1989) and public roads. The state of repair of the British roads was very poor, and the network lacked coordination. Equally heterogeneous and uncoordinated, but more profitable, was the system of internal navigation, based on private canals. The great protagonist of the transport revolution in Britain was the railway, based on long-term concessions by the government to private train operators, who had to finance the construction of the infrastructure. The railroad industry was the object of an investment fever from the late 1830s, excited by the expectations of high demand and profits. Fixed investment costs were, however, very high and competition severe, and bankruptcies and consequent service disarray created wide public concern. There was a common saying at the time that either the state would run the railways, or the railways would run the state. Over forty years, government and Parliament reacted to an increasingly unstable industry structure through a series of bills that culminated in the Railway and Canal Act of 1874. As a result of this legislative activity, the British transportation system, which had originally been totally private, became minutely regulated and largely subsidized by public contributions. Things did not go as far as nationalization, but the competitive freedom of companies in Britain's transportation sector lasted only through an initial disorderly and unsustainable phase of early capital accumulation.

3. Labor Protection. Concern with safeguarding workers in Britain goes hand in hand with the development of the workers' movement in

the country, but early Victorians were really concerned with the social impact of industrial development. As early as 1819, a law had been passed forbidding the employment of minors younger than nine years of age in the cotton mills and limiting the working day for children under sixteen years of age to twelve hours. The Trade Union Act (1824) recognized workers' right to form associations. The Factory Act of 1833 broached the problem of educating the children who worked in Britain's textile mills. In 1847, Parliament passed the Ten Hours Act, which limited the length of time spent working daily. In 1842, the Mines Act was passed, forbidding women and children to work in mines, and by 1852, there were already signs of social-welfare legislation. The first Trade Unions Congress was held in 1868, and from then onward, British trade unionism became an integral part of the unwritten constitution of the empire. A revised Trade Union Act in 1871 acknowledged the new legal status of the unions.

4. Taxation. As of 1842 (after a debut with William Pitt in 1798 as an emergency war tax), income taxes (under the Peel government) began —timidly, under the profile of progressiveness—to undermine the role of the debt as the leading source of public finance. This was also the beginning of the erosion of the social status of the rentiers, who had to pay taxes instead of earning income from interest on their loans to the Exchequer (but a century elapsed before Keynes suggested euthanasia for them!). Between 1689 and 1820 this social group financed an average of 30 percent of public expenditures. The income tax signaled a turning point. In 1867 the electorate increased to over two million men (Reform Act). In 1884, the electorate was further enlarged to almost five million voters. The access to vote of a larger number of people reinforced the political support for the increasing substitution of the more progressive income tax for debt finance and indirect taxation.

These illustrative examples suggest that the new responsibility of the state toward society in the Victorian period had its deep roots in the age of individualism itself. The process of building a comprehensive public intervention was mature around 1870. In that year, for the first time, a public competition was held for admission to the home civil service, just a symptom of an important series of political-administrative reforms starting in the 1860s. The perception of the state, largely negative among earlier political thinkers, including economists, whose target was the old system, changed along with the state itself. There was less patronage and inefficiency than previously, and the perception of government's taking an active role became more positive. A great British historian of the old generation, George Macauley Trevelyan, wrote:

A characteristic of the new national machinery, fully apparent towards the end of Queen Victoria's reign, was the close interrelationship that had grown up on the one end between private philanthropic effort and State control, and on the other end between local and central government.... [This] complicated and constantly shifting relationship was rendered possible by the evolution of the permanent nonpolitical Civil Service of Great Britain with its accumulated stores of knowledge, experience and sound tradition. In the third quarter of the century, the Civil Service was removed from the field of political jobbery by the adoption of open competitive examination as the method of entrance, a device that seemed as strange as it has proved successful. (Trevelyan [1942] 1959, 463)

1.1.3   The Growth of a New Government, the Decline of an Old Empire

In the previous section, I mentioned some of the interventionist trends in Britain before 1870. The growth of a new public sector paralleled the decline of British economic supremacy among the nations of the world.

In the first decades of the nineteenth century, international openness was seen by the British ruling elites through the eyes of an imperial power. Britain was proud of its technical superiority over the rest of the world. Gradually, however, awareness spread among investors about the increasing competitiveness of other countries, especially Germany and the United States, but also of some of the British colonies. In fact, as Landes (1965) documents, British entrepreneurs had lost their leadership in international business before World War I, also perhaps because of the inability of the third generation of industrial revolution capitalists to manage the new competitive age and because of the bureaucratic behavior of management in British firms.

From this perspective, the years leading up to World War I, that is, until 1913, can be seen as a cumulative process of socialization of capitalism within a liberal macroeconomic policy. This socialization was not, however, without uncertainties. It is possible to grasp single aspects, rather than a coherent picture, of this phase of transition from the Victorian welfare state to the new age of extensive public intervention.

I have already mentioned the important role of local government in Britain as a factor driving change in the economic role of the state. Municipal corporations were active in a wide variety of sectors, from roads and trams, to water, gas, and electricity, to refuse collection, public housing, public parks, school meals, and the like (Foreman-Peck and Millward 1994; Millward 2000). Parliament granted local authorities the power to levy local taxes, however, only to a very limited extent. Muncipal service tariffs usually covered service costs. In 1914, each of the over three hundred local authorities in Britain supplied one or more public services on a commercial basis, to such an extent that one spoke of the trend toward "municipal socialism."

Transport in Britain was increasingly placed under public control. In 1873, the first example of a British regulatory authority, the Railway and Canal Commission, was established. Tariff control, while already in force in the previous three decades of railway development, became more systematic. The commission had the task of amalgamating transport firms and of coordinating the network of canals and railroads. The first modern public corporation in Britain was the London Port Authority (1909), a forerunner of the port authorities privatized eighty years later.

Another increasing trend in Britain at the time was the regulation of labor markets. In 1905, with the Unemployed Workmen's Act, local authorities were given the power to take measures to create jobs. In 1909, "labor exchanges" (offices in charge of job placement at the industry and local levels) were created. The previous year, the state had assumed responsibility for welfare with the Old Age Pension Act, which entitled those who had not made any contributions to pension funds to collect a pension of five shillings a week once they reached the age of seventy. Other measures in this area that preceded World War I involved technical education, unemployment, solving labor disputes, occupational diseases of workers, job placement, public houses and town planning, establishing fair wages and subsequently also minimum wages, and national health insurance, among others. Education offers perhaps the clearest example of large-scale public provision of a universal service in Britain. Whereas in 1870 there were 16,800 teachers in primary schools, after subsequent Elementary Education Acts, the number of teachers rose to 50,700 in 1890 and 132,000 in 1900. Between 1870 and 1913 the teacher/pupil ratio in British schools fell from 1:85 to 1:33 (Schremmer 1989).

To finance the new arrangements for the provision of public services, taxation became more progressive. In 1894, after various reforms to the previous tax system, a progressive inheritance tax was introduced. The marginal rate was just 8 percent, but by 1913, the tax—which at the time was considered to be radical—was to account for almost 17 percent of the country's tax revenues.

Most of these late Victorian and post-Victorian reforms were only partly an effect of the spread of leftist ideas, first of Chartism, and then of socialism. Largely they represented rather an independent evolution of the British institutions and of the mentality of those who had to run them, in a context in which one could clearly see the tangible shortfalls of private action in many fields. In the words of Trevelyan ([1942] 1959, 529–30): "As Sir William Harcourt said as far back as 1894, 'we are all socialist now'. At any rate, by whatever name you call it, this system of State assistance to the life of the poorer citizens is a great fact of modern English life." Moreover, the feeling that the empire was under attack by the new international competitors helped to shape a political consensus across the political spectrum. Britain was having to struggle abroad for commercial supremacy and therefore could not afford disruptive internal struggles.

Whereas in the rest of Europe, revolutionary Marxism attracted the workers' movement and a large number of intellectuals, British socialism had acquired its own peculiar moderate features. Workers' claiming of their rights, after earlier radical origins, can be traced back to the course of a democratic-parliamentary battle in one sense, and to the design of schemes to reform the functioning of capitalism in another.

The socialization of productive resources was an essential ingredient of Fabian socialism, as it was of Marxism. As shown below, however in a position that was in many ways ambiguous, Fabians quite often invoked social ownership for efficiency reasons, rather than as an aspect of class struggle and income redistribution. This orientation of the Fabian ideology ended up giving the postwar Labour nationalization an administrative and technical stamp rather than a political and social one.

Tomlinson (1994) defined the attitude toward socialism of the neoclassical economists themselves, *in primis* Marshall, as "skeptical sympathy." Persistent hostility to the idea of government involvement in general economic activities did not prevent widespread acceptance of the need for considerable specific intervention in economic matters. We are now a long way from the earlier suspicion of a state that is hostile to the individual, a widespread sentiment among classical economists. The champion of neoclassical orthodoxy, Arthur Cecil Pigou, who followed Alfred Marshall as the professor of economics at Cambridge, was ready to admit that without public intervention, the market, in many cases, for example, in urban development, produces undesirable effects.

We cannot therefore accept the orthodox periodization, which sees the era of individualism triumph between 1820 and 1870 and the era of collectivism establish itself thereafter. In mid-nineteenth century, individualism in running firms was a phenomenon in decline. Public intervention was precocious and pragmatic. Market and state interacted and changed in complex ways. These changes appear to be a case of gradual shifts without net caesuras. A biologist might describe this process as symbiosis and coevolution of two species.

1.1.4   *The State between the Wars*

World War I marked a crisis and the passage to large-scale public intervention in the economy. The year 1917 saw the birth of the Ministries of Food and Labour. In 1918, the number of voters had reached twenty million. There were other important policy changes during the war years. Women over the age of thirty were allowed to vote if they were married or the head of a family. The mines came under government control. The Ministry of Ammunition planned vast sectors of the economy.

The postwar period marked a break in government interventionism. Despite contemporaries', especially Keynes's, acute critical perception of this policy reversal, however, the attempts to return to laissez-faire (and to the prewar monetary regime) do not appear to have been so strong. The interlude between the two wars was above all in Britain a social crisis, particularly in the form of mass strikes. Especially important was the general strike of 1926. The government responded to these strikes by intensifying the legislation aimed at settling the social conflict between the working class and the owners and managers of the large corporations (particularly in the mining, steel, textile, and transport industries) through organs of control of industrial relations and health and welfare institutions.

Economic orthodoxy crumbled after occasional attempts had been made up to the early 1930s to return to the previous Victorian and Edwardian order: The gold standard, free trade, and a balanced budget ceased to be the compulsory reference point for any government economic policy that could command parliamentary consensus. An attempt in 1925 by the Conservatives, led by Winston Churchill, to return to the old social order based on relatively weak unions and to constrain the working class proved totally unrealistic and resulted in the return to power of a Labor government (headed by Ramsey MacDonald).

In 1919, the Ministry of Health was set up. In the same year, the British government raised old-age pensions and extended state education secondary schools. The Housing Act increased housing subsidies, and the Housing and Town Planning Act was passed, financing the construction of 170,000 new houses by local authorities. Numerous other laws followed that led to the construction of 1.3 million subsidized dwellings between 1919 and 1939. In 1920, the Unemployment Insurance Act granted twelve million workers public protection against loss of work. The measure was extended in 1927. In 1929, the existing Poor Law unions (totaling about 600) were dissolved, and welfare assistance became part of local authorities' ordinary responsibilities. Local authorities by 1936 were providing welfare assistance to 1.6 million people. The welfare system had already become broad and comprehensive in 1939, well before William Beveridge's reforms.

While the role of the state as public services provider increased, the type of company in which ownership and control were separate firmly established itself in the private sector. Imperial Chemical Industries (ICI) was founded in 1926 from the merger of four large firms, modeled on the kind of multidivisional decentralized organization illustrated by Alfred Chandler for the United States (Payne 1978). Industrial concentration in Britain was such that in 1935, the 135 largest companies in the country controlled 25 percent of total employment. In thirty-three industries, the top three firms accounted for over 70 percent of employment.

In parallel, the national government was establishing its own direct role in the large-scale supply of essential services. This went a lot further than Victorian municipal socialism and the sporadic acquisition of strategic companies, like the future British Petroleum (BP), originally the Anglo-Iranian Oil Company, a government acquisition backed by Churchill in 1912. Prewar state companies included the British Broadcasting Corporation (BBC) (1927) and British Overseas Airways Corporation (BOAC) (1939), the nucleus of the future British Airways.

Government plans were proposed by the ministries to tackle the perceived declining performance in Britain's coal, steel, railway, cotton, and shipbuilding sectors, plans that included proposals for nationalization of industries in these sectors, also with a forerunner of subsequent regional policies (Special Areas Act, 1934). These plans and the related new legislation appear to run parallel to those on the continent, with the establishment of large public companies at the height of the Great Depression, even though the democratic political context and the liberal tradition give these British policy trends specific features, particularly as compared with authoritarian state interventionism in Nazi Germany and Fascist Italy.

One leading example of this specificity (i.e., of a search for a compromise between outright nationalization and private ownership) is the Electricity Supply Act of 1926, which created a peculiar centralized system of coordination of the electricity market through a public body, the Electricity Board, which controlled a large majority of the country's private and municipal power plants. In the opinion of Hammond (1992), in certain ways the 1990 privatization of electricity in Britain was a return to the system put in place by the act.

The London Country Council in 1933 was able, without effective opposition, to take the London bus and underground system into public ownership. Herbert Morrison, later an influential member of Attlee's cabinet, designed the institutional framework for London Transport. This framework became a model for postwar nationalization, and I discuss it further below.

In 1926, in *The End of Laissez-Faire*, Keynes wrote: "For more than one hundred years our philosophers ruled us because, by a miracle, they nearly all agreed or seemed to agree on this one thing [individualism and laissez-faire]. We do not dance even yet to a new tune. But a change is in the air" (272). Perhaps that century-old undisputed intellectual kingdom never existed. In 1936, when Keynes published his *General Theory of Employment, Interest and Money*, the orthodoxy against which he fought was still influential, and laissez-faire was still the ideology of a large part of the economic and political elite. It was perhaps by now, however, a vestige of a waning social order, rather than a consistent policy option.

1.1.5 British Socialism and Clause IV

Clause IV of the Labour Party Constitution of 1918 summarized the role of public ownership in British socialist doctrine. The clause returned to the limelight recently when Tony Blair's New Labour repealed it. Sidney Webb, founder of the Fabian movement (and of the London School of Economics [LSE]; see the official LSE history by Dahrendorf [1995]) probably drafted the text. It read: "To secure for the producers by hand or brain the full fruits of their industry, and the most equitable distribution thereof that may be possible, upon the basis of the common ownership of the means of production, and the best obtainable system of popular administration and control of each industry and service."

This rather elaborate formula was very careful in its choice of wording. For example, it referred to "producers by ... brain" as well as "by hand." It made a distinction between the specific question of distribution and equity and the appropriation of the fruits of labor of the working class, and the "upon the basis of common ownership" formula itself was open to a number of operative solutions.

According to McDonald (1989), the version of Clause IV that was approved was the broader one of the two proposed. The more moderate wing of the party would have preferred a reduced version that talked about "common ownership of all monopolies and essential raw materials" (more or less what was to happen subsequently).

Webb felt that the most appropriate method for common ownership should be decided for each individual case. It was clear from the beginning that various forms of common ownership were possible, from departmental enterprise, under the responsibility of a ministry (the prototype was the Post Office), to forms of municipal ownership and management, to workers' and consumers' cooperatives.

As to which sectors to nationalize, the recurrent ones in the Labour proposals were land, railways, and mines, and the arguments for nationalizing these industries often had a Ricardian flavor. The existence of rents in these industries, rather than profits, simultaneously created inefficiency and inequity in the distribution of income from them. Public ownership of these industries was therefore justifiable also in the light of classical economics. Support for public ownership of these industries could have been found not only among the working class, but also among the productive bourgeoisie, who would have benefited from energy and transport at lower prices than were offered by private management.

Perhaps the most detailed, and in the end most influential, version of the Labour vision of what common ownership could signify in practice is the type of public corporation proposed by Herbert Morrison in *Socialisation and Transport* (1933). This book goes far beyond what its title suggests. Largely it is a discussion of the London Passenger Transport Bill, worked out by Morrison when he was Minister of Transport for the Labour government between 1929 and 1931. It also, however, outlines the model for the British public corporation, which was subsequently fully implemented by the Attlee's government.

The core of the Morrisonian model is a public body whose board is nominated by—but functions independently of—the government. The public corporation must, Morrison felt, be subject to parliamentary control and managed by people with considerable professional experience who consider themselves "high custodians of the public interest." The idea that became popular fifty years later of being able to regulate the market by granting a small group of people (the directors of the regulatory offices for nationalized firms) ample discretionary powers is not very far from Morrison's model, which entrusts the public interest to the "good chaps" in the boards of the nationalized firms (Helm 1995).

Morrison's model had several strong points at the time he proposed it: From an ideological point of view, it fit in with the socialist tradition; from a practical point of view, it offered a concrete and well-defined institutional framework. Its weak point was its lack of democratic governance.

Morrison's draft was the finishing line in a debate within the Labour movement. On one side of the debate was the radical idea of public ownership as a fundamental method of exercising the power of the workers. On the other was the revisionist idea of public ownership as just one possible mechanism for social control of the economy. In the Morrisonian model, the workers themselves were excluded from participation in the boards, as they likewise were from representation on the boards of sector interests. According to Morrison's model, the boards had to be organs of top administration, subordinate to the government, but with a dominant technical-managerial element.

Thus there was a simultaneous refusal of the self-management governance, linked in many ways to guild socialism or to some forms of trade unionism, and of the departmental enterprise, based on the example of the Post Office, which was considered bureaucratic and inefficient. Keynes, certainly not a socialist, was sympathetic to the Morrisonian ideas. In *The End of Laissez-Faire* (1926), he advocates a role for a new form of public corporation, as a cure for the divergence of private and social interest. Keynes says that "progress lies in the growth and recognition of semi-autonomous bodies within the State" and mentions as examples the universities, the Port of London Authority, and "even perhaps the railways companies" (289).

The militarization of the British economy in World War II led to the public administration's management of different strategic sectors. In this perspective, the great Labour nationalization, which I shall describe in the next section, appears to be more the epilogue of a long season that started in the early Victorian era than the beginning of a new phase.

1.2 The Great Labour Nationalization, 1946–1951

1.2.1 The Attlee Government

After the short-lived experience of the first MacDonald cabinet in 1923–1924, Labour was back in office in 1929–1931, again under MacDonald, who then led a national coalition government (1931–1935). Except in those years, the Conservatives were always in office until the end of World War II. Labour returned to power in the United Kingdom with the first postwar election in July 1945, bringing with it an ideology that was clearly in favor of public ownership. The nationalization program that Labour implemented in a remarkably short space of time came as no surprise to anyone who knew the Labour constitution. With the exception of the banking and cotton sectors, the government nationalized those industries that the Labour Party had envisaged "socializing" in the 1930s, a program subsequently blocked by electoral defeats leading to sustained Conservative majority in the decade 1935–1945. Subsequent Conservative governments until 1979 did not overturn the public economic structure created by Labour in the postwar years.

In 1946, the British government took under public ownership the Bank of England, the nation's coal industry, and civil aviation. In 1947, most transport and electricity was brought under state control, followed by gas in 1948. As of that year, the nationalized sector accounted for 10 percent of the workforce, 17 percent of GDP, and 19 percent of investments.

After these achievements, in its electoral platform for 1950, Labour announced its intention to proceed further by nationalizing the sugar and cement sectors, and in general, private firms that were allegedly not operating in the public interest. During Labour's two years in power (1950–1951), however, it did not implement these measures.

In his monumental study of the postwar Labour government experience, Chester (1975) reconstructs the nationalization process that led to a public sector with over 2.3 million employees in 1951, a long way from the small public sector of the Victorian period. Although

Table 1.1
Employment in nationalized firms, 1951

Sector	Employees
British Airways	23,300
Bank of England	6,700
Cable and Wireless	9,500
Electricity boards	176,200
Gas boards	143,500
British Steel	292,000
North Coal Board	765,000
North Scotland Hydroelectricity Board	2,700
Transport Commission	888,000
of which Railways	600,000
Total	2,306,900

Sources: Chester 1975; Gourvish and Day 1991; and other sources.

nationalization was the realization of a fundamental aspect of received British socialist doctrine, perhaps the partisan dimension was not as important as one might think.

As table 1.1 shows, a considerable share of employment in the nationalized sector as of 1951 derived from industries that a Conservative government had already subjected to state coordination during the war: coal, steel, transport, electricity, and gas. The government was quite well versed in the problems of these sectors, and the change from a wartime system of controlled supply prices to one of direct government control did not appear to be subversive to the large majority of the public.

The great postwar nationalization was not reducible to an essentially technical-administrative phenomenon, as would perhaps emerge from Chester's reconstruction. There was, however, a broad consensus across the political spectrum about the need for state-led reconstruction and rationalization of national industries. This was certainly the case for the railways and coal, both sectors that suffered much from the war and in which national reconstruction appeared to be indispensable to recovery, but it is also at least partly true for the other sectors that were nationalized. In the case of the railways, for example, in their final year under private ownership, they sustained substantial losses that had to be covered with public subsidies.

The core motivation behind nationalization seemed to have become achieving efficiency through amalgamation plus a dose of national planning. The main argument concerned technical scale economies that would have been lost through fragmentation in ownership, not only private, but also municipal. The policy discourse was about nationalization rather than socialization. The transformation of social relations played a minor, although not entirely marginal, role.

For example, the gas sector, nationalized in 1948, was above all a case of amalgamation. At the time there were 1,046 private and municipal gas companies operating. The establishment of twelve regional gas boards, which were later merged to form British Gas, seemed sensible and long overdue (O'Neill 1996). Even the names of the new corporations were drawn from the experience of the electricity boards set up in 1926 by a Conservative government (electricity companies at the time numbered 550).

Oil and gas deposits were already the property of the Crown, so the companies in these sectors operated in a regime of concessions. The nationalization of both the gas and the electricity sectors had already been recommended, for reasons of efficiency, in 1936 and 1944, respectively, by parliamentary commissions with a Tory majority.

In the case of nationalization of the coal industry, the social dimension of this policy was more important than in other sectors, where technical and coordination aspects prevailed. Perhaps it is worth stopping for a moment to reflect on the role of coal miners in a country that from the start of the industrial revolution, through steam technology, was to be highly energy intensive.

On October 13, 1992, British Coal announced it was closing thirty-one of its remaining fifty mines. At that point, coal miners had practically disappeared as a social group. But when Sidney Webb wrote Clause IV in 1918, there were 1,133,700 coal miners in Britain, and of these 250,000 were ex-servicemen. Miners had been by far the most highly represented social group in the British army during World War I (Kernot 1993).

As far back as 1842 the British government had seen the need to intervene in the regulation of working conditions in the mining sector with the Mines Act, which prohibited the employment of women and children in the mines. Between 1856 and 1886 there were a series of trade union protests about the extremely hard working conditions in British coal mines (deaths through accidents were no fewer than a thousand a year). A climate of proud class solidarity, bordering on self-isolation, among miners is the one constant feature of industrial relations in the coal sector that caused long nationwide strikes among miners (particularly in 1926, as in 1972, and to the last lost battle in 1984–1985, led by the coal union leader Arthur Scargill).

But in 1946 nationalization of the coal industry could have been seen more as a rational measure to reorganize an industry that in practice was already under indirect public control than as an act of social justice. In that year, the Coal Board merged more than 800 mines, with a total workforce among them of 716,500. Huge numbers of layoffs and intense industrial action followed nationalization. Ministries, not private shareholders, appointed the management of the National Coal Board that forty years later would have the last word in the industry and eventually defeated the unions.

1.2.2   The Technocratic Drift

Gradually the structure derived from the great Labour nationalization was evolving into a complex organization mainly driven by technical and financial considerations, developing its own internal logic, without any clearly stated political-social mission (apart from occasional government interference in pricing and employment decision making). Public and private enterprise seemed able to coexist in Britain without major tensions.

If there was a wide consensus about the existence of a large array of public corporations, in other ways the government emphasis on the purely technical aspects of their management was a limitation. One hint of this limitation was the different positions taken (and solutions offered) on the subject of who should effectively control the boards or these corporations. Only a minority position in the Labour cabinet favored greater involvement of the workers in the decision making. The compromise reached between those who held more technocratic views and those who favored a more democratic corporate governance was that the government had to appoint the managers of public corporations, but with parliamentary control.

Therefore, public corporations lacked a clear definition of their strategic objectives, in the framework of well-designed industrial policies. Moreover, the government did not pay much attention to the public corporations as a way to change the economic structure of the country and the distribution of income and power among social classes, as in the traditional socialist view. According to Sassoon (1996): "By nationalizing public utilities the Labour government acquired a potentially formidable weapon for restructuring the private sector. As part of an overall plan, or at least a fairly comprehensive industrial policy, nationalization could have played a major role. The Labour government had, however, no comprehensive plan. It simply maintained the financial and physical controls it had inherited from the wartime coalition" (154).

Despite this crucial failure in the nationalization design, the inclusion of a large part of the working class within the public sector was in fact an important change in British society, a change that had consequences for industrial relations, wages, and public spending priorities. The tension between the social and economic role of the nationalized industries was probably a crucial factor in the crisis involving them in the 1970s (more on this subsequently). Successive governments never established a transparent way to trade off the corporations' two functions, social and economic. Over the next thirty years, without any fundamental differences between periods of Conservative and Labour governments, the public corporation gradually lost its social and strategic dimension. The "commanding heights" of the economy were apparently under the control of the new owners, but they were not willing to use this power.

For example, in the case of the Transport Commission, the statutory objective of the public corporation was very generic: to provide an "efficient, adequate, economic and properly integrated system of public transport." No government, however, offered a strategic support plan to give the objective any concrete form, and there was no clear indication of coordinated tariff policy across the different transport modes, but each corporation was under a statutory obligation to break even each year. This obligation originated from the increasing role of H.M. Treasury as the department in charge of the control of the nationalized industries and reflected the budgetary perspective of the Exchequer. (I discuss this point in detail in chapter 7.)

As we shall see, a comparison between the legislation and statutes concerning the nationalized industries in the 1950s and those that established regulatory bodies in the years of privatization shows a similar vagueness of objectives. Successive governments never stated in a clear way the true, hard decisions that needed to be made about the national transport system, particularly the balance that needed to be struck between the investment in infrastructure across different transport modes: rail, buses, cars, and so on. The Transport Commission (like the future regulators in the transport sector) had in fact no strategic guidance concerning investment priorities and pricing policy.

The government's own ability to influence the investment programs of the nationalized sector soon proved to be limited. The mechanism for consulting workers to improve industrial relations was also found to be ineffective. The trade unions, although involved in the day-by-day management of public corporations through frequent meetings with the executives, were mostly interested in pay and working time, not in the overall strategy of the nationalized industries and their relationship with consumers. On several occasions, industrial relations proved to be worse in the public than in the private sector.

Subsequent White Papers from H.M. Treasury (1961, 1967, 1978) established rules for the behavior of management of public corporations that were oriented more toward financial or budgetary targets than toward economic policy criteria, for example, in terms of social costs and benefits of the public corporations' investment programs. The financial criteria included the obligation to break even on an annual basis (subsequently, every five years); the determination of a test discount rate (TDR)[1] for investment projects (8 percent, which was believed to be comparable to that for low-risk projects in the private sector); fairly mechanical attempts to impose price rules for the nationalized industries' output, rules based on marginal cost (which under increasing returns to scale could bring about a loss and thus contradict the required rate of return in excess of TDR); the requirement to evaluate the burden of social responsibilities (for example, the low fares for some disadvantaged users) with a shadow price;[2] and, lastly, the imposition of cash limits (external financial limits),[3] which created rigid ceilings to firms' ability to recur to borrowing to finance investment or cover losses.

A year before the turning point under Thatcher, the White Paper of 1978 adopted a required rate of return of 5 percent for investment programs undertaken by public corporations (rather than for single projects). It also required "performance indicators" (especially productivity and unit cost indices) to be published for every sector. In the end, this combination of general rules was no substitute for a national development plan or a consistent strategy for the provision of public services. It neither transmitted nor maintained a sense of social change among workers and users or a sense of clear mandate or mission in management.

Among the Labour ranks, the new idea of a "competitive" public corporation (i.e., a state-owned enterprise that had to compete in the market with private firms) was catching on. One result of that market-oriented approach to public ownership was to be the establishment of the National Enterprise Board (NEB). The Labour Party envisaged creation of the NEB during opposition years 1970–1974. The initial grand design for the NEB included public ownership of twenty-five of the country's hundred largest companies. When it was actually established, the NEB's role was limited to being a shareholder in British Leyland and to offering venture capital for small, research-intensive companies and eventually "a hospital for sick companies" (Sassoon 1996, 515). Harold Wilson's government, although it did nationalize shipbuilding and aircraft, was very far from the early view embodied in Clause IV.

1.2.3 Crisis of the Nationalized Industries

Probably the government's occasional interference in controls on the prices of public services caused the greatest damage to nationalized firms. This interference was part of a more general income and price control policy implemented by the government. Restraint of wages and tariffs, however, was particularly strong in the public sector. Such interference only aggravated state-owned companies' financial position, making the budget cost of such companies visible to the taxpayers, whereas the social benefit of containing inflation was obviously limited and "one-off." Perhaps the image of inefficiency in public corporations in fact appeared, in the case of Britain, to be linked mainly to their pricing policy rather than to excessive costs. This image of inefficiency was coupled with scarce consideration for customers' needs by the management of public corporations, because of a lack of clear targets from the government.

Foreman-Peck and Millward (1994) observe that the long-term trend of productivity in Britain's nationalized sector was no lower than that for private firms. Moreover, the profitability crisis of state-owned firms and thus the capacity for self-financing in the 1970s left the public corporations wide open to subsequent attack by Thatcher.

A historic assessment of the role of the nationalized industries in economic growth and crises in Britain between World War II and the 1980s will be less severe than many seem to believe nowadays (Millward 2000). (I discuss productivity trends before and after privatization in chapter 4.) It can be conjectured, however, that from the moment the criterion for evaluating the performance of the nationalized sector became, in the final analysis, simply its financial viability and consequently its profitability, public ownership lost its raison d'être. This shift had already begun before the arrival of the Thatcher government. The National Economic Development Office (NEDO) (1976) report depicts a sector with an identity crisis more than one in financial difficulty. In conclusion, I suggest that the roots of the collapse of the nationalized industries in Britain lie outside the corporations, in the inability or refusal of successive governments to provide the management of these corporations with a consistent policy framework and strategic planning.

1.3   The Great Divestiture, 1979–1997

1.3.1   Background

In the period between the great postwar nationalization and the great privatization of the 1980s and 1990s, there were only marginal changes in the extent of public ownership of British corporations as table 1.2 shows. For example, the government of Edward Heath sold Thomas Cook travel agency and some council houses in 1970–1974.

Some of these marginal changes were simply oscillations of a pendulum. Burk (1988) documents the story of the first privatization, that of British Steel, which was nationalized in 1949, denationalized in 1953, renationalized in 1967, and denationalized again in 1988. This is, perhaps, an extreme case of ebb and flow of public ownership. One cannot say, however, that the Conservative governments of the period intended to dismantle public firms. Although a Labour government in 1974 nationalized (to avoid bankruptcy) British Leyland and Jaguar, the Conservatives had done the same with Rolls-Royce in 1971. The Conservative Heath government nationalized the water industry in 1973.[4]

It is also worth remembering how the large private firms had developed in postwar Britain. They continued to merge and separate ownership from management. About a hundred leading holding companies that controlled 24 percent of GDP in 1935 were controlling roughly 45 percent by 1970 (Prais 1974, 283; see table cited by Payne [1978]). Already in 1950, two-thirds of firms were no longer managed by their owners, but by directors. This is probably the main difference between the British economic structure and the one prevailing in most of continental Europe after World War II.

Table 1.2
Nationalization and privatization by British governments, 1945–1997

Prime minister	Majority	Years in office	Main nationalizations and denationalizations
Attlee	Labor	1945–1951	Nationalizations: British Airways, Bank of England, Cable and Wireless, electricity boards, gas boards, British Steel, North Coal Board, North Scotland Hydroelectricity Board, Transport Commission
Churchill	Conservative	1951–1955	Denationalization of British Steel
Eden	Conservative	1955–1957	
Macmillan	Conservative	1957–1963	
Douglas-Home	Conservative	1963–1964	
Wilson	Labor	1964–1970	Renationalization of British Steel
Heath	Conservative	1970–1974	Nationalization of Rolls-Royce, water industry
Wilson-Callaghan	Labor	1974–1979	Nationalizations: British Leyland and Jaguar, British Shipbuilders, British Aerospace. Partial divestiture of British Petroleum
The great divestiture (see Appendix for more detailed chronology)			
Thatcher	Conservative	1979–1982	British Petroleum, National Enterprise Board holdings, British Aerospace, Cable and Wireless, Britoil
Thatcher	Conservative	1983–1986	British Telecom, British Gas
Thatcher	Conservative	1987–1988	British Airways, Rolls-Royce, British Airports Authority
Major	Conservative	1989–1993	Water, Electricity
Major	Conservative	1993–1997	Coal, Railtrack
Blair	Labor	1997–2004	NATS (air traffic control), public-private partnerships, bail out of Railtrack and National Air Traffic Service

Source: See text.

The majority of the directors of private firms came from the upper classes. They often had had a humanistic education at Oxford or Cambridge and some experience in the accounting field. It was not exceptional for them to have been in the civil service (Payne 1978). In short, those managing private firms usually did not have an entrepreneurial or technical background.

By the time Anthony Crosland, a leading Labour politician, published *The Future of Socialism* in 1956, the perception of the bureaucratic nature of the modern large firm was widespread. In 1964, Robin Marris, an academic, published his illuminating contribution on the managerial firm, *The Economic Theory of "Managerial" Capitalism*, largely founded on his observation of large British corporations. In the intellectual climate created by these works, the view that there were fundamental differences in efficiency between nationalized and private firms would have had little credibility. After all, the same type of person could appear to be in control of both types of firms.

The premonitory signs of the change in perceptions of corporate governance and efficiency that would affect the destiny of the public firm in Britain over the next twenty years were weak. On an international level, a political swing to the right definitely occurred in many countries at the time, particularly in the United States (Hood 1994). The change in climate was also in response to considerable increases in tax burden in Britain because of policies put in place to control budget deficits in the second half of the 1970s, following the trade union battles of those years.

Chile was the first laboratory among significant world economies of large-scale privatization. In 1975 the government of Chile hired economic advisors from Chicago who proposed a "shock therapy" for Chile based on a monetary squeeze, reduction in public spending, large-scale privatization, deregulation of public services, and liberalization of foreign trade. The government of General Augusto Pinochet, which had seized power in 1973 with a military coup, implemented the recommendations of the U.S. advisors, with the backing of the International Monetary Fund (IMF). Of the five hundred firms that had been nationalized in the space of a few years by the previous government, headed by Salvador Allende, Pinochet's government left in public hands only twenty-seven. Chile may have looked to many like a special political case,[5] but American economists influenced a new breed of British free-marketers.

In 1976, in her *The Right Approach* policy statement, Thatcher did not mention privatization. The Labour government, on the other hand, in the same year, when faced with a recession and budgetary crisis, felt the necessity of turning to the IMF for an emergency loan. To meet the IMF's conditions for assistance, the Chancellor of the Exchequer had to sign a Letter of Intent that, among other things, precluded transfers to nationalized firms. To raise additional cash to cover the government budget deficit, shares in British Petroleum were sold, an *ante litteram* privatization out of necessity.

The British Conservative manifesto (Conservative and Unionist Party 1979) offers no hint of a great plan for divestiture of the nationalized industries. It concentrates on some specific denationalizations: British Shipbuilding, British Aerospace, and National Freight. A review of the status of Britoil, limitations on the scope of the National Enterprise Board in the acquisition of stakes in private firms, and a greater financial discipline for nationalized firms were also considered. There was speculation about broadening the policy of licenses for private buses and selling a large share of council houses (public housing). That was all the manifesto proposed or even hinted at, although it is highly likely that in some circles there were already ideas that were much more ambitious. One example of these more ambitious ideas was the Ridley Report (Boardman and Ridley 1979), a working document produced by an authoritative group within the Conservative Party that proposed axing the welfare state, passing anti-union legislation, and denationalizing some public corporations. The report had remained officially unpublished for tactical reasons, but *The Economist* disclosed it.

Thatcher's political ideas, in fact, can be traced back to her association with the Institute of Economic Affairs (IEA, founded in 1957) and the Centre for Policy Studies (CPS, founded in 1974), two right-wing think tanks. The tenets of the new Conservative thinking were the perception of big government as an obstacle to growth and liberty, a commitment to monetarism, and the rejection of income policies. Hence, there was an outright rejection of a special relationship between government and the trade unions. Other ingredients were the willingness to restore profit incentives to the private sector through a reduction of taxes and a cut to public expenditures, including the welfare state and subsidies to nationalized industries.

Having gained the majority, in Parliament the Thatcher government in 1979 adopted a policy that went far beyond the electoral program proposed in the manifesto, reflecting the deep convictions that had developed during the long years of crisis in the governments of Harold Wilson and John Callaghan, and perhaps also an intolerance for the moderate, paternalistic approach of previous Conservative governments. The shift toward a more radical approach, however, was initially gradual and pragmatic. Again, the manifesto of the Conservative Party of 1983 spoke only of a partial privatization of British Steel, and for electricity and gas, preference was given to liberalization over privatization. A Thatcher supporter, Sir Keith Joseph, Secretary of State for Industry, wrote:

We came to office convinced that the structure of the nationalized industry contributed to the national malaise ... in all too many cases, particularly when the nationalized industry commanded a monopoly, those concerned did not see themselves as living under the healthy necessity of satisfying the customer in order to survive; they had no incentive to cut costs to beat competitors; they were free of risk of liquidation ... Such was our diagnosis; what was our aim? our aim [was] to abate inflation and to create a prospering social market economy—that is, a mainly free enterprise economy. (quoted in Miller 1995, 85)

These convictions influenced a policy approach that could be defined as "pedagogic." Nigel Lawson, Thatcher's Chancellor of the Exchequer, declared that through the policy of privatization adopted by the Thatcher government, the public attitude toward private ownership, entrepreneurship and the values of a free-market economy would have to become more positive.

According to Braddon and Foster (1996) this attack on public intervention in the economy had a cultural foundation that must be sought in the reemergence within the British political elite of the old tension between the ideals of the "good society" and the "good person." This tension was reflected in Berlin's (1969) two concepts of liberty: the fundamentally positive "socialist" one, and the fundamentally negative "liberal" one. For those who believed that the ideal of the "good society" had overcome that of the "good person," privatization should have contributed to the destruction of the "dependency culture." Moreover, the latter was the degeneration, or perhaps the inevitable consequence, of an excess of positive liberty (i.e., the freedom from destitution and poverty that was one possible justification of the welfare state and the public provision of basic goods and services through the nationalized industries). Maybe: But why did these ideas, which were certainly not new, become popular at the end of the 1970s?

It has been claimed that neoliberal ideology, of which privatization is an essential ingredient, became popular because of a crisis of the Keynesian-type economic policies. This crisis occurred in the context of a crisis of accumulation sparked by the oil shocks of the 1970s. According to Foreman-Peck and Millward (1994), this policy shift could be traced back to high unemployment coupled with high inflation in the mid-1970s, a combination of macroeconomic diseases that could not be cured through Keynesian demand management. A more specific view is put forward by Galal et al. (1994, 173):

> The UK divestiture program of the 1980s arose because of a decline in the efficacy of government management of public corporations. Over the 1970s this became especially acute, with successive governments facing conflicts between macroeconomic and microeconomic objectives. The macroeconomic pressures diminished the availability of investment funds and exerted pressure for monopoly pricing; both these results were in direct conflict with underlying microeconomic principles. This ultimately led to the introduction of a large-scale divestiture program.

These explanations are interesting, but probably incomplete. Privatization was in fact part of a broader agenda.

If we look back to the parallel growth pattern of industry and state in Britain since early Victorian times, the neoliberal agenda was probably more than a break in the postwar social policy. It was an ambitious attempt to revive a golden age of individualism, reversing a secular trend. Privatization should be examined as part of this public-policy project.

1.3.2 Privatization Policy: Facts and Interpretation

In October 1979, only a few months after coming into power in May, the Thatcher government inaugurated its privatization program with the sale of 5 percent of the shares in British Petroleum, which was already listed on the stock exchange. As previously mentioned, a Labour government had done the same thing some years before. Between 1979 and 1983, the years of the Conservatives' first term in office under Thatcher, twelve public firms were partially or totally privatized, and the sale of council houses was launched. These early divestitures were of relatively small companies, some of which had been supported by the National Enterprise Board.

The Thatcher government's second term, 1983–1987, saw the privatization of twenty-four major state-owned enterprises. In its third term,

1987–1991 (the last for Thatcher, who resigned in November 1990), forty major corporations were privatized, including the twelve regional electricity companies and the ten water and sewerage companies. The two successive terms of Conservative government, under John Major, saw the almost complete integration of the program.

We can identify four methods of privatization practiced in Great Britain under the governments of Thatcher and Major and subsequently widely copied abroad: placement of a corporation on the stock exchange, with an initial fixed price by public offering or with a minimum price tender (accounting for around 40 percent of British privatization operations); employee or management buyouts (25 percent); trade sales (30 percent); and private placement (5 percent). In some cases, there was a bulk sale of 100 percent of the corporation's shares (for example, British Airways); in other cases the operation was split into installments (British Telecom). In some companies, the government remained a shareholder with special powers through the "golden-share" formula (British Aerospace, British Airports Authority, British Gas, and British Telecom). The special, "golden" shares that the government held were formulated differently from case to case; in general they gave the Treasury the power to block hostile takeovers or acquisitions by foreign investors in some sectors, usually only for a limited period.

Ex post, the privatization program could be said by its supporters to have had a number of results. The large majority of British public firms were sold off. Over a million employees were transferred to the private sector (in 1979, public firms in Britain employed around 1.5 million people). The percentage of GDP attributed to public firms, which was originally over 9 percent (more than 11 percent of fixed investments), fell to less than 3.5 percent in 1990 (investments dropped below 3 percent). The percentage of the workforce employed in the public sector, which was 7.2 percent in 1979, had fallen to just 1.9 percent in 1992, and presumably was less than 1 percent in 1997.

The main sectors involved in the privatization effort were energy, transport equipment and services, telecommunications, and water. Some other specific sectors such as steel (British Steel) were also involved. A hodgepodge of particular firms were also privatized (e.g., hotels belonging to the railways and some factories producing arms).

An estimate of the government's gross receipts from the divestiture of public corporations and sale of debt is in the region of £86 billion (see appendix) in constant sterling (1995). In one particular year, 1989, receipts from privatization were the equivalent of 4 percent of the British public debt. Whereas in 1979 the British government had to provide for the financial requirements of public firms by way of loans to the tune of £3 billion, privatization greatly reduced those requirements. Furthermore, although the real return on equity in the nationalized sector was close to zero in 1979, privatized firms would have had a higher average profitability than the share market. In turn, higher profits would have generated additional tax receipts for the government through corporate taxes.

Privatization should have facilitated liberalization in some sectors previously in a public-monopoly regime. This did happen in part, but a new regulated private sector also emerged. The regulators of this sector were given broad powers in areas such as the determination of prices, transfer of ownership, specification of the services that the firms were required to provide, and qualitative standards for those services. At the end of the privatization process, the regulated industries accounted for capital of £80 billion and 400,000 employees.[6]

Despite the initial doubts of some financial experts regarding the capacity of the stock exchange to absorb the share placements of the privatized firms, private national investors showed themselves more than willing to absorb the issue of shares. In fact, generally they were oversubscribed. This created an army of millions of new, small shareholders. Between 1979 and 1993, the number of individual shareholders in British corporations rose from three million to over eleven million, or from 7 percent to 22 percent of the total adult population. Moreover, perhaps 90 percent of the employees of privatized firms purchased shares of the firms in which they worked. The demutualization of some building societies[7] and other mutual life assurance companies is relevant here (the demutualization of Abbey National was a prominent example, resulting in the creation of millions of new shareholders).

As a result of privatization, there were significant reductions in prices in real terms and improvements in the quality of the service provided in telecommunications, gas, electricity, air transport, and so on. In contrast, there were sizeable increases in prices in the case of water. On the other hand, as we shall see, the interpretation of the data on prices and productivity is a delicate and controversial subject.

To the promoters of privatization and their followers, this record of achievements was beyond doubt a success story and a major opportunity for changing the pattern of British economic history.

1.3.3   The Historical Perspective

The privatization policy of the Conservative governments in the period under study consisted of a hodgepodge of declared objectives. Literature on the subject, partly based on official documents (H.M. Treasury 1989, 1993) or on declarations by government representatives, including biographies of key politicians (Thatcher, Lawson, Ian Walker, Cecil Parkinson), have identified lists of varying numbers of objectives. For example, Miller (1995) identifies thirteen objectives based on twenty-four empirical works (a rather heterogeneous sample as regards quality and coverage):

• reduce the size and scope of government
• reduce government control of business
• reduce political interference in management decisions
• free government funds
• create a free-market economy
• promote domestic investment
• benefit the economy through higher returns on capital in private business
• generate new sources of tax revenues
• reduce the government budget deficits
• broaden domestic equity ownership
• promote equity ownership among employees
• provide consumers with improved service, better quality, more choices, new products, and lower prices
• improve the efficiency and performance of the privatized firms through competition or other means.

According to Miller, there was perhaps a fourteenth objective, which was never made official: to reduce the power of the trade unions. There is little doubt that privatization and contracting out actually had this more or less hidden objective as well.

I take a closer look at each of these objectives and the evaluation of the results in later chapters. The evidence of a great success in achieving these objectives appears to many to be so overwhelming that any further analysis is deemed superfluous. *The Economist* (1995), however, offered the following commentary:

One of the Conservatives' clearest triumphs over the past 15 years has been the privatization of state-owned companies. Fat nationalized industries have been transformed into fit and profitable enterprises. Huge subsidies have been eliminated. The prices of phone calls, electricity and gas have dropped in real terms. Services have improved strikingly. Eager to learn from this success, scores of governments have studied the British example and much of Europe is now following in Britain's footsteps. Curiously, the only group which remains unimpressed is the British public. Many Britons still do not believe they have benefited from privatization.

On a more general level, one could ask what legacy the policies developed and implemented in accordance with the policies of five Conservative government passed on to the following generation and what the relationship of those policies was with previous history. From this angle, four points are important: trends in public spending and taxation, distribution of incomes, national productivity, and regulation.

John Hills (1998) observes that New Labour, which came into power in May 1997, inherited a welfare state that was in some ways different from that of 1979 but nonetheless had surprising elements of continuity with the welfare state of that time. The share of public spending on GDP in the crucial sectors of the welfare state (education, health, social security, housing, personal social services) had risen slightly between 1979 and 1997, a surprising result from the point of view of those who had declared the objective of rolling back the state to be an absolute priority. Although spending on housing and education diminished over the two decades, spending for social security increased more than proportionally. Table 1.3 shows the breakdown of public expenditure in Britain by functions as a percentage of GDP since 1890. Table 1.4 offers the breakdown of social expenditures in Britain since 1960.

If public spending is considered as a whole, the Conservative governments of the period achieved a modest reduction of the expenditure/GDP ratio, mainly through cuts in spending for public investments, which dropped from 6.4 percent of GDP in 1975 to 0.9 percent in 1997. Furthermore, on a long-term view, the breaking point in the growth of government spending came in 1976, under a Labour government, because of the conditions imposed by the IMF on the granting of its emergency loan.

Figure 1.1 shows the long-term trends of British GDP and public expenditures. Figure 1.2 shows expenditures as a percentage of GDP in the United Kingdom since 1850. Evidence suggests that public expenditure growth closely correlates to output growth since the beginning

Table 1.3
Breakdown of public expenditure in Britain by functions (percentage of GDP)

Year	Administration and other	National debt	Law and order	Defense	Social services[a]	Economic services	Environmental services	All services
1890	1.07	1.62	0.61	2.37	1.85	0.98	0.34	8.87
1895	1.05	1.47	0.54	2.78	2.56	1.19	0.48	10.13
1900	0.85	1.01	0.51	6.98	2.62	1.88	0.62	14.53
1905	0.94	1.17	0.54	3.02	3.26	1.88	0.66	11.54
1910	1.00	0.91	0.58	3.35	4.01	1.70	0.65	12.25
1915	0.79	1.70	0.40	21.13	2.75	1.05	0.37	28.25
1920	1.16	5.26	0.54	8.42	6.67	3.29	0.41	27.38
1925	1.28	6.57	0.69	3.57	10.82	3.17	0.65	26.75
1930	1.07	6.59	0.67	2.74	11.89	2.69	0.73	26.38
1935	1.07	5.52	0.72	2.70	14.05	2.72	0.92	27.69
1955	1.49	3.99	0.61	8.90	11.60	3.57	0.81	30.98
1960	2.20	3.80	0.78	6.92	13.74	5.70	1.25	34.47
1965	1.66	3.86	0.94	6.14	16.00	5.98	1.52	36.09
1970	2.38	3.96	1.09	5.38	15.58	7.21	1.83	40.33
1975	5.15	3.76	1.38	4.79	18.31	5.71	1.95	43.66
1980	3.17	4.36	1.51	4.72	23.99	4.73	1.60	44.08
1985	3.02	4.90	1.76	5.17	25.06	4.58	1.13	45.63
1990	3.40	3.95	1.84	4.40	22.81	2.46	0.86	39.72
1995	3.50	3.15	2.25	3.78	26.27	2.66	0.68	42.28

Sources: 1890–1935: author's elaboration on Peacock and Wiseman 1961; 1955–1995: author's elaboration on Liesner 1989; ONS, n.d.
Note: 1890–1920: yearly data; 1925–1995: five-year-average data.
[a] See table 1.4.

Table 1.4
Breakdown of social expenditure in Britain (percentage of GDP)

	Education	Health	Social security	Housing	Total social services	Total public expenditure
1960	3.4	3.2	5.7	1.9	14.2	34.5
1965	4.1	3.4	6.3	2.2	16.0	36.1
1970	4.7	3.8	7.3	2.5	15.6	40.3
1975	5.5	4.4	8.0	3.7	18.3	43.7
1980	5.5	4.7	10.3	3.4	24.0	44.1
1985	5.3	5.2	12.9	1.7	25.1	45.6
1990	4.9	5.0	11.9	1.0	22.8	39.7
1995	5.3	5.7	14.3	1.0	26.3	42.3

Source: Author's elaboration on ONS (n.d.-a) data.
Note: Five-year averages.

of the period. Moreover, in contrast to widespread perceptions, the ratio of public expenditures to GDP since the late 1960s does not show a clear increasing trend. Between 1920 and 1960 the ratio increased from 20 percent to 40 percent. In the following forty years, it fluctuated around its previous level, with occasional increases in the 1970s best explained by the oil shocks of that time period and other rather exceptional circumstances. From this long-term perspective, it is difficult to attribute a major role in public-expenditure restraint to the Conservative governments after 1979.

A perhaps even more important aspect of the Conservative legacy was that fiscal pressure on the taxpayers did not decrease in the last two decades of the twentieth century. Although there was a reduction in the income tax rate and in other taxes on income, there was an increase in the value-added tax (VAT) and in national insurance contributions. I discuss these trends in chapter 8.

One of the fundamental reasons for the Conservative governments' failure to cut back the welfare state during their nearly twenty years in power was the explosion in the demand for welfare services, especially as a result of the increase in the rate of unemployment among men (the trend was similar for women, but the levels lower), from roughly 5 percent in 1979 to peaks of 13 percent and 14 percent in 1986 and 1993, respectively. At the same time there was in Britain, as there was elsewhere in Europe, a noticeable aging of the population, but also—to a degree that was unparalleled in other European countries—an

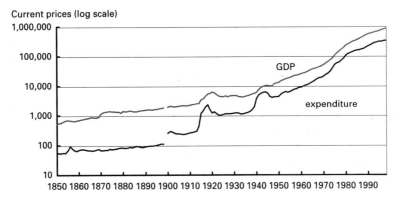

Figure 1.1
Public expenditure and GDP in Britain, 1850–1998.
Sources: 1850–1899: central government expenditure and GNP—Mitchell 1988; 1900–1947: total public expenditure—Middleton 1996; GDP—Liesner 1989; 1948–1998: general government expenditure and GDP—ONS, n.d.-a.

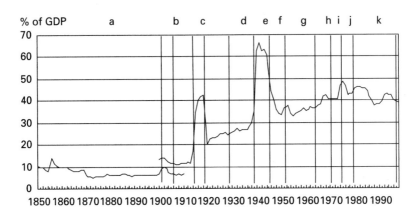

Figure 1.2
Public expenditure as a percentage of GDP in Britain, 1850–1998. a: Victorian age; b: foundation of Labour Party—Lloyd George government; c: World War I; d: the Great Depression; e: World War II; f: Labour government (Attlee); g: Conservative government (Churchill, Eden, Macmillian, Douglas-Home); h: Labour government (Wilson); i: Conservative government (Heath); j: Labour government (Wilson-Callaghan); k: Conservative government (Thatcher, Major).
Sources: 1850–1899: central government expenditure share of GNP—Mitchell 1988; 1900–1947: total public expenditure—Middleton 1996; GDP—Liesner 1989; 1948–1998: general government expenditure share of GDP—ONS, n.d.-a.

explosion of family disintegration and poverty. Between 1979 and 1995 the proportion of lone-parent families with children in Britain doubled, from 12 percent to 23 percent, and 80 percent of these families were dependent on public assistance.

Equally surprising is the fact that the attitudes of the electorate, far from being increasingly supportive of government policies to control spending, actually showed the opposite trend. The results of the British Social Attitude Survey, conducted over a number of years, show that in 1995 over 60 percent of interviewees were in favor of increased taxation and spending, and just 5 percent were in favor of further cuts (Hills 1998). Lawson's pedagogy does not appear to have been very successful.

Seen at this first level, the results obtained by the policies of the Conservative governments were less profound than could have been expected. From the point of view of controlling public spending, privatization played a very modest role (I discuss this in detail in chapters 3 and 8).

On one aspect of the economy and of British society, the politics of the Thatcher and Major governments did have a profound effect: the distribution of income and wealth. As official data show (ONS 2000b), in 1979 the proportion of the British population below 50 percent of median income was slightly more than 5 percent; in 1997, it was around 15 percent. The percentage of the population under 60 percent of median income doubled over the same time period. This dramatic change in the social structure had various causes, including increasing wage inequality, a phenomenon known to a similar extent only in the United States and partly due to the decline in the role of the trade unions (and of minimum wages established by the wage councils); an increase in long-term unemployment and in the number of families dependent on public assistance; changes in the government policies for indexing benefits to the disadvantaged; and a tax policy that was generous with capital income, increased indirect taxation, and diminished the progressivity of the income tax.

At the end of a social experiment that promoted "popular capitalism," in 1996, 1 percent of the U.K. population owned 20 percent of the kingdom's marketable wealth (about £388 billion), and around 50 percent of total wealth was owned by 10 percent of the population. In 1997–1998, around one-third of households had no savings at all, and over half had less than £1,500.[8]

I discuss in chapter 3 the available evidence on output and productivity trends in the United Kingdom. As I show there, it seems difficult to say to what extent the set of economic policies implemented in the 1980s and 1990s affected the country's growth path. I present evidence at the firm level in chapter 4.

If privatization was to have been the prelude to a full restoration of a free-market economy, in which regulation played only a transitory role, then Conservative expectations were in some ways disappointed. Regulation does not seem to be a transitory phenomenon at all. The progressive liberalization in some sectors, for example, in telecommunications and in electricity, was neither a necessary prerequisite for nor a necessary consequence of privatization, as other countries' experience shows. In fact, in some cases it appears that public utilities liberalization in Britain has probably been deferred and limited to pave the way for placing shares on the stock exchange and to preserve the stability of management. Neither does it appear that privatization broke the penetrating role of higher public bureaucracy in these sectors. This role draws its raison d'être from a complex regulatory game between ministries, regulators, and top managers. Ownership of listed corporations may be private, but the actual owners of the corporations are not the great numbers of individual shareholders. Ironically, pension funds, other financial institutions, and foreign groups, including French state-owned enterprises in the electricity and water sectors, now control most of the British privatized industries in those sectors. A new breed of bureaucrats has taken the place of the old one. Quite often, the game they play is not plain competition, and for good economic reasons.

More generally, if the "Thatcher revolution" was a radical attempt to change the secular route of coevolution of state and market in British economic and political history since the Victorian era, as discussed in this chapter, the attempt cannot be said to have succeeded fully. It certainly reshuffled ownership rights and some rules of the game and determined a new social equilibrium, but it did not revive the conditions for a golden age of a free-market economy. Big government and intrusive regulation are still present, wearing new clothes. From this angle, it is interesting to ponder why the result of the social experiment was different from that envisaged by its proponents. To understand this, we must go beyond privatization rhetoric and turn to economic analysis.

1.4   Further Reading

Hannah (1994) offers a review of evidence on the nationalized industries. See also Polanyi and Polanyi 1972 and Polanyi and Polanyi 1974. Hood (1994) has an interesting chapter on possible general explanations for the policy reversal from public enterprise toward privatization. The issue of a "political economy of privatization" is discussed by several contributors in Clarke and Pitelis 1993. Worcester 1994 is an account on the role of marketing and public relations advisors in privatization.

There is a huge scholarly literature on British economic history. In this chapter I have cited just a very small sample. Additional references may be found in Moggridge 1989; Pollard 1978; Ashworth 1991; Tomlinson 1994; Millward and Singleton 1995; Foreman-Peck and Millward 1994; Floud and McCloskey 1993; and Millward 2000, 2002.

Ample literature exists on the Thatcher government's record, including Thatcher's own memoirs (1993) and serious academic research by contemporary historians, public-policy scholars, and other social scientists. Seldon and Collings (2000) provide a short and readable account, with a chronology of 1979–1990, abstracts from selected documents, and a bibliography. See also Browning 1994; Glennerster 2000; Dunleavy 1986; Hare and Simpson 1996; Haskel 1992; Jenkin 1995; Johnson 1991; Kay 1987; Kay, Bishop, and Mayer 1984; Mac Avoy et al. 1989; Miller 1997; and Walters 1989.

Selected case histories include Bailey and Baldwin 1990 for British Airways; Beesley 1996 and Beesley 1997 for the utilities; Bradshaw 1996 for the bus industry; Bradshaw 1997; Bradshaw and Lawton-Smith 2000; and Welsby and Nichols 1999 for rail and transport; see also Estrin and Whitehead 1987; Foster 1992; and Hoopes 1994 on oil assets. On postal services, see Waterson 1992 and London Economics 1994. For a survey of liberalization in the United Kingdom, see Pollitt 1999; Ramanadhan 1988; and Yarrow 1993.

Appendix

Table 1A.1
Privatization database (1979–1997) (constant 1995 million pounds)

	Business	Years privatized	Methods of privatization[a]	Proceeds[b]
Amersham International	Chemicals	1982	FPO	124.0
Associated British Ports holdings	Transport	1983	FPO	83.3
Associated British Ports holdings	Transport	1984	TO	83.9
Atomic Energy Authority Technology	Energy	1996	FPO	204.6
Belfast International Airport	Transport	1994–1997	MBO/EBO	48.0
British Aerospace	Manufacturing	1981; 1985	FPO	633.4
British Airports Authority	Transport	1987	FPO + TO	1,697.2
British Airways	Transport	1987	FPO	1,262.2
British Coal	Energy	1994–1997	TS + MBO/EBO	937.4
British Gas	Energy	1986–1993	Redemption of debt	3,259.0
British Gas	Energy	1986	Sales of shares: FPO + TS	7,568.0
British Petroleum	Energy	1979	FPO	691.7
British Petroleum	Energy	1983	TO	940.3
British Petroleum	Energy	1981; 1987–1990	Public offer	7,014.2
British Steel	Steel	1988	FPO	3,151.5
British Sugar Corporation	Manufacturing	1981	TS	85.3
British Technology Group	Manufacturing	1992	MBO/EBO	27.5
British Telecom	Telecommunications	1984–1987	Loan stock	1,389.0
British Telecom	Telecommunications	1986–1989	Redemption of preference shares	1,075.6
British Telecom	Telecommunications	1984; 1991; 1993	Sales of shares: FPO + TO	16,873.4
Britoil	Energy	1985	FPO	665.6

Company	Sector	Year	Method	Value
Britoil	Energy	1982	TO	1,112.4
Cable and Wireless	Telecommunications	1981; 1985	FPO	1,252.3
Cable and Wireless	Telecommunications	1983	TO	455.4
Chessington Computer Centre	Services	1996–1997	MBO + TS	10.6
DTELS (formerly Home Office Directorate of Telecommunications)	Telecommunications	1993–1994	TS	5.2
Drivers, Vehicles, and Operators Information Technology (Department of Transport)	Services	1993–1994	TS	12.4
Electricity companies[c]	Energy	1991–1995	Redemption of debt	2,406.9
Electricity companies: England and Wales[c]	Energy	1995	Sales of shares: FPO	11,327.9
Electricity companies: Scotland[c]	Energy	1991	Sales of shares: FPO	2,915.4
Enterprise Oil	Energy	1984	TO	631.8
Forestry Commission	Forestry	1982–1995	TS	279.1
Forward	Services	1993–1994	TS	4.1
General Practice Finance Corporation	Services	1989	TS	90.3
Harland and Wolff	Manufacturing	1989	MBO/EBO	10.1
Her Majesty's Stationery Office	Manufacturing	1996–1997	TS	1.9
Insurance Services Group	Services	1991–1992	TS	18.0
Land Settlement Association	Services	1983–1987	TS	35.2
Motorway Service Area leases	Services	1982–1993	TS	31.5
National Enterprise Board holdings	Various	1979–1980	TS	647.6
National Freight Corporation	Transport	1982	MBO/EBO	9.7
National Seed Development Organisation	Agriculture	1987	TS	93.6
National Transcommunication Ltd.	Telecommunications	1991	TS	76.9
Northern Ireland Electricity[c]	Energy	1992–1993	Redemption of debt	72.5
Northern Ireland Electricity[c]	Energy	1992–1993	Sales of shares: FPO + MBO + TS	725.8

Table 1A.1
(continued)

	Business	Years privatized	Methods of privatization[a]	Proceeds[b]
Nuclear power industry[c]	Energy	1996	FPO	653.3
Professional and Executive Recruitment	Services	1988–1999	TS	6.7
TSA (building management)	Services	1993	TS	20.6
Railtrack[c]	Transport	1996	FPO	2,235.7
Recruitment and Assessment Services	Services	1996–1997	TS	6.7
Rolls-Royce	Manufacturing	1987	FPO	1,485.2
Rover Group	Manufacturing	1989–1990	TS	188.6
Royal Ordnance Factories	Manufacturing	1987	TS	267.7
Short Brothers	Manufacturing	1989–1990	TS	37.7
Transport Research Laboratories	Transport	1996–1997	TS	2.9
Water	Water	1989–1990	Redemption of debt	91.8
Water[c]	Water	1989	Sales of shares: FPO	3,896.3
Wytch farm (British Gas Onshore Oil Association)	Energy	1984–1985	TS	178.8
Privatized companies' debt, various	—	1992–1998	—	4,091.1
Residual share sales, various	—	1995–1998	—	1,907.6
Miscellaneous	—	1979–1997	—	813.9
Total	—	—	—	85,926.5

Sources: H.M. Treasury 1997c, table 3.13; ONS 2000c, table 2.1G; Vickers and Yarrow 1988a; Bishop, Kay, and Mayer 1994; Veljanovski 1987; NAO, various years.

[a] Methods of privatization: FPO: fixed-price offer; MBO/EBO: management/employee buyout; TO: tender offer; TS: trade sale.

[b] Proceeds (1995 prices) are Treasury net proceeds deflated using GDP deflator (1995 = 100).

[c] Detailed data about electricity, rail, and water companies are provided in table 1A.2.

Table 1A.2
Gross proceeds from privatization of water, electricity, and railways companies

Company	Date privatized	Gross proceeds (millions of pounds, current prices)	Gross proceeds (millions of pounds, 1995 prices)
Water Companies			
Anglian Water	December 1989	707	904
Northumbrian Water	December 1989	157	201
North West Water	December 1989	854	1,092
Severn Trent	December 1989	849	1,086
Southern Water	December 1989	392	501
South West Water	December 1989	293	375
Thames Water	December 1989	922	1,179
Welsh Water	December 1989	346	442
Wessex Water	December 1989	246	315
Yorkshire Water	December 1989	472	604
Total (water)		5,238	6,699
Electricity: Regional electricity companies (RECs)			
Eastern Electricity	December 1990	648	770
East Midlands Electricity	December 1990	523	621
London Electricity	December 1990	523	621
Manweb	December 1990	285	338
Midlands Electricity	December 1990	503	597
Northern Electricity	December 1990	295	350
Norweb	December 1990	415	493
Seeboard	December 1990	306	363
Southern Electricity	December 1990	648	770
South Wales Electricity	December 1990	244	290
SWEB	December 1990	295	350
Yorkshire Electricity	December 1990	497	590
Total		5,182	6,153
Electricity: Generating companies			
National Power	March 1991	2,231	2,482
PowerGen	March 1991	1,367	1,521
Scottish Power	June 1991	1,956	2,176
Scottish Hydro	June 1991	920	1,023
Northern Ireland Electricity	June 1993	726	736
Total (electricity)		12,382	14,091
Railways			
Railtrack	May 1996	1,950	1,888

Table 1A.2
(continued)

Company	Date privatized	Gross proceeds (millions of pounds, current prices)	Gross proceeds (millions of pounds, 1995 prices)
Rolling stock companies (presale dividend)	September 1995	800	800
Rolling stock companies (sale proceeds)	January–February 1996	1,822	1,764
Freight operators	September 1995–March 1997	255	247
Track renewal	February–July 1996	48	46
British Rail infrastructure service companies	February–May 1996	171	166
British Rail Maintenance Ltd.	April–June 1995	32	32
British Rail Infrastructure Services Design Offices	July–December 1995	8	8
British Rail Central Services	February 1994–December 1996	70	70
Other companies	1995	144	144
Total (railways)		5,300	5,165
Total (water, electricity, railways)		22,920	25,955

Sources: Author's elaboration on ONS, n.d.-b; Hayri and Yilmaz 1997.

2   Privatization Theories and Cost-Benefit Analysis

2.1   Beyond Rhetoric

A theory of privatization should be the counterpart of a theory of public ownership. This, in turn, should be an integral part of an economic theory of the state. Neither one exists in a satisfactory form, in spite of several contributions to a wide literature.

Economists are not at their ease with analyzing the growth of government. At the beginning of the twenty-first century, public spending and taxation are typically between around 40 percent and 60 percent of GDP in most advanced countries. One century ago, this proportion was five to ten times lower (Florio and Colantti forthcoming). Government has become by far the largest owner of fixed capital and the largest employer in capitalist economies. Transfers, particularly for pensions and welfare, have been increasing faster than national income for decades. Public provision of services, taxation, or regulation influences all prices in an economy directly or indirectly. The economy, as we observe it, is a complex interplay of market forces, government actions, and social institutions' and agents' behaviors.

Some think that big government is a political phenomenon that mainly generates redistribution effects and harms collective growth and welfare. Others conjecture that the growth of government obeys an economic logic and is a socially efficient answer to collective needs (see, e.g., the entertaining debate between Buchanan and Musgrave [1999]).

Opinions on this subject are deeply divided. We do not have a consensus about the optimum size of government from the point of view of growth and welfare. Neither is there perhaps any real sense in posing the problem in these terms, as do those who are convinced that the best state is the one that does "less," as opposed to one that does "more."[1]

In spite of the lack of a general economic theory of the state, some strands in economic literature aspire to offer a theory of privatization. The objective of such a theory is to explain why the state sells, or should sell, to the private sector the assets that it has appropriated in the past. The aspiration often does not appear to be very conclusive, since a large proportion of the contributions to this literature are based on questionable assumptions. Some propositions in this area are, however, interesting and testable. Economics, with all its limitations, can contribute to the understanding and evaluation of policy reforms.

In fact, privatization is above all a policy change, often pursued by very determined governments and driven by elementary convictions, expressed more in rhetoric than in analytical form. The Thatcher government was no exception. Decisions of huge economic importance were made on the basis of documents and parliamentary debates that, if reread today, appear to be surprisingly simplistic. The economists' theories about privatization often came later than actual privatization policies and sometimes betray a *post hoc ergo propter hoc* reasoning. There seems to be little point in offering here a comprehensive review of these economists' contributions, as others have already done so.[2]

In what follows I limit myself exclusively to a discussion of some general propositions that may be of guidance in the empirical survey of the British experience with privatization. The propositions in which I am interested are rooted in different strands: first, in traditional neoclassical doctrine; second, in theories of property rights, public choice, and the Austrian view; third, in agency theory; and fourth, in a welfare economics framework of analysis. I develop the last of these in some detail, because I deem social cost-benefit analysis to be the most useful perspective for an evaluation of the British experience with privatization. Moreover, this application of cost-benefit analysis to the evaluation of a large-scale divestiture policy can be relevant for other country case studies. An appendix offers some simple cost-benefit formulas and completes the chapter.

2.2   Positive Theories

2.2.1   *The Orthodox Doctrine*

Although it encountered some difficulty in providing a general definition of the firm, orthodox microeconomic doctrine, founded on neoclassical assumptions, attempted to formulate a theory about the public enterprise. In a mirror-like way, one can use this doctrine for the analysis of privatization.

The traditional microeconomic view regarding public enterprise is as follows: The market is not always able to generate competitive equilibrium because of "market failures," which can be of four types: natural monopoly, public goods, externalities, and incompleteness of information. Public intervention is justified only when one of these types of market failure is present.

In the simplest market failure case, natural monopoly, we observe economies of scale. The existence of decreasing average costs (or rather, subadditive production functions) forces profit-maximizing firms to apply prices that are higher than the marginal and average costs. The public firm can instead apply cost rules that simulate competitive equilibrium. The state budget covers any possible loss in the case of applying the rule of marginal-cost pricing. Alternatively, Ramsey pricing is the second-best solution for public firms constrained to a balanced budget. A more general case, following the Baumol-Panzar-Willig approach, considers economies of scope as well as economies of scale of a contestable multiproduct firm.

A second market failure case occurs when the private sector is unable to offer the optimum amount of Samuelsonian goods for which consumption is neither rival nor excludable. This happens because of the free-rider problem and the difficulty of true revelation of individual preferences. There may be partial solutions to this second type of market failure through private provision of public goods. If, however, agents consider these goods collectively desirable, and private firms do not supply them, a public provider can offer them and finance the cost through taxation. Public procurement in some cases can substitute for public production.

Third, market failure can occur in cases in which the existence of important externalities in production or consumption can create conflicts that cannot be solved through transactions between private parties. There are different possible solutions to this type of market failure. Public production can redress situations of this type by internalizing the different interests at stake.

In the fourth type of market failure, the existence of incomplete markets distorts price signals or can even prevent potential markets from developing. Public production can eliminate this problem by creating conditions of more complete information and of more effective enforcement of contracts, for example, through public provision of compulsory insurance against certain risks.

When none of these types of market failure is present in a particular sector, the public firm has no role, and privatization of that sector is justified.

This traditional doctrine (as presented in textbooks, e.g., Atkinson and Stiglitz 1980) can offer a first building block of privatization theory in a simple way. One can subject the existing public provision of goods and services in a given country to a market failure checklist based on the four types of market failure outlined above. If the public provision of a good cannot be justified by a market failure, privatization can only improve efficiency, since public intervention is seen here as a costly and imperfect market substitute.[3]

Traditional microeconomic doctrine regarding public enterprise has suffered strong criticism on many fronts. Objections include the following propositions. The concept of natural monopoly at firm level should not, it is argued, be arbitrarily extended to all phases of network industries, even to those such as conventional production of electricity in which economies of scope and of scale are not relevant. The benefits of public management can only be small in comparison to the costs. Pure public good is a very special occurrence that does not involve the typical nationalized sectors (transport, energy, water, etc.) or many of the services of the welfare state (health, education, and social security). There is no reason why public production in cases of externalities should be a better remedy than other solutions (for example, corrective taxes and incentives to the private sector). In cases of incomplete markets from the informative standpoint, public production should not be a better alternative than defining service standards or other means of intervention.

In the end, the broad issue with the traditional view is that "policy failures" can be greater than market failures. The door is thus open for a reconsideration of the tenets of the traditional view.

There is no doubt that many of the criticisms of the traditional doctrine with regard to public enterprise, although often suspiciously unilateral, hit the mark. Traditional doctrine cannot be revived today; neither was it universally agreed upon in past times. To explain public ownership and privatization, we must therefore look at other lines of research, some of which had long coexisted with neoclassical orthodoxy, before meeting with much greater interest recently.

2.2.2   *Property Rights*

The theory of property rights can be traced back to Coase (1937) and was subsequently developed by a number of authors.[4] The reasoning goes as follows. In the case of private ownership, property rights are well defined, and there is a clear incentive for owners to control managers and workers so that they maximize profits. In the case of public ownership, the situation is more confused. Public firms are formally the property of the state, and their profits belong to the state. The state is, however, an abstraction. Ministers or bureaucrats have no specific incentive to guarantee the rights of the public owner. Conversely, they may have their own specific interests of a political nature, or concerning prestige and personal power, which overlap and interfere with the public owner's rights. The latter view, in turn is at the core of the public-choice theory.

The different strength and specification of property rights in the two types of firms leads to a prediction. The state-owned firm is intrinsically less efficient than the private one, since the firm's management in the latter case answers to an owner who has a lot to gain from minimizing costs.[5] Let us take a closer look.

The central proposition of the theory of property rights is that the performance of firms is a function of the regime of ownership in which they operate: "The most important ownership distinction is between state (public) and private ownership" (Alchian and Demsetz 1973, 18). To be verifiable the proposition requires two definitions: what we mean by the variable to be explained (*performance*) and what we mean by the explanatory variable (*ownership*).

Starting with the latter, the theory of property rights classifies ownership as a right, or a series of rights, belonging to the much broader category of individual property vis-à-vis other people (Pejovich 1990, 27). In the Hart-Moore version, the "owner" is the person who can claim the "residual rights." The reference point of this perspective is the individual, who appears to be the only subject involved. Joint ownership, in turn, requires the definition of decision rules. This is far removed from the neoclassical vision in which the firm as such is viewed as an "empty box"; on the contrary, in the property rights approach, only the individual may have rights, and so only the individual can make decisions.

In this context, ownership rights are seen as made up of a group of specific individual rights:

• the right to use a good
• the right to appropriate the fruits of the good itself
• the right to alter it, including the right to transfer one or more of the above rights and the property itself to third parties

For an individual who wants to maximize his utility, the incentive is clearly to exercise his rights in such a way as to achieve maximum efficiency. This includes the sale of the good to a third party who can gain a greater benefit from it, so that the seller may share the results with the more efficient owner.

The previous argument is used in a symmetric way to ascertain that in the case of public ownership the achievement of efficiency is hindered by the following factors:

• The nontransferability of public property implies that it is impossible to assign the good to someone who can manage it better.
• The dilution of the benefits of the economic results of ownership for the "public" weakens the stimulus to achieve them.
• The lack of individual entitlement of property rights (or that of a group of individuals) makes it difficult to measure the economic results of ownership, inasmuch as this is a costly process that is justified in view of the appropriation of the benefits.

The prediction that interests us here, with reference to the British experience, is unambiguous: Privatization will usually improve the performance of firms in itself, that is, more or less independent of other accompanying policies such as liberalization or regulation (which may, however, interfere with the prediction). In any case, one problematic aspect of this prediction involves identifying which performance indicator is most coherent with the approach of the theory of property rights itself.

If we remain within the framework of methodological individualism, we must suppose that the individual intends to maximize a nonvisible variable, which is her utility. This variable may or may not coincide with the firm's profits. Coincidence is not necessary, as, in turn, the firm's profitability is not the same thing as firms' productivity.

An instructive example of dissociation between the utility of a firm's owner and its profits can be found, in a sense paradoxically, in the case of individual owners, for example, the farmer or artisan or the professional person. He or she sees the property of assets as a projection and complement of his or her own person (human capital), instrumental to the execution of an activity that gives him or her income, a certain status, and intrinsic satisfaction. This is just a simple example. The key prediction of the theory of property rights, apparently a clear and sensible one, is in fact too general and vague to be translated into applied analysis because of the uncertainty surrounding the precise definition of the variables at stake (owner, property, performance, efficiency).

Symmetrically, looking at it from the point of view of methodological individualism, the theory of property rights defines public ownership only in negative terms, as the realm of nonrights of the individual. What public ownership is, in general terms, we do not know, because if only individuals may hold rights, in a sense public ownership cannot exist except as an envelope of weak and diluted individual rights.

At a historic level, perhaps, such type of public property existed in the form of the commons, the traditional right of common use of land, forests, and so on. Abundant economic literature has aimed at showing the negative implications of the commons, resulting from the lack of exclusivity of access and the like. This literature, in fact, is not always balanced. Certain types of commons have been sustainable for centuries because of elaborated rules about their use. The tragedy of the commons often occurred when some external factor had disrupted traditional systems for exploiting the commons.

In any case, the public ownership that established itself in the nineteenth and twentieth centuries has very little to do with the commons. It is a set of institutions, regulated by local or national laws and statutes. The set of rules associated with modern public ownership is not based on diluted individual rights. There is no individual ownership right to the road system of a country, to its water network, or to its hospital facilities, when these are the property of a public body. There are individual rights of users-taxpayers, but these cannot be construed as property. In some cases, there are individual voting rights to elect public administrators, who will in turn be responsible for the management of public services or the appointment of managers. In general, however, the holders of those rights that are similar to (but in fact not concurrent with) those of private property are collective subjects, not individuals (Barzel 1997). (This brings us to the study of how these collective subjects function. I deal with this in the next section, which is dedicated to public-choice theory and the contribution it can make to the study of privatization.)

To conclude with the theory of property rights, privatization itself paradoxically constitutes a kind of counterevidence with respect to the abstract nature of the theory in its more dogmatic versions. The large-scale transfer of public property to the private sector shows that it is not true that such property is nontransferable. Public subjects that hold property rights can, when the law allows and electors agree, sell them. If they wish to do so, they can sell the publicly owned goods to the highest bidder or make a gift of them. If the law does not allow them to do this, then they can change the law, something that the private sector cannot do. Therefore, the thesis of nontransferability of state-owned enterprises, with all its crucial implications, is questionable. On a closer look, both private and public property are the envelope of a range of property rights. These rights, including the right to transfer ownership, may be more or less well defined for either private or public agents. What we can predict about the resulting incentive structures and performances depends upon the specific objectives and constraints of the agents.

2.2.3   Corporate Governance

To the advocates of the theory of property rights, it is clear that the large firm is not the place for the self-rule of individual owners. The raising of huge amounts of capital from thousands (later to become hundreds of thousands and millions) of individual shareholders implies that managerial decisions must be delegated (Berle and Means 1933; Coffee 1999, 2000; Demsetz 1988; Jensen and Fama 2000). This opens the door to the risk that owners will not be able to monitor closely how their rights are affected by managers' decisions. For example, managers can siphon off part of the firm's profits in the form of high salaries or other benefits.

There is, however, a counterargument to this view. The right to confer and to cancel the mandate to manage the firm remains with the firm's shareholders. If they are not satisfied with the firm's performance, they can transfer their property rights, that is, sell their shares to third parties. Therefore, if the shareholders feel that changing managers is a costly decision to implement, they have a way out. Any resulting decrease in the value of the firm's shares will make it easier for teams that are more efficient to take over. It follows that the managerial market and property rights can operate in an integrated way to ensure, in fact, roughly the same results as would have been obtained in a less complex context (Jensen and Ruback 1983; Grossman and Hart 1980).

The observation that apparently there is no inverse correlation between diffuse share ownership and share values seems to confirm property rights theory. The corporate governance literature, however, goes much farther than these simple predictions.[6] Studies in this area typically focus on five issues:

- the impact of the law and behaviors on the separation of ownership and control
- monitoring by owners and third parties
- contracts and their legal enforcement
- takeovers and managerial effort
- bankruptcy as a credible threat

The empirical findings cast doubts on the one-way conclusions of the theory of property rights. These findings show that a number of outcomes are possible under different ownership structures.

First, there is evidence, particularly in transition economies, that managers of privatized companies can expropriate shareholders, without risking a takeover. In fact, there are obvious incentives for executive directors to form a coalition with a control group and to share among them the benefits of ownership. Other shareholders, however, can exit only if they actually have better alternatives. Paradoxically, recognition of good company performance may give a small, risk-averse shareholder an incentive to sell to make a profit, whereas a poor performance may lead to the apparently irrational decision to hold (in actuality, a situation of being trapped).

Empirical research on corporate governance of privatized firms, particularly in transition economies and less-developed countries, has widely shown how difficult it is to make general predictions about the impact on firms' performance of actual corporate governance mechanisms. Formal legislation is important as a factor in governance structure, but actual behaviors are too. Unfortunately, good empirical research on ownership versus control in state-owned enterprises is scarce. Anedoctal evidence shows that the management of public corporations does respond to incentives from those corporations' collective owners. A clear example is the British experience under the Thatcher government. As I show in chapter 6, following new directives by ministries in Thatcher's time, managers in the nationalized industries suddenly changed industrial relations habits and procurement routines. This led to huge downsizing under public ownership, even before the announcement of divestiture.

Another example of corporate governance issues is monitoring. Because monitoring is usually costly for an individual shareholder, the corporate governance literature explores the role of other agents, particularly of banks or financiers, in monitoring. Again, it seems difficult to say that monitoring of a privatized firm by banks will always be more effective than such monitoring of a public corporation. Public corporations may or may not recur to bank loans or to corporate bond issues. There is ample evidence, in Europe and elsewhere, that financial institutions can effectively monitor public corporations. On the other hand, lack of transparency can hinder monitoring in either public or private ownership.

The bankruptcy argument against public ownership runs as follows. The state-owned firm cannot go bankrupt, thanks to soft budget constraints. The exposure of private companies to the threat of bankruptcy gives managers the right incentives. They know that mismanagement or simply lack of effort may be extremely dangerous. Many very large private firms, however, also do not face bankruptcy, at least in the conventional meaning. In the United States, the European Union, and elsewhere, there are a number of safety nets for large firms, including banks (e.g., Chapter 11 legislation in the United States, receivership, and bailouts). Moreover, those who actually bear the risk of a firm's potential bankruptcy are not its managers, but its creditors, its employees, and its less-informed shareholders. On closer inspection, the bankruptcy argument against public ownership needs a lot of qualifications to hold.

2.2.4 Public Choice

The public-choice approach dates back to the contributions of Downs, Niskanen, Tullock, Buchanan, Mueller, Frey, and several others reviewed by Mueller (2003).[7] These authors stress the divergence of objectives between the public owner and the private. Whereas for the latter the objective of economic activity is well defined, the traditional maximization of profits, there is a plurality of economic and political objectives for the public owner. Some of these objectives can be attributed to the preferences of those that the political system puts in a position to nominate, monitor, or recall the managers of public firms. These objectives can diverge from the maximization of profits or minimization of costs. Managers of public firms use resources differently and in general less efficiently than they would in a regime of private ownership.

We can extract a number of specific propositions from the public-choice literature. First, methodological individualism applies to the analysis of the public sector in the same way as it does to the analysis of private organizations. Politicians and bureaucrats wish to maximize their own utility and do not necessarily serve the common good. According to Niskanen (1971), three "p-variables"— pay, power and prestige—approximate individual utility in the public sector.

Second, the manager of a public firm, like any holder of public office, will try to maximize those variables that correlate with his or her utility. These may include revenues, sales, budget (revenues plus transfers), employment, or investment. There is no incentive to minimize costs, hence the intrinsic inefficiency of the public firm.

Moreover, the monopoly power typically enjoyed by public firms allows insiders and especially top management to use the information they possess in a manipulative manner. The informative costs for users and citizens in general prevent them from monitoring the management of public firms. (I deal with this subject in more detail in my discussion of the principal-agent approach in section 2.2.6.)

Finally, in the public firm there will be a widespread tendency toward rent seeking, not only on the part of the management, but also on the part of trade unions. On the other hand, the political system will be able to exercise greater control over management in public firms than in private. This greater control will not, however, necessarily have beneficial effects on efficiency. Conversely, the firm may become a functional instrument for maximizing the consensus of incumbent politicians, with the imposition of objectives (for example: employment objectives) that have little to do with the firm's mandate to supply services at minimum cost. In the end, the firm may end up being captured by groups with common interests that condition the politicians. These in turn condition the firm's management.

Privatization takes the firm away from groups with external interests or from rent seeking by insiders or opportunistic behavior by politicians. Under private ownership, efficiency increases. From here onward, the argument is similar to the one based on the theory of property rights.

Thus, the two strands of theory, that of property rights and that of public choice, converge: Both start from methodological individualism, then apply it in different contexts and reach similar predictions. The principal weakness of both these currents is, however, precisely their dichotomous nature. Apart from the merit of single propositions deriving from the two theories, the fundamental contraposition of public and private property in both theories, although historically founded, is analytically ambiguous. Many of the problems raised by the two theories are also relevant to the private sector, especially in the context of large firms.

Tittenbrun (1996) and Martin and Parker (1997) observe that there seems to be a continuum of firm ownership between public and private, rather than a net separation of the two types of ownership. Perhaps this is going too far. The distinction between private and public ownership is helpful at an abstract level, but for purposes other than those for which public-choice theory uses it.

In a democracy, public institutions are part of a political system based on voting rights. This is a purely formalistic vision of how a real-world political system works, however, and here methodological individualism appears to be inadequate. Politicians may have their private agendas, but these agendas may include their vision of the common good. In turn the formation of ideas about what constitutes social welfare is a complex process. Individuals react to a number of collective factors. The attempt to build an economic theory about the functioning of the state based on the axiom of methodological individualism appears to be far-fetched.

On the other hand, consider the following array of examples: a public firm captured by its management, which de facto behaves like a "residual claimant" of the firm's profits (perhaps hidden); a private firm controlled by a very small coalition of insiders and owned by millions of shareholders who never see a balance sheet and are happy with a satisfying dividend; a public enterprise the share capital of which is controlled by the Treasury, but with a large part of its capital placed on the stock exchange, that is exposed to competition, and that is run by a professional management; or a private firm operating in a strict regime of regulation. These and several other possible examples show that the concept of public versus private in much of the literature mentioned previously is somewhat blurred and lends itself to different interpretations.

Besides, again, privatization paradoxically contradicts public-choice theory. If politicians or the management of a public firm were interested in maximizing their own utility, and the public firm were a part of this plan, why at a certain point would they decide to implement a policy of large-scale privatization? Do the politicians who privatize pursue the public interest (especially greater efficiency), and those who nationalize pursue their own personal interests? Alternatively, do the public and private interests of the policymakers who privatize coincide in some way, whereas they diverge when policymakers establish or manage a public firm?

2.2.5 The Austrian Perspective

Another interesting strand of literature to emerge from the privatization debate is the Austrian approach, associated with Menger, Wieser, Boehm-Bawerk, and Hayek, for some aspects also with Schumpeter, and in later years with contributions from Machlup, Kirzner, Shackle, and others. Some protagonists of the British privatization, including Thatcher and Professor Stephen Littlechild, an influential adviser to the Conservative government, explicitly acknowledged that Hayek's works had influenced their views.

The Austrian approach shares with the theories of property rights and of public choice methodological individualism as an epistemological axiom (in a philosophically much more sophisticated form). Although it reaches the same conclusions for public policy as those two theories, some of its propositions are original and offer a specific perspective.

The crucial aspect of the functioning of the economy in the Austrian conception, in contrast to that in the neoclassical vision, is not the efficient allocation of scarce resources under complete information, but the introduction of continuous innovations under conditions of uncertainty. The public firm disregards those market signals that should orient the continuous activity of discovery and adaptation that substantiates the role of the entrepreneur.

There are two possible explanations as to why the public firm ignores market signals. First, freedom to search for revenues is weakened in the public firm, both because of the existence of regimes of legal monopoly and because of the statutory limits imposed on the public firm that prevent it from diversifying. Second, the pricing rules for the public firm (e.g., the rule of matching price to marginal cost) weaken the role of nonparametric, or disequilibrium, prices. For example, monopoly prices and profits by some firms are powerful signals to all other agents to adapt their behavior following new circumstances. Thus, marginal-cost pricing, based on known information, inhibits the chance of discovering new information about costs and exploiting it. Cost is a subjective quantity, because it involves expectations of future values and not an objective calculation based on certain data.

The imposition of predetermined budgetary rules on the public firm (e.g., the obligation to break even, and also soft budget constraints [Kornai 1980]) eliminates profits and losses from the scenario and thus wipes away other crucial signals for entrepreneurial activity. The impossibility of the firm's going bankrupt prevents freedom of exit from the market and obscures situations in which the public firm's organization and operation have been surpassed by technological and market evolution.

The public firm is a hostile environment for innovation and for the trial-and-error mechanism that is the heart of the economy itself, according to the Austrian vision. Only private property and competition can generate an appropriate process of experimentation with innovative solutions, according to the perceptions of individual operators.

The philosophical basis of the Austrian doctrine is an extreme subjectivism, which poses considerable epistemological problems. The contribution that this subjectivism offers to privatization theory does not go much farther than stating that public firms have often difficulty in adapting to change. The lack of entrepreneurs in such firms implies insufficient stimuli to innovation.

The theoretical status of this proposition is, however, doubtful. Is it an empirical observation linked to specific methods of organization of the public sector, or is there some deeper connection, as some of the previous remarks would imply?

In fact, the proposition raises quite a few misgivings. In the vision of Joseph Schumpeter, who has made the greatest contributions regarding the socioeconomic role of the entrepreneur, the function of the capital owner is indeed conceptually and historically separated from that of the entrepreneur. Furthermore, innovators may not be an individual but a team, as they are in effect to an increasing extent in complex private organizations. The conditions that allow the entrepreneurial type to flourish in a certain society have undoubtedly been historically associated with capitalism and still are. An example is the interaction between entrepreneurs in industries based on the Internet and venture capital and the stock exchange. However, this historical association between entrepreneurship and capitalism should not lead to a confusion between the roles of the entrepreneur and the capitalist, which remain at least conceptually quite separate.

In other contexts, for example, one may speak of political, social, or even religious entrepreneurs. These individuals show innovative capacities and, wherever the institutional environment allows it, they implement changes. They often do not claim ownership of the resources that third parties make available to them. Most scientists, for example, are innovators in their field, with only limited ownership of or economic rights to the fruits of their discovery or invention. They have other incentives to innovate.

Thus, managers of public firms may have greater or lesser entrepreneurial aptitude than their counterparts in private firms. A number of factors play a role in this aptitude, including the internal and external rules of the organization's functioning, the degree of autonomy the managers have from the political system, the system for remunerating managers, the existence of competitive challenges to the firm from other organizations, and reputation aspects (i.e., the good reports and credit acquired during one's managerial career in the public sector). Historically, some of the most innovative firms have been either state-owned or under strict control of governments. Symmetrically, in appropriate conditions, the manager of a private firm can be a bureaucrat who minimizes risk and uses all his energy to put up defenses of his monopoly power against potential competitors. An example that I indirectly consider later within the British Telecom case history (chapter 9) is the behavior of the management of a regulated monopoly (or asymmetric duopoly). In such a case it may pay for the managers to behave in such a way as to convince the regulator to postpone the entry of competitors. Rent seeking is a perfectly rational behavior for a profit-maximizing private firm in certain circumstances.

2.2.6 The Principal-Agent Approach

The agency theory framework may offer a different approach to privatization (Vickers and Yarrow 1988a). In large organizations, both private and public, there is informative asymmetry between owners and managers, as well as different objectives. We can model principal-agent problems in terms of incentive and information structures (Sappington and Stiglitz 1987; see also the agency problems described in Laffont and Tirole 1993, 2000; and Shapiro and Willig 1990). Theorization based on ownership alone cannot solve this class of problems. It can, however, play a role in their solution.

Different agents may engage in mutual relationship in defining the objectives of the firm and determining how it will be run. For a nationalized firm, policymakers appoint managers and answer to the voters. Public bureaucracy, including top management, answers to the policymakers. For a large private firm, the management answers to the shareholders. Under a given regulatory environment, however, the management may also answer to regulators. The latter, in turn, although partially independent of policymakers, operates on their mandate. Sometimes trade unions, consumers, or workers may be involved in the decision-making process as well. Each agent has his own objectives, information that the others do not share, certain powers, and costs of monitoring and of contract enforcement. (See, e.g., Shapiro and Willig 1990; Bös 1991, 1994; Bös and Peters 1991; Hart, Schleifer, and Vishny 1997; Schleifer 1998; and Laffont and Tirole 2000b)

Game-theoretic models formalize the relationships between the agents in this decision-making framework. These models usually introduce strong conceptual simplifications into the hypotheses about and characterization of the economy that they employ. In the simplest case they are partial equilibrium settings, with only one good and one subgroup of relationships, typically including only games played by two kinds of agent, and so on. More complex models are available, however, in the theoretical literature (e.g., Laffont and Tirole 1993; Bös 1994, chaps. 28–32).

A well-known example of this approach is Laffont and Tirole 1993. In Laffont and Tirole's benchmark model, an indivisible public project is implemented by a monopolist, whose cost function includes an efficiency parameter and a managerial-effort parameter. The regulator can reimburse the production costs to the firm, but the firm accepts the procurement contract only if the regulator allows a reservation utility level that can be standardized as a normal profit. This contract setting may imply an additional transfer from the regulator to the firm. Public funds involved in this transaction require shadow pricing because of distortionary taxation. Social welfare is a function of the consumer surplus, the managers' utility, and the shadow price of public funds. The firm's utility is equal to the transfer from the regulator, less the disutility of managerial effort. The regulator can easily derive the optimal contract in welfare terms, if he or she knows the firm's efficiency parameter and is ready to meet the incentive constraints (i.e., the manager should get not less than his or her reservation utility). If, however, the government has less information than the firm's management on the efficiency parameter and knows only that the parameter can take a range of values with a given probability distribution, a problem of asymmetric information arises. It is easy to show that in such a situation, the regulated efficient firm will earn socially costly rents that are increasing in the exogenous efficiency parameter. The firm might be either a public corporation or a private regulated firm with taxation of excess profit at the 100 percent rate.

Now, as a variation on this basic model, suppose that profits are taxed at less than 100 percent and that shareholders can offer a contract to the firm that parallels the transfer that the regulator can offer. There are now two principals, and management should accept both offers to start production. In this context additional rents arise:

First, private regulated firms suffer from the conflict of interest between shareholders and regulators. For instance each principal fails to internalize the effect of contracting on the other principal and provides socially too few incentives for the firm's insiders. Second, while the managers of private firms invest more on non-contractible investments, public sector managers invest less, because of the risk of expropriation (e.g., in the form of additional social goals, such as promoting regional development, containing unemployment, etc.). (Laffont and Tirole 1993, 654)

The implication of this double-principal framework is that results are ambiguous, and we cannot establish in general the relative efficiency of private versus public firms (including the quality of output). There are several possible variations on these simple models.

The principal-agent literature, unlike that of the property rights, public-choice and Austrian school theories, does not lead to unilateral predictions. The analytical results obtained through research in this area are strongly dependent on the specific configuration of the problem under study, and empirical research in this area is still in its infancy.

Nevertheless, many of the topics raised by agency theory are conceptually interesting. The theory suggests that we should not define privatization (or nationalization, if these policies are examined in the same way) as a transfer of formal property rights. Policy reforms bring about a change in informative structures and in incentives. Ownership change is a vehicle of this more complex transformation of the economic environment. For example, within this framework one can study the equivalence conditions for public and private ownership (Sappington and Stiglitz 1987) and the implications of incomplete contracts (Schmidt 1996).

2.3   Some Welfare Economics of Privatization

The research strands I have described up to this point offer many useful intuitions about the economic effects of privatizations to which I shall often refer in my discussion of empirical aspects of the U.K. experience. The strength of these ideas, however, lies more in their suggesting certain interpretations rather than in their offering a detailed analytical framework that can be applied to studies of specific countries. Moreover, propositions about the superior efficiency of the private firm compared to the public one are often dogmatic.

What I want to do, here, is to evaluate privatization in terms of social welfare, without relying on strong a priori assumptions. For example, it cannot be taken for granted that reducing the allocative distortions in a sector increases aggregate welfare. This is not always true, as optimal-taxation theory shows. Moreover, a number of models employ strong simplifications. For example, principal-agent models often address purely illustrative objective functions. The predictions offered by these simple models can suggest some empirical tests, but real-world economy is too complex to be studied through the assumptions of one specific theory. On the other hand, one would like to explore what one can say about the changes in social welfare (appropriately defined) brought about by privatization in a given economy and time.

It is not necessary to assume, in exploring these changes, that the government, in Britain or elsewhere, intends to maximize social welfare; it is sufficient to say that this objective function expressed in terms of social welfare is in itself of interest. In other words, examining social changes that result from privatization does not necessitate making any specific assumptions about the self-interested or benevolent nature of policymakers. Social welfare is defined and the impact of policy reforms is observed (or guessed) on our conventional measure. One might also wish to use sensitivity analysis to provide an alternative welfare measure and discover whether results are robust. From this point of view, the evaluation of a public divestiture project requires tools of applied welfare economics similar to those used in the cost-benefit analysis of public investments.

2.3.1   Cost-Benefit Analysis

The compulsory references for a systematic exposition of the theory in the field of cost-benefit analysis remain Drèze and Stern 1987 and 1990. The authors offer a useful approach to the problem under consideration, in the framework of the broader theory of reform.[8] They maintain that privatization implies a transfer of a stream of profits from the public to the private sector as well as changes in technology and production levels of privatized industries. In principle, we can evaluate the first aspect like any other transfer of income, by the use of welfare weights that transform private benefits into social welfare and by the distribution characteristics of consumption goods. Evaluation of the remaining aspects requires the use of the shadow prices of the good produced before and after privatization.

According to Drèze and Stern (1990), the first aspect will usually weigh negatively in the evaluation of a privatization reform. Profits from privatization accrue to high-income social groups, whose welfare weights are lower (on the social-welfare function) than those of the beneficiaries of transfers from the public sector. The other evaluation aspects will have ambiguous signs, since they depend on the structure of the incentives, on the previous integration of nationalized firms into public policies, on the efficacy of these policies and their coherence with the general objectives as embodied in the social-welfare function, and so forth.

In what follows I try to build on Drèze and Stern's approach, by presenting (informally) the basic concepts of a cost-benefit analysis of privatization. Readers who wish a more formal treatment may consult the references cited within the discussion and notes.

The first and most important step in the appraisal (ex ante) or evaluation (ex post) of a public divestiture is to measure the effects it has on consumers. To this end, it is advisable to consider explicitly the direction of price changes resulting from the divestiture for goods and services produced by the privatized firms. Price changes as a result of privatization should be compared to those of the same firms in a regime of public ownership, under specific assumptions about the market and regulatory environment. It is therefore necessary to make a projection of prices with and without privatization and compare any difference in the conjectured prices in the two scenarios.

Obviously, a privatized and regulated firm that has an obligation to satisfy all demand at optimal prices and whose possible profits are taxed at 100 percent is virtually indistinguishable from an optimally planned public firm. In theory, for a public firm, the optimal prices at which to manage transactions are shadow prices, which the planner computes by solving the problem of constrained maximization of a social-welfare function (SWF). We can specify this function using indices of aggregate individual welfare with appropriate distributive weights (one can think of more complex SWFs, but I focus here on the standard case). The regulator might then perform the same calculation for a privatized firm. In practice, however, things can work differently from this optimal scenario, for the following reasons.

For state-owned enterprises, a typical second-best case studied in the literature on optimal tariffs, beginning with the classical contribution by Boiteux (1956),[9] is the existence of budget constraints. Public firms, however, can be subject to a variety of additional restrictions, such as quantity constraints, which arise when there is credit rationing. In the case of the United Kingdom in the period prior to the privatizations there was a specific version of cash limits, the "external financial limits," so that state-owned firms could incur debts only up to a certain ceiling fixed by the government. Such cash limits ration public funds and may be inconsistent with shadow price formulas that ignore this constraint (cf. Florio 1990). Other typical quantity constraints arise when the government imposes limits on the mobility of workers, the aim being, for example, to help preserve employment in a certain area or industry. An additional constraint again of a quantitative nature (on production factors or joint products) results from the imposition of standards for the environment and for the quality of goods produced that are more stringent than those for the private sector. Similarly, there may be restrictions on the localization of investments and so on.

As has often been observed, firms in the public sector are not generally able to apply simple formulas of optimal pricing, à la Ramsey or Boiteux, perhaps because the above-mentioned additional constraints considerably complicate the welfare-maximization problem from both the analytical and the informative point of view. Moreover, managers and politicians may have their private agendas that interfere with public goals.

Some of the additional constraints mentioned above were stringent in the experience of the nationalized sector in the United Kingdom in the 1970s. Public firms formulated their decisions concerning investments, employment, and pricing in a much more complicated manner than that suggested by the standard theory. Thus when hypothesizing a scenario without privatization, one must bear in mind any possible divergences between effective tariffs in the nationalized sector and optimum tariffs. Alternatively, one can conceive of two scenarios, one in which privatization is compared with a counterfactual, suboptimal nationalized industry and another in which for comparison a benchmark of optimal planning, or equivalently, optimal regulation, is used.

Under suboptimal regulation, price distortions may result in relative prices' being higher or lower than the corresponding shadow prices. For example, in a situation of nonregulated symmetric oligopoly, destructive competition (Kahn 1989) may momentarily prevail, with decreasing prices, worsening of the quality of the goods (cf. Kamerma and Kahn 1989), bankruptcy, and industry disarray (the railways and airlines industry in Britain offer some examples). Many other outcomes are possible and probable, however: for example, the establishing of a private monopoly or collusive oligopoly characterized by prices that include a considerable monopolistic rent, the likelihood of which increases as the possibility of price discrimination increases. Obviously, it is also possible that the government eliminates the public monopoly at the same time of liberalization. Then competition develops, with falling prices and net benefits for the consumers. As I show particularly in chapter 7 in the case of the United Kingdom, however, this may come about with totally different timing and modalities from sector to sector. In a sense, this is good for empirical research, because it offers variations in reform regimes. For example, we may observe privatization with price regulation but without liberalization, then private ownership with price regulation and liberalization, and eventually private ownership without price regulation and with full competition. Thus in general one cannot say whether with a large-scale privatization that involves various sectors, relative prices of the privatized industries will on average increase or decrease; neither can one say whether this is socially desirable compared to the previous situation under public ownership.

There are some clues that may help one to understand what happens when we observe the privatized industries. Particularly, the formation of monopoly profits may signal divergence between average unit revenues and marginal costs. In principle, there are good theoretical arguments for supposing that long-term marginal costs are good proxies for shadow prices in the privatized industries. If the average production costs in the privatized industries are not too different from marginal costs and implicitly from shadow prices, as may be the case under constant returns to scale, then a rate of return on capital in the privatized sectors that is constantly higher than the average for the economy is probably an indication that regulation is weak. Perhaps the regulated firm has captured the regulator, or the latter has been surprised by unexpected demand or technology shocks. In these or other cases, if we evaluate the benefits of privatization by using shadow prices based on costs, instead of actual distorted prices, the picture we obtain is quite different from the conventional one. We may wish to compare this wedge between prices and social-opportunity costs under privatization and under nationalization (observed in past times or as a counterfactual).

The previously mentioned example of monopoly profits under constant returns should convince us that it is not possible to say a priori whether a particular preprivatization vector of prices and quantity was "better" than the corresponding postprivatization one. Neither is there any justification in the presumption that the welfare of consumers (measured with some appropriate metric or even with the simple and inaccurate consumer surplus) will invariably increase under privatization, at least after a momentary adjustment. Everything will depend on the degree of distortion at the beginning and that of postprivatization prices. Readers should keep this argument in mind when I discuss, in chapter 7, the effects of privatization on prices in the U.K. experience, in sectors such as water, telecommunications, and energy.

In the framework of the approach described above, it will in any case be necessary to specify a criterion of social welfare to keep count of redistribution effects. In fact, we cannot refer to a representative consumer for this purpose. Changes in prices affect not an average or median consumer, but consumers with different levels of income and welfare. The achievement of greater aggregate welfare for the users of public services provided by the privatized utilities (whatever way it is measured) depends on the starting and finishing lines of the set of consumer prices; on whether or not price discrimination exists for different categories of consumers; and on any possible concurrent redistribution of incomes. In the United Kingdom, the effect of the second of these factors was not negligible.

All this discussion constitutes a reason for being cautious in the evaluation of privatization policies. If the market is imperfect and the prevailing price structure within a particular nationalized industry prior to privatization was not very different from marginal costs (obviously minimum or efficient marginal costs), then the wider the privatization policy, the greater the risk of its introducing distorted prices into the economy. Obviously the inverse relationship is also true. If prior to privatization production costs were too high and prices were strongly distorted, and if after privatization the government is able to steer the system toward a competitive equilibrium or toward a regulated market with tariffs near optimum, then a policy of public divestiture will increase social welfare.

The interpretation of variations in prices and costs therefore represents the heart of the problem that I am discussing. As Hicks (1946) wrote clearly many years ago, the only reason for aggregating quantities through market prices in forming a nation's accounts is the presumption that those prices are near the marginal rates of substitution between goods. If prices are not correlated with measures of individual welfare, the macroeconomic data tell us little about social welfare. The income statements of privatized firms, too often the only basis for the public debate, tell us even less.

Government should implement a public-investment project only if it guarantees a social profit. The project should show a positive difference between the values of its outputs and inputs, evaluated using accounting prices that reflect the social-opportunity cost of the goods used and produced. In the same way, welfare-maximizing governments should not carry out a public divestiture if the social profit from divestiture is negative, independent of any possible increase in the firm's profit at market prices.

Let us now examine some of these points in more detail.

2.3.2   Redistribution Effects: Consumers, Shareholders, and Taxpayers

Let us suppose for a moment that shadow prices do not change with privatization, as would be the case in a marginal privatization project, which by definition does not modify objectives of, constraints on, and solutions to the social-optimum problem. Then it is clear that the evaluation of the privatization project in terms of social welfare depends only on the effects of quantity and of redistribution. Both types of effects have a causal link with the passage from a regime of public tariffs to one of competitive or regulated prices. In other words, given a set of shadow prices and distributive weights for the economy, the increase or decrease in social profit following the divestiture of a particular industry is determined by the long-term increase in consumption and by distribution aspects.

In an economy of the Diamond-Mirrlees (1976) type, characterized by constant returns and conditions of competitive equilibrium, profits calculated at production prices, without distributive adjustments, are greater than those computed by weighting the redistributed added value with an appropriate system of weights of social preferences. In these conditions, the social evaluation of privatization will generally be lower than that at market prices, unless compensatory policies are implemented by means of appropriate taxes and transfers, virtually taxing the capital gains and profits from privatization of the higher income groups and subsidizing the lower income groups. Note here that the compensation must be "effective," and not potential, à la Kaldor-Hicks. One remedy in terms of actual compensation is presumably the windfall gains tax of privatized firms introduced by the Blair government when it took office in 1997. On the other hand, as I discuss in chapters 5 and 8, it was a tardy remedy, and on top of that, one that was scarcely consistent with the framework of regulation inasmuch as it revealed its unreliability. Other redistribution effects, as noted previously, pass through changes in prices (and rationing). An example is tariff rebalancing, for example, in telephone services, which may favor high-volume business users in comparison with low-volume residential users, for example, pensioners, see chapter 7.

Privatization may also result in redistribution of producer surpluses between the incumbent, competitors, and suppliers and in indirect changes in the profits of business customers of the privatized utilities. These effects usually either are small or compensate for one another and consequently require limited welfare adjustment. There may, however, be more sizeable cases.

Finally, another social group comes into play, the taxpayers, which form the largest group of all those considered. Nationalized firms belong to them in the form of virtual collective property. Any possible losses by such firms will worsen the net assets of the state; any possible profits will improve them. With privatization, capital gains may fall on the buyer or on the seller, or the transaction can be neutral. I discuss this point in detail in chapter 8, along with its implications for social welfare.

2.3.3 Efficiency Effects: Firms and Workers

Redistribution effects should be traded off against any possible increase in productive efficiency. For any such valuation to be coherent, we must again measure gains in productive efficiency using a suitable system of accounting prices. In general this system will not be based simply on production prices, as in the simple case mentioned previously, since the majority of privatized activities do not have the characteristics required by the Diamond-Mirrlees model.

Moreover, it is quite unreasonable to assume that shadow prices and production prices generally coincide, because of the existence of increasing returns, externalities, and public goods. One must explicitly bear in mind that a large-scale privatization, altering the state of the economy, changes the general equilibrium. If this is a non-Walrasian equilibrium, with constraints of quantity, unemployment, and other macroeconomic imbalances, shadow prices change according to the change in the state of the economy.

This subject is very complex (see Starrett 1988). It will only be touched on in the discussion of the U.K. experience, since it is also of relatively limited practical interest, because, perhaps surprisingly, the effects of privatization on firms' productivity appear to be empirically modest. Why this came about I discuss mainly in chapter 4.

So far, I have touched on some problems that affect first consumers, and second savers who have purchased shares in privatized firms and taxpayers (who virtually are the sellers). Another group whose welfare is typically influenced by divestiture is the workers of the previously nationalized sector. If there was excess employment, wages, or both in the state-owned enterprises of that sector, then layoffs and reductions in real wages may take place when those enterprises are privatized.

Here we must ask ourselves whether there are any effective differences in the two scenarios (with and without privatization) from the point of view of social welfare and if so, how to evaluate these differences. In principle for this evaluation, it will be necessary to consider the gap between effective wages and shadow wages. Obviously much depends on the hypotheses that can be formulated about the productivity of laid-off workers and their destiny after privatization. Chapter 6 offers a discussion of these issues.

2.3.4   The Macroeconomics of Privatization

The effects I have talked about can be analyzed in terms of variations in the welfare of the single agents (consumers, firms, shareholders, workers, and taxpayers). In addition to such microeconomic evaluation, theoretically, one can fall back on a macroeconomic transformation of the traditional social-welfare function of the Bergson-Samuelson type.[10] Following such an approach, any change in social welfare can be broken down into the sum of four variations: prices, output, employment, and an inequality index (see the appendix to this chapter).

I suggest an evaluation of the impact of privatization on social welfare through these same four components. From now on I suppose that the economy is closed, or alternatively that the foreign sector is not allowed to purchase shares in the firms in the economy, and that there are no second-order impacts on trade with the rest of the world. (Such a restriction on share purchases is not allowed by European Union regulations, but it was implemented in some transition economies.) Otherwise it would be necessary to subtract from social welfare the benefits transferred abroad. Alternatively, we may consider the rest of the world as if it were a national agent. In some cases this is acceptable; in other cases it is inappropriate.

Let us now suppose at first that production prices can change, but that they continue to be representative of shadow prices. In this case, privatization is socially beneficial only if its possible positive effects on GDP and employment compensate for any possible fall in the distributive index and possible inflationary pressures, namely, aggregate price changes. Under the hypotheses given previously, this offers an approximate measure of the costs and benefits of privatization.

2.3.5   Privatization, Public Finance, and Social Welfare

I turn now to a complementary approach to the evaluation of divestiture. In fact, the prior discussion also lends itself to a reformulation in welfare terms of the change in public-finance accounts following privatization.

Consider the time-discounted budget of the public sector. In a simple model, the government budget may depend on the indirect taxes on privately produced goods, the tariffs on publicly produced goods, the profits in the private sector and the average rate of tax on profits, and transfers or lump-sum taxes for each taxpayer. In other words, the time-discounted budget for a closed economy is the net present value of direct and indirect tax revenues, transfers, and the balances of the public firms. The single addends are net public spending or public revenue, according to the sign of the parameters under government control. The values for each year are discounted at a rate that expresses the opportunity cost to the government of the numeraire in a given time horizon. Here it is not relevant how the rate is calculated. It could also be, in a first approximation, the real interest rate on additional public debt.

With the time-discounted budget balance thus defined, possible short-term proceeds from privatization are added to future decreases in tariff revenue and with possible additional proceeds from an increase in profit taxes and so forth. The lump-sum revenue is equal to the transfers from the state plus the quota of profits distributed to the private sector, net of tax.

The time-discounted public balance equals the difference between the net product of the public sector and the net consumption of the private sector, where quantities are all evaluated at shadow prices. According to Walras's law, in fact, under certain conditions if $n-1$ markets balance in correspondence with a vector of prices, the closing equation, in this case the public balance, is also satisfied by the same vector.

Suppose now that the government is not capable of imposing optimum production prices because there are externalities, quantity rationing, and so on. In this case, the price vector that we should use in evaluating the privatization programs is again the vector of shadow prices and not that of actual prices. We would then have a shadow budget balance that depends on two components. The first is the net production of the public sector evaluated at accounting tariffs. The second is the contribution to the government budget of private consumption, evaluated using the spread between market price and shadow price (in other words, with optimum indirect tax, à la Diamond and Mirrlees 1971a, 1971b).

Obviously if the shadow price and the production price coincide, the budget balance of the public sector evaluated at actual prices and evaluated at shadow prices will in turn coincide (the shadow tax is nil). Therefore, we can also evaluate the welfare effects of privatization programs in principle by examining the government budget balance, but correcting the effective prices and tariffs pre- and postprivatization with appropriate accounting prices.

For a marginal privatization the time-discounted budget remains in equilibrium with the previous value of shadow prices if, and only if, the increase in net demand of the private sector is such that it compensates for the decrease in public production. (The net worth of the public sector may offer a crude empirical proxy for what I have in mind; see chapter 8). This remark provides a measure of how much productive efficiency must increase and/or how effective the public regulation of the market must be to compensate for the fall in net supply of the public sector during privatization.

Finally, for the welfare-maximizing government, the "right" sale price of a marginal public firm equals the increase in net product in the private sector as a result of privatization, evaluated at shadow prices, with the loss of net product in the public sector, also evaluated at shadow prices, having been deducted.

2.4   Summing Up

The evaluation of a large-scale privatization policy can be viewed as a problem of applied welfare economics. This does not exclude testing propositions taken from other approaches such as the theory of property rights, the corporate governance literature, public-choice theory, the Austrian school, agency theory, and even traditional neoclassical doctrine. I do not, however, take any of these approaches as justifications for unilateral predictions. I suggest testing theoretical propositions at an empirical level and trace them back to a comprehensive evaluation, as far as possible. I use cost-benefit analysis as my accounting framework.

Three converging strategies of cost-benefit analysis are possible:

1. One can calculate the changes in welfare for single groups of agents (consumers, shareholders, workers, and taxpayers) and aggregate these changes with an appropriate microeconomic SWF.

2. Alternatively, one can use a macroeconomic transformation of the same function and break down the effects of privatization into four aggregate indices—product, prices, income distribution, and employment —then aggregate the impacts using appropriate weighting coefficients.

3. Finally, one can use Walras's law to calculate the aggregate effect of privatization on the budget balance of the public sector, time-discounted and evaluated at shadow prices.

Under appropriate conditions, these three welfare change measures must yield the same result.

I consider this framework simply as a way of establishing some ideas. Daunting practical difficulties arise if one wishes to proceed to the evaluation of studies of specific countries. These difficulties do not, however, authorize us to return to accounting measures that are unsatisfactory for testing social-welfare changes, such as the short-term financial impact on the government budget, or on the firm's profitability.[11]

The strategy that I follow will be to pin down the conceptual reference model described above, but to proceed in a pragmatic manner, allowing for shortcuts and digressions. I present available empirical evidence, taken from the copious but often heterogeneous literature about British privatization, as well as some new evidence. I structure the presentation bearing in mind very freely the changes in welfare for the different groups of agents or the possible changes in aggregate indices, which are important for social welfare. I do not abandon—for the sake of the construction of a theoretical model—a discussion of the real-world complexity of the problems being studied.

From here onward, the reader must not expect any concession to an abstract model. The theory presented within the chapter serves only as a criterion for organizing the collection and analysis of empirical data, and it would be unrealistic to expect calculations carried out with the rigor required by the cost-benefit analysis approach discussed here. Such rigor is simply impossible when we need to evaluate a large-scale, complex policy reform.

The theory discussed in the chapter may serve as a compass, but navigation will be erratic, and the result not altogether certain. At the end of this book, I hazard an overall evaluation (chapter 10). However, it will be after all, a conjectural interpretation, exposed to many possible criticisms. I will consider it already to be a satisfactory result if others react with different calculations. My aim is to shift attention from accounts of privatized firms to accounts of society as a whole. Others will be able to produce more precise evaluations than mine, for Great Britain or for other countries.

2.5   Further Reading

Additional helpful references in privatization theoretical literature include Bös 1999 on incomplete contracts. Newbery and Stern (1987) offer a simple framework for the evaluation of policy reforms; Pirie (1988) restates the neoliberal critique of public enterprise; see also Shirley and Walsh 2000. For an early view on the benefits of public ownership (in the United States), see Thompson 1925. Waldron (1990) proposes a general theory of the right to private property. Yarrow and Jasinsk (1999) collect a wide set of important papers on public versus private ownership in a global perspective. See also Yergin and Stanislaw 1998; and Bös 1993, 1997.

Appendix

I present here, selectively and informally, some simple formulas for the cost-benefit analysis of privatization. As I mentioned in the chapter, there are three convergent ways to look at the welfare impact of privatization: a macroeconomic-welfare approach, public-finance welfare accounting, and a microeconomic cost-benefit approach, and I examine each in turn. I also mention some partial equilibrium formulas.[12]

The Macroeconomic Welfare Approach

Following Drèze and Stern (1987), I assume a Bergson-Samuelson social-welfare function

$$SWF = W(V_1, V_2, \ldots, V_n), \tag{2.1}$$

where V_i, $i = 1, 2, \ldots, I$ are individual welfare indexes. V depends upon the vector of consumption prices q with its dimension, lump-sum income m, and for any given level of exogenous wages w, upon the rationed quantity of labor services supplied by each consumer, l. By convention, labor supply is a negative demand. Working time is distributed according to a rationing function that assigns a maximum to each consumer, and nominal w is sticky. Under involuntary unemployment, w, in numeraire, is a distorted measure of the substitution rate between leisure and work time. In general, if w_s is the money disutility of labor and $\bar{w}$ is a fixed wage, we may have $w_s < \bar{w}$, given that the individual is involuntarily unemployed.

The welfare function has arguments m_i, x_i, and l_i, weighted by their appropriate prices: m_i with a price equal to one, because lump-sum income is already expressed in units of numeraire; consumption goods demand x_i with the price vector q; and l_i with the wedge $(\bar{w} - w_s)$. More generally, the difference between actual non-market-clearing prices and virtual prices is an exact measure of the marginal change of expenditure necessary to keep the consumer at the same utility level. Similar wedges will appear if there are additional quantity constraints (Starrett 1988).

Welfare weights are first partial derivatives of W to a marginal increase of lump-sum income of the *i*th consumer:

$$\beta_i = \frac{\partial W}{\partial V_i} \frac{\partial V_i}{\partial m_i}. \tag{2.2}$$

β_i may be a positive parameter, estimated by the observation of marginal rates of income taxation or by the inverse optimum approach (Ahmad and Stern 1984), based on indirect taxation. Alternatively one can test for a set of alternative values, reflecting different political orientations.

I use the following welfare differential (see Drèze and Stern 1987, 935):

$$dW = de + \sum_i (\beta_i - 1) \, de_i - \left(\sum_i \beta_i x_i \right) dq + \sum_i \beta_i w_{si} \, d\bar{l}_i. \tag{2.3}$$

Expenditure of the ith consumer is $e_i = m_i - \bar{w}\bar{l}_i$. Thus national expenditure is $\sum_{i=1}^n e_i = e$. The interpretation in the context of this book is the following. For a closed economy, the welfare impact of a marginal privatization reform can be decomposed into changes of national income, de; of an inequality index $\sum_{i=1}(\beta_i - 1) \, de_i$; of a welfare-weighted price vector, $\sum_i (\beta_i x_i) \, dq$; and of welfare-weighted employment, $\sum_i \beta_i w_{si} \, d\bar{l}_i$.

Although the British privatization program was very large, it was small relative to the economy, and second derivatives can therefore be disregarded. Thus I can simply look for proxies of the four terms of the above decomposition. These proxies may simply be changes of GDP, of the Gini index, of the GDP deflator, and of unemployment, weighted by appropriate macroeconomic welfare weights (see Florio 1990b).

The Public-Finance Welfare Approach

Following Drèze and Stern (1990), let R be the net present value of the government budget; τ are indirect taxes levied on consumption goods x; p are prices; publicly produced goods are z; π are the profits of the private sector; γ is the average rate of corporate taxation; and r_i are lump-sum transfers or taxes for each taxpayer, $1, \ldots, n$. Thus the net present value of the budget is

$$R \equiv \sum_{t=1}^m \left[pz + \tau x + \gamma \pi - \sum_{i=1}^n r_i \right] (1 + \sigma)^{-t}. \tag{2.4}$$

Each term could be negative or positive and interpreted accordingly as net taxation or net expenditure. The social discount rate is σ in the time horizon $t = 1, 2, \ldots, m$.

With a production prices vector p, and with y being the net output, the pretax private-sector profit is $py = \gamma\pi + (1 - \gamma)\pi$. Consumers own the private sector and get net profit as income. Hence, consumers face the budget constraint

$$qx - \sum_i r_i + (1 - \gamma)\pi = 0. \tag{2.5}$$

To simplify notation, all prices can be expressed in terms of net present value of the numeraire, that is, uncommitted public income. Thus by substitution in (2.4) and obvious change of notation, we have that the government budget is zero if

$$R = p^*(z + y - x), \tag{2.6}$$

or if a vector p^* exists such that markets clear. For Walras's law, if $(n - 1)$ markets are in equilibrium for a given price vector, the closing equation, here the government budget, is satisfied for the same price vector.

Suppose now that the government (or the regulator, for privatized companies) is unable to plan $p = p^*$, because of externalities, quantity constraints, monopoly power, and other market imperfections. We thus need to use a set of shadow prices. Let υ be such a vector. The shadow budget is then

$$R^* = \upsilon z + (q - \upsilon)x + \gamma\pi - \sum_i r_i + (\upsilon - p)y. \tag{2.7}$$

The first term on the right-hand side is public revenue at shadow prices; the second term is the contribution of private consumption to the budget, evaluated by the difference $(q - \upsilon) = t^*$, a vector of optimal indirect taxes; the third and fourth terms are the same as in (2.4); and the last term may be optimal taxes at production level (Diamond and Mirrlees 1971a, 1971b).

Consider now the differential

$$dR^* = \upsilon(dz + dy - dx). \tag{2.8}$$

For a marginal privatization the net present value of government budget is still in equilibrium for unchanged shadow prices if and only if private netput change $(dy - dx)$ compensates for the decrease in public production: $dz < 0$. This gives an exact measure of how much the private sector should achieve under privatization/regulation. The price the government gets for the marginal privatized company should be equal to the increase of the netput of the private sector evaluated at shadow prices, less any lost income for the public sector, also evaluated at shadow prices. In this framework, any increase of monopoly profit under privatization with lax regulation does not influence project evaluation.

The Microeconomic Approach

Finally we can consider the welfare change for each agent and for each privatized company. Suppose welfare components of agents can be considered separately as

C = consumers' surplus

T = taxpayers' utility

S = shareholders' utility

L = workers' utility

Obviously an individual can appear here at the same time under different categories; for example, a taxpayer may be also a consumer, and so on. Thus welfare change as a result of a divestiture is

$$dW = \sum_{i=1}^{n} \beta_i (dC_i + dT_i + dS_i + dL_i) \tag{2.9}$$

β coefficients weigh the change of social welfare of different individual consumers, different taxpayers, and so on. The basic idea here is that the cost-benefit test for a divestiture is the same as for public investment. The project should generate positive social profits. It can be shown that under some conditions, including the use of consistent SWFs and constraints, the same set of shadow prices solves the problem of welfare maximization across agents, macroeconomic objectives, and public-finance welfare accounting.

Jones, Tandon, and Vogelsang (1990) have offered a useful partial equilibrium approach to the cost-benefit analysis of privatization (see also Galal et al. 1994). I shall refer to this, for short, as the "JTV framework." Under this approach, which I summarize here, there is a fundamental divestiture formula:

$$\Delta W = V_{sp} - V_{sg} + (\lambda_g - \lambda_p)Z, \tag{2.10}$$

where ΔW is the welfare change generated by a privatization, V_{sp} is the social value of the firm under private operation, V_{sg} is the social value of the firm under continued government operation, λ_g and λ_p are, respectively, the multipliers of public and private funds, and Z is the actual divestiture price.

Social values are defined here as the net present values of the future streams of consumers' surpluses C, corporate profits Π, and government revenues R. Thus in general

$$\Delta W = \lambda_c \Delta C + \lambda_p \Delta \Pi + \lambda_g \Delta R, \tag{2.11}$$

where without loss of generality, a convenient normalization rule is $1 = \lambda_c$.

Thus if consumers' welfare is the numeraire, there is an expectation that $\lambda_g > 1$ under distortionary taxation. According Jones, Tandon, and Vogelsang (1990), it may be the case that $\lambda_p > 1$ as well if investment is suboptimal: Thus, if the investment level is suboptimal, the social value of private profits exceeds the social value of consumption.

It will then be just an empirical issue to determine the relative value of the two multipliers. When (as may usually be the case, we suggest) $\lambda_p < \lambda_g$, the cost-benefit analysis rule is to sell if

$$Z > (V_{sg} - V_{sp})/(\lambda_g - \lambda_p). \tag{2.12}$$

An implication of (2.12) is that under $\lambda_p = \lambda_g$, or indifference between private and public funds, the sale price does not matter. Privatization is thus seen as a pure transfer, without a welfare impact.

There is a substantial theoretical and empirical literature on the marginal excess burden of taxation that supports the view that $\lambda_g > 1$ for most countries, although the estimates vary a great deal (a typical middle estimate for the United States, e.g., is 1.33). In this framework there is a fundamental trade-off between allocative and cost efficiency. This trade-off is apparent when we consider that prices and quantities, costs, profits, taxes, and consumers' surpluses may change after divestiture.

Under constant returns we may simply write that

$$\Pi_g = (P_g - c_g)q_g \quad \text{and} \quad \Pi_p = (P_p - c_p)q_p,$$

where P are prices, c are costs, and q are quantities. Private valuation is then expressed as perpetuity of net-of-taxes profits:

$$V_{pp} = (\Pi_p - T_p)/\sigma, \tag{2.13}$$

where T are taxes on profits, and σ is the discount factor.

The corresponding social value for each year is

$$V_{sp}(t) = \lambda_p V_{pp} + S_p(t) + \lambda_g T(t), \tag{2.14}$$

where S is consumers' surplus. In turn, for each year, the social value of continued public ownership will be

$$V_{sg}(t) = S_g(t) + \lambda_g \Pi_g(t). \tag{2.15}$$

The intertemporal version of the basic divestiture equation is thus found by substitution. This leads, after some simple manipulation, to the perpetuity value

$$\Delta W = [\Delta S + \lambda_g \Delta \Pi - (\lambda_g - \lambda_p)(Z_p - Z)]/\sigma, \tag{2.16}$$

where $Z_p = V_{pp}$, or the maximum willingness to pay by the private buyer. If the government is able to extract from the buyers all their willingness to pay, so that $Z_p = Z$, then the welfare change is simply the change of consumer surpluses and company profits, with the latter, however, evaluated according to the shadow multiplier of public funds.

Under perfect competition, prices are exogenous either for public or for private firms, and thus consumers' surpluses are unaffected, whereas profits may change because of cost savings:

$$\Delta W = \{\lambda_g[(c_g - c_p)q_g + (P - c_p)(q_p - q_g)]\}/\sigma. \tag{2.17}$$

More interestingly, a trade-off arises under monopoly (without regulation). Under this condition, the monopolist may have an incentive both to save on costs and to raise prices. In such a case, the consumer surplus will be affected. In general, for small changes and linear demand:

$$\Delta S = \Delta P(q_p + \Delta q/2). \tag{2.18}$$

The firm in this case should be divested only if the negative change in relative surplus is compensated for the change in profits.

The JTV framework is attractive because it is simple, and what I do in this book is broadly consistent with it. A crucial aspect of this approach, however, is the role of profits in this framework.

In the Drèze-Stern framework (i.e., in general equilibrium), monopoly profits play no role in the calculation of social-welfare changes. Whereas normal profits are included in long-run marginal costs, monopoly profits disappear, when all outputs and inputs are evaluated at shadow prices. If actual prices are going to be used in empirical ex post evaluations, extra profits should be deducted if we want to transform actual prices into shadow prices. Under this view, the JTV framework should be used carefully when evaluating large privatizations, affecting millions of consumers and several industries, because the partial equilibrium and one-consumer-equivalent-economy shortcuts may be misleading. Another way to see this issue is the following: Whereas the JTV framework focuses on a counterfactual (continued public versus private ownership), the Drèze-Stern framework focuses on shadow prices around the constrained social optimum.

A microeconomic approach more consistent with the general framework of the macroeconomic decomposition mentioned above is the one proposed by Newbery (2000). In that approach, the impact of a change of the jth price following privatization/regulation is seen as the sum of net demands of each individual, weighted by the appropriate welfare weights. We have for each good

$$\sum_i (\beta_i x_{ij}) = -\frac{\partial W}{\partial q_j},$$

or for each good

$$BD_j Q_j = -\frac{\partial W}{\partial q_j}, \tag{2.19}$$

where B is the average value of β and Q is the aggregate value of demand. Thus we compute D, the distributive characteristic of the jth good as

$$D_j = \frac{\sum_i (\beta_i x_{ij})}{BQ_j}. \tag{2.20}$$

If we know the distributive characteristic of the good and the profile of the welfare weights, the calculation of the welfare impact of price changes is easy (see chapter 7).

Laffont and Tirole (1993, 2000b) also use consumer surplus in their theory of regulation, in a one-consumer-equivalent-economy setting. They use a shadow price for taxation and show that excess profits should be subtracted when calculating aggregate welfare change. Their basic model is as follows:

$$W = S - (1 + \lambda)(t + C) + U, \tag{2.21}$$

where W is social welfare; S is gross surplus; C are project costs, including a net transfer t by government to the firm, evaluated with 1 plus the shadow price of public funds; and U is firm's utility. The latter is defined as

$$U = t - \varphi(e), \tag{2.22}$$

where the second term on the right-hand side is the disutility of effort of firms' managers (an unobservable variable). Thus

$$W = S - (1 + \lambda)(C + \varphi(e) - \lambda U. \tag{2.23}$$

This implies that leaving a rent to the firm (or to its shareholders and top managers) is socially costly. Under symmetric information, government may need to leave an information rent to the firm to ensure incentive compatibility and delivery of the good.

In the British case this model is obviously relevant when there are direct transfers to private firms, and also when there is underpricing or lax regulation, because in these cases there is a hidden transfer to firms.

3   Macroeconomic Trends

3.1   Topics for Discussion

Whereas in this book most of the analysis is in a microeconomic setting, in this chapter I discuss British privatization as a major policy reform in the context of the country's macroeconomic performance. I have three reasons for pursuing this line of inquiry.

First, the British economy changed considerably in the twenty or so years since 1979 that I consider here. Therefore, it is interesting to see denationalization in a wider perspective, as a part of a policy package that generated or reacted to macroeconomic signals.

Second, cost-benefit analysis for individual agents may fail to capture indirect effects and externalities, that is, net benefits or costs to third parties. In principle, a set of shadow prices offers all that we need for a general equilibrium evaluation. In practice, however, we must often rely on proxies and on partial equilibrium assumptions. Looking for aggregate impacts may be a way to check whether there are major spillovers from the effects of privatization into other sectors.

Third, in the last chapter I suggested that in principle a large-scale policy reform can be evaluated using a macroeconomic welfare function, including as arguments output, prices, income distribution, unemployment, and a set of welfare weights as parameters. Therefore, it is helpful to look at changes in these variables.

The structure of this chapter, as of subsequent ones, is as follows. I start with some topics that may be relevant for the discussion, then present the evidence, and eventually comment on the results. This structure does not imply that the chapter covers all relevant topics or all the available evidence. I need to be selective, and this constraint is particularly binding in this chapter. The rest of this section presents some simple ideas on how we can look at a large-scale privatization as a macroeconomic shock.

In the short run, following divestiture, we may observe mainly demand effects, and an (IS-LM) framework[1] may be appropriate, in spite
of its well-known limitations, for the study of the immediate impact
of privatization on the macroeconomy. In the medium term, we need
to consider supply-side effects. Productivity, costs, and prices may
change, and we turn to an (AS-AD) framework.[2] In the long run, we
should look to sustainable output growth, and for that, we need a
growth framework. A full specification of these three frameworks for
the British economy would be a daunting task far beyond my research
scope in this book. I simply suggest a mental experiment.

To begin, and to simplify, suppose we are in a closed economy.
In the short term, output matches demand of consumption goods, of
investment goods, and of public expenditures. Broad money supply
matches money demand, which in turn depends on output, prices, and
interest rate. Prices are fixed. When we move to a dynamic setting and
consider a sufficient time span, we need to explain price changes. In
the familiar AS-AD context, the supply side of the economy results
from consistent wage setting in the labor market and price setting by
firms. The former depends upon expected prices and costs, current unemployment rate relative to its structural rate, and labor protection by
legislation or unionization. In the longer run, we should look at sustainable economic growth and its proximate causes, labor force, capital, and knowledge (or other suitable definitions of innovation drivers).

Privatization may potentially have an impact on several macroeconomic variables, in the short run as well as in the long run, particularly on output, employment, investment, and total factor productivity
(TFP), and hence on costs and prices. I present here, informally, just
some examples of possible impacts of privatization shocks on the economy, with the proviso that several other cases are possible.

Privatization, which I consider here as a one-time sale of assets,
amounts initially to changing the ownership shares in the existing
stock of domestic assets. On the demand side, one crucial variable is
the differential between the present value of income of a public and a
privately owned enterprise, "the public-private valuation differential"
(see MacKenzie 1998). This difference may be negative, positive, or
zero. This sets three possible cases: indifference pricing, overpricing,
and underpricing.

With underpricing (overpricing), the government sells its assets as
equity capital at a price less (more) than the expected net present value
of the future stream of income under a public ownership regime, dis-

counted by the discount rate of uncommitted public funds. At the same time, the sale price is less than the private valuation of the assets (otherwise, private agents will not buy). Indifference pricing occurs when the sale price is exactly equal to the net present value of assets to the owner and there is coincidence with value to the buyer.

A second important variable is the method of financing the acquisition by the private sector. The following illustrative financing cases are compatible with the preceding valuation cases:

• Bond/equity swap: buyers acquire equities by selling government bonds they own (we exclude here sale of corporate bonds).

• Equity/equity swap: investors sell other equities and buy privatization shares.

• Money/equity swap: reduction of money balances (I exclude here financing acquisitions by loans) finances the acquisitions.

A third important variable is the way in which the government uses the privatization proceeds (for example, for reducing the public debt, reinvestment, or financing current expenditure). The government may buy back bonds and reduce its net debt, or it may use the proceeds of privatization to pay for new public-investment goods or to finance current expenditure, or it may reduce taxation, without changing its fiscal stance.

If there are several privatization initial share offerings, the government may in some cases select a combination of these options for one divestiture decision and another combination for another, so that we observe a mixture of cases. I disregard this possibility here, however, and focus on a one-shot, large-scale divestiture decision. Moreover, government may accompany divestiture with lax or binding price regulation (or liberalization).

Because there are three variables and three possible values for each of them, as well as two regulatory regimes, there are then $27 \times 2 = 54$ possible combinations, probably all with different macroeconomic impacts. For example, we can observe indifference pricing cum equity/equity swap cum public investment increase and tough regulation, or overpricing cum money/equity swap cum tax decrease and lax regulation.

I focus here on just two illustrative combinations: privatization with underpricing and public-debt redemption, with and without lax regulation (or liberalization). Government sells its assets as equity capital at a price less than the expected net present value of the future stream of income and less than the private valuation. Privatization proceeds are committed to buy back bonds. Savers finance their acquisition of new equities by selling government bonds.

This case has several macroeconomic consequences. In the short run, private wealth increases, because although the savers have to sell bonds up to the value of the sale price, they receive a windfall capital gain. I show in chapter 5 that in the U.K. privatizations of the 1979–1997 period, this capital gain may have been as much as 20 percent in twenty-four hours. Such a bonanza may give a push to demand. Because in the short run, government taxes are unaffected, whereas the level of public investment falls, fiscal policy is restrictive. The increase of private consumption and investment, however, may counteract this negative impact. The IS curve shifts upward, whereas the LM curve is unaffected. We may observe an initial demand shock, proportional to divestiture value and to the extent of underpricing.

In the medium term, the picture changes. First, if the private discount rate is greater than the social discount rate, as it often may be, indifference pricing or underpricing implies that the stream of real income generated by the privatized companies is higher than that generated by the corresponding nationalized companies, because the valuation is inversely related to the discount rate.

There are two different scenarios. Private owners may expect higher productivity as a result of privatization. This, in turn, if the markup is constant (or decreasing because privatization is compounded with greater competition or strict price regulation), implies a decrease in output prices. For a large-scale privatization (in the United Kingdom in the period under study, the output of privatized corporations was around 10 percent of GDP; in transition economies it is a higher share), this reduces the general price index. Hence, real money increases, and the LM curve shifts downward. Aggregate demand shifts, and we have a new equilibrium with an increase of output and a decrease of interest rate. Cost decrease implies that the AS curve shifts downward, and this allows higher output with a price decrease. This sequence confirms the initial impact on demand. Employment may temporarily decrease, but higher output may counteract this initial impact.

Alternatively, with lax regulation and weak competition, we may observe a different scenario. Profit expectation after privatization may be based on a prediction of higher relative prices. Private investors forecast undemanding price regulation and unconstrained market power.

In the AS-AD framework, the result of a higher markup over costs may be inferior output equilibrium. Thus, although privatization has a limited impact on the IS curve, because both public and private wealth are unaffected, it may have a negative impact on output in the longer term, following changes in relative prices.

Thus, there are two new possible equilibria, one clearly expansionary, the other one recessive. These equilibria depend on the origin of profit expectation: higher productivity or higher markup. In the higher-productivity scenario, we have favorable effects of both demand and supply. In the higher-markup scenario, the positive impact on demand is counteracted by an adverse supply shock. A range of combinations between the two scenarios is possible, and there are some caveats.

First, the government has lost net wealth, or the net present value of future incomes, less privatization proceeds. In the long run, if it wants to restore its net wealth, it needs either to raise taxes, perhaps in the form of capital gains taxation (as with the Labour windfall tax), or to reduce current expenditures. This tax policy may counteract the expansionary impact of underpricing policy.

Second, privatization may have a negative impact on private investment, because underpricing is in fact a subsidy to buyers of already existing assets. This subsidy increases the return to equity of owners of privatized companies compared to that of owners of other companies and may in the long run displace investment in other sectors. Third, cost savings may counteract increased markups.

Summing up: In the short run, with underpricing, the impact is expansionary, government net worth is diminished, private net worth is increased, and privatization is not very different from a public transfer financed by debt. In the longer run, the increase of output might be further sustained by strict regulation or increased competition, but it might also be reversed by an increase of company markup. Government may limit the demand effects if it taxes away the capital gains that accrue to buyers or raises other taxes in the future to recoup the wealth it has lost.

Incidentally, note that with underpricing and higher markup, there is a regressive redistribution of wealth from the taxpayers and consumers to the shareholders. This may bring down consumption and output in the long term (particularly if some of the shareholders are foreign investors). An alternative or complementary path for bringing down the AS curve is to force down wages, perhaps through a decrease of labor protection (e.g., limiting the power of unions and the scope of labor legislation). This may have been important in the British experience in the time period under study, as I show in chapter 6.

Finally, in an open economy with a regime of flexible exchange rates, a wide privatization program may attract capital from abroad, and thus we may observe appreciation of the local currency. If there are inflationary effects associated with divestiture, however, the opposite may happen. The sign of the exchange rate change is therefore ambiguous.

All this looks rather complex, but in a sense, it amounts simply to restating the obvious. In the short term, privatization may have mainly demand effects, and in the medium term, mainly supply effects. This may change equilibrium output. There will be an output increase if there is underpricing (without expectations of subsequent capital gains taxation), plus a productivity increase, and no markup increase. Without an initial productivity shock, the impact of public divestiture on output will probably be negligible or negative. In fact, the expected privatization productivity jump may not materialize because of slack regulation and weak competition and because the effect of ownership change per se is small.

In the long run, a permanent change in productivity performance is needed to sustain a new growth pattern. As Schipke (2001, 11) points out:

The extent to which a reduction in government activity has implications for output growth depends on whether and to what degree privatization affects the national savings rate, the level of capital investment (both physical and human), the efficiency with which the resources are used, and the rate of technological progress. Furthermore, whether the divestment of public enterprises has a one-time or transitory impact or instead affects economic growth permanently depends on which model captures growth process most adequately.

According to endogenous-growth theory, higher savings and investment, because of the accompanying decrease in the public deficit, may sustain a long-term increase in the growth rate. Therefore, if privatization contributes to better financial conditions in the public sector and to faster adoption of new technologies in the private sector, we should be able to discern not just an output increase, but also an output growth increase in the long run. The economy will change its development trajectory. However, the *if* conditions are very important here, as my previous examples show.

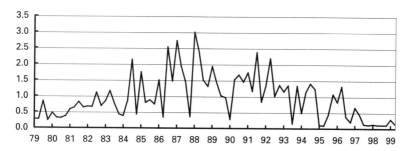

Figure 3.1
Proceeds of British privatizations as a percentage of GDP (quarterly data).
Source: Author's calculations based on ONS, n.d.-a.

I turn now to empirical evidence. I briefly review aggregate output and productivity trends, investment, employment, inflation, and income distribution in the United Kingdom before and after privatization and propose a simple test of its macroeconomic impact.

3.2   Empirical Evidence

3.2.1   Privatization Proceeds

To test the macroeconomic impact of privatization, we need an explanatory variable representative of divestitures. The most obvious candidate is the time series of privatization proceeds, for which data have been collected quarterly since 1979. I added to these data (net proceeds for sales of public corporations) proceeds from the sales of council houses. Figure 3.1 shows quarterly data for the proceeds as a percentage of GDP. See also figures 3.2 and 3.3.

First, I look at the time profile of each of the macro variables and briefly comment on each of them. Second, I test some simple models in which I focus on output and privatization proceeds and use a set of other macroeconomic variables as controls. I also use a time series of underpricing (more on this later).

3.2.2   Output

The years between 1950 and 1979 were a period of relative decline for the United Kingdom. Around 1950, the United Kingdom was third in the world, after the United States and Switzerland, in terms of real

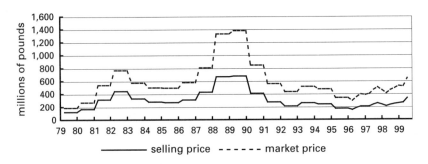

Figure 3.2
Value of dwellings sold for owner occupation, England (current prices).
Source: Author's calculations based on DETRA 1999, table: "Value of Dwellings Sold for
Owner Occupation: England—Local Authorities."

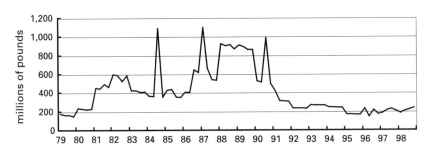

Figure 3.3
Underpricing of public assets at privatization.
Source: Author's calculations based on ONS, n.d.-b; OECD, n.d.; and Datastream, n.d.

per capita GDP (in purchasing-power-parity [PPP] dollars, 1990, based
on Maddison [2001] data). By 1979, the United Kingdom had fallen
to eleventh, after Belgium and Austria, whereas France and West Germany had risen to third and fourth, respectively, in the rankings. Between 1979 and 1996, there was a further small drop, and the United
Kingdom ranked twelfth as of 1996. According to Crafts (1998), the
Conservative years were, if not a miracle, at least the end of the decline
in real per capita GDP.

This achievement does not, however, seem impressive. Rankings
are not a very good measure of actual performance. It seems better to
compare actual levels. At the end of the 1970s, the per capita GDP of
the United Kingdom was still 10 percent *higher* than the average for
OECD countries. In 1996, it was 8 percent *lower*. The OECD survey
(1998, figure 11) shows that the gap in per capita GDP between the

United Kingdom and the United States between 1960 and 1996 was virtually unchanged (in fact, on average the gap was smaller in the first twenty years than after 1979).

The best comparison is probably with EU countries. If we take the British per capita income in 1960 to be 100, the other countries in the European Union recorded a level of 80 in that year. These countries were recording over 100 in 1980, and after some distancing in the following years, had overtaken the United Kingdom again by the 1990s.

To understand relative changes in income per person, we should consider GDP growth in different countries. Crafts (1998) observes that GDP grew 2.3 percent yearly in the United Kingdom in 1950–1979 and 1.7 percent in 1979–1996. He argues that this took place in the context of an international retardation of growth during which the British economy slowed a lot less than that of many other countries. This may be true, but it is not an indication of good performance. Real GDP yearly growth in the United Kingdom 1960–1973, before the first oil shock, was more than 3 percent; it was only 1.4 percent in 1973–1979. It is fair to say that after those troubled years, the growth rate of the British economy simply converged to the low rate of most other developed countries.

After an initial slowdown, probably because of monetarist policies in the 1980s, the annual rate of growth of GDP in the United Kingdom in the last decade of Conservative years was around 2.5 percent. This growth rate for the United Kingdom was probably close to its average for the last fifty years (Maddison 2001).

It is true that in 1950–1979, the British growth rate was only two-thirds of the average growth rate of OECD countries. That average, however, included excellent performances in some countries, such as the growth rates of Japan (6.8 percent), West Germany, or Italy (both around 4.5 percent). In the following twenty years, growth in the United Kingdom was still marginally *below* the OECD average. This does not look like a British growth miracle. It appears instead to be a return to the old pattern, after the slump in the 1970s. At the same time, it reflects the fading of the true miracle in other countries.

3.2.3 Productivity

According to OECD (1998), privatization, liberalization, and deregulation of the labor market in the United Kingdom had a substantial impact on productivity: "The wide-reaching program of structural reform over the past couple of decades has probably helped UK productivity levels to catch-up with best practices although a substantial gap remains" (54). In fact, productivity per employee and per hour worked increased between 1985 and 1996 in the United Kingdom at a higher rate than that of other G7 countries, enabling the country to reduce the gap between it and the United States. If we take 100 to be the value added per hour worked (or per worker) in the manufacturing sector in the United States, in the United Kingdom it was 45.0 in 1960, 53.6 in 1973, 59.7 in 1985, and 69.7 in 1995.

Other authors suggest that the productivity growth in the 1980s in the United Kingdom was genuine and largely due to reduction of union power (Oulton 1995; Brown, Deakin, and Ryan 1997) but masked by poor macroeconomic management and adverse demand-side conditions. Again, this may be true, but labor productivity can increase for two different reasons. Sustained output growth can exceed employment growth. Alternatively, the denominator of the output/employment ratio can drive the process, and stable or modestly increasing output can face sharply decreasing employment. As I show later in the chapter, in the United Kingdom there was wide deindustrialization in the 1980s, and actual and disguised unemployment tripled in a few years. Hence, labor productivity growth exceeded output per capita growth.

Obviously, demand has an important role in productivity trends. In fact, the relative gain in productivity was relative to the United States 16 percent in the last ten years of the period considered, during which the policies of the Conservative governments were fully unfurled. However, it was 19 percent in the thirteen years before the first oil shock, years in which the political situation was quite different, with powerful trade unions and a large nationalized sector. In the intervening period, between 1973 and 1985, the relative increase in productivity was 11 percent.

International comparisons offer mixed evidence that the Conservative years mark an aggregate productivity jump. In 1960, the size of the productivity gap between France, a country often considered interventionist, and the United States was similar to that between the United Kingdom and the United States. By 1995, France's index of relative productivity had increased by almost 90 percent (the cumulative increase for the United Kingdom over the same period was just over 55 percent). In addition, Germany, Belgium, Finland, and Sweden, countries that pursued a mix of structural policies different from the United Kingdom (and each one different from the others) closed their productivity gaps with the United States more than the United Kingdom over the period considered. Thus, it is true that in the last decade, labor productivity growth in the United Kingdom was greater than in other developed countries, but looking at it over the longer term, it doesn't appear to be any more than a partial recovery of the gap accumulated in the past.

From table 3.1, it is clear that in the long run (1960–1997), the trends in TFP and labor productivity of the United Kingdom do not show a better performance than those of most EU countries. The result is much better for capital productivity, but so it was also in 1960–1973 and 1973–1979 (see figure 3.4), a result probably explained by low levels of investment (see section 3.2.4).

Moreover, when we consider separately the manufacturing sector and marketed services, the story is different. In the former, the monetary squeeze and recession in the early 1980s provoked substantial labor shedding and then raised capital per employee. Labor productivity growth in manufacturing increased substantially, whereas there was no change or decrease in the service sector, which includes most of the privatized industries.

3.2.4 Investments

In the 1990s (cf. OECD 1998, table A, p. 176), public investments in the United Kingdom declined at an average annual rate of 0.8 percent, with a cumulative effect of falling from a modest 1.3 percent in 1988 to 0.98 percent in 1997, perhaps the lowest level of all OECD countries (see Kamps 2003 for new, comparable data). Such a phenomenon is to be expected if the proceeds from divestitures under a large-scale privatization policy are not used for infrastructure investments but rather for public debt redemption or financing current expenditure (see the appendix to chapter 1 and Newbery 2002).

We can ask ourselves whether private investment fully or partly substituted for public investment. The rate of growth of private investments over the period averaged 2.5 percent (2.9 percent of residential construction). Despite this rate of growth, however, gross nonresidential investment in the United Kingdom, as a share of GDP, is the lowest in the European Union. The OECD (1998, 18) survey on the United Kingdom states that "low investment, especially by companies ... [in

Table 3.1
Productivity trends in the business sector, 1960–1997 (percentage changes at annual rates)

	Total factor productivity			Labor productivity			Capital productivity		
	1960–1973	1973–1979	1979–1997	1960–1973	1973–1979	1979–1997	1960–1973	1973–1979	1979–1997
United Kingdom	2.6	0.5	1.1	4.0	1.6	2.0	1.7	−0.3	0.6
United States	1.9	0.1	0.7	2.6	0.3	0.9	0.4	−0.5	0.1
Japan	4.9	0.7	0.9	8.4	2.8	2.3	−2.3	−3.6	−2.0
Germany	2.6	1.8	1.2	4.5	3.1	2.2	−1.4	−1.0	−0.5
France	3.7	1.6	1.3	5.3	2.9	2.2	0.6	−1.0	−0.5
Italy	4.4	2.0	1.1	6.4	2.8	2.0	0.5	0.3	−0.6
Canada	1.1	−0.1	−0.5	2.5	1.1	1.0	−1.9	−2.6	−3.6
Total of the above countries	2.9	0.5	0.8	4.5	1.4	1.6	−0.2	−1.2	−0.6
Austria	3.3	1.1	0.9	5.9	3.1	2.3	−1.7	−2.9	−1.9
Belgium	3.8	1.3	1.0	5.2	2.7	1.9	0.6	−1.8	−1.1
Denmark	2.1	0.6	1.2	3.9	2.3	2.1	−1.5	−2.6	−0.7
Finland	4.0	1.9	2.6	5.0	3.2	3.5	1.4	−1.6	0.2
Greece	2.7	0.8	−0.2	9.0	3.4	0.7	−8.8	−4.2	−1.9
Ireland	4.5	3.8	3.7	4.8	4.3	4.1	3.4	1.8	1.9
Netherlands	3.5	1.7	1.0	4.8	2.6	1.5	1.0	−0.1	0.1
Portugal	2.6	−1.0	1.0	7.5	0.5	2.4	−6.0	−3.8	−1.6
Spain	3.1	0.6	1.6	5.9	2.8	2.7	−4.4	−5.4	−1.6
Sweden	1.9	0.0	1.1	3.7	1.4	2.0	−2.2	−3.2	−1.0
Total of above EU countries	3.2	1.2	1.4	5.4	2.6	2.3	−1.2	−1.8	−0.6

Source: Author's elaboration on OECD 1998.

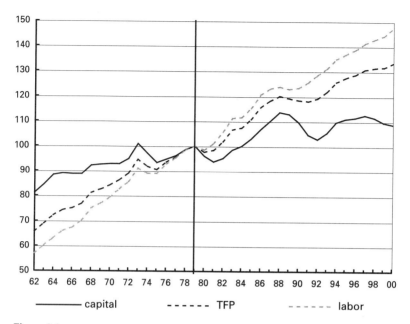

Figure 3.4
Productivity in the business sector (1979 = 100).
Source: Author's elaboration on OECD (n.d.) data.

the] manufacturing and public sector ... has become, in conjunction with sluggish labor supply, a barrier to sustained expansion." According to OECD data, on the arrival of the Thatcher government in the United Kingdom, the ratio of investment to GDP was in the region of 18 percent; in 1997 it had fallen to below 16 percent (with a peak of over 20 percent in 1989).[4]

3.2.5 Employment

As I showed in the chapter 2, the 1980s in the United Kingdom witnessed a decisive attack by the government on elements of rigidity in the labor market. Senior Conservative politicians considered privatization partly, if not primarily, as a move with which to weaken the trade unions.

The subject of structural changes in the labor market over the past twenty years in the United Kingdom and in many other countries is important, and I return to it in chapter 6. One could note here that of

the 7.5 million individuals in the United Kingdom who are of working age but economically inactive, a substantial percentage are people
either taking early retirement or defined as disabled.

The second group, especially, have recorded a spectacular increase
since privatization. Over the twenty years under consideration here,
the absolute increase in the number of those defined as disabled was
1.5 million people, or 4 percent of the population. As a result, although
unemployment fell over the period, and also because of the increased
participation of women, the number of people with a history of work
who were excluded from the labor force, especially adult males,
increased.

On average, between 1988 and 1997, the unemployment rate in the
United Kingdom was 8.1 percent, and at the end of the period, it was
7.1 percent. This is a quite a low figure compared to those in a number
of other countries in continental Europe. If a large part of the increase
in the number of disabled and early-retired is disguised unemployment, then involuntary unemployment in the United Kingdom was
actually over 10 percent during the period—no better than that of
other European countries. It seems reasonable to conjecture that a part
of the involuntary unemployment disguised as invalidity or early retirement can be traced back to the large-scale downsizing of privatized
firms in the 1980s and 1990s (in reality already launched before divestiture, as I show in chapter 6).

3.2.6   Public Finance

I discuss the implications of privatization for public finance in detail in
chapter 8. Here I limit myself to a brief overview of the main trends:

Looking at the budget balance of the U.K. public sector, there is
evidence of a deterioration in the 1970s, followed by a policy of fiscal
contraction in the 1980s, which coincides with Thatcher's three terms
in office, then a worsening in the 1990s under the government of John
Major, and finally a net improvement in the most recent years of our
time horizon. The ratio of public debt to GDP contracted in the 1970s,
falling by a good twenty points, remained stable in the first half of the
1980s, decreased in the second half of the decade by almost another
twenty points, and then increased again (by roughly ten points) in the
1990s. The net worth of the public sector (which includes both financial
liabilities and real assets) deteriorated considerably over the period,
from a maximum of 82 percent of GDP in 1979 to a minimum of 13.7

percent of GDP in 1998 (I discuss the link between privatization and this spectacular drop in chapter 8).

Between 1979 and 1997 the ratio of taxation to GDP increased by two percentage points; over the same period total public spending fell from 43 to 39 percent; the average reduction, if we compare the 1970s, 1980s, and 1990s, does not appear to be an impressive one for a government strongly committed to "rolling back the state." Moreover, as mentioned in chapter 1, a large part of the cuts in spending resulted from the decline in public investments.

3.2.7 *Inflation*

The inflationary process in the United Kingdom is a long-term phenomenon that, despite the monetarist policies of the first phase of the Conservative governments, has been a constant feature over the past twenty years. H.M. Treasury (1998a, 10) summarizes the U.K. inflation phenomenon in the latter part of the last century as follows: "For most of the past 30 years, the UK's inflation record has been poor. During the 1970's, inflation averaged 13 percent, peaking at almost 27 percent in August 1975. Inflation averaged 7 percent during the 1980s and reached over 9 percent in the early 1990s. From 1980 to 1997 the UK had the second highest average inflation rate of the G7 countries, and it had greater variability in inflation than all countries but France and Italy." In this context, we can ask ourselves whether the sectors that were first nationalized and then privatized contributed to containing inflation, if they were neutral with regard to their effect on inflation, or if in fact they amplified it.

A disaggregate analysis for some privatized sectors is carried out in chapter 7. As I show in that chapter, when we control for demand and input prices, the privatized sectors did not experience output price trends that were terribly different from the long-run performance of the nationalized industries. Furthermore, although some of these sectors may have recorded reductions in prices in real terms (for example, telecommunications), others recorded increases (e.g., water, buses, and railways).

3.2.8 *Distribution of Income*

Over the period under study, inequality of incomes increased in all OECD countries. The trend was a general one, but it occurred to a far greater extent than average in the United Kingdom, regardless of whether one considers family income, spending, or wages (Gootshalk and Smeedling 1997).

In 1979, the share of total income held by the tenth decile was 4.5 times that held by the first decile; in 1995 it was 8 times. The gap between those with the highest and lowest incomes widened basically because whereas the richest decile saw its income grow by 50 percent in real terms over the period, the poorest decile suffered a drop in real income of 14 percent.

The composition of the poorest section of the population in Britain has changed noticeably: Whereas in the past it had been made up predominantly of pensioners, nowadays 70 percent of the low-income families are unemployed people, single parents, invalids and the infirm, and the "working poor," that is, those who work for very low wages. A third of the children in the United Kingdom live in families in conditions of poverty, the largest proportion in the European Union.

One effect of this situation is that the number of families on Supplementary Income Support doubled over the period under study. The 2.8 million of 1979 had become 5.6 million by 1996: quite a paradoxical outcome for a set of policies whose declared intent was to eradicate the country's "dependency culture" (OECD 1997).

Some of the reasons for the increase in the number of disadvantaged persons in need of social benefits are the increase in unemployment and in nonparticipation in the labor market and the sustained increase in the number of part-time and self-employed workers (Burniaux et al. 1998). The change in the country's industrial structure played a considerable role, with the decline of the traditional industries and the role of the less-skilled workers in those industries.

There are three reasons why privatization may have contributed to this increase in the number of people receiving welfare support:

1. The restructuring of state enterprises and the subsequent privatization brought about the loss of over 500,000 jobs after 1979, especially in the old industries (coal, steel) (see chapter 6 for a detailed discussion): There is little doubt that the families involved in this industrial restructuring process suffered a drop in income, even if we consider the increase in government subsidies.

2. The part of the workforce and management who stayed with the privatized firms recorded higher than average wage increases (again, see chapter 6).

3. Privatization allowed for considerable financial gains for the purchasers of shares placed by the British government at substantial underpricing (i.e., under their market value), and a quite permissive regulation regime allowed for further gains in the dividend account and in the capital account for the holders of shares in the larger privatized enterprises (in general, as I show in chapter 5, the yield of stocks of privatized companies was higher than that for other companies quoted). The financial gains from holding shares of privatized companies involved millions of shareholders, especially families in the upper and middle classes, but it did not touch the lowest deciles of the population.

3.2.9   Testing

I turn now to a simple test of the long-run impact of privatization on output in the United Kingdom based on a paper I coauthored (Florio and Grasseni 2003). In that paper, our test focuses on real GDP and its determinants as controls for the role of privatization. (For details, see the appendix.)

We test a log-linear regression equation of the form

$$y_t = \mu + \beta Priv_t + \gamma z_t + \varepsilon_t, \tag{3.1}$$

where y_t is real GDP, $Priv_t$ are privatization proceeds, z_t is a vector of explanatory variables, and ε_t is an error term. The variable of interest is $Priv$; a positive and significant estimate of the parameter β would therefore suggest a positive long-run elasticity between privatization and output for the U.K. economy.

Based on the previous discussion and data availability, the variables we have selected as controls include, for different specifications of the empirical models we test: government expenditures, taxes, investment, export, import, broad money supply, inflation, interest rates, unemployment, number of working days lost because of industrial actions, price of shares, and surplus per employee (see figures 3.5 and 3.6). We use quarterly data, and the period covered is 1979–1999. We transform nominal values in 1995 constant pounds using the appropriate GDP deflators.

One of the main issues related to the estimation of time-series data concerns the stationarity of the variables involved. We report in the appendix the results of standard tests for integration, and we describe there also the cointegration approach we use. We find that the error

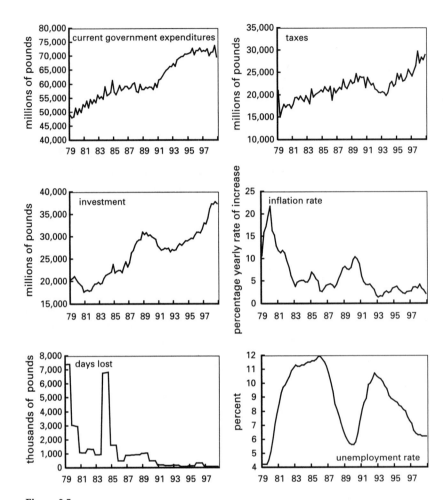

Figure 3.5
Selected macroeconomic variables.
Sources: ONS, n.d.-b; OECD, n.d.; and Datastream, n.d.

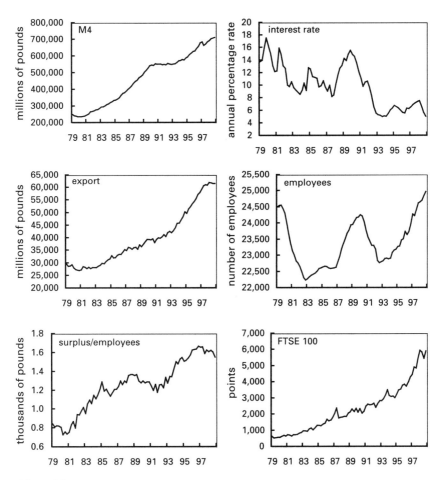

Figure 3.6
Selected macroeconomic variables (continues).
Sources: ONS, n.d.-a; OECD, n.d.; and Datastream.

correction model (ECM) estimation, based on the residuals of regression (3.1), supports the assumption of cointegration.

Obviously care needs to be taken in the interpretation of this test, because a simple reduced-form equation of the U.K. economy is being tested, and there may be several omitted variables. Having said this, we find a statistically significant positive parameter for privatization proceeds, but it is very close to zero. GDP elasticity to privatization proceeds is around 0.003 and 99 percent significant, in our best empirical models.

In other models, in which we consider cumulated proceeds or in which we use a Hodrick-Prescott (HP) filter for GDP or other explanatory variables, the parameter estimates are even lower or not significant. These coefficient estimates, taken together, suggest that, at least until 1999, privatization per se had a very modest macroeconomic impact on GDP in the United Kingdom. Therefore, we can exclude the existence of major growth externalities in our time horizon, and we can turn to the microeconomic approach.

3.3 Discussion

To sum up, my findings are the following. First, public-sector investment in the United Kingdom fell quite drastically over the period considered for two distinct reasons: (a) because as state-owned enterprises gradually disappear, so do their investments; and (b) because of the adoption of restrictive budgetary measures. Private investment did not substitute for decreasing public investment. Although after a long period of stagnation, private investments in the United Kingdom picked up at the end of the 1990s, coinciding with the increasing business cycle in the whole OECD area, the investment/GDP ratio in the United Kingdom was low in comparison with that of EU countries. This hindered output growth.

Second, despite the liberalization of the labor market in the period under study and the transfer of a large number of workers from the traditionally very unionized public sector to the private one, the participation rate did not increase. Involuntary unemployment, bearing in mind disguised forms of unemployment due to early retirement or invalidity, did not decrease and was no lower than that of many EU countries.

Third, long-term inflation in the United Kingdom was no lower, and often higher, in this period than that of other European countries. The prices of the services of some privatized utilities dropped, but prices of services of others increased. Even conceding that the average price index of privatized firms was falling in comparison with the retail price index, overall the productivity change in the service sector was modest, and the real price decrease was lower than its potential.[4]

Moreover, one specific channel for transmission of inflationary shocks suggested by the U.K. experience is the development of an unexpected capital gain by households because of underpricing of privatization shares and council houses. To accommodate this "shock" of unexpected enrichment, the families' marginal propensity to save should rise, if only provisionally. What actually happened was that during the period considered, the rate of saving of families plummeted, and there were occasional booms in consumption and real estate investments.

In the first phase of the British privatization policy, underpricing, public-investment cuts, and tax reforms, faced with rigidity of supply, because of the prolonged stagnation of private and public investments, contributed to inflationary trends and to large deficits in the trade balance.

Fourth, there is no clear evidence that positive shocks on the supply side from the change in ownership per se did anything to divert economic growth in the United Kingdom from its long-term trend. It is also difficult to identify any effect of those shocks on the level of GDP and on productivity changes in the long run. The "miracle" apparently was just the end of decades of relative decline in comparison to other countries. This was more, however, the effect of the fading of exceptionally high growth elsewhere than of a good performance of the British economy.

Finally, income redistribution in the period under consideration was regressive. The causes of this regressiveness were many, but privatization probably played a role in the sense of encouraging the trend rather than impeding it. There is little doubt that, to consider only the extreme cases, the position of the top and bottom deciles of the population in terms of per capita income respectively improved and deteriorated, in both relative and absolute terms.

The conclusion, in light of my approach of reclassifying the macro data in terms of social welfare, is that the variation in GDP attributable to privatization was very small. Privatization's effects on employment were, to say the least, moderately restrictive. Its inflationary impact was probably neutral. An adverse redistribution effect was present. Thus for any set of reasonable welfare weights, it is difficult to say that the British privatization policy was an unambiguous Paretian improvement in terms of social welfare, at least for any moderately egalitarian macroeconomic social-welfare function.

I repeat that these are just conjectures that are scarcely demonstrable at this stage. It appears, however, to be equally difficult with the data that we have reported to demonstrate the opposite position: that

privatization over the past twenty years had a positive macroeconomic impact on the country's growth and welfare.

Two possible objections are worth considering here. One might acknowledge that there is no macroeconomic evidence of a supply-side
shock as a result of privatization but consider this to be because the
impact, albeit positive, is small and cannot be captured by aggregate
variables. A related, but somewhat different, objection is that the positive impact of privatization on growth is masked by other adverse
changes in the economic condition of the country (Oulton 1995).

As for the first objection, the issue seems to be how we can say that a
supply shock is "small" relative to the economy. If we use the ratio of
privatization proceeds to GDP as the relevant explanatory variable, its
dimension is certainly not negligible, as in some years it is more than
2 percent of GDP. This dimension is comparable with those of fiscal
reforms that are usually tested by standard macroeconometric models
of the British economy. For example, Wallis (1987) reviews simulations
of macroeconomic impacts of seven econometric models of the U.K.
economy in the 1980s and finds that

• a 3.25 percent increase in public expenditures financed by high-
powered money increases GDP by 0.6–0.9 percent for most models;

• a 5 percent decrease in the marginal rate of income tax (e.g., from 30
percent to 28.5 percent) has a typical impact of around 0.2 percent of
GDP;

• a 10 percent decrease in the VAT rate (from 15 percent to 13.5 percent) has an impact of around 0.2 percent of GDP.

These examples (among many possible ones) have a budgetary dimension similar or inferior to that of the yearly flow of privatization proceeds in most years.

Moreover, if we consider that the privatized industries in Britain
account for around 10 percent of GDP, a labor productivity increase of,
say, 10 percent should generate a permanent potential increase in GDP
of around 1 percent. An increased productivity growth should generate higher output profiles over time. If we do not see this impact with
standard tests, the impact should probably actually be much smaller
than 1 percent of GDP. In fact, this exactly is what I show in subsequent chapters, in which I turn to a discussion of productivity changes
in individual industries resulting from privatization.

The second potential objection noted is similar in spirit, but it ad-
vances the doubt that positive and negative shocks cancel one another

out. There is little doubt that monetary policy and high exchange rates in the 1980s damaged the British economy, particularly exports. There is also little doubt that there was an investment slowdown in Britain for most of the 1990s. Our empirical models support the view that GDP in the United Kingdom is highly dependent on the rest of the world and on investment. According to Oulton (1995), without the British participation in the exchange rate mechanism (ERM) and without budgetary mismanagement by the Exchequer in the 1990s, we might have been able to observe the positive impact of the supply-side shocks, including industrial legislation reform, privatization, and higher participation in education and vocational training. My empirical tests control for fiscal stance, exports, and investments, however, and I cannot confirm anything more than a very modest impact of privatization per se.

At this point, we must turn our backs on a method of analysis that cannot give us very much, and we must consider the microeconomic effects of privatization on the single agents. The purpose of this chapter was simply to sow some seeds of doubt in the mind of the reader about the overall impact of privatization on the British economy.

3.4 Further Reading

There is a huge literature on long-term productivity trends in the United Kingdom. Most recently, see O'Mahony 1999, which offers some evidence that Britain's productivity lags behind that of the United States, France, and Germany, and that the gap in productivity per hour worked between Britain and the latter two countries is around 30 percent. This is partly attributable to higher investment in France and Germany than in Britain: Capital per hour worked is respectively 50 percent and 70 percent higher in those countries than in Britain. From this angle, low unemployment (and lower wages) in the United Kingdom are the flip side of low capital per worker. Empirical tests on the macroeconomic impact of privatization include Favero 1988; Barnett 2000; Mackenzie 1998; Chisari, Estache, and Romero 1999; Gylfason 1998; and Bennett et al. 2003.

Appendix

This appendix draws from Florio and Grasseni 2003. We test empirical regressions of the general form of equation (3.1), reproduced here for convenience:

$$y_t = \mu + \beta Priv_t + \gamma z_t + \varepsilon_t, \tag{3.1}$$

where y_t is real GDP, $Priv_t$ are privatization proceeds, z_t is a vector of explanatory variables, and ε_t is an error term. For all variables, quarterly data cover the period 1979:2–1999:1. Value data are at constant 1995 prices and seasonally adjusted. Data at current prices have been deflated by the GDP deflator. The empirical regression equation (3.1) is in log-linear form, causing the coefficient of the variables to be elasticities and reducing heteroscedasticity. GDP is gross domestic product at market prices, in millions of pounds at constant prices. The main sources for privatization proceeds are ONS 2000c and H.M. Treasury 1997c.

The controls we consider are

GOV: total current expenditure;

TAX: public-sector taxes on income and wealth;

GNET: total net government expenditures less taxes on income and wealth (the difference between GOV and TAX);

INFLATION: the inflation rate;

RPI: the percentage change in the retail price index over twelve months—all items;

SURPLUS: gross operating surplus per employee;

EXPORT: total exports, in millions of pounds at 1995 prices;

UNEMPL: unemployed percentage of labor force yearly data transformed into quarterly data based on quarterly employment data [Source: OECD Statistics Directorate, n.d.);

INV: Gross fixed-capital formation, in millions of pounds at 1995 prices;

M4: broad money stock, end-of-period, level;

INTEREST: three-month yield, Treasury bills;

FTSE 100: Financial Times Stock Exchange price index [Source: Datastream, n.d.);

DAYLOST: working days lost because of industrial actions;

UNDER: underpricing of privatized stocks and other assets (see table 5A.2).

All data are from ONS except for unemployment and FTSE 100.

The test for cointegration is in two steps, following Engle and Granger (1987) procedure. First, after testing the integration of the individual series, we run the cointegrating regression linking the several series in levels in equation (3.1). Once equation (3.1) is estimated, the residuals, ε_t, are recovered and subjected to the usual unit-root test using an augmented Dickey-Fuller (ADF) test and/or a Phillips-Perron (PP) test. If the residuals are stationary, cointegration can be assumed. The cointegrating regression represents the long-term equilibrium, and the cointegrating error term ε_{t-1} serves as a measure of disequilibrium. If evidence in support of cointegration is found, we estimate an ECM (3.1) and its lagged residuals, as follows:

$$\Delta y_t = \mu + \beta \Delta Priv_t + \gamma \Delta z_t + \theta \varepsilon_{t-1} + u_t, \tag{3.2}$$

where u_t is a random-error term. A negative and statistically significant estimate for θ would suggest convergence of the model to a long-run equilibrium, and in such a case, the coefficient θ can be interpreted as the speed of the convergence.

The residuals generated from the cointegration equation are tested for stationarity using ADF and PP tests, and the test statistics generated from equation (3.1) for the data previously identified are presented in table 3A.1. For these specifications the tests indicate that the residuals are stationary, and therefore this suggests that cointegration is present. Hence, there generally exists a significant long-run relationship between GDP and the several variables included in the model.

As for our variable of interest, *Priv*, we find that in most specifications the coefficient β is positive and statistically significant but very close to zero, suggesting a weak impact of privatization on the growth of the country. In some models we use the rate of interest instead of M4 as the control variable . In these cases, the coefficient β is never significant, and the ADF and PP tests suggest that a weak cointegration is present among the variables involved.

To examine the short-term process of adjustment to deviation from the long-run equilibrium relationship, the parameters of the error correction model are presented in table 3A.2. The results show that β, which indicates here the short-run effect of privatization proceeds on GDP, is not statistically significant. Table 3A.2 reports the results of a standard diagnostic test (Ramsey's Reset).

Table 3A.1
Estimates of the cointegration regression model (3.1) with log-GDP as dependent variable

Variable	(1)	(2)	(3)	(4)	(5)
C	6.15***	6.959***	6.438***	6.167***	6.653***
	(27.35)	(17.69)	(16.47)	(19.06)	(15.24)
Priv	0.001	0.003**	0.005***	0.001	0.003*
	(0.74)	(2.16)	(2.91)	(0.74)	(1.87)
GNET	0.025	0.051**	0.058**	0.025	0.064**
	(1.20)	(2.15)	(2.29)	(1.18)	(2.13)
INV	0.212***	0.28***	0.286***	0.211***	0.287***
	(8.52)	(11.76)	(9.40)	(7.57)	(11.13)
EXPORT	0.187***	0.165***	0.171***	0.186***	0.172***
	(10.27)	(6.99)	(6.28)	(8.30)	(6.64)
M4	0.115***			0.114***	
	(6.79)			(5.97)	
INTEREST					−0.007
					(−0.99)
INFLATION	−0.011***	−0.010**	−0.008*	−0.011***	
	(−3.10)	(−2.28)	(−1.70)	(−3.01)	
UNEMPL	−0.024***	−0.037***	−0.027***	−0.025***	−0.029***
	(−3.50)	(−3.65)	(−2.54)	(−2.90)	(−2.97)
DAYLOST	−0.004**	−0.012***	−0.007***	−0.004**	−0.012***
	(−2.34)	(−6.70)	(−3.64)	(−2.27)	(−6.15)
UNDERPRICING					0.002
					(0.57)
SURPLUS		0.092***			0.088***
		(4.12)			(3.76)
FTSE 100			0.036***	0.001	
			(2.56)	(0.08)	
Adj. R^2	0.99	0.99	0.99	0.99	0.99
DW	0.83	1.35	1.15	0.84	1.35
ADF	−2.66	−3.94	−2.85	−2.65	−4.11
PP	−4.63	−6.45	−5.83	−4.62	−6.70

Note: *t*-statistics in parentheses. Critical values of the ADF and PP statistics computed in accordance with MacKinnon 1991 at the 1, 5, and 10 percent level are −3.51, −2.89, −2.58, respectively. C = constant.
*statistically significant at the 1 percent level.
**statistically significant at the 5 percent level.
***statistically significant at the 10 percent level.

Table 3A.2
Estimates of the error correction model (3.2) with first difference of log-GDP as dependent variable

Variables	(1)	(2)	(3)	(4)	(5)
C	0.001	0.003***	0.003***	0.001	0.003***
	(1.55)	(4.35)	(4.41)	(1.39)	(4.27)
$\Delta Priv$	−0.0005	−0.0004	3.06E −05	−0.0005	−0.0003
	(−0.77)	(−0.68)	(0.04)	(−0.77)	(−0.45)
ΔGNET	−0.002	0.01	0.002	−0.001	0.009
	(−0.12)	(0.69)	(0.15)	(−0.10)	(0.60)
ΔINV	0.073***	0.07***	0.082***	0.070***	0.076***
	(3.27)	(2.99)	(3.43)	(3.15)	(3.01)
ΔEXPORT	0.112***	0.115***	0.118***	0.103***	0.112***
	(3.78)	(3.63)	(3.58)	(3.35)	(3.31)
ΔM4	0.181***			0.182***	
	(4.29)			(4.32)	
ΔINTEREST				−0.002	
				(−0.34)	
ΔINFLATION	−0.004	−0.009***	−0.006*	−0.003	
	(−1.27)	(−3.07)	(−1.85)	(−1.08)	
ΔUNEMPL	−0.063***	−0.064***	−0.07***	−0.065***	−0.057***
	(−4.50)	(−4.50)	(−5.15)	(−5.11)	(−4.38)
ΔDAYLOST	−0.002*	−0.004***	−0.003**	−0.002*	−0.004***
	(−1.85)	(−3.06)	(−2.16)	(−1.89)	(−2.85)
ΔUNDERPRICING					−0.0005
					(−0.21)
ΔSURPLUS		0.051***			0.044***
		(3.63)			(3.00)
ΔFTSE 100			0.011	0.008	
			(1.46)	(1.10)	
ECM(−1)	−0.374***	−0.30***	−0.299***	−0.379***	−0.303***
	(−4.84)	(−4.25)	(−4.40)	(−4.90)	(−4.13)
R^2	0.65	0.63	0.59	0.66	0.60
Adj. R^2	0.60	0.58	0.54	0.61	0.54
DW	1.91	1.89	1.72	1.89	1.74
Test RESET	1.78	0.50	2.20	2.80	0.65
	prob	prob	prob	prob	prob
	(0.19)	(0.48)	(0.14)	(0.10)	(0.42)

Note: t-statistics are in parentheses. C = constant.
*statistically significant at the 1 percent level.
**statistically significant at the 5 percent level.
***statistically significant at the 10 percent level.

4   Firms

4.1   Topics for Discussion

The previous chapter shows that the evidence for a structural impact of privatization on aggregate output and productivity in the United Kingdom is small or dubious. In this chapter, I turn to assessing productivity at a microeconomic level. The chapter's first section deals with some conceptual issues. I then turn to presenting evidence in the second section, and I comment on that evidence in the concluding section. I single out four areas of study: profitability, productivity of labor, productivity of capital, and TFP, for both individual firms and industries. I briefly discuss in the remainder of this section some conceptual issues related to these performance indicators.

A number of empirical studies on privatization focus on profitability, which can be measured by conventional balance sheet indicators such as return on investment (ROI), return on sales (ROS), return on equity (ROE), and return on assets (ROA), among others. Perhaps more precisely, the internal rate of return on net cash flows can be used, or the net present value of cash flows.

These measures of profitability are the most interesting ones to the private owner (and indirectly to his creditors, suppliers, and employees). They do not, however, constitute proof that the firm uses its economic resources in the least costly social way. Greater profitability may result from different causes, including a reduction in input unit costs or an increase in the output price in real terms. These changes may, in turn, have different causes (e.g., dynamic scale economies, increase in the degree of monopoly, exogenous changes of technology or of demand), in addition to greater productivity. The welfare implications are different for each potential cause. It is therefore necessary to explain the specific causes of any increase in profitability in order to ascertain its impact on social welfare.

Moreover, as noted, profitability can be measured in different ways. The economic meaning of profitability may differ across different indicators. For example, returns gross of interest, tax, and depreciation will usually be more interesting for welfare analysis than net profits, the latter being the result of particular financial and accounting circumstances and conventions.

Thus, we should avoid common misunderstandings about the correlation between profitability and efficiency. If a privatized firm operates in a monopoly regime, then we should evaluate the increase in profitability, as shown empirically, according to a higher ROE or ROS than the average for the sectors exposed to competition as a social cost.

In principle, we could consider socially efficient a transitory monopoly profit linked to innovation (by a well-known Schumpeterian argument). On the other hand, a persistent wedge between marginal prices and costs is comparable to an indirect tax. The loss of welfare for the consumer because of this "private tax" is, however, greater than the loss resulting from public taxes. For the latter, the levy from taxes returns to consumers in the form of public spending; hence, the loss of welfare to consumers is solely the burden in excess of taxation. Monopoly profit implies a first-order welfare effect. It therefore becomes crucial to know whether the social-welfare function that I assume assigns the same weight to the welfare of the consumer and of the monopolist. The fact that shareholders in the privatized firm and the other stakeholders may be numerous does not alter the nature of the problem. Taxation of monopoly profits, even if at a 100 percent rate, cannot wipe out the excess burden to consumers of distorted monopoly prices.

In this sense, increases in profitability for companies that operate in noncompetitive conditions determine a loss of social welfare and are therefore socially inefficient, whereas transitory profits correlated to higher productivity are a completely different, and more socially desirable, performance. It is not profitability per se that is important, but some of its possible drivers. Increased productivity is the most important among them.

Here, again, we need to be careful. In general, what we observe empirically at firm level are some indices of average productivity and their variations over time. These indices are of various kinds; often they are ratios in which the numerator is a measure of the output and the denominator a measure of a factor (or an aggregated measure for TFP). These measures have their problems, for one or more of the reasons below.

Marginal labor productivity, according to the microeconomics text-book definition, is the partial derivative of a function of production. It is the increase in real output obtained under a marginal increase in labor when the quantity of other factors is kept constant. The empirical observations of output that are usually available are often associated with changes in other inputs, including capital. Therefore, we need to exercise caution in considering the rough figures before and after privatization. This may be particularly important in considering the British experience, in which firms often increased investment and contracting-out after government divestiture. Empirical observations of output and employees in some cases would exaggerate the actual increase in labor productivity of privatized industries.

Moreover, physical output is not always measurable in obvious ways (number of computers, weight of cars, etc.). Even labor is not a homogeneous factor (for example, after privatization there may be more white-collar workers and fewer blue-collar).

For multiproduct firms, additional delicate problems of aggregation arise. The use of prices as a weighting coefficient creates sensitive issues. For example, changes in the relative prices of various products and services (e.g., local and international telephone calls) before and after privatization will noticeably influence the result of firms' productivity estimates. If prices are distorted (in the sense discussed in chapter 2), then the weighted production index in turn will be distorted. Therefore, the very frequent use in the literature of ratios of deflated turnover (and value added) to number of workers, even where the numerator is deflated by some price index, may have an ambiguous significance.

Eventually, and contrary to the mental picture that many have of the meaning of the term "labor productivity," this concept does not necessarily have anything, at least directly, to do with the effort and the organization of a firm's labor force or management. As noted, labor productivity, empirically observed by simple output/employment ratios, can increase because capital or energy intensity increases. Other factors being equal, it may increase because there is an increase in demand. Consequently, the same labor force will be able to respond to an increase in production, as often happens in network industries such as the supply of drinking water or electricity.

Moreover, the expectation that privatization increases the incentive for management to squeeze labor efficiency is reasonable, within certain limits. Effort and organizational changes are variables difficult to measure. In addition, in some cases, executives of large regulated corporations may have an incentive for "quiet-life" management. I touch on some of these points in section 4.3 and in later chapters.

Similar considerations apply to the measure of productivity of capital, with an additional complication. It is more difficult to measure input here than in the case of labor. In the privatization process, the evaluation of assets is subject to drastic changes. The measure of productivity of capital is quite different depending on whether one considers the historical cost, the value at the time of privatization, or the current value. As I show in chapter 5, for some British utilities, especially water, the importance of underpricing was so great that it forced the regulator to introduce conventional values for capital ("the regulatory asset base") to calculate the return.

In principle, the most appropriate measure for showing the level and change in productive efficiency is total factor productivity. TFP, however, poses the usual conceptual problems that result from aggregation of the factors (usually resolved by resorting to indices of prices for the factors themselves) and practical problems of availability of information.

Finally, as for other issues in this book, one must carefully distinguish between changes in productivity linked to privatization per se and those with different causes.

With these broad questions in mind, in this chapter I survey the available evidence on output and productivity in the nationalized and privatized industries. As noted, my objective is to determine whether the impact of privatization on productivity, which is ambiguous at a macroeconomic level, manifests itself more clearly at the firm or industry level.

4.2   The Empirical Evidence

4.2.1   The Performance of Public, Private, and Privatized Firms

A vast amount of empirical literature exists about the comparative performance of public and private firms at an international level. Tittenbrun (1996) examines eighty-seven empirical works dealing with a large number of countries and twenty-seven sectors. The list of these sectors is itself interesting: airlines, bus services, banks, cleaning services, construction, debt collection, electricity, the fertilizer industry, forestation, hospitals, housing, insurance, manufacturing, payroll processing, railways, refuse collection, road maintenance, ship repairs, slaughterhouses, steel, telecommunications, urban tree maintenance, turf maintenance, various industries, water, weather forecasting, and the weaving industry. As did many other reviews that preceded it, Tittenbrun's study concludes that the impact of market structure on performance is probably greater than that of ownership in itself. For an opposite view, see Shirley and Walsh 2000, which surveys the empirical literature and concludes that "ownership matters."

Other general surveys include, for example, Millward and Parker 1983; Ferguson 1988; and Yarrow 1986. According to Sawyer and O'Donnell (1999), most reviews support the proposition that when we compare firms operating in the same industry and in a similar environment, comparisons of efficiency give mixed evidence. A number of studies exist that, instead of a synchronic comparison between public and private firms (which is often quite improper when comparing different industries), propose a comparison between the same company before and after privatization.

Turning to the works that refer specifically to the United Kingdom, the contributions that I consider most relevant for their broad coverage include Millward 1991; Foreman-Peck and Millward 1994; Hannah 1994; and Martin and Parker 1997. I consider several other works that tackle the subject for specific sectors, periods, or company cases in section 4.4 or elsewhere within the chapter. My references are far from exhaustive. The variety of methods, periods, and sectors examined in these studies is wide, as is their quality. I try to distill from this heterogeneous empirical literature the main results about profitability and productivity. Megginson and Netter (2001) offer a review of the literature in this area (see also section 4.4).

4.2.2   Profitability

I discussed in section 4.1 some reasons why profitability may not be the most relevant performance indicator for economic analysis of policy reform. With this reservation, it is, however, useful nonetheless to observe profitability.

Earlier comparative studies have shown that the profitability of public firms in the United Kingdom was generally lower than that of private firms in the same sector.[1] Practically all the studies agree on this assessment. The greater profitability of private companies, however, does not appear to be attributable with any certainty to lower costs or greater productivity, as I show later in this section.

Studies based on time series, in general, observe an increase in the profitability of U.K. privatized industries in the 1980s. The trend was observed even before privatization, and consequently it is not always easy to establish a causal relationship between change of ownership and change in profitability. In any case the results of these studies were unambiguous (Hutchinson 1991; Bishop and Kay 1988, 1989; Haskel and Szymanski 1990, 1991, 1992, 1993a, 1993b; Hartley, Parker, and Martin 1991; Bishop and Green 1995). The interpretation of what happened, however, was complex. According to Bishop and Kay (1988), although it may be true that privatized companies have been faster growing and more profitable, the causation seems to run from growth and profitability to privatization, rather than the other way round.

I would like to explain the underlying causes of profitability. Therefore, I turn first to production cost studies, then to productivity studies. (I come back to profitability in chapter 5, where I focus on shareholders.)

4.2.3   Production Costs

Profits depend on revenues and costs. I discuss revenues together with prices in chapter 7; here I focus on costs. Costs depend upon prices of inputs and productivity. Evidence does not suggest that production costs are clearly and always lower in the public sector than in the private sector, when comparison is possible (e.g., Foreman-Peck and Waterson 1984 on the producers of electricity between the two wars; Millward and Ward 1987 on the gas sector in the nineteenth century).

Lynk (1993) and Hunt and Lynk (1995) study the relative efficiency of the firms operating in the U.K. water sector before privatization (1989). At the time, there were ten regional water authorities (public) that pursued an integrated river basin policy, operating in sectors such as the supply and distribution of drinking water, sewers, and environmental services. Nevertheless, there were also twenty-eight private water-only providers. Thus, this is a clear case in which comparisons between public and private firms are sensible. The approach followed by the authors is to use a stochastic cost frontier, which computes the spread between the minimum theoretical cost assigned to input and the effective cost. The period studied was from 1979 to 1988, with the use of dummies for each region and for each year. The private firms were found to have costs greater than their frontier value in the region of 11.5 percent. Public firms were found to have a much lower excess of costs, in the region of 2 percent. In other words, the latter were determined to be more efficient. One fundamental reason for the superior technical efficiency of the public corporations seems to have been the existence of economies of scope in the water industry that were not exploited by the private firms.[2]

I am not aware of wide-range studies on cost performance before and after privatization, but some specific studies are particularly interesting and worth mentioning here. They refer to the electricity industry, British Airways, and British Steel and to changes in procurement organization.

Newbery and Pollitt (1997) show that in the case of the U.K. electricity sector, the privatization of the Central Electricity Generating Board (CEGB) would in fact, compared to a counterfactual scenario, have led to an annual reduction of 5 percent in costs. This would have been equivalent to a return on capital of 40 percent, but the producers and their shareholders would have entirely appropriated the benefits, and the government and the consumers would have lost out. This implies socially inefficient prices (I return to this subject in chapter 7) (see also Domah and Pollitt 2001).

Eckel and Singal (1997) discuss evidence on British Airways (BA), whose restructuring began in 1980 with the nomination of Lord (John) King of Wartnaby as chairman, whereas privatization took place in 1987. The decline in the share prices of the company's U.S. competitors (in the region of −7 percent) in the ten years following the announcement of BA privatization (1985–1995), together with the decline in tariff rates (−14.3 percent) over the same period, would seem to be sufficient evidence of an improvement in performance. The authors study only the market for international traffic, which is less influenced by the regime of regulation. They assume that the lower tariffs and lower operating costs that enabled BA to present itself more aggressively on the market were due to changes in internal organization. These changes seem, however, to have very little to do with any improvement in corporate governance (monitoring by majority shareholders, structure of the board, etc.). They seem linked instead to changes in pay incentives for the firm's top management (introduction of plans for executive stock options, seven-fold increases in the CEO's salary) before divestiture; obviously competition (e.g., with entrants such as Virgin) played a major role as well.

Aylen (1988) analyzes in detail the evidence on British Steel Corporation (BSC). The author sees the resurrection of BSC as one of the most important cases of restructuring in business history. In 1980–1981, the company was losing £1 billion out of a turnover of £3 billion, a result worthy of the *Guinness Book of Records*, with a cost per ton that was a third greater than its German competitors. Less than a decade later, British Steel was making a profit of £0.4 billion on a turnover of £3.8 billion. Management achieved this result by doubling productivity (in fact reducing the workforce by half), taking steps to save energy, and other methods of rationalization. The result is even more noteworthy in comparison with international competitors, placing British Steel, after restructuring, at the top of the world ranking in terms of efficiency (measured as cost per ton). The turnaround, however, is not attributable to privatization, according to Aylen, but to a change in objectives and incentives within the public management: "before the 1980s there was an overlap between government and BSC finances with losses accepted for social reasons. In particular there was close political scrutiny over input decisions such as investment, plant closure, employment levels and domestic coal consumption, and attention to politically sensitive outputs such as steel prices during periods of inflation.... Overall enterprise efficiency was subordinated to immediate, short term political concerns" (23).

After 1980, still in a regime of public ownership, the picture changed dramatically. The government established clear commercial objectives for the company that took priority over social objectives. A new top manager (Ian Mac Gragor) was appointed. The company was required to publish performance ratios, based on indexes of labor productivity, energy efficiency, and utilization of capital. The system of salary negotiation changed, with quarterly bonuses, linked to productivity, that added as much as 20 percent to salaries. Aylen concludes that the dramatic turnaround in British Steel's fortunes was due to changes in management and workforce incentives. In fact, it was government, not the new private owners, that changed the incentives for management.

Finally, I mention changes in procurement as a result of privatization. Harris, Parker, and Cox (1998) collected evidence on such changes by sending a questionnaire to forty-eight privatized companies. Twenty-eight of these companies replied, including ten firms operating in the electricity sector and seven water utilities. Twelve companies, it was found, centralized procurement after privatization; another twelve decentralized it; and four made no change to the structure. In fifteen of the twenty-eight firms, employment in the procurement branch decreased after privatization, with an average reduction from 123 to 79 workers. The most commonly cited causes for the destaffing were the need to contain costs, general downsizing, and increased efficiency. In twenty of the twenty-eight firms, a strategic mission was defined for the procurement function, and there was greater recourse than previously to managerial techniques, from negotiation, to the accreditation and formal selection of suppliers, to benchmarking, and so on. In general, the strategy was to be more collaborative with suppliers. There had been a strong swing to outsourcing in twenty-three of the firms. The sectors most affected by this outsourcing were information technology, engineering, cleaning, catering, and security. The reasons most commonly given for the outsourcing were cost reduction and the expectation of greater efficiency. Two-thirds (nineteen) of the firms reported a great improvement in the performance of suppliers (price competitiveness, quality, flexibility, etc.).

In conclusion, a noticeable improvement in procurement in formerly public British firms was evident after privatization of those firms. During the 1980s, however, apparently in all large firms, great attention was paid to procurement, perhaps in public corporations as well, but I am not aware of comparative studies on this.

I suggest that taken together, the three studies on production costs and the research on organization of procurement point to strong causal links between decreasing costs and managerial effort. The causal link between the latter and ownership change is much weaker. I turn now to an examination of productivity.

4.2.4 Labor Productivity

Regarding productivity trends, Millward (1991) and Foreman-Peck and Millward (1994) compare the long-term growth of the productivity of public firms in the United Kingdom with that of the manufacturing sector. The legitimacy of such a comparison is debatable, since the nationalized industries were mainly in the service and nonmanufacturing sectors, with different demand growth and dynamic economies of scale. From another point of view, however, the comparison can nevertheless be interesting. In many developed economies in the postwar period manufacturing was the sector that recorded the greatest increases in productivity. We can therefore see it as a benchmark case. As far as labor productivity is concerned, the main results of the two studies are the following. The rate of growth in labor productivity in the United Kingdom between 1951 and 1984 (before the start of the great privatization) was higher in the public firms than in the manufacturing sector, perhaps because of the huge cuts in employment pursued in the public firms for the whole of the period considered.

Hannah (1994) considers the period 1948–1988. Again, with manufacturing used as a benchmark, the Millward results are confirmed. Disaggregation by sectors helps us to understand which nationalized industries recorded better productive performances than manufacturing: airlines, electricity, gas, telecommunications, and, just for the period 1978–1985, steel, coal, and railways. Poorer productive performances than for manufacturing were recorded for road transport, buses, the Post Office, and the railways.

Other studies confirm this picture. Hutchinson (1991) considered seventeen firms in five sectors during the 1970s. He found higher rates of growth in labor productivity in the public firms than in the private ones, with some exceptions. Paradoxically, in the Conservative period after 1979, the evidence on productivity was even more clearly in favor of the public sector.

NEDO 1976 also compared the trend in productivity of U.K. public firms and the manufacturing sector (see table 4.1).[3] The firms consid-

Table 4.1
Nationalized Industries: Ratio of selected firms' growth rates (percentage per annum)/ total manufacturing growth rates in corresponding years

	British Airways 1960–1974	British Gas 1960–1975	Electricity 1960–1975	Post Office: Telecommunications 1960–1975	Total manufacturing 1960–1975
Output	11.0	7.4	4.7	9.9	2.7
Employment	3.6	−1.4	−1.6	2.1	−0.7
Capital stock	3.4	6.2	5.0	6.1	3.5
Gross domestic fixed capital formation	5.2	3.3	−4.0	10.1	1.8
Output per head	7.1	8.9	6.3	7.7	3.4
Output per unit capital	7.3	1.1	−0.3	3.6	−0.8
Capital per head	−0.1	7.7	6.7	3.9	4.2
Total factor productivity	7.2	5.1	1.7	6.4	2.3

Source: Author's calculations based on NEDO 1976, Background paper 3, table 2.7.

ered were British Airways, British Gas, British Rail, British Steel, the CEGB, the National Coal Board (NCB), the Post Office (subdivided into telecommunications and the rest), National Bus, and National Freight Corporation (NFC).

If one examines the average growth of the per capita product in the long term, disregarding the cyclic variations, which in some cases are sizeable, one observes that

• labor productivity in the manufacturing sector increased between 1960 and 1975 at an average annual rate of 3.4 percent;

• for some public firms, average growth was slower: 1.7 percent for the NCB; 0.4 percent for the Post Office (excluding telecommunications); 2.1 percent for NFC; 1.1 percent for National Bus (1970–1975); and −1.4 percent for British Steel;

• for the remainder of the public firms, the trend was much higher than in the manufacturing sector: 7.1 percent for British Airways; 8.9 percent for British Gas; 5.8 percent for British Rail; 6.3 percent for the CEGB; and 7.7 percent for the telecommunications portion of the Post Office.

The increase in productivity is partly attributable to demand growth. What is perhaps more notable is the fact that productivity increases, in firms in which they occurred, often was the result of generally larger cuts in employment in the public sector than in manufacturing. In the latter, the output increased by only 2.7 percent annually, whereas employment declined by 0.7 percent annually. On the other hand, except for BA and the Post Office, in which employment increased, all the other public firms cut employment more drastically than the manufacturing sector.

Turning to more recent times, Molyneux and Thompson (1987) for the period 1978–1985 and Hartley and Hooper (1990) for the period 1979–1990 find that the annual increase in productivity in the nationalized sector as a whole was 4.4 percent, greater than that of the manufacturing sector (4.1 percent) and of the economy as a whole (1.9 percent).

Unfortunately, an obvious limit to many of the works cited is the limited number of years considered before and after privatization. To get an overall view of long-term average productivity trends in some of the main nationalized-privatized industries, I tried to extend the NEDO 1976 labor productivity index series with data collected from

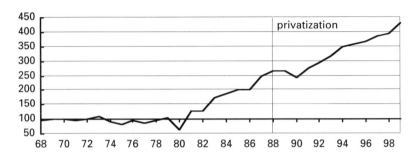

Figure 4.1
Steel: Labor productivity index (1970 = 100).
Sources: Employment: Eurostat, Iron and *Steel* (various issues); output: Mitchell 1998.

various recent sources: company reports, Office of National Statistics (ONS), Eurostat, and other international agencies. I present here some raw labor productivity indexes using data on employment and some measure of output (either in physical or value terms). Only limited original data on labor productivity were available. (The employment counterpart of this exercise is presented in chapter 6.)

I checked the consistency between NEDO and subsequent data by overlapping periods and using comparable methods. Consistency varies from case to case, but it is enough to guess the long-term trend in productivity before privatization for some nationalized industries. I have singled out six industries for which raw data comparable to those used for the NEDO study exist: steel, coal, gas, telecommunications, railways, and CEGB (electricity generation), both as nationalized industries and as their privatized followers.

1. Steel. As in the case of coal, NEDO's *value output per employee* and my *physical output per employee* indexes are quite comparable in the overlapping period. After stagnating from 1968 to 1979 (see figure 4.1), labor productivity grows during the 1980s and keeps growing at the same rate before and after privatization (the vertical line in the figure).

2. Gas. Data on employment and (physical) output, available for the entire period 1962–1993, were used to construct the index, which is in thousands of cubic meters per employee. The series (see figure 4.2) shows two major periods of growth in labor productivity: 1965–1975 and 1984–1993.

3. Coal. Although the two indexes used here to measure productivity in the coal industry are different in their definition (NEDO's index measures value output per employee; my index measures physical out-

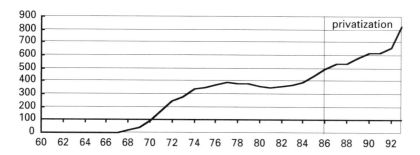

Figure 4.2
Gas: Labor productivity index (1970 = 100).
Sources: Employment: Martin and Parker 1997; output: Mitchell 1998.

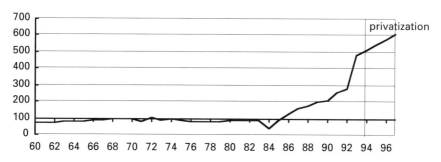

Figure 4.3
Coal: Labor productivity index (1970 = 100).
Sources: Employment: Eurostat, *Coal Bulletin* (various issues); output: Mitchell 1998.

put per worker), they share the same trend in the overlapping period. The overall picture is clear. Until the mid-1980s, labor productivity remained constant or even slightly decreased, then started to grow, with a sensible jump before privatization period (see figure 4.3).

4. CEGB. The productivity measure used for the electricity sector is gigawatt-hours (GWh) per employee. The long overlapping period (1970–1980) ensures good consistency between NEDO data and sources that are more recent. Figure 4.4 clearly shows an increase in the rate of labor productivity growth shortly before and after privatization. This coincides with a major change in technology, following the fading of the necessity of buying coal for the electricity generators (More on this in chapter 7).

5. Telecommunications. In this case, I use two different productivity indicators: the *main lines per employee* indicator happens to coincide with the NEDO series in the overlapping period (1970–1975) and

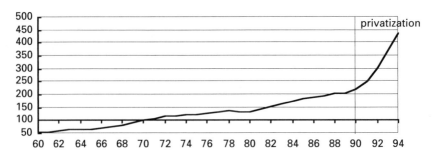

Figure 4.4
CEGB: Labor productivity index (1970 = 100).
Sources: CEGB *Annual Report* (various years).

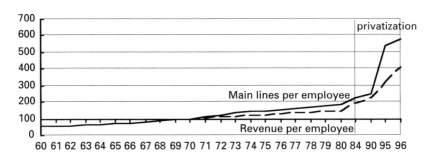

Figure 4.5
Telecommunications: Labor productivity index (1970 = 100).
Sources: Employment: Eurostat 1997; British Telecom, *Annual Report* (various years); output: ITU, *Yearbook of Statistics* (various years).

shows an acceleration of the rate of productivity growth in the industry since the early 1980s (see figure 4.5). The *revenue per employee* index, in constant pounds, covers the period 1970–1996 and shows a similar trend. (I discuss the British Telecom [BT] data in detail in chapter 9.)

6. Railways. I use different indicators for the passenger business and for the freight business in this industry, respectively, *passengers per km per employee* and *tons per km per employee*. In this case, overlap with the NEDO series data is limited, and compatibility is also. This does not allow for long-term comparisons; regardless, both series reveal an increase in the rate of growth of productivity since the early 1980s (see figure 4.6), a slowdown in the early 1990s, and a final increase corresponding to the first years after privatization.

These simple examples, with all their limitations, show how difficult it is to say that the British privatization of the late twentieth century

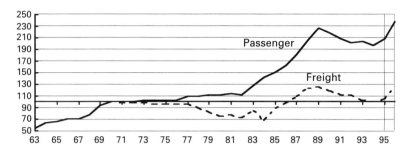

Figure 4.6
Railways: Labor productivity index (1970 = 100).
Sources: Employment: DETRA 1996; DETRA 1997; output: Mitchell 1998; UIC 1999.

always changed labor productivity trends dramatically. The evidence is mixed, and accurate empiral analysis just confirms this. I comment here some examples of such analysis.

Burns and Weyman-Jones (1994b) use mathematical programming techniques to study the increase in productivity in the distribution of electricity. They use a nonparametric estimation technique, based on the Farrell (1957) approach, which allows one to construct Malmquist productivity indices that incorporate multiple inputs and outputs. These inputs and outputs are defined as the ratio of the value of the input distance function after an event to the value of the input distance function before the event. The event they consider is divestiture of the regional electricity companies (RECs), and the period considered is 1971–1993. They use as inputs the number of workers, the kilometers of circuit of the distribution network, and the circuit reinforcement capacity, expressed in megavoltamps. Five output variables are used: number of customers, kilowatt-hours (kWh) supplied to domestic consumers, kWh supplied to commercial users, kWh supplied to industrial clients, and maximum simultaneous demand (again in kWh).

The results of this empirical analysis are mixed:

In one company there was a productivity decrease after privatization, in five others the productivity increased at a lower rate than before privatization, and in the remaining six, productivity growth increased. Based on test statistics conducted on the logarithm of the change in the Malmquist index, the authors are not able to reject the null hypothesis of equal productivity before and after privatization: In other words, according to Burns and Weyman-Jones, after allowing for the secular trend in productivity, the industry aggregate efficiency did not improve significantly. Note that if there is a cost decrease, as recorded by Newbery and Pollitt (1997), but no overall productivity increase, input prices may have been falling. This has limited relation to privatization. The falling prices depend on changes in technology and decreasing government protection of the coal industry.[4]

A totally different result was shown by a similar study of the twelve regional subdivisions of British Gas, in which productivity appears to have doubled after privatization and the result is statistically significant (Waddams Price and Weyman-Jones 1993). Inspection of figure 4.2 shows, however, that productivity trends in the gas sector increased several years before privatization.

Taken together, these two studies, which are good representations of the available literature, show on the one hand that the initial management conditions and performance of two public monopolies can be very different. On the other hand, they show that the effects of privatization on the productivity trend of an industry can vary from insignificant, as in the case of electricity supply, to sizable, as in the case of gas.

4.2.5   The Productivity of Capital and TFP

According to Millward (1991), the long-run rate of growth of the stock of capital over the period 1950–1970 was greater in the private sector than in the nationalized industries. Paradoxically, productivity of capital in the manufacturing segment recorded constant decline, whereas in the public sector, it showed continuous growth, albeit at very low rates. The NEDO study (1976) offers solid support for this view (see table 4.1). In fact between 1960 and 1975, the output per unit of capital declined in the manufacturing sector at a rate of −0.8 percent annually. In the public sector, there was only one case of a decline, and it was a slight one (−0.3 percent, for the electricity sector); for the other public firms, growth rates were high (British Airways, +7.3 percent; Telecommunications, +3.6 percent, etc.)[5] Moreover, according to Millward's (1991) results, TFP was always higher in public firms than in the manufacturing industries. Hannah (1984) reaches the same conclusions.

The basis for these assertions can be found in NEDO 1976, which shows how TFP in the manufacturing sector increased by roughly 28 percent in the space of fifteen years. This performance was comparable to that of the public electricity firms (+28 percent), but much lower that that of other nationalized industries: 245 percent for BA, 216 percent for British Gas, and 225 percent for telecommunications. On the other hand, estimating TFP in the case of public firms (and in general) raises particular methodological problems.[6]

Bishop and Thompson (1992b) study nine companies from the early 1970s (BA, British Airports Authority, British Coal, British Gas, British Steel, BT, British Rail, CEGB, and the Post Office). They find that although labor productivity in British public firms was lower than that in the economy as a whole in the 1970s, in the 1980s productivity levels in public firms increased, overtaking that of the economy as a whole around 1985. This turnabout was due to the substitution of capital for labor, as is confirmed by the fact that in the 1980s the TFP of the nine firms grew much more slowly than labor productivity. Overall, the authors claim that it is difficult to attribute the increase in TFP in the firms to a single factor, such as scale economies resulting from increased demand or technical progress. What is true for one firm is not true for another (coal and telecommunications are indeed different).

Boussofiane, Martin, and Parker (1997) study the productive efficiency in the same nine privatized firms using the data envelope analysis (DEA) method. They test three models: one with constant returns to scale, one with variable returns, and one including "environmental" variables to take into account the economic cycle and the technological trend. They conclude that there is evidence of improvement before and after privatization in some cases, but little discernible effect in others.

Parker and Saal (2001) study TFP trends in water and sewerage companies in England and Wales. The study covers the years 1985–1990 and offers aggregate and company-level calculations. It rejects the hypothesis that privatization and the resulting regulation improved efficiency at the industry or company level. It also rejects the hypothesis that observed improvement in these firms' profitability can be primarily attributed to TFP growth rather than to an increase in the price of output relative to the price of inputs.

Haskel and Szymanski 1993a tried to control productivity trends using different factors. The authors use panel data for twelve firms and control for demand, union power, market power, changes in ownership, and regulation and find productivity improvement at the time of restructuring before privatization. The study identifies for each company key facts, such as new regulation and new management. Privatization is found not to have changed TFP, and competition is determined to have played a limited role as a factor in TFP change as well. The study shows that the most important factors in TFP growth were restructuring preprivatization and labor shedding.

Green and Haskel (2001) compare the results of six studies on TFP or on TFP growth, including Bishop and Kay 1988; Bishop and Thompson 1992a, 1992b; Bishop and Green 1995; Martin and Parker 1997; and Waddams Price and Weyman-Jones 1993. They conclude that in all six studies, there is evidence that TFP rises before privatization, but not after. Green and Haskel also present their own TFP growth calculations for six corporations (British Airways, British Coal, British Gas, British Steel, British Telecom, and the Post Office, with the last still public). The time series spans the period between 1972 and 1999. They find a TFP growth increase after privatization for British Airways and a decrease for British Gas, British Steel, British Telecom, the Post Office. They also find a very high increase in TFP growth for British Coal, but it occurs before privatization. They conclude that firms improved their productivity significantly in the run-up to privatization, but the faster growth rate after privatization was not sustained. In their words this performance was a productivity catch-up rather than a permanent change of pace.

Moreover, we should consider that the 1970s were weak growth years for the British economy. If we include the 1960s, as we did above, the comparison between TFP growth before and after privatization does not show evidence of a structural break in the data time series.

4.2.6   The Study by Martin and Parker

Martin and Parker (1997) examine four different performance indicators for eleven different privatized companies (British Airways, British Airports Authority, Britoil, British Gas, British Steel, British Aerospace, Jaguar, Rolls-Royce, NFC, Associated British Ports, and BT). Their results are particularly interesting and deserve a detailed discussion. Their study considers not just utilities but also other corporations. The indicators considered are the rate of growth in labor productivity, the rate of growth in TFP, the rate of growth in value added, and the rate of profit (cf. Martin and Parker 1997, chap. 7).

For each of the companies studied, the figures considered were taken from balance sheets or other company sources, examined over a time span that covers both the years immediately before and after nationalization and subsequent years, usually until between 1992 and 1995. This time span allows five different subperiods to be identified: the period in which the company operated as a nationalized company, the years between the announcement of the intended privatization and the actual divestment, the early postprivatization years, the recessive cycle of 1988–1992, and the more recent past.

The authors attempt to summarize their results, counting the number of instances for each company in which there was an increase or a reduction in a particular performance indicator. They repeat this for each of the four indicators, comparing each pair of periods (nationalization compared to each of the other four):

- nationalization versus preprivatization
- nationalization versus postprivatization
- nationalization versus the recession
- nationalization versus the latest period

In total, there were 159 comparisons, which showed the following:

- Privatization does not appear to have had significant effects on increases in labor productivity. It had mainly negative effects on TFP and mainly positive effects on value added per worker and on profitability.
- When the periods are compared, the indicators are somewhat better in the nationalization period than in the postprivatization period or in the recession, and they were worse under nationalization than in the preprivatization period and more recently.

The results of the summary show that overall, of the 159 comparisons, 82 showed improvements in the performance indicators compared to the period of nationalization and 77 deterioration.

The study's method of determining which comparisons to make and count is open to obvious criticism, as the authors acknowledge. Nevertheless, overall, the time series of balance sheet data for these eleven firms support the authors' conclusions. The cases in which there is evidence of an improvement in company performance after privatization or after the announcement of privatization offset the other cases in which evidence of deterioration is found. Hence we cannot reject the null hypothesis, which is that privatization in itself did not have a statistically detectable effect on the variables examined. This conclusion is compatible with most of the empirical studies mentioned previously, which in turn may be considered an observation sample.

To reassess the conclusions of Martin and Parker (1997), I pooled their data into a single sample of 66 observations (6 periods × 11 organizations). Thus, I ended up with seven series corresponding to the following performance variables: labor productivity of the organization and a relative productivity index (ratio of the former to the labor productivity of the manufacturing sector or to the whole economy, where appropriate), total factor productivity (also relative), rate of profit (also relative), and value added (relative). For each of the seven variables, I estimated an ordinary least-squares (OLS) regression on a constant term (capturing the average value of the dependent variable during the nationalization period) and five dummy variables, constructed so as to represent the effect of each period with respect to the nationalization period (i.e., our baseline period). Table 4.2 summarizes the estimation results: Nearly all of the estimated dummy-variable coefficients fail the conventional significance test, so that the null hypothesis that the coefficient is equal to zero must be accepted.

This empirical test is admittedly simple and crude. The number of observations is small. One could wish for a larger sample and try more serious econometrics. The results, however, are clear and sensible. In fact, although the dummy variables for the subperiods generally have an estimated coefficient not statistically different from zero, there are the following reasonable exceptions:

1. TFP decline in recession years: This is compatible with a faster slowdown of output than of production factors.

2. Return on capital: Postannouncement there is an increase; probably an increase of profits was reported to make privatization easier.

3. Added value: There is a positive impact of the dummies for the last period and a negative one for the recession period.

These results are statistically significant and have the expected sign. Thus, they confirm that although the business cycle has a discernible effect on performance, privatization per se has no visible impact, except for the announcement effect.

4.3   Discussion

The long-term study of productivity and profitability in British privatized firms does not confirm the expectation that transfer of ownership has an unambiguous effect of increasing efficiency. I think the evidence supports the following propositions.

First, until the 1970s, labor or capital productivity and TFP usually increased more in Britain's nationalized industries than in the manufacturing sector. Exceptions were some protected industries in struc-

Table 4.2
Estimation results on Martin and Parker (1997) data set (66 observations)

Dependent variable	National- ization period	Popriva- tization period	Post- announcement period	Postpriva- tization period	Recession period	Latest period	Adj. R^2
Labor productivity	7.3*	0.3	−0.2	−3.5	−4.2	0.7	0.06
	(2.3)	(3.3)	(3.3)	(3.3)	(3.4)	(3.5)	
Labor productivity (relative)	4.5*	−0.1	0.0	−3.6	−3.3	0.0	0.05
	(2.2)	(3.1)	(3.1)	(3.1)	(3.1)	(3.2)	
Total factor productivity	3.9	0.2	−1.6	−2.0	−6.3*	−1.1	0.14
	(1.7)	(2.4)	(2.4)	(2.4)	(2.4)	(2.5)	
Total factor productivity (relative)	3.0	−1.0	−2.7	−3.5	−6.4*	−2.7	0.13
	(1.6)	(2.3)	(2.3)	(2.3)	(2.4)	(2.5)	
Rate of profit	9.0	8.4	15.4*	10.8	−4.2	0.7	0.15
	(5.1)	(7.2)	(7.2)	(7.2)	(7.4)	(7.6)	
Rate of profit (relative)	1.7	1.3	2.1	0.9	−1.2	−0.6	0.14
	(0.9)	(1.2)	(1.2)	(1.2)	(1.3)	(1.3)	
Value added (relative)	1.5	1.3	3.1	−3.2	−7.2*	8.7*	0.28
	(2.5)	(3.6)	(3.5)	(3.5)	(3.6)	(3.8)	

Source: Author's elaboration on Martin-Parker 1997, tables 5.1, 5.2, 5.3, 5.4, 6.1, and 6.2.
Note: Standard errors in parentheses.
* coefficients significantly different from zero

tural crisis, like coal and several public corporations during the slump following the first oil shock. Second, in a cross-section comparison between public and private firms, the latter are observed to have generated higher profits, as one would expect because of the different objectives of the two types of firms. Third, the profitability of the formerly nationalized industries increased immediately before and after privatization. We cannot rule out, however, that this was more because of wider markups over costs than because of productivity growth. Fourth, following privatization, productivity, however it is measured, improved in some firms, but not in others. There is no overall evidence of a structural break in the time series.

I cite here the conclusions of just one typical paper among many empirical papers on the subject. Liu (1995) studies an uncommon object in privatization research, ports. There are three hundred ports in Britain, and they offer a unique example of a variety of ownership structures: private (before and after the privatization of Associated British Ports), municipal, and owned by trusts. Government interference is limited, and there is some competition on relatively fair grounds (apart from the location advantage of some ports, particularly those on Britain's east coast). The study, based on a sample of twenty-eight major ports and a rather straightforward econometric approach, reaches a conclusion that I feel is appropriate as a general comment for the subject of this chapter:

In the case of British Ports we fail to identify ownership as a significant factor of production and the evidence does not establish a clear-cut pattern of efficiency in favor of one or another type of ownership. Needless to say, one piece of empirical evidence is rarely decisive; rather it is added to the body of evidence which researchers use to evaluate the worth of different economic theories. But the finding does echo those of many previous comparative studies. The British "experiment" of mixed port ownership provides additional backing for the view that that the superiority of the control system for private enterprises is a weak proposition. (273)

As noted, labor productivity, even when it is measured very crudely with indexes based on the average observed productivity, does not show an impact attributable to privatization. Productivity of capital and TFP, which are more difficult to measure, appear even to show deterioration in some privatized industries. Even if we may attribute some of these observations to errors in measurement, the evidence at a microeconomic level does not contradict that at a macroeconomic level.

To the best of my understanding of previous research and available evidence, there is no clear and general evidence in the research findings of a productivity micro shock.

How can one explain these results for Britain, the cradle of privatization? I suggest here a first tentative interpretation that I shall try to substantiate in the rest of the book. In the British historical experience, as I showed in chapter 1, private ownership typically assumes the form of dispersed shareholding, with shareholders not very well informed and hardly involved in company decision making. Small and medium-sized enterprises are less common in Britain than elsewhere. Very few large firms are under the control of entrepreneurs. The financial dimension, with its specific habits, is pervasive. Decision making is largely the privilege of autocratic top executives, under the scrutiny of other executives, those representing institutional investors. Utilities have additional bureaucratic masters, the regulators. Therefore, private ownership in Britain is a rather loose and complex governance structure.

The establishment of regulated oligopolistic markets can provide incentives to control costs, but to what extent this happens cannot be predicted without a number of qualifications. Monopoly power or the existence of (even tacit) collusion among the oligopolists may allow management to offload extra costs onto the consumer and to offer a satisfactory extra profit to shareholders. If regulators allow this, the incentive to increase productivity is less than under full competition. Continuous managerial efforts to raise productivity may even risk being counterproductive. Regulators may watch and put management under pressure. Highly profitable companies risk regulatory squeeze. Managers' quiet life, and convenient pay, will be disturbed. The best course of action for them is perhaps to report "satisfactory" profit results and avoid "maximizing" efforts. This is not terribly different from what the management of public corporations should do under a budget constraint and a required-rate-of-return regulatory framework. Therefore, the incentive system for the privatized firm may differ from that in the public corporation, but not by so much.

At this stage, these are just conjectures. Other explanations are possible. To elucidate the causes behind the observed productivity trends, we need to look into production factors: labor and capital. On the one hand, the effects of privatization on the labor and management factors needs to be assessed. On the other hand, the transfer of ownership rights and the resulting shareholding structure needs to be analyzed.

Hence, why the actual leap forward in the productivity of privatized firms in Britain was small can be better understood from within the firm.

My preliminary interpretation of this relatively modest performance points to corporate governance issues, which were not unknown in nineteenth-century Britain. At the early dawning of the modern large enterprise, John Stuart Mill observed: "Individuals acting for their own pecuniary interest are likely to be in general more careful and econom-ical than a public board; but the directors of a Joint Stock Company are not acting for their own pecuniary interest, but for that of their con-stituents. The management of a company is representative manage-ment, as much as that of an elected public board, and experience shows that it is quite as liable to be corrupt or negligent" (quoted in Harris 1959, 609).

4.4   Further Reading

Although I have cited in this chapter many empirical works, the litera-ture is so wide that I had to be selective. In this section, I mention some additional useful references, but the list is not exhaustive. A recent review of comparative productivity studies according to type of own-ership, Villalonga 2000, considered a wide array of cross-sectional studies. Whereas a simple count would give the feeling that studies that find evidence of greater efficiency associated with private owner-ship had the edge (104 against, 35 neutral and 14 in favor of public ownership), the evidence, according to Villalonga, is inconclusive. Usually the studies do not distinguish the explanatory power of mar-ket structure as a separate factor from ownership and fail to use ap-propriate efficiency measures. Moreover, only a very limited number of studies allow for appropriate statistical analysis. Megginson and Netter 2001 offers many additional references and a summary of re-sults of international research trends in this area.

International comparisons of productivity growth are difficult, but interesting. The studies by Hannah and Millward that I mentioned previously show that in a number of sectors, the level of labor produc-tivity was much higher in the United States and Germany than in the United Kingdom. The gap was similar both for the manufacturing sec-tors and for the nationalized sectors (e.g., electricity, gas, railways, water). According to Millward (1991), in 1950–1985, TFP growth was similar in the United Kingdom and the United States (between a minimum of 1.3 percent annual growth and a maximum of 2.4 percent). A comparison between the two countries in the mining, gas, electricity, water, transport, and communications sectors, however, almost always shows a net higher pace for the U.K. industries, predominantly nationalized, compared to the United States, predominantly private. O'Mahony (1999) compares labor productivity for gas, electricity, and water in United Kingdom, United States, Germany, France, and Japan and finds evidence that the United Kingdom caught up with the other countries studied after the 1990s. She thinks this may suggest evidence of an impact of privatization or of tight regulation. She does not, however, disentangle the former from the latter or from other possible factors.

Comparative trends for productivity in public and private firms often seem to correlate with industry-specific business cycles and structural differences. In some periods, the increase in labor productivity and TFP in Britain has been much greater in the public sector than in the private (Pryke 1971 for the subperiod 1948–1968). It was clearly greater in the private sector, however, in other subperiods (Pryke 1981 and Pryke 1982 for the period 1968–1978) or for some sectors (Ashworth and Forsythe 1984 for civil aviation; Rowley and Yarrow 1981 for the steel industry after nationalization). Taken as a whole these studies refine rather than contradict the picture. In general, the statistical evidence of an increase in TFP due to privatization is weak (Burns and Weyman Jones 1994a, 1994b, 1994c for the electricity sector; for gas, Waddams Price and Weyman Jones 1993; Bishop and Thompson [1992a, 1992b, 1993] observe improvements in productivity in nine firms, both privatized and public, during the 1980s compared to the 1970s; Foreman-Peck [1989] and Foreman-Peck and Manning [1988] do not observe any improvements in productivity in the case of BT; the results vary from case to case for Vickers and Yarrow [1988a] and for Yarrow [1986, 1989]). Other contributions to productivity literature before and after privatization include Ashworth and Forsyth 1984; O'Mahony and Oulton 1994; Hamilton 1971; Polanyi 1968; Polanyi and Polanyi 1972, 1974; Pryke 1971, 1981, 1982; Rowley and Yarrow 1981; Foreman-Peck and Waterson 1984; Foreman-Peck and Manning 1988; Millward and Ward 1987; Millward 1990; Molyneux and Thompson 1987; Bacon, Blyton, and Morris 1991; Parker and Martin 1995; Parker, Martin, and Boussofiane 1997; Lynk 1993; Cubbin, Domberger, and

Meadowcroft 1987; Hartley and Hooper 1990; Hutchinson 1991; Kay, Mayer, and Thompson 1986; Yarrow 1986; Vickers and Yarrow 1988a, 1988b; Bishop and Kay 1989; Beesley and Littlechild 1989; and Caves 1990. NERA 1996 reviews some of these contributions. I have cited other more recent works in the previous sections of the chapter.

5   Shareholders

5.1   Topics for Discussion

In this chapter, I examine the economic impact of privatization through the financial market and shareholding. Several interesting research issues arise in this context.

The government can manage the transfer of assets from the public to private sector in several ways. In the United Kingdom, the most important channel was through placements of shares in the stock exchange. Public offerings of stock in formerly public companies aim at reshuffling the financial portfolio of investors. The government or its agents must persuade investors to buy privatization shares by offering conditions that are at least as advantageous as those offered by the secondary market.

Empirical research in finance has frequently observed that underpricing occurs with any initial public offering (IPO). The financial literature traces back these causes to different theories:

- Principal-agent theory: Financial intermediaries (underwriters) know the market better than the firm (principal) and are interested in undervaluing the firm to minimize their sales effort and to maximize the probability of success of the public offering.

- Information asymmetry theory: Subscribers are split into one more-informed and one less-informed group. The latter subscribes to all IPOs, whereas the former subscribes only when they expect a positive initial return. In general, IPOs have to be underpriced in order to attract the more-informed investors. The greater the uncertainty about the value of the firm, the greater the underpricing must be to attract these investors.

- Reputation-building theory: Underpricing may be a way of indicating the issuer's determination to attract prestigious underwriters.

When the sale is in installments, the firm indicates that it has the financial strength to allow itself an initial underpricing, which it will recoup in subsequent placements.

• Investor sentiment theory: There may be irrational elements—in particular, excessive optimism—in the behavior of the markets. These elements become apparent after the placement. Often an initial underpricing culminates in underperformance in the longer term.

Hence, one key issue I wish to discuss in this chapter is the extent of underpricing for British privatization and the long-run performances of the shares of privatized companies on the London Stock Exchange, possible explanations for these two phenomena, and their impact on the financial markets.

When the underpricing of an offering is sizable, the first vintage of shareholders realizes substantial capital gains. Small savers may decide to cash out the profit. They can use the revenue from the realized capital gain to replenish their previous portfolio of financial activities or to purchase other shares. They can buy real estate investments, durable goods, or even luxuries. In this case, the effect of privatization would be, unexpectedly, that of boosting consumption and investments, albeit in a different way from increased public spending or reduced taxes. In fact, these spending behaviors arise through a phenomenon of financial illusion (the decrease in public-sector net worth, a subject I discuss in chapter 8).

The increase in stock exchange capitalization as a result of privatization creates a larger market, which is usually thought to be beneficial for the financing capacity of firms and thus for investments and growth. The relationship, however, between the amount of savings invested in shares, on the one hand, and the performance of firms' real investments, on the other, is rather complex. The inflow of private savings into the stock exchange makes the financing of investment projects less costly for the firms than debt. To assess the efficiency of this financing mechanism, it is necessary to evaluate the capacity of the share market to channel savings toward those firms that have the best investment projects. This process is far from smooth.

The diffusion of shareholding among a large number of small savers, or so-called popular capitalism, can broaden the market and change the economic perceptions of large sections of the population. Nevertheless, such diffusion may have the effect of increasing financial markets' irrationality and inefficiency, because of the behavior of uninformed operators.

Another aspect of popular capitalism as practiced in Britain has been the distribution of shares to employees of formerly public corporations at a discount. Some have claimed that employees' holding shares provides an incentive for them to increase their working effort. Whether this actually occurs depends, however, on the size of the shareholding of the workers. If individual shareholding is small, then its incentive effect may be negligible. If it is big, ample literature exists that shows that the control of privatized companies by insiders may have negative effects on the companies' productivity.

Dispersed share ownership amplifies corporate governance issues. Top executives and coalitions of relatively small shareholder groups can take control of large firms, imposing choices on the firms that do not maximize the value of the investment for the majority of the firms' shareholders.

A further aspect that is worthy of attention in this context is the relationship between privatization and international finance. Privatization placements of stock at privatization occur in a global circuit of share issues and trade. The implications of this international dimension for national shareholders, and more generally for savers, may be important. For example, international investors may be less committed than national ones to long-term investment strategies.

Finally, the value of the shares of privatized firms depends on potential investors' expectations of profit. In the case of regulated utilities, the seller finds himself in a peculiar position. Governments are able to exert considerable influence on profit expectations through the announcement of a more or less strict regulation in terms of the allowed price cap or implicit rate of return. Subsequently, this power to influence the share price of regulated firms is divided between the government and the regulator. A weak regulatory environment may determine abnormal returns in the long run. This fact reinforces a vast category of rentiers, with important redistributive effects and perhaps with an overall distortion of the market. The shares of the regulated utilities compete with those of other companies that are more exposed to competition and therefore may be less profitable.

In the next section, I present empirical evidence on selected topics. I am particularly interested in the financial size of initial placements of stock of British privatized firms and their impact on the structure of shareholding; market size, information and efficiency; transaction costs; underpricing and long-run performance of privatization shares; and corporate governance. Section 5.3 concludes the chapter with an evaluation of the evidence.

5.2   The Empirical Evidence

5.2.1   *Shareholding and Markets*

At the end of 1997, the British government privatized forty-three major firms by fixed-price offer or tender, with fifty-five separate sales transactions (in some cases there were seasoned offerings). In fact, there were thirty major offers, since in some cases, for example the RECs, placement of some firms occurred simultaneously. The estimated nominal proceeds from privatization in this form were over £70 billion (Curwen and Hartley 1997; Martin and Parker 1997). I presented in the Appendix to chapter 1 my own comprehensive estimation of the proceeds at around £86 billion at 1995 prices, including tender offers, management/employee buyouts, direct sales, and debt redemption (I do not consider here the sale of council houses).

Individual participation in the offerings varied from a minimum of 8,000 subscribers for Associated British Ports (ABP) (1982) to a maximum of 4.5 million for British Gas (1986). Roughly half the proceeds for the Exchequer from stock placement of the former nationalized industries came from institutions and half from the public. A clawback mechanism envisaged that if public subscriptions to the offerings exceeded a certain threshold, then the quota reserved in advance by the Treasury for financial institutions diminished. In twenty-nine cases, the offerings allowed the public to pay for the shares they purchased in two or three installments. There was also in some cases a loyalty bonus of one free share for every ten or fifteen purchased for those who kept their shares for a year after purchasing them. The bonus doubled for some utilities if the purchasers were the utilities' own customers. Employees frequently received free shares in addition to those reserved for them (at times) at reduced prices. The value of this incentive was, on the other hand, rarely more than £500.

About forty other firms were divested through trade sales, without placement on the stock exchange, but by means of direct negotiation. There were also over two hundred buyouts, the majority of them management buyouts, but there were also a number of employee buyouts (the most famous case was that of the National Freight Corporation).

By any standard, the financial size of the program was huge. For example, the British Telecom IPO was by far the biggest ever on the London Stock Exchange. As I show in chapter 8, the ratios of proceeds to GDP and public-finance variables were sizable (see also chapter 3).

In the rest of this chapter, I focus on public offerings.

One of the constitutive elements of Conservative policy during the Conservatives' eighteen years in office was the maximum possible diffusion of shareholding, presumably seen as a way to make capitalism popular and especially to increase support for privatization itself. Some have argued (see, e.g., Dobek 1993) that within this policy there was an element of electoral calculation in terms of an expectation that new shareholders would vote Conservative and oppose any possible renationalization of the firms the Conservatives were privatizing. Although this may be true, I will not discuss here the political economy of share ownership. This is not to deny that this is a crucial subject, but it is simply outside the scope of the present research.

The data available, thanks to sample surveys in various years (ONS 1999, table A), allow us to form a picture of the long-term trends of share ownership in the United Kingdom. These data should, however, be interpreted with caution, since the companies' registration of the status of shareholders may be in indirect forms (nominee accounts) that do not always allow one to discover the identity or nature of the owners.

We can observe clear trends in the data. Privatization did not stop the relative decline in individual ownership of shares. In 1957, individuals owned almost two-thirds of the shares of listed companies. In the past forty years, the value of the stocks owned by individuals has fallen from over a half to just over a sixth of the total, as table 5.1 shows. Ownership became an indirect phenomenon, with shares man-

Table 5.1
Ownership of U.K.-listed equities (percent)

	1963	1975	1981	1989	1997
Individuals	53.8	37.5	28.2	20.3	16.5
Pension funds	6.5	16.9	26.7	32.0	22.1
Insurance companies	10.1	15.9	20.5	20.0	23.5
Unit and investment trusts	12.6	14.6	10.3	8.0	8.6
Public sector	1.5	2.6	3.0	2.0	0.1
Rest of world	7.0	5.6	3.6	12.8	24.0
Others	8.5	6.9	7.7	4.9	5.2
Total	100.0	100.0	100.0	100.0	100.0

Sources: Author's calculations based on ONS 1999.

aged by insurance companies, pension funds, and other financial institutions. Furthermore, in the 1980s, there was a sustained increase in shareholding by the foreign sector, which in 1997 became the largest owner of shares, in relative terms, with ownership reaching a quarter of the value of the securities.

The picture might appear different if we look at the number of owners rather than the number of shares owned. Successive British governments and some researchers have often cited these figures in a very optimistic way. In 1979, there were 2.5 million individual shareholders of British corporations; in 1992 there were 11 million. This would appear to confirm the success of popular capitalism. The assessment can be rendered more realistic, however, by considering that many of the new individual shareholders since privatization began hold shares in just *one* company (usually one of the privatized utilities). The average size of these share portfolios is only a few thousand pounds (ONS 1999, annex G).

The holders of portfolios worth less than £100,000, almost all of which are individuals, are very numerous. These small portfolios, however, represent just 10 percent of the value of the listed shares. On the other hand, it is interesting to observe that alongside these small shareholders, there are indeed some holders of large portfolios. At the end of 1997, about 2 percent of the total capitalization of the stock exchange, worth some £26.4 billion, belonged to individuals whose assets in securities were worth more than £100 million. (This figure may include some nominee accounts.) However, 54 percent of individual shareholders own shares in only one company, 20 percent have shares in two, 9 percent in three, and only 17 percent in four or more (*Stock Exchange Quarterly*, Summer 1991, quoted in Gaved and Goodman 1992). The equity ownership of these small shareholders is generally limited to the privatized firms. There has been virtually no spread of shareholding to other listed companies.

At the end of the first phase of mass placement, in 1990, the percentages of share ownership among various social groups were as follows (Connolly and Munro 1999, based on General Household Survey data):

Unskilled manual workers	6 percent
Professionals	43 percent
Council tenants	7 percent
Homeowners	53 percent

The majority of those who purchased shares on issue had sold them within the year. For example, the percentages of original shareholders of certain privatized firms who still owned shares after one year were as follows (Jackson and Price 1994):

Cable and Wireless first offering	17.3 percent
Amersham International	13.2 percent
British Telecom	73.6 percent
British Airport Authority	48.7 percent
British Gas	70.6 percent
British Airways	38.2 percent
Jaguar	43.3 percent
Associated British Ports	34.4 percent
Rolls-Royce	46.2 percent
twelve RECs	40.0 percent
Scottish Power	67.0 percent
British Aerospace	17.0 percent

During the second half of the 1980s, a number of studies estimated that between 10 and 23 percent of the adult British population owned shares of stock in at least one company. For example, there were 2.4 million holders of British Gas shares, and 0.8 million BT shareholders. Around 1.6 million people owned shares in the company for which they worked (Vickers and Yarrow 1988a). In the 1990s, these numbers increased.

Impressive as these figures may be, the phenomenon of share ownership was not truly "popular." Of the approximately forty-five million adults in the United Kingdom at the end of the 1990s, only two million own shares in more than three companies. Individual shareholding is a social trend that has largely not involved the middle- and low-income sectors of the population. It probably mainly involves the 10 percent with the highest income, and only touches the next 10 percent. In 1990, only 13 percent of individual shareholders had purchased stock on the secondary market.

I estimate that at the end of 1997, fewer than two million individuals—less than 5 percent of British adults—participated more or less actively in popular capitalism. The others became shareholders through initial issues, inheritance, or distribution of shares to employees. There was far more growth over the 1980s and 1990s in the weight of the foreign sector, insurance companies, and pension funds, as the figures above show.

I have already mentioned that at the end of 1997 the foreign sector was the largest shareholder in British firms in relative terms, accounting for roughly a quarter of stock exchange capitalization. Of the £295 billion shareholding of residents abroad, £151.2 billion was of U.S. origin, compared to just £60 billion for the whole of the European Union (according to data quoted by ONS [1999, tables 6–8]). The sectors in which capital from abroad has acquired a particularly important position include electricity and water, in which there is an especially strong presence of capital from France.

In twenty-four cases of privatization, the Conservative governments resorted to the issuing of special shares, which, in addition to the limits to the quota of capital allowed to single shareholders, frequently placed limits on ownership by foreign subjects (Curwen and Hartley 1997). However, this provision had no impact on foreign penetration.

A number of privatized firms have been acquired by foreign capital: Ford (United States) acquired Jaguar in November 1989; Avon Energy Partners (United States) acquired Midlands Electricity in 1996; Lyonnaise des Eaux (France) acquired Northumbrian Water in December 1995; Texas Utility acquired Eastern Group in 1998; Cal Energy acquired Northern Electric and Gas in 1996; Central and South West (United States) acquired See board in 1996; American Electric Power acquired Yorkshire Electricity in 1997; and Southern Company (United States) acquired Western Electricity in December 1996. Ironically, the French public monopoly Electricité de France (EDF) now owns London Electricity, the utility that supplies electricity to 10 Downing Street.

The sizable penetration of foreign capital into British companies occurred as a result of a combination of circumstances, not all of them attributable to privatization. The macroeconomic and monetary conditions surrounding privatization certainly played an important role, but divestitures offered welcome opportunities to international investors. The consequences of this foreign investment for the British capitalist system were apparent only in subsequent years. For example, when the United Kingdom was debating whether to join European Monetary Union, an element was predicting the possible reactions of international investors in U.K.-based firms to whichever decision was ultimately made.

5.2.2 *Information, Efficiency, and the Size of the Market*

One can ask whether individual shareholding in the privatized British firms could have been more extensive and significant, as perhaps was the intention of the Thatcher policy. To encourage small savers to invest in equities, the government had to remove information barriers to shareholding in addition to providing generous tax relief (Gaved and Goodman 1992). I discuss this tax relief in chapter 8; as for the removal of information barriers, it does not seem realistic that simply issuing a better sale prospectus or other communication tools will overcome lack of information among savers about the investment opportunities (and risks) offered by shareholding. The campaigns undertaken by the U.K. government to market firms being privatized were certainly aggressive and reached millions of potential purchasers. Nevertheless, after a certain point the information provided in regard to firms placed on the market can become too technical and move beyond the grasp of the public.

For example, the placement prospectus for the RECs (Kleinwort Benson Ltd 1990), consisted of 800 large pages of small print, divided into thirteen sections, one of a general nature and one for each of the RECs. The glossary of technical terms alone is seven pages and contains over one hundred terms. The first chapter introduces the reader to the mechanism of the regulated electricity market. It is difficult reading for any professional economist who is not specializing in energy economics. It is hard to see how this type of document could be useful to anyone outside the sphere of professional readers. Mini-prospectuses were available as well, but probably the large majority of new shareholders of privatized British firms based their purchases on simple advertisements. They probably know little more than the name of the firm and the sector in which it operates (as was the case for purchasers of the public offerings one century ago; see chapter 1). Social-attitudes studies show that although as much as a quarter of the adult population became shareholders upon the privatization of British nationalized firms, there was no change whatsoever in the fundamental investment behaviors of savers: According to Gaved and Goodman (1992), the privatization crusade turned out to have a negligible impact on social attitudes toward shareholding.

One also wonders whether the opening up of the market to these new shareholders was actually beneficial from the point of view of efficiency. Hayri and Yilmaz (1997) explore this question and find that the distribution of shareholding after privatization contributed to inefficiency in the market. According to literature on the efficiency of financial markets, individual investors with non-diversified and relatively small portfolios are the best candidates to behave like "noise-traders." This suggests that British privatization, by broadening this category of shareholders, created a tendency for prices of shares in privatized firms to diverge from their basic values to a greater degree than for other shares.[1] Small shareholders with portfolios that are not very diversified have little access to quality information. According to Hayri and Yilmaz (1997), they react to pseudosignals, such as an editorial in a newspaper and suggestions from acquaintances. They make their investment decisions based on noise as if it were information. One of the consequences is the tendency to develop adaptive behavior (e.g., to "jump on the bandwagon" when there is news of an increase in prices). The result can be mispricing of the shares most widely held by the noise-traders. The effect of this investment behavior would appear to confirm the hypothesis that the prices of the shares of privatized British firms, unlike the rest of the FTSE-100 shares, show a strong deviation from a random walk.[2]

To the extent to which it is desirable that the Stock Exchange be efficient in forming prices, mass shareholding may have had undesirable side effects. For example, it can amplify speculative bubbles.

Finally, I want briefly to discuss the impact of privatization on the size of the market. Between 1983 and 1998 the capitalization of the stock exchange in the United Kingdom went from US$226 billion to US$2,372 billion: a tenfold increase at current prices and exchange rates. In the United States, without any privatization, over the same period capitalization increased from US$1,898 billion to US$12,926 billion (a sixfold increase, but starting from a much higher capitalization size than in Britain). Overall capitalization of the world stock exchanges rose from US$3,384 billion to US$26,520 billion (almost eight times as much). At a global level, the annual volume rose from US$1,227 billion in 1983 to US$19,485 billion (Megginson and Netter 2001, based on Federation of International Stock Exchanges data available at www.fibv.com).

As one can see, the increased size of the stock market is a global trend that has a multitude of explanatory variables. In the absence of an analysis that tests these variables, it is not prima facie evident that privatization in the United Kingdom was the sole or major factor in the increase in the size of the stock market. Undoubtedly the British stock exchange showed more growth in capitalization and transactions in the 1980s and 1990s than the United States or even the aggregated world stock exchanges. Privatized firms may have played a part in this growth (and they counted for 14 percent of the value of the FTSE-100 at their peak), but so did the strong pound, the international position of London, and Britain's political stability during the period in question. The reverse may also be true: Strong financial markets in Britain may have helped large-scale government divestitures. An indirect proof of this contention is that in recent years, with decreasing share prices, privatization placements have decreased dramatically everywhere.

Moreover, it is difficult to say whether the "popular capitalism" policy helped firms find external finance and select better investment projects. As I showed in chapter 3 regarding macroeconomic conditions, the years I consider were characterized by considerable deindustrialization of the country. Significantly, the privatized firms, even when they had large investment programs (as was the case with water), did not issue new shares to finance themselves. Partly, this was the consequence of the writing-off of debt at divestiture, but in most cases, increased profitability played a major role.

5.2.3 Transaction Costs

Mass public offerings do not come without substantial transaction costs. Up to 1994 at least £780 million had been paid in fees and commissions to bankers, advisers, consultants involved in privatization (Vickers and Yarrow 1988a).

For 1981–1987, the National Audit Office indicated that the following percentages of the gross proceeds of privatization for the listed firms had been spent on promotion, advisory fees, and underwriting fees (Helm 1995, quoting a National Audit Office study):

Cable and Wireless	3.1 percent
British Aerospace	3.8 percent
Amersham	4.6 percent
Britoil	3.2 percent
ABP	11.2 percent
Enterprise Oil	2.8 percent
BT	6.8 percent
British Gas	6.4 percent
BA	4.7 percent

These percentages refer purely to the costs incurred by H.M. Treasury and do not include the costs incurred directly by the companies, which include the consultants' costs and the time and effort dedicated by the companies' management to the privatization plan. Some of the costs incurred were particularly extravagant in economic terms. For example, given the substantial underpricing of IPOs of privatized firms and the consequent need to ration the number of shares that were put up for sale, expenditures for advertising and underwriting were in fact often superfluous (Vickers and Yarrow 1988a).

International evidence exists that puts the cost of the issue of private shares in large quantities at around 4.5 percent of their value. Average data on individual operations cited above and experts' opinion confirm that 4 percent may be a prudential estimate for British government placements. Based on my estimates of proceeds in constant 1995 pounds, I suggest that the overall transaction costs of British privatization may have been in the region of £3 billion.

5.2.4 Underpricing

One popular business intelligence source asks the question: "Why should privatizations be good investments?" The answer, to the benefit of prospective investors, is the following:

Governments frequently provide state enterprises with a "dowry" of debt write-off or other financial support before launching them in the private sector; and when the launch is made they provide a fair wind by insuring that the price is not too demanding.... Government owned companies have dominant market positions (and) because of their size may be less risky then some other investments ... a composite index of privatized stocks showed a rise of over 165 percent between the beginning of 1989 and end of 1992: this compares with 65 percent for the S&P 500 index. (Privatization International 1994)

In short, the great attraction of the shares of privatized firms is first, financial restructuring and underpricing, and second, a dose of monopoly power. Investors should know that the government grants the privatized utilities dominant positions in their markets when divestiture is only partially and gradually accompanied by liberalization.

I define underpricing here as a price at placement that is below the equilibrium market price in a given time horizon (e.g., after the first trading day). Some authors acknowledge that the initial shares of privatized firms in Great Britain were underpriced but claim that such underpricing was limited. Boyfield (1997), in his apology for British privatization, observes that an underpricing of 12 percent is typical for new private issues. In the case of British privatization, this premium even reached 45 percent, which was extremely high, but in some ways inevitable, to encourage buyers.

In part, according to some authors, underpricing of initial share offerings is the cost of a strategy: that of encouraging those who are reluctant to do so to buy shares. Rock (1986) says that a discount was necessary to attract uninformed investors. Boyfield (1997) also observes, with unintentional wit, that the City was "disinclined" to participate in tender sales (that is, in competitive procedures aimed at minimizing underpricing). In this section I confine myself to the question of underpricing, that is, the immediate capital gain for an investor who buys at placement and sells twenty-four hours later, and deal with the long-term gains from a buy-and-hold strategy in section 5.2.5.

Vickers and Yarrow (1988a, table 7.1) raised the subject of underpricing, based on their observations of the first divestitures of the Thatcher government.[3] In the fifteen cases they studied, the unweighted average underpricing of the shares of the privatized companies was in the region of 19 percent. The average weighted by the amount of undervaluation was higher, thanks to the considerable weight of BT, which recorded a price difference of 33 percent after the first trading day on the first placement (subsequent tranches were less underpriced). Vickers and Yarrow show that for placements based on tender offers (ABP, British Airport Authority, BP, Britoil, Cable and Wireless, Enterprise Oil) underpricing was nil.[4]

With IPOs, some categories of purchasers also received a series of additional benefits. For example, those purchasing shares in British Gas (BG) also received a voucher of £40 for each 400 shares they purchased. As I have already noted, in many cases one free share was offered as a loyalty bonus for every ten or fifteen purchased and retained for one year from the date of purchase.

Not surprisingly under these conditions, price could not ration demand, which was in fact often a multiple of the value of the shares offered. An extreme case was probably that of British Airways, where the demand for stock was thirty-two times the number of shares offered. For placements in the 1980s in the form of offers for sale, demand for shares was typically seven to eight times greater than the number of shares offered, excluding extreme cases.[5]

Table 5.2, based on Cawthron 1999 data, shows the internal rates of return (IRRs) for holders of shares in various privatized British firms

Table 5.2
Internal rates of return from shares held until May 31, 1997, and for shares bought on May 31, 1997

| | Real internal rates of return[a] | | | |
| | a | b | $c = b - a$ | c/a |
	Bought at initial sale; sold on May 1, 1997[b]	Bought after first day's trading; sold on May 1, 1997[b]	Difference	Percentage
BT				
Tranche 1	14	10	−4	−29
Tranche 2	12	9	−3	−25
Tranche 3	8	5	−3	−38
British Gas	11	8	−3	−27
British Airports Authority	16	13	−3	−19
Anglian Water	21	16	−5	−24
Northumbrian Water	35	27	−8	−23
North West Water	22	17	−5	−23
Severn Trent	23	18	−5	−22
Southern Water	29	24	−5	−17
South West Water	22	17	−5	−23
Thames Water	21	17	−4	−19
Welsh Water	24	19	−5	−21
Wessex Water	23	17	−6	−26
Yorkshire Water	22	18	−4	−18
Eastern Electricity	42	34	−8	−19
East Midlands Electricity	34	27	−7	−21
London Electricity	32	26	−6	−19
Manweb	38	29	−9	−24
Midlands Electricity	40	32	−8	−20
Northern Electricity	36	30	−6	−17
Norweb	44	35	−9	−20
Seeboard	45	38	−7	−16
Southern Electric	32	25	−7	−22
South Wales Electricity	40	31	−9	−23
SWEB	41	32	−9	−22
Yorkshire Electricity	35	27	−8	−23
PowerGen				
Tranche 1	29	23	−6	−21
Tranche 2	16	15	−1	−6

Table 5.2
(continued)

	Real internal rates of return[a]			
	a Bought at initial sale; sold on May 1, 1997[b]	*b* Bought after first day's trading; sold on May 1, 1997[b]	$c = b - a$ Difference	c/a Percentage difference
National Power				
Tranche 1	30	23	−7	−23
Tranche 2	23	21	−2	−9
ScottishPower	14	10	−4	−29
Scottish Hydro	14	10	−4	−29
Northern Ireland Electricity	23	17	−6	−26
Railtrack	87	75	−12	−14
British Energy	25	31	6	24
Average (unweighted)	28	22	−6	−20

Sources: Cawthron 1999 and my calculations.
[a] Internal rates of return are calculated from "real" cash flows adjusted in line with the RPI. Internal rates of return shown are therefore the annual percentage returns received over and above the rate of inflation. Returns shown are gross. Investors may be liable for income tax and/or capital gains tax.
[b] Or at takeover, if earlier.

at May 31, 1997. The assumption is that investors purchased the shares at the issue price or on the secondary market twenty-four hours later. The difference between the two rates gives us a measure of the underpricing of the initial offering. The absolute difference in the real IRR varies from a minimum of 3–4 points to over 10 (on average, 5.7 points). In percentage terms, compared to the IRRs for those who purchased on the secondary market, the average unweighted IRR for those who purchased on placement is 25 percent higher than that for those who purchased twenty-four hours later.

When confronted with such a sizable underpricing phenomenon, one must look into the causes. We should ask whether this spread between the IRR at purchase and that for purchase a day later correlates to privatization or to the fact that the IPOs involved were large and in sectors and at times that were particularly vulnerable to underpricing.

Levis (1993) examines 712 IPOs in the United Kingdom over the period 1980–1988, roughly the same period as that studied by Vickers and Yarrow (1988a), and finds that the average abnormal adjusted IRR after twenty-four hours is 14.3 percent. He uses the following measure:

The first day adjusted return for issue is defined as the percentage change in price from the offering date to the close of the first day of trading (r_i) less the equivalent change in an appropriate benchmark (r_m)

$ar_i = r_i - r_m$.

The benchmark used is the weighted daily Financial Times All-Shares (FTA) Index. Although not a large sample in terms of the number of initial public offerings, the twelve privatizations considered in Levis's sample account for 76 percent of the total new equity capital collected through IPOs on the London market between 1980 and 1988.[6]

Compared to an average value of abnormal returns for IPOs of 14.3 percent, these placements recorded 37.25 percent. Placements in all the other sectors were well below 20 percent, with the sole exception of those in "publishing and printing" (24.63 percent). We may therefore assume that *excess* underpricing specifically attributable to the first vintage of privatization was in the region of 23 percent.

A more recent work (Huang and Levich 1999) allows us to corroborate these results and examine possible explanations for them. The study is an international comparison (thirty-six countries) covering 1979–1996, and it deals with 330 IPOs and 177 seasoned public offerings, with an income for the sellers of US$352 billion. The sample includes fifty-seven privatizations in the UK. The index for the return is not adjusted by the benchmark of the market or for the special conditions offered to certain categories of purchasers. This gross return is the dependent variable, considered as a proxy for underpricing. It is then regressed on a set of possible explanatory variables, such as the volatility of prices prior to the offer, the price trends in the previous month, those of the offer, a dummy if the controlling share is sold (50 percent or more of capital), the percentage of stock offered to the foreign sector, and a Gini index of income distribution, among others. The attempt is to verify various possible hypotheses for the causes of underpricing.

The international sample of 297 transactions related to privatized firms shows an immediate unadjusted return of 25.6 percent on average (with a median around 10 percent), which becomes 32.1 percent for the 220 IPOs, whereas the return on seasoned offerings is only 7.17 percent. The difference is statistically significant at the 95 percent level, which is seen as confirmation of the theories of reputation building and information asymmetry (see section 5.1) (although the first of these two interpretations seems more convincing).[7]

As regards the forty-two cases of British privatization IPOs, Huang and Levich find an immediate return of 17.7 percent, whereas for a sample of 2,133 IPOs in the United Kingdom, the average is 12 percent. The difference in return between the privatization and other IPOs is six points and is 99 percent statistically significant. These results confirm that there is a noticeable difference between underpricing of privatization IPOs and ordinary underpricing in the case of the United Kingdom.[8]

I report findings on underpricing from a study I coauthored (Florio and Manzoni 2002), based on a sample of fifty-five U.K. privatization operations (including both initial and seasoned offerings), in the appendix.[9] In that study, my coauthor and I find evidence of unweighted average abnormal return on the first day of around 13 percent (see table 5A.2). This is somewhat lower than other findings I cited previously, because of the smoothing effect of the seasoned offerings. However, a company-by-company examination confirms that underpricing of privatization IPOs of around 18.5 percent can be observed. This in turn confirms earlier results by Huang and Levich. For some of the main privatized companies, the underpricing was more than 20 percent, and it was 30 percent for the British Telecom IPO in 1984.

Summing up, I point to overwhelming evidence that the underpricing of British privatization IPOs was far greater than the usual underpricing for ordinary placements.

5.2.5 Abnormal Returns in the Long Term

I want now to determine whether underpricing fades away in the longer term through *negative* abnormal returns or is frozen at an initial level or amplified by positive abnormal returns. International empirical literature shows that with ordinary IPOs, subsequent negative abnormal returns correct the initial underpricing.

According to Levis (1993), the empirical evidence for almost every capital market in the world is unequivocal in two conclusions: IPOs provide significant abnormal returns in the first day of trading, and this constitutes evidence of deliberate underpricing. The same author quotes a series of empirical studies that show evidence of underperformance of IPO shares in the long term in the United States, Germany, Brazil, Mexico, Chile, and Finland, and he proposes to verify whether data for the United Kingdom confirm these results. He concludes that for a period of thirty-six months after the initial offering there is evidence of underperformance also in the case of the United Kingdom.

The test here is simply an extension of the index already specified for the return after twenty-four hours to include the difference between the return at thirty-six months from the IPO and a benchmark index (without any risk adjustment). Although the author is mainly interested in showing underperformance in the case of the United Kingdom for IPOs as a whole, we are more interested here in the case of privatized firms.

The result (see Levis 1993, table 11) is that after three years, the cumulated abnormal return of the IPOs as a whole was 55.72 percent, and that of the privatized firms was almost double: 96.91 percent. In fact, the ratio of the IPO shares price index to the benchmark indexes was lower than one for all three benchmarks and for the sample as a whole (712 cases). In the case of privatization, however, it was well above one for the FTA and Hoare Govett Smaller Companies indexes, and marginally lower than one for the All-Share Equally Weighted index.[10]

Given the size of the privatized firms in Britain, I think that the comparison with the FTA index seems definitely the most relevant of the three attempted. This gives us a significantly high ratio: 1.157 for the privatized firms compared to 0.958 for the IPOs as a whole (obviously the deviation is less if the comparison is without the privatized firms in the benchmark).

In the space of ten years, privatized firms, which at the time were capitalized at £145 billion or 20 percent of the total value of the share market, recorded an average increase in price of 276 percent (not corrected by dividends). A strategy of buy and hold for the forty-nine stocks considered, with an outlay of £100 per security in 1984, would have led to an initial cumulative outlay of £4,900 that would have achieved a value of £18,400 in 1994. This performance is higher than those of the best international investment funds, at least for categories of equivalent risk.[11]

Cawthron (1999) offers a different, but convergent, approach. He considers the real rate of return from investing in one share after the first day of its offering and compares it with the FTA. He calculates the performance at May 31, 1997, for the shares of all the privatized companies. With the exception of BT, there is ample evidence of internal rates of return for these shares far higher than the benchmark index. In

Table 5.3
Abnormal returns calculated for some sectors

Firm	100 days	1 year	4 years
Water	31	58	93
Electricity (RECs)	26	23	124
Electricity (Generation)	28	27	109
BT	51	52	18
BG	10	22	32
British Airports Authority	43	39	69
Railtrack	3	15	n.a.

Source: Chennells 1997.
Note: n.a. = not applicable.

the case of the 12 RECs, the difference is seventeen points on average; in the case of the ten water authorities, the average difference is twelve points. I should note that the IRR of the FTA index between 1984 and 1996 was, in real terms, on average over 15 percent, which is undoubtedly high both in historical terms and by international comparison. Therefore, the abnormal returns of privatized companies in fact exceeded a stock exchange performance, which was in itself particularly good.

Chennells (1997, 281) offers other interesting estimates. Still using the FTA, abnormal returns were increasing over time for water, electricity, gas, and railways and decreasing for BT (see table 5.3).

A colleague and I (Florio and Manzoni 2002) repeated the exercise of calculating abnormal returns for a sample of privatized firms (fifty-five cases, including five tenders and some secondary offerings). We have extended the analysis to different periods: one year, two years, three years, five years, and ten years (for the last, the sample comprises fourteen cases only) (see figure 5.1). We use the FTA index as a benchmark and as share prices the monthly Datastream values corrected by dividends and other operations). Moreover, we have tried to disentangle possible explanatory factors for the observed performance of the share prices. We report this decomposition in the appendix.

As a result of analysis, we can confirm that there is evidence of abnormal returns in the long run. For our sample, the cumulative abnormal returns are 21 percent at one year, 30 percent at two years; and 57 percent at 5 years.[12] Abnormal returns are negligible for secondary issues and very high and persistent for IPOs (see figure 5.2). The values are statistically significant and confirm that the returns on shares of

Cumulative average adjusted return

Figure 5.1
Cumulative average adjusted returns for entire sample of U.K. privatized firms, 1977–1996.

Cumulative average adjusted return

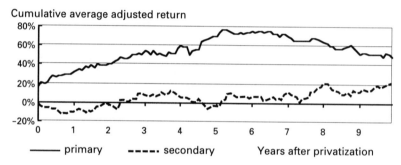

Figure 5.2
Performance by primary or secondary issue.

privatized firms, after the initial underpricing, outperformed the market. Moreover, paradoxically, underpricing and outperformance are positively correlated: Placements with the highest abnormal returns in the long run are also those with the highest initial underpricing.[13]

The empirical evidence thus confirms the rather cynical comment from within the City mentioned at the beginning of section 5.2.4. Beyond the initial "dowry," the market appreciated the protection of the monopolistic position granted by the government to the privatized firms. It is no coincidence that sectors such as electricity and water showed particularly high abnormal returns,[14] whereas manufacturing firms, operating in a more competitive environment, showed normal returns (see figures 5.3 through 5.6). I discuss the corrective impact of the windfall tax on abnormal returns on the shares of the privatized industries in chapter 8.

Cumulative average adjusted return

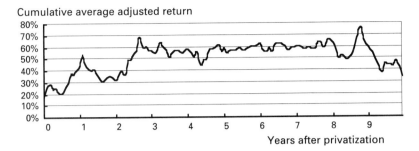

Figure 5.3
Water industry performance.

Cumulative average adjusted return

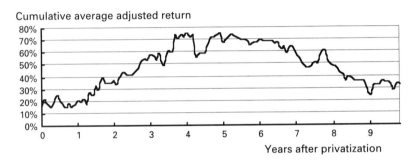

Figure 5.4
Electricity industry performance.

Cumulative average adjusted return

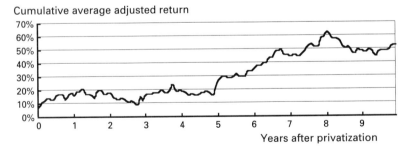

Figure 5.5
Telecommunications industry performance.

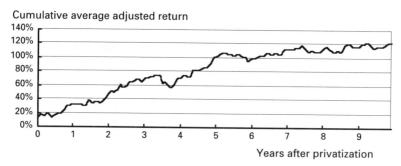

Cumulative average adjusted return

Years after privatization

Figure 5.6
Transport industry performance.

5.2.6 Corporate Governance, Privatization, and Regulation

When faced with shareholders who are partly dispersed and partly made up of financial institutions, such as pension funds and insurance companies, it is easy to foresee that the management of a company will assume considerable power. Elsewhere (chapter 6), I show that a clue that this is the case are the enormous increases in the salaries of companies' CEOs and other board members and of top management. From this perspective, the structure of ownership in many privatized industries poses specific corporate governance problems.

It is a widely held opinion that in large British firms, corporate governance is not very transparent, because of the reluctance of institutional investors to assume managerial responsibility. In certain cases, they even abstain from nominating nonexecutive directors. Consequently, managerial decisions and their economic and financial impact are monitored more through informal channels (one-on-one meetings) than through formal ones (shareholders or board of directors meetings).

These observations form the basis of the Cadbury Report, and that of the Greenbury Report, written at the end of the inquiry of two official commissions operating at the beginning of the 1990s (cf. Gregg, Machin, and Szymanski 1993). The Cadbury Commission was set up "to investigate the financial aspects of corporate governance, and followed a number of high profile corporate scandals and collapses. These were typically characterized by a combination of fraud, inadequate financial controls, poor quality financial reporting, the concentration of boardroom power in the hands of one person in the dual role of Chairman and Chief Executive Officer (CEO), weak and ineffective boards, and substantial investor losses" (OECD 1998, 129). This picture of corporate mismanagement emerged several years before the Enron and other scandals in the United States. When we think about the relationship between management and shareholders in the British privatized firm, we should duly consider this governance issue.

There are few empirical studies in the area of British corporate governance. An important and often quoted one is Cragg and Dyck 1999b. Cragg and Dyck examine the relationship between managers and shareholders in 114 British firms between 1970 and 1994, including state-owned, privatized, and ordinary listed companies. The research focus is on the turnover of top managers and on voluntary resignations, dismissals, and company performance. Management resignations are conceptualized as a function, per unit of time, of the financial performance of the company (measured as the ROA), of the type of ownership, of the personal characteristics of the manager (age, etc.), of the specific variables of the industry in which the firm operates, and of the time period considered and the distance from privatization. The key findings are that

• the turnover of managers is higher in privatized firms than in state-owned ones;

• in public corporations, dismissals of managers are less frequent than in private firms;

• a reduction in performance equivalent to one standard deviation increases the probability of dismissals in privatized firms by 50 percent, whereas it has no consequences in public corporations.

The conclusions that the authors reach seem to be quite strong in relation to the data that they use. For example, they find the annual rate of resignations in privatized firms to be 16.1 percent and only 14.3 percent in state companies; it is 12.6 percent in other companies listed on the stock exchange. These differences are small and not statistically significant.

It is apparent that the incidence of dismissals is greater in privatized firms than in state companies. It is also greater in privatized firms, however, than in private companies quoted on the stock exchange; consequently it is not clear how this variable can discriminate between public and private ownership. It is instead probably a symptom of restructuring and change of control. Moreover, if one studies the influence of the sector variables on dismissal, one observes that in the case of regulated privatized firms, the impact of privatization on managerial turnover, though positive, is not statistically significant.

As a whole, Cragg and Dyck 1998 should provide reassurance about the problems of corporate governance mentioned at the beginning of this section. (Incidentally, Cragg and Dyck's analysis would support the theory of property rights; cf. chapter 2.)

I suggest a rather different reading of this interesting empirical evidence. Cragg and Dyck tried to distinguish between voluntary resignations and firings. They assure us that they have identified the cases that can be identified with certainty as one or the other (for example, death or serious illness in some cases and company announcements in others). Anecdotal evidence suggests, however, that quite often resignations for health (or personal) reasons are in fact dismissals, and sometimes dismissals of top management "for poor results" are due to different causes, for example, the advent of new coalitions in groups that control the firms. The authors themselves interpret the high turnover in nationalized firms as promotions, a completely different interpretation from that which they advance for the turnover in the other types of company. In the public sector, however, promotions are often a way to present changes of management. The surprising aspect of the Cragg and Dyck study is how *small* is the difference in management turnover in the three types of firms they consider. Therefore, the message is rather one of similarity than of difference.

To clarify corporate governance issues in different types of organizations, what would in fact be needed is an empirical analysis of the actual configuration of property rights of shareholders and managers and the exercising of them after privatization. This subject has been studied more for Eastern European countries, where there have been obvious abuses of power by minority control groups, managers, and other insiders, but perhaps has been investigated to a more limited extent for the United Kingdom and other developed countries. For example, we would like to know more about the actual incentives to deliver cost-saving managerial effort in complex organizations under different governance mechanisms.[15]

Another proposition of property rights theory that deserves empirical scrutiny is the role of takeovers as a way of protecting shareholders and of promoting efficiency. One crucial aspect of the British experience is a tradition of financial markets inclined to hostile takeovers. In the United Kingdom during the 1980s, there were about two hundred

episode each year of merger and acquisition, compared to half that
number in France and a quarter in Germany.

Surprisingly, there is no clear evidence to show that the companies
that were victims of acquisitions in the 1980s were those with the worst
performances. Franks and Mayer (1997) show that along with these
acquisitions came changes in top management and company restructuring, but that there was little evidence that the acquired companies
had recorded unsatisfactory performances prior to being acquired.

A further point that is worth remembering is the role of fund managers in the corporate governance of companies listed on the stock
exchange. In a study of sixteen large firms, the holders of large blocks
of shares in those firms, defined by the study's authors as interests of
£1 million or more, controlled 60 percent of the firms' capital (Gaved
and Goodman 1992). The power of the fund managers was found to be
enormous. In 1990, the top ten British financial investors administered
funds throughout the world worth £500 billion, and the rate of growth
of those funds was faster than that of the smaller funds, although their
performance was no better. The concentration of capital in the hands of
the funds' managers, and of company shares in the hands of holders of
large blocks, seem to be trends that proceed in parallel. This is a source
of concern on two fronts: first, from the point of view of volatility of
share prices, because there is some empirical evidence that this volatility correlates with the percentage of shares held by institutional investors; and second, from the point of view of performance, inasmuch as
this correlates negatively with the importance of institutional investors.

British law formally protects the property rights of firms' shareholders. These rights include the right to receive information by way of
the annual report, the right to participate in meetings, the right to vote
on binding resolutions, the right to present motions and in certain case
to call shareholders meetings, and the right to receive dividends and
freely transfer shares. In point of fact, however, some of these rights are
void of any practical content:

· In shareholders meetings some binding resolutions require a majority
of 75 percent, which is practically unattainable.

· Institutional investors do not participate in meetings.

· An official report (Myners Committee 1995) concluded that virtually
all participants in our consultation exercise viewed the Annual General
Meeting as an expensive waste of time and money, attended only by
small shareholders to discuss marginal questions.

• An analysis of 4,750 resolutions approved in shareholders meetings (OECD 1998) shows that voting at these meetings has a purely formal character. Only half of the institutional investors voted, including proxy votes. Not a single resolution was defeated in 1997, and on average, the votes against were just 1 percent.

• Institutional investors often do not even appoint representatives to the company's board.

• For institutional investors the most frequent practice for exerting their influence over top executives is to resort to informal one-on-one meetings with top management, usually about questions of long-term strategy.

• Institutional investors virtually never exert pressure for the replacement of directors, except in extreme cases.

In the case of the United Kingdom, with 2,070 listed companies in 1994 and a capitalization of 114 percent of GDP (at the time in the United States it was only 75 percent of GDP), there were almost as many fund managers. In 1995, the latter controlled financial activities worth US$1,789 billion, equivalent to 162.3 percent of Britain's GDP, of which 69 percent was in shares. At the time, fund managers in the United States had only 36 percent of their activities in shares. In 1995, 42 percent of the shares owned by fund managers were controlled by the top twenty-five organizations, with a much higher concentration than in other countries. Considering the overall value of the market in 1996, a group of fifty institutions controlled 50 percent of the total. With limited exceptions, privatized companies are now firmly under the control of these financial shareholders and of foreign groups.

5.3   Discussion

The available empirical evidence allows for some unambiguous conclusions and some conjectures. First, the British government offered shares in the firms it privatized in the 1980s and 1990s at initial public offering that were considerably underpriced. In my sample of fifty-five placements, the twenty-four-hours underpricing of British privatization IPOs was around 18.5 percent, definitively higher than that of private IPOs. The average, weighted by the value of proceeds, was around 20 percent. For some large placements, such as the British Telecom IPOs, the underpricing was as 30 percent or more. The transaction costs for promotion expenses, advisors, underwriters, consultants' fees, and the like was in the region of 4–5 percent.

As Vickers and Yarrow (1988a) observed, underpricing implies a change in the distribution of wealth. The winners from this under-pricing were those who bought privatized shares on issue, and the losers were the taxpayers. Vickers and Yarrow give five reasons for believing that this effect was undesirable:

· the arbitrariness of the resulting wealth redistribution, which as such had no socially useful function

· the development of rent-seeking activities

· the benefit to the foreign sector, which corresponds to a loss of national wealth

· the additional effect connected to the loss of welfare for the taxpayer caused by distortionary taxation

· The cost provoked by a possible renationalization

These critiques are still valid more than ten years later. The British government could have avoided most of these costs by recurring to tenders or other forms of sale. I estimate that the government has virtually transferred £14 billion from the taxpayer to shareholders in the privatized firms, including foreign investors. Another three billion pounds in transaction costs were mostly a transfer to the City. I return to the welfare impact of these transfers in the book's final chapter.

Moreover, and in my opinion more important, there is the subsequent outperformance of the stocks, especially in the case of some regulated utilities. To a certain degree underpricing is a typical phenomenon of all IPOs, worth in the region of 12–14 percent in many countries. Usually for ordinary IPOs, however, the excessive initial gain fades away through subsequent underperformance. For British privatization placements, the opposite occurred. The purchaser of a portfolio of shares of privatized companies, each with identical weight in the portfolio's asset composition, would have greatly exceeded the return of the FTA stock exchange index, as well as other benchmark indices. Such an investor would have obtained a return that was far higher than that from the other private IPOs. In some cases (the electricity sector) the real average annual return was double that of the FTA index. This outperformance was particularly intense in sectors, such as water and energy, in which the market power of the firms

remained considerable. It lasted for at least ten years after initial placement. There is evidence of slow convergence toward the benchmark at
the end of our time horizon (and more clearly after 1997, as I discuss
subsequently).

Second, the mass diffusion of shareholding as a result of privatization of British nationalized firms had a limited or perhaps an adverse
impact on the functioning of the country's financial market. Estimates
of the number of individual shareholders vary, but the maximum is 11
million, around a quarter of the country's adult population. Demutualization of building societies (see note 7 in chapter 1) also played a role
in the building of popular capitalism, and this was a rather passive
process. Customers of building societies became their shareholders.
In the United Kingdom at the end of 1997, presumably the numbers
of individuals holding shares were lower (and probably they were
inflated by double counts),[16] but it is still true that millions of people
purchased shares for the first time in privatized British firms.

Who were they? Sociologically these new shareholders belong to the
higher income brackets, essentially the top two deciles. Shareholding
is virtually insignificant among the working class in Britain, people
living in rented houses, and so on. The new owners are part of the
upper middle classes, who previously invested their savings in state
bonds or building-society accounts. It is doubtful that this change in
the composition of their portfolios was of economic significance.

This investment was in the majority of cases only a small amount,
limited to a few thousand pounds, with reduced portfolios of only
three and sometimes only one security, and limited in time. A profit
having been realized, the shares that were purchased were often sold
(and in part were substituted for by new privatization issues). Many
employees bought, on special terms, shares in the companies in which
they worked. Many public utilities sold small amounts of their stock to
their customers at a discount.

Economic theory would say that from the point of view of risk diversification, these were dubious choices, although they were in fact
beneficial to those who made them, because until 1997 regulation and
liberalization were often soft. At the end of 1997, only two million
shareholders, less than 5 percent of adults, had share portfolios with
more than three securities. Only 14 percent of the shares owned by
individuals were purchased on the secondary market.

There is no evidence that all of this purchasing (and selling) of shares
in privatized firms brought about any great change in the social posi-

tion or psychological attitude toward entrepreneurial risk of the millions of marginal purchasers. At least one serious study shows that the resulting abundance of uninformed shareholders determined market inefficiency. It resulted in excessively adaptive behavior (noise trading) and a systematic deviation from the random walk of share prices around fundamental values.

The relative position of individuals among the various types of shareholders in U.K. firms is now a modest one. It is, on the other hand, highly probable that privatization had a strong influence on making the foreign sector stand out as the largest shareholder among British firms, in addition to confirming the growth of the role of fund managers and pension funds and of other forms of professionally managed saving. The Tory governments themselves offered greater tax relief to managed savings than to individual share ownership.

On the other hand, if all the companies privatized had been placed with tender sales reserved for institutional investors, this would presumably have generated less substantial underpricing, lower transaction costs, and greater efficiency of the financial markets. It is nevertheless doubtful that this would have had any effect in the long term on the extra profits that accrued to those who bought shares in the privatized firms when they were initially offered. I have shown that privatization shares outperformed the market for many years after placement. This implies that the market, until 1997, my time horizon, expected that these companies could deliver higher profits than the rest of the companies listed on the London stock exchange. Because the observable or foreseeable change in firms' productivity after privatization was modest, as I documented in chapter 4, the expectation of extra profits should be attributed to confidence in continued market power. This in turn implies that regulation until the end of the 1990s was unable or unwilling to control excess returns of privatized companies. I return to this topic in chapter 7, in which I discuss price trends before and after privatization.

There is no empirical evidence that shows that the privatization of British public companies improved the efficiency of the financial market as a whole, or that it was a factor in the enlargement of the financial market (indeed, perhaps the causation in this case is inverted), or that it made a measurable contribution to lowering the privatized companies' investment costs. In fact, after privatization, companies made little recourse to share issues to finance their investment plans. They could manage without such issues, for the simple reason that their capacity for self-financing increased enormously thanks to the rise in the long-term profitability. At the end of this section, I return to recent financial trends.

Finally, I turn to corporate-governance issues. Here we are on ground that is more conjectural. Small shareholders play an insignificant role in corporate governance in the British context (as they do everywhere), although there is no systematic evidence that they have suffered because of this limited role. Profits of privatized firms were so high until the end of the 1990s that it is difficult to say whether top management of these firms maximized profits or there were further margins for gain.

For many years, the majority of the boards of the privatized firms comprised the same people appointed by the government before privatization. Change in the composition of these boards came more slowly than anticipated. There is some evidence that the turnover rate of top management in nationalized industries, privatized firms, and established public-stock companies in Britain is virtually the same. In the last two types of firms, however, variations in the firm's performance increase the probability of management dismissal. In this sense, the shareholders have had an efficient mechanism for safeguarding their profits. This evidence, however, contradicts the concern expressed by several authoritative official reports on corporate governance issues, which show that large listed companies have developed peculiar governance mechanisms that give management great power and relegate the role of shareholders meetings and other formal control mechanisms to almost marginal positions.

I suggest that in Britain privatization marked a further passage from capitalism based on individual participation in company risk, albeit a very diluted participation, to a new type of fund-managers capitalism. Government bribed the middle classes by underpricing of stocks in privatizing companies and protection of rents, but the essential beneficiaries were the financial bureaucrats, whether Britons or foreigners, and their constituencies.

Managerial capitalism had already emerged in the 1930s, long prior to the British privatizations. This transformation of enterprise governance was the subject of the classic reflections of Marris and others mentioned in chapter 1. Even under managerial capitalism, however, managers were still accountable to individual shareholders, at least to the most influential among them. In the last decades of the twentieth century, the chain became longer. Individuals increasingly entrusted their savings less to firms and more to fund managers. They in turn decided how to structure their portfolios, what kind of relationship to establish with the internal management of the companies in which they invested, if and when to exercise their property rights in the form of the "voice" (for example, firing managers), and when they should exercise the ultimate form of property right, the right to exit by selling their shares.

One implication of this situation is that the main listed companies are under the control of the same kinds of subjects and often actually by the same network of vested interests. Half the shares on the London Stock Exchange are owned by fifty institutions. This model managerial corporate governance therefore foresees a contract, often implicit, between two groups of managers, that is, between two groups of bureaucracies: one "internal" and the other "external" to the company.

It is possible that some British Conservative politicians were genuinely convinced that privatization was a way of relaunching a capitalism that was closer to the classic values of individualism than the mixed economy with a large nationalized sector as it existed in Britain between the 1950s and the 1970s. It is also possible that popular capitalism was a rather opportunist rhetorical contrivance. In any case, from the point of view of corporate governance and actual property structure, the result was an acceleration of fund-managers capitalism. As previously noted, one can even ask oneself whether the cause and effect in this case was not actually the reverse.

Margaret Thatcher (or her advisors) invented privatization as a policy, ideology, and rhetoric. This policy, however, was encouraged or at least captured by an evolution of British capitalism that began in the 1970s. This transformation expressed itself in the hegemony of the fund manager over the corporate manager, who in turn had taken over from the individual entrepreneur during previous decades. Private ownership (like public ownership) has several faces. Not all of them convey the same corporate values and incentives. I return to these issues in chapter 6.

In recent years, additional evidence has surfaced of the complex interplay among the financial structure of British capitalism, privatization, and regulation. At the end of the 1990s the political climate around the privatized industries changed. The New Labour government's windfall tax, clearly an ex post admission that the privatized utilities had earned excess profits, was a signal of this change. I return to the windfall tax in chapter 8.

Fiscal pressure is not the only reason to consider that a change of regime happened at the end of the 1990s. Regulators' attitudes also became more demanding. I show in chapters 7 and 9 that regulators, who had observed privatized firms' extra profits, frequently after some years imposed an increasingly tough cap on the prices of public services or made other decisions to the same effect. One response of the regulated utilities was to change their capital structure and increase gearing. This is convenient because of the difference in the tax treatment of equity and debt. A "flight from equity" resulted from the tighter regulatory stance, and some utilities have created a separate company that owns assets, mostly financed by debt. For example, in the water industry, often a different company from the owner of the infrastructure operates the assets, with small equity. The ownership structure of these privatized utilities is consequently complex and blurred. According to Cave (2002), "From a 'privatisation perspective,' these changes are disquieting, from the point of view of both incentives and risk transfer. It is hard to see how debt holders can exercise the same effect on management as equity holders. In relation to risk, the question is raised as to whether debt holders or consumers will ultimately assume the risks previously shouldered by equity holders" (6). In fact, for several years after privatization, the latter risks were minimal, because the regulatory and business climate was undemanding. Shareholders enjoyed both an initial political kickoff bonanza, and for many years abnormally high returns (in fact, monopoly rents). As soon as taxation and regulation became more demanding and tried to squeeze monopoly rents, debt substituted for equity.

5.4   Further Reading

Biais and Perotti (2002) discuss the "Machiavellian" underpricing hypothesis in a political economy framework. Caves (1990) discusses privatization and corporate governance issues. Chapman (1990) focuses on underpricing in the United Kingdom. Lopez-de-Silanes (1997) offers an empirical analysis of privatization prices. On the Private Finance Initiative, see Millward and Benson 1998. On popular capitalism, see Redwood 1998.

Appendix: The Short- and Long-Run Performance of U.K. Privatized Firms, 1977–1996

The sample my coauthor and I use in Florio and Manzoni 2002 includes fifty-five privatization offerings that occurred in the United

Kingdom over the period 1977–1996.[17] The sample comprises the allocation of both majority stakes and minority stakes. First-issue share offerings (primary offers) and secondary-issue share offerings (secondary offers) are also included in the sample to control for this factor. In the latter case, the initial offer is followed by one or more seasoned offers. Price series have been collected from Datastream International Ltd., and we referred to Company Analysis for accounting information about the sample firms. Table 5A.1 presents detailed information about single privatization issues, which is mainly taken from two Price Waterhouse (1989a, 1989b) publications. Specifically the table presents the name of the firm, its industry sector, the first trading day for its shares, net proceeds for the government from the sale of shares (at 1995 prices), offer price, percentage of equity sold (size of the offer), and method of sale.

The methodology we employed is the standard event study approach and is totally consistent with the methodology used in Levis 1993 to analyze the performance of U.K. IPOs. We have calculated three different performance measures for each privatization offering (either primary or secondary):

1. The first-day abnormal return (ar_i) for each individual issue i. This is the percentage change in price between the offering date and the close of the first trading day[18] (r_i) less the equivalent change in an appropriate benchmark (FTA) occurred over the same time period (r_m):

$$ar_i = r_i - r_m. \tag{5.1}$$

2. The first-month abnormal return (ar_{it}) for each issue i. This is the return from the offering price to the last calendar day of the first trading month (r_{i1}) less the equivalent benchmark return[19] (FTA) (r_{m1}). The time interval over which we have computed the returns varies from one to thirty calendar days, according to the day of the month on which the privatization actually occurred:

$$ar_{it} = r_{i1} - r_{m1}. \tag{5.2}$$

3. The long-run return is computed using monthly prices and is based on prices on the last day of the month on which the stock is traded. These prices are not adjusted for splits, rights, or scrip offerings. For each issue i the monthly abnormal return (ar_{rt}) from the second trading month is computed as follows:

$$ar_{rt} = r_{it} - r_{mt}, \tag{5.3}$$

Table 5A.1
Privatized firms: Dates, industry sector, proceeds, prices and percentage of equity sold

Company name	Industry sector	First trading day	Proceeds at 1995 prices	Offer/tender price	Offer rate	Method of sale
AEA Technology	BSS SUPP	9-26-96	224.0	280	n.a.	n.a.
Amersham International	CHEM	2-25-82	124.0	142	100.0	O
Anglian Water	WATER	12-12-89	n.a.	240	98.4	n.a.
Associated British Ports (I)	TRANSP	2-16-83	83.3	112	51.5	O
Associated British Ports (II)	TRANSP	4-19-84	83.9	270	48.5	O
British Aerospace (I)	MANUF	2-20-81	91.2	150	51.6	O
British Aerospace (II)	MANUF	5-14-85	542.2	375	59.0	O
British Airports Authority (I)	TRANSP	7-28-87	1,697.2	245	95.6	O
British Airports Authority (II)	TRANSP	7-28-87	1,697.2	290	95.6	T
British Airways	TRANSP	2-11-87	1,262.2	125	97.5	O
British Energy	ENERGY	7-15-96	653.3	198	87.8	O
British Gas (sales of shares)	ENERGY	12-8-86	7,568.0	135	96.6	O
British Petroleum (I)	ENERGY	10-0-77	n.a.	845	49.0	O
British Petroleum (II)	ENERGY	11-12-79	691.7	363	5.2	O
British Petroleum (III)	ENERGY	9-26-83	940.3	435	7.2	T
British Petroleum (IV)	ENERGY	10-30-87	6,998.7	330	36.8	O
British Steel	STEEL	12-5-88	3,151.5	125	100.0	O
British Telecom (I)	TLC	12-3-84	5,819.2	130	50.2	O
British Telecom (II)	TLC	12-10-91	5,597.0	335	25.9	O
British Telecom (III)	TLC	7-19-93	5,457.2	410	20.7	O
Britoil (I)	ENERGY	11-23-82	1,112.4	215	51.0	T

Company	Sector	Date	Value	Percent	Code
Britoil (II)	ENERGY	8-12-85	665.6	59.0	O
British Technology Group	BSS SUPPORT	7-6-95	n.a.	n.a.	n.a.
Cable and Wireless (I)	TLC	11-6-81	350.8	49.4	T
Cable and Wireless (II)	TLC	12-5-83	455.4	22.3	O
Cable and Wireless (III)	TLC	12-13-85	901.6	31.1	O
East Midlands Electricity	ELECTR	2-11-90	523.0	97.5	O
Eastern Electricity	ELECTR	12-11-90	648.0	97.6	O
Enterprise Oil	ENERGY	7-2-84	631.8	100.0	T
Jaguar	ATM	8-10-84	294.0	100.0	O
London Electricity	ELECTR	12-11-90	523.0	97.5	O
Manweb	ELECTR	12-11-90	285.0	97.5	O
Midlands Electricity	ELECTR	12-11-90	503.0	97.7	O
National Power (I)	ELECTR	3-12-91	2,231.0	60.9	O
National Power (II)	ELECTR	3-6-95	n.a.	38.3	O
Northern Electric	ELECTR	12-11-90	295.0	97.5	O
Northern Ireland Electricity	ENERGY	6-18-93	725.8	96.5	O
Northumbrian Water	WATER	12-12-89	157.0	98.4	O
Norweb	ELECTR	12-11-90	415.0	98.4	O
PowerGen (I)	ELECTR	3-12-91	1,367.0	59.5	O
PowerGen (II)	ELECTR	3-6-95	n.a.	36.6	O
Railtrack	TRANSP	5-20-96	2,235.7	98.0	O
Rolls-Royce	MANUF	5-20-87	1,485.2	96.7	O
Scottish Power	ELECTR	6-18-91	1,956.0	96.4	O
Seeboard	ELECTR	12-11-90	306.0	97.5	n.a.
Severn Trent	WATER	12-12-89	849.0	98.4	O
South Wales Electricity	ELECTR	12-11-90	244.0	97.5	O

Table 5A.1
(continued)

Company name	Industry sector	First trading day	Proceeds at 1995 prices	Offer/tender price	Offer rate	Method of sale
South Western Electricity	ELECTR	12-11-90	295.0	240	97.0	O
Southern Electricity	ELECTR	12-11-90	648.0	240	97.5	O
Southern Water	WATER	12-12-89	392.0	240	98.4	O
Trustee Savings Bank	BANKS	10-10-86	1,360.0	100	n.a.	n.a.
Thames Water	WATER	12-12-89	922.0	240	97.4	O
Welsh Water	WATER	12-12-89	346.0	240	98.4	O
Wessex Water	WATER	12-12-89	246.0	240	98.4	O
Yorkshire Electricity	ELECTR	12-11-90	497.0	240	97.5	O

Note: BSS SUPP = Business Support; CHEM = Chemicals; TRANSP = Transports; MANUF = Manufacturing; TLC = Telecommunications; ATM = Automobiles; ELECTR = Electricity; T = tender; O = offer; n.a. = not available.

where r_{it} and r_{mt} are the monthly return in month t for the firm i and for the market, respectively.

To allow comparisons with previous empirical findings we use the same measures of long-run performance as Ritter (1991) and Levis (1993). Thus, the average abnormal returns (AR_t) on a portfolio of n firms for month t and adjusted for the market performance is computed as follows:

$$AR_t = \frac{1}{n} \sum_{i=1}^{n} ar_{it}. \tag{5.4}$$

The cumulative abnormal return ($CAR_{1,s}$) from the beginning of the first full calendar month of trading to every month s is the sum of the average abnormal returns (AR_t):

$$CAR_{1,s} = \sum_{t=1}^{s} AR_t. \tag{5.5}$$

The statistical significance of CARs is assessed by means of a simple t-statistic computed for each period as follows:

$$t(CAR_t) = \frac{CAR_t}{S.E.(CAR_t)}, \tag{5.6}$$

where $S.E.(CAR_t)$ is the standard error of the average cumulative abnormal return on period t and $t(CAR_t)$ is the t-statistic (with two degrees of freedom) for the null hypothesis that CAR_t is equal to zero.

In the underpricing analysis, we measure the degree of underpricing as the percentage change in the offer price and the unadjusted closing price on the first trading day (see table 5A.2). In table 5A.3, we show the coefficient estimates from the linear regression of the underpricing on some explanatory variables. All the coefficients appear to be statistically significant. The variables that turn out to be helpful in explaining the underpricing are firm size on the day of the privatization (SIZE), the return on the capital employed (ROCE), the percentage of shares sold out (OFFER_RATE), the firm leverage or indebtedness (DEBT_EQUITY), the method of sale (O_T), and a dummy equal to one if the offer is primary and zero otherwise.

As described previously, the short-run performance of U.K. privatized firms is measured in terms of average abnormal return on the

Table 5A.2
Underpricing and short-term performance of U.K. privatized firms

Company	First-day price	Offer price	Under-pricing	Market trend	First-day abnormal returns	First-month company returns	First-month FTSE returns	First-month abnormal returns
Aea Technology	323.5	280	0.15	-0.00	0.15	0.13	0.00	0.13
Amersham International	188	142	0.32	-0.00	0.32	0.32	-0.01	0.33
Anglian Water	288.5	240	0.20	0.00	0.19	0.27	0.02	0.24
Associated British Ports (I)	138	112	0.23	-0.00	0.23	0.25	-0.03	0.28
Associated British Ports (II)	266	270	-0.01	-0.00	-0.00	-0.03	0.01	-0.04
British Aerospace (I)	170	150	0.13	-0.00	0.13	0.19	0.02	0.16
British Aerospace (II)	416	375	0.10	-0.00	0.11	0.05	-0.00	0.06
British Airports Authority (I)	291	245	0.18	0.01	0.17	0.18	0.01	0.17
British Airports Authority (II)	291	290	0.00	0.01	-0.00	0.00	0.01	-0.00
British Airways	169	125	0.35	0.00	0.34	0.36	0.05	0.30
British Energy	192	198	-0.03	-0.00	-0.02	-0.00	-0.01	0.01
British Gas	147.75	135	0.09	0.00	0.08	0.11	0.03	0.07
British Petroleum (I)	912	845	0.07	0.00	0.07	0.10	0.02	0.08
British Petroleum (II)	356	363	-0.01	-0.01	-0.00	0.06	0.02	0.04
British Petroleum (III)	436	435	0.00	-0.00	0.00	0.00	-0.01	0.01
British Petroleum (IV)	265	330	-0.19	0.03	-0.23	-0.19	-0.02	-0.16
British Steel	127.25	125	0.01	-0.00	0.02	0.00	0.01	-0.00
British Telecom (I)	172	130	0.32	0.02	0.30	0.42	0.05	0.36
British Telecom (II)	327	335	-0.02	-0.00	-0.01	-0.01	0.02	-0.04
British Telecom (III)	413.5	410	0.00	0.00	0.00	0.01	0.03	-0.01
Britoil (I)	196	215	-0.08	-0.00	-0.08	-0.12	-0.02	-0.09

Britoil (II)	203	185	0.09	0.00	0.09	0.21	0.04	0.17
British Technology Group	251	195	0.28	0.00	0.28	0.42	0.02	0.39
Cable and Wireless (I)	197	168	0.17	-0.01	0.18	0.17	0.03	0.14
Cable and Wireless (II)	271	275	-0.01	-0.00	-0.01	0.01	0.02	-0.00
Cable and Wireless (III)	585	587	-0.00	0.00	-0.00	0.01	0.02	-0.00
East Midlands Electricity	290.5	240	0.21	-0.00	0.21	0.19	-0.01	0.20
Eastern Electricity	288	240	0.20	-0.00	0.20	0.15	-0.01	0.17
Enterprise Oil	185	185	0.00	0.00	-0.00	-0.02	-0.02	0.00
Jaguar	179	165	0.08	0.01	0.06	0.09	0.03	0.05
London Electricity	282	240	0.17	-0.00	0.18	0.16	-0.01	0.17
Manweb	306	240	0.27	-0.00	0.28	0.27	-0.01	0.28
Midlands Electricity	284	240	0.18	-0.00	0.19	0.15	-0.01	0.17
National Power (I)	212.5	175	0.21	-0.00	0.21	0.18	-0.00	0.18
National Power (II)	456.5	476	-0.04	-0.00	-0.03	-0.10	0.03	-0.14
Northern Electric	282.5	240	0.17	-0.00	0.18	0.19	-0.01	0.21
Northern Ireland Electricity	126.5	100	0.26	0.00	0.26	0.35	0.00	0.34
Northumbrian Water	297	240	0.23	0.00	0.23	0.30	0.02	0.28
Norweb	292	240	0.21	-0.00	0.22	0.20	-0.01	0.21
PowerGen (I)	212	175	0.21	-0.00	0.21	0.16	-0.00	0.16
PowerGen (II)	491	512	-0.04	-0.00	-0.03	-0.09	0.03	-0.12
Railtrack	409.5	380	0.07	-0.00	0.07	0.07	-0.00	0.08
Rolls-Royce	232	170	0.36	-0.01	0.38	0.28	-0.00	0.29
Scottish Power	255.5	240	0.06	-0.00	0.06	0.02	-0.04	0.06
Seeboard	282	240	0.17	-0.00	0.18	0.17	-0.01	0.19
Severn Trent	271	240	0.12	0.00	0.12	0.18	0.02	0.15
South Wales Electricity	304	240	0.26	-0.00	0.27	0.28	-0.01	0.30

Table 5A.2
(continued)

Company	First-day price	Offer price	Under-pricing	Market trend	First-day abnormal returns	First-month company returns	First-month FTSE returns	First-month abnormal returns
South Western Electricity	290	240	0.20	–0.00	0.21	0.20	–0.01	0.21
Southern Electricity	290	240	0.20	–0.00	0.21	0.17	–0.01	0.18
Southern Water	281	240	0.17	0.00	0.16	0.21	0.02	0.18
Trustee Savings Bank	85.5	100	–0.14	–0.00	–0.14	–0.17	0.01	–0.19
Thames Water	276	240	0.15	0.00	0.14	0.24	0.02	0.21
Welsh Water	281	240	0.17	0.00	0.16	–0.05	0.02	–0.08
Wessex Water	294	240	0.22	0.00	0.22	0.29	0.02	0.26
Yorkshire Electricity	299.5	240	0.24	–0.00	0.25	0.24	–0.01	0.26

Note: First-day abnormal returns and first-month abnormal returns are computed as in equations (1) and (2), respectively.

Table 5A.3
Results of cross-sectional multiple regression analysis for underpricing[a]

Explanatory variable	Coefficient	t-statistic
Constant	0.7478***	3.315
SIZE	−0.0512***	−3.922
P_S	0.3008***	3.553
DEBT_EQUITY	−0.0004***	−4.172
OFFER_RATE	−0.0029*	−1.933
ROCE	−0.0033***	−3.213
O_T	0.1927***	11.971
R^2	0.786	
Adj. R^2	0.733	
F-value	14.72***	

[a] Underpricing $= \beta_0 + \beta_1$ (SIZE) $+ \beta_2$ (P_S) $+ \beta_3$ (DEBT_EQUITY) $+ \beta_4$ (OFFER_RATE) $+ \beta_5$ (ROCE) $+ \beta_6$ (O_T) $+ \varepsilon$, where Underpricing $=$ market-adjusted first-day return; SIZE $=$ natural logarithm of the total assets of firm prior to offering; P_S $=$ dummy variable equal to one in the case of a primary offering, zero otherwise; DEBT_EQUITY $=$ total debt to total assets ratio in percentage; OFFER_RATE $=$ percentage of equity offered to the public; ROCE $=$ return on capital employed; O_T $=$ dummy variable taking on the value one if the method of sale is a public offer and zero if it is a tender offer.
* significant at the 10 percent level.
*** significant at the 1 percent level.

first trading day. The long-run performance is measured by average CARs computed over one, two, three, five, and ten years after privatization. Following the methodology of Levis (1993), we have studied the first-day return and the long-run return. We are particularly interested in the correlation between method of sale, percentage of equity sold, and year of privatization, industry sector, and firm size. The objective is to capture possible and significant differences between partitions of the sample.

Within a multivariate perspective, the results show that underpricing decreases as (1) firm size increases, (2) leverage becomes larger, (3) profitability rises, and (4) the equity stake sold increases. Moreover, the level of underpricing is significantly higher for primary offers than for secondary offers, and for public offers than for tender offers. As expected, underpricing is larger for smaller firms, which may be explained in terms of asymmetric information about the firm's value. In addition, the lower the percentage of equity offered, the higher the liquidity risk, and the larger therefore is the underpricing that investors require for taking on this risk. The linear model we have used explains approximately 73 percent of the variations in the underpricing (dependent variable), and the F-test is able to reject the null hypothesis that all of the slope coefficients (excluding the constant or intercept) in the regression are zero.

The cumulative abnormal return computed over the whole sample appears to be significantly different from zero starting from the first three months after the privatization (CAR_3M = 14.5 percent). CARs seem also to increase over time, reaching 21 percent after one year, 42 percent after three years, and 57.3 percent after five years. After six years from the privatization date, CARs seem to reverse their trend and decrease to 38.5 percent at the end of the tenth year. Because of the small number of observations, we cannot analyze the CARs' behavior beyond ten years.

The analysis of the cumulative abnormal returns computed for the various subsamples leads to the following results. Breaking down the sample according to the year of privatization, it emerges that offerings in the years 1989–1990 have higher positive CARs than those in other years. Moreover, privatized firms within the water, electricity, and transport industries outperform other industry sectors.

6 Employees

6.1 Topics for Discussion

Property rights theory suggests that private owners convey greater efficiency incentives to managers and workers than do ministries. The argument boils down to the following. The aim of the "owner" of nationalized firms is not to maximize profits, but to achieve a jumble of political objectives. This does not provide the boards of directors of nationalized firms with clear incentives to minimize costs. On the other hand, private shareholders, being able to appropriate profits, can adequately motivate management to minimize costs, including labor costs.

Hence, various authors maintain that labor costs are destined to be excessive in a public corporation. Privatization, in this perspective, should therefore have foreseeable consequences in terms of the quantity and remuneration of labor. First, after divestiture, we should observe a trend toward a reduction in the number of the firm's employees for the same amount of output. Second, salaries should fall in real terms or relative to those of other private firms. Third, worker and manager effort should increase, and their organization should change.

The need to achieve results in one or more of these three directions hastens managerial action to reduce the power of trade unions within privatized firms. From the point of view of the theory of property rights, one can also forecast what the efficiency effects of employees' shareholding in a firm will be. This policy of promotion of employee shareholding was one ingredient of privatization in Great Britain, as in other countries. Employee participation in company profits is expected to have positive effects on employees' attitudes toward work.

Moreover, one can ask what effects large-scale privatization may have on the labor market as a whole, for example, through the indirect effects linked to the changing role of trade unions, reduction in personnel, and containment of salaries. According to standard macroeconomic theory, as noted in chapter 3, privatization can be considered a positive shock to aggregate supply, thus increasing output and employment.

For some of these questions the empirical evidence, as I show in this chapter, is anything but unambiguous. The picture that emerges from this evidence seems nevertheless quite different from that foreseen by property rights theory.

6.2   Empirical Evidence

6.2.1   Labor Market Policies in the United Kingdom after 1979

A discussion of employment, wages, and industrial relations in British firms before and after privatization fits into the broader context of the shift in Britain's labor policies after 1979 (Brown, Deakin, and Ryan 1997; Gregory 1997). Britain's income policies in the 1970s foundered in a situation of simultaneous high inflation and unemployment. These policies had their final manifestation in the "Social Contract" of the last Labour government prior to privatization, against which there were appalling waves of highly unpopular strikes, especially in the public sector and in essential services (from refuse collection to funeral services). This type of militant trade unionism consequently became an easy target for Tory policy. At the end of the 1970s, a swing to the right created a political climate clearly favorable to the reduction of "big government," to the rejection of the prevailing income policies, and to changes in industrial-relations legislation.

Unemployment began to rise in the United Kingdom at the end of the 1960s, but it quadrupled at the end of the 1970s. The monetary policy of the first Thatcher government aimed primarily at curbing inflation. Because there was a considerable increase in the oil revenue from the North Sea at the same time, however, this created a combination of high interest rates, a government seen as tough on inflation, and a strong currency. Sterling appreciated by 40 percent in real terms in four years (it had been floating since 1973, in a regime of total liberalization of capital since 1979). Consequently, a large part of the country's industrial base was displaced, and output fell 9 percent and employment fell 15 percent in the space of two years. During the recession of 1980–1981, 1.3 million jobs were lost, equal to 5 percent of the workforce, with unemployment peaking at 3 million (11 percent) in 1986.

The Thatcher government assumed an attitude of noninvolvement in wage conflicts in the private sector, rejecting the "corporatist" approach of the income policy of the previous twenty years. At the same time it introduced a series of legislative acts aimed at weakening the trade unions in the United Kingdom (primary legislation on labor issues was passed in 1980, 1982, 1984, 1986, 1988, 1989, 1993, and 1995).

This legislation implied a restriction of the cases of legitimate "industrial action." A secret vote of union members became necessary to decide on a strike. Moreover, a certain length of time had to elapse (typically seven days) between such a decision and the beginning a strike. Secondary picketing was made illegal.[1] If a court declared a strike illegitimate, the trade union was responsible for the damages incurred (this led to some pilot procedures with huge fines, even millions of pounds, levied on the unions and to the seizure of their property). The unions' ability to achieve closed-shop systems, according to which employment in some firms automatically implied membership in the union, was also restricted. Finally, the laws also regulated unions' election procedures and in particular the secret vote for the election of officers and delegates.

The effects of this shift in government attitude toward the unions, together with high unemployment and the orientation of a very large part, perhaps the majority, of public opinion, did not take long to manifest themselves. In 1979, the rate of unionization in Britain was 55 percent of those employed, which was equal to 8.5 million members. At the end of the 1990s, the rate of unionization was just 30 percent (23 percent in the private sector), including the privatized firms. It is highly probable that privatization has in fact contributed considerably to the decline in union membership through a "composition effect". According to Gregory (1997), employment has plummeted in the traditional union heartlands of manufacturing, the steel industry and public corporations, and there has been no offsetting unionization of fast-growing industries such as financial services and leisure industries. In parallel, there was a decline in employee recognition of union representation. In 1984, 66 percent of workers were employed in factories in which a union was recognized; by 1994, this figure had fallen to 48 percent (and just one third in the private sector).

Collective-bargaining coverage is now lower in the United Kingdom than at any time since World War II. Therefore, the decline in coverage of workers through union bargaining is even more pronounced than the decline in membership. Moreover, the frequency of strikes in the country has dropped sharply since the approval of the new labor legislation.

Although it is not conclusive, there is some evidence about general trends in wages in the United Kingdom over the period under study. The statistically significant difference between wages in unionized firms and those in nonunionized firms is currently between 0 and 10 percent. This may confirm the erosion of any previously existing "union wage premium." On the other hand, there is also evidence that in the more competitive sectors, wage dynamics are such that they eliminate the role of the union in determining wages, which thus remains confined to the noncompetitive sectors (Stewart 1990).

As stated previously, the Thatcher government took a neutral attitude toward negotiation in the private sector. The government repealed norms for the protection of minimum wages, in particular, the Fair Wages Act of 1946 and subsequent norms implemented by Labour governments. Some of these norms forced all contractors operating in the public sector to pay at least the same wages as those specified in the major collective contracts. The abandoning of this law also entailed the United Kingdom's repeal of its agreement with the International Labor Office convention on contracting out, aimed at preventing competition based on lower wages in tenders for procurement to the public sector.

In 1993, the Major government abolished twenty-six wage councils that had survived the repeal of the minimum wage legislation. The councils dated back to the beginning of the century and covered about 2.5 million workers in sectors in which wages were typically low (retail trade, hotels, clothing, etc.). Their task was to monitor labor conditions in these industries and to fix minimum standards of pay.

Other important reforms restricted unemployment benefits. Moreover, the reforms of the labor market in the United Kingdom implemented in the last two decades of the twentieth century led to lower costs for hiring and firing than in other developed countries.

The macroeconomic, structural, and legislative changes mentioned previously probably contributed to a deep structural reform of the labor market in the United Kingdom. One effect of this change was a marked increase in wage inequality and a reduction in official unemployment. (The share of the workforce that was no longer involved in the market also increased greatly, however.) The pay differentials among employees in each industry have increased dramatically in the United Kingdom in the past twenty years and produced a wage distribution that was the most unequal of any period in the twentieth century.

The British labor market, following the radical transformations introduced over the last twenty years, is now one of the most deregulated in developed countries. In 1997, the unemployment rate was 6.4 percent of the workforce, which was very low compared to those of other EU countries (OECD 1998, 69ff). Nevertheless, there were perhaps 2.3 million people, or an additional 6.5 percent of the population of working age, who would have been willing to work if they could find employment, although they were not classified as unemployed.

Furthermore, there has been no increase in the size of the British labor force over the period under study. We can explain this apparent contradiction between low official unemployment and large disguised unemployment by the considerable increase since the 1980s in the number of people living on some kind of benefits. In the United Kingdom the number of "long term sick and disabled" has risen substantially in the past twenty years to 1.5 million, which is equal to 4 percent of people of working age.

The phenomenon is particularly concentrated among unskilled males. We have no data about the work history of members of this group, so it cannot be established whether they came from the privatized sector, although this would appear to be probable (for example, ex-steelworkers or ex-miners could easily obtain recognition as disabled).

Since 1977, the greater flexibility of the U.K. labor market in regard to pay and tenure of jobs has contributed to a large increase in the Gini coefficient of family income, which rose from less than 0.23 at the end of the 1970s to over 0.32 in 1991, reversing the stability or slight decline of the 1960–1970s. The trend of the past two decades toward inequality in earnings is a global widespread phenomenon, but in the United Kingdom, it happened earlier and with a greater intensity than elsewhere. In 1979, the ratio of the incomes of the first decile in the distribution of family income to the tenth decile was 4.5. In 1994, it was 8. Whereas for the population as a whole, real incomes grew by 35 percent between 1979 and 1991, those of the richest decile rose by 50 percent, and those of the poorest fell by 14 percent in real terms. Seventy percent of those in the poorest decile are unemployed, lone parents, disabled, or "working poor."

A third of the children in the United Kingdom live in poor families (those with incomes less than half the median), more than in any other country of the EU. Between 1979 and 1995, the number of people receiving Supplementary Income Support doubled, reaching 5.5 million. When the families of these people and other people of working age who are de facto unemployed are included, this figure rises to 10 million, a fifth of the population (and 70 percent of those in this group are pensioners). With regard to the working poor, studies reported by the OECD (1997) show that 10 percent of those employed at the time received a gross wage of less than £3.50 per hour and that 30 percent received between £3.50 and £4.50.

Much of the rising inequality in family income in Britain comes from a combination of rising unemployment in the 1980s, the freezing of some social security benefits (including pensions in real terms), regressive taxation reform, and increasing pay differentials. On the latter point, pay inequality in the United Kingdom increased since the 1970s more than in any other OECD country except the United States, probably partly because of the decline in bargaining coverage discussed previously.

Changes in labor conditions in privatized firms must be viewed in this broader context of rising income inequality.

6.2.2   Employment Trends in Privatized Companies

Stories of unemployment in the 1980s have been the subject of popular British films such as *Thank You, Mrs. Thatcher* and *The Full Monty*. These are about workers from privatized sectors (steel and coal). The success of these movies was just one sign (among others) of a national trauma. In fact, privatization was only part of the explanation for large-scale downsizing of the former nationalized industries. Tables 6.1 and 6.2 present evidence on employment trends in selected privatized companies in the United Kingdom since 1979.

At the end of the period under study, in about 1996, employment in the firms in the tables—excluding British Rail, the electricity generators, and Cable and Wireless, for which the data are incomplete, and the Post Office, which was never privatized—was roughly 517,000. In the same firms, employment in 1979 stood at around 1,320,000: This 60 percent decrease is therefore a case of gargantuan downsizing, with over 800,000 jobs lost. At the time of privatization, however (which varied from firm to firm, and therefore the total has a purely indica-

Table 6.1
Employment changes in selected companies, 1979–1995

Firm	1979	At privatization date	1995
Associated British Ports	11,571	9,085 (1983)	2,253[a]
British Gas	101,600	91,900 (1986)	69,971[a]
British Telecom	233,447	244,592 (1984)	148,900
Rolls Royce	57,800	42,000 (1987)	43,500[a]
British Steel	191,500	53,720 (1988)	39,800
British Coal	183,000	17,000 (1993)	11,000
British Railways	244,084	122,100 (1996)	130,600
British Airways	57,741	40,440 (1987)	53,060
British Airports Authority	7,298	7,462 (1987)	8,171
Cable and Wireless	n.a.	10,750 (1981)	39,636
National Freight Corporation	35,922	24,305 (1982)	33,989[a]
Water companies	63,221	46,728 (1989)	54,200[a]
RECs	95,800	82,485 (1990)	74,457[a]
Electricity generators[b]	n.a.	24,553 (1991)	11,737[a]
Post Office	178,397	not privatized	155,000[a]

Sources: Boyfield 1997; Martin and Parker 1997; and Pendleton 1999.
Note: n.a. = not available.
[a] 1994.
[b] PowerGen and National Power only.

Table 6.2
Employment in public corporations: Average percentage annual growth rate

	Nationalization period	Prepriva-tization period	Postannounce-ment period	Postpriva-tization period	Recession period	Latest period
British Airways	3.1	−9.7	−5.4	7.2	7.8	−0.5
British Steel	−6.9	−7.9	0.0	−0.8	1.3	−8.7
British Gas	−0.9	−3.8	−3.8	−3.3	−1.1	−6.0
CEGB	−1.5	−1.5	−0.2	−12.9	−3.8	−16.5
British Telecom	2.1	0.5	−0.2	−0.9	0.1	−10.9
Post Office	0.4	n.a.	n.a.	n.a.	−1.2	−2.3
National Freight	−6.3	−17.9	−17.9	−3.7	4.6	0.2
British Railways	−5.0	0.0	−2.9	−4.3	−3.3	−2.7
Jaguar	−3.2	0.5	11.6	7.4	−4.2	n.a.
Rolls-Royce	−3.2	−5.2	1.1	13.0	11.2	−10.9
National Coal Board	−6.5	−20.9	−35.5	−13.6	−13.5	−20.9
Britoil	27.6	22.8	13.2	−1.3	n.a.	n.a.
Associated British Ports	n.a.	−4.0	−5.3	−11.2	−17.3	−6.5
British Aerospace	5.6	5.6	5.6	−0.5	8.7	−21.5
British Airports Authority	−0.3	−0.1	0.0	7.5	10.1	−6.7

Sources: My elaboration on NEDO 1976; Martin and Parker 1997.
Note: Periods differ for each organization, except for recession period (1988–1992) and latest period (1993–1997). n.a. = not available.

tive significance), employment had fallen to 638,000. Consequently, seven-eighths of the downsizing for these firms happened under state ownership.

The picture is quite clear. For the large sample of firms considered in the tables, divestiture does not denote a structural break in employment trends, except in specific cases. In general, whenever there are drastic changes in the number of employees, these are the result of exogenous factors, such as changes in regulations, demand conditions, or market structure.

Several privatization studies have considered a relatively small number of years before divestiture and often observe no more than the effect of the privatization announcement. I have tried to go back as far as possible, and the picture changes accordingly.

I constructed a series of the average annual growth rate of employment for fifteen privatized firms, covering 1960–1997. Figures 6.1 through 6.3 show long-term employment trends, in some cases since 1960. The available evidence is fragmentary, and data for some years are missing, but overall the data reject the hypothesis that privatization of these firms reduced employment,[2] when subperiods or GDP growth are controlled for. Let us examine some examples.

1. Transport services (figure 6.1) accounted for a substantial part of the nationalized industries. British Airways made considerable cuts in personnel between 1979 and 1984. Before privatization (1987) or its announcement, BA laid off 20,000 workers out of almost 58,000, following financial crisis and increasing competition. Recovery in employment began in 1985 and continued. Since 1988, the employment figure for BA includes 7,000 employees of British Caledonian, the acquisition of which reinforced the dominant market position of British Airways.

In the same air transport sector, when there was no competition, the effect of privatization was negligible: British Airports Authority recorded little change in employment during the final years of public ownership. Subsequently employment increased, both through the acquisition of other companies and as a result of the need to improve security standards in British airports. In the case of Associated British Ports, employment sharply decreased, from 11,000 to 2,000, as a result of the liberalization of the labor market in the nineteen ports previously under the monopoly system, as elsewhere in Europe. In contrast, employment at the National Freight Corporation increased from 24,000 at divestiture in 1981 to 34,000 in the mid-1990s, whereas it had

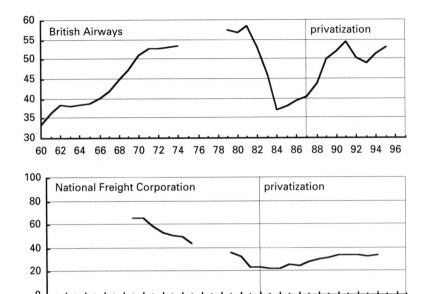

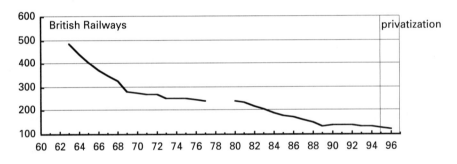

Figure 6.1
Transport: Employment (in thousands).
Sources: Author's elaboration on NEDO 1976; Martin and Parker 1997; Eurostat; and ONS.

decreased under public ownership by two-thirds (employees numbered 66,000 in the 1960s). Employment at British Railways decreased by more than 50 percent (around 120,000 employees) well before divestiture.

2. In the energy sector (figure 6.2), there was a substantial downsizing among the electricity companies in the period considered, most of it following a change in power generation technology (substitution of gas for coal). Employment halved from 45,000 at divestiture to 24,000 in the mid-1990s. Nevertheless, under public ownership it had already decreased by 25,000 units since 1970. At Britoil, employment was stable both before and after privatization, and subsequently it fell only because of the drop in international oil prices in the period under study. British Gas witnessed a sharp reduction in employment over the period considered, partly because of widespread contracting out of some services (e.g., maintenance), from 88,000 to 70,000. Again, privatization (1987) did not mark a structural break in the long-term trend: The drastic decline in recent years coincided with the liberalization of the sector, ten years after divestiture. Under private ownership, employment decreased from 85,000 to 70,000 in seven years. Under public ownership, it slowly but constantly decreased by 40,000 units between 1960 and 1987. British Coal is another obvious example. But NFC, and electricity companies as well, all recorded substantial downsizing under public ownership.

3. It is also very interesting to observe what happened in some other manufacturing and services firms (figure 6.3). British Steel lost more than 150,000 workers over the period studied, equivalent to 79 percent of the company's 1979 workforce, but under public ownership following the structural crisis in the sector (particularly because of the substitution of other materials for steel as input in many industries), it had lost around 200,000 jobs (1968–1989). For British Aerospace, the time series is difficult to interpret because of numerous acquisitions of other companies during the period under study, but overall there is no evidence that divestiture had a significant influence on employment (which almost doubled eight years after divestiture). Employment at both Jaguar and Rolls-Royce increased after divestiture.

Employment levels at British Telecom, which I discuss in detail in chapter 9, did not change for seven years after privatization. Employment then fell drastically, by more than 100,000 units, only because of the market entry liberalization for national and local calls and increasing competition for international calls and mobile phones, as well as

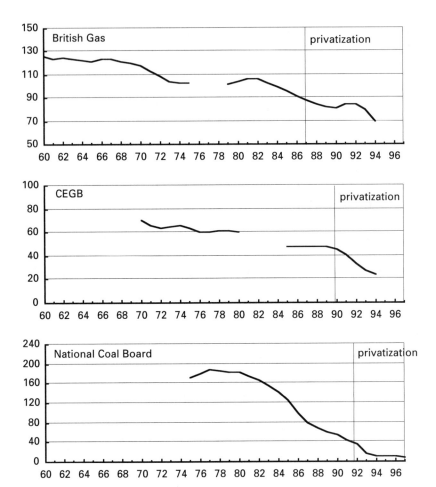

Figure 6.2
Energy: Employment (in thousands).
Sources: Author's elaboration on NEDO 1976; Martin and Parker 1997; Eurostat; and ONS.

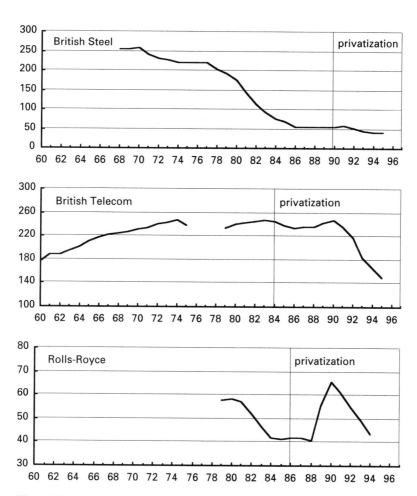

Figure 6.3
British Steel, British Telecom, and Rolls-Royce: Employment (in thousands).
Sources: Author's elaboration on NEDO 1976; Martin and Parker 1997; Eurostat; and ONS.

Table 6.3
Increases in nominal wages in selected companies, 1980–1988

Privatized company	Wages (percentage)
British Airports Authority	+68.6
British Airways	+79.0
British Gas	+62.3
British Coal	+82.1
British Rail	+85.4
British Steel	+120.1
British Telecom	+114.4
Electricity generators	+89.5
London Regional Trasport	+101.6
Post Office	+42.4
Water authorities	+81.0
Scottish Transport Group	+64.8
Average privatized[a]	+67.1

Sources: Salama 1995 (average data); Haskel and Szimanski 1992b (company data).
[a] 1979–1988.

more severe price regulation by the Office of the Telecommunications Regulator (OFTEL).

I return to interpretation of this evidence in section 6.3.

6.2.3 Wages

Salama (1995) claims that between 1970 and 1983 wage increases in nationalized firms in Britain were higher than those in the private sector, but without a corresponding increase in productivity. This dynamic is still in evidence if privatized industries during 1979–1988 are examined (see table 6.3). Several studies confirm this evidence (for a survey, see Pendleton 1999).

Based on Martin and Parker's (1997) data for eleven companies, which show wage levels in the periods before and after privatization, standardized with respect to the wages of the manufacturing sector or with the averages for the economy as a whole, table 6.4 shows that privatization did not alter the relative position of the average employee in the denationalized industries in regard to pay conditions as compared with that of the average employee in British industry as a whole or in the manufacturing sector, with the single notable exception of British Steel. Average wages in the majority of cases are higher at the

Table 6.4
Wages per employee relative to those in the economy as a whole

Organization	Nationalization period	Preprivatization period	Postannouncement period	Postprivatization period	Recession period	Latest period
Energy[a]	166	166	169	165	112	135
Transport services[b]	135	136	135	138	137	141
Transport goods[c]	124	125	124	122	118	123
British Steel	130	126	118	111	113	115
British Telecom	141	144	143	141	142	154

Source: My calculations based on Martin and Parker (1997) data.

Note: Data are for wages per employee in each organization relative to wages per capita in the U.K. economy or manufacturing industry expressed as a percentage (e.g., a figure of 154 means that wages were 54 percent higher in the organization than in the economy or manufacturing in the period studied). For British Gas, British Steel, British Aerospace, Jaguar, and Rolls-Royce, wages are expressed in relation to wages in manufacturing. For the other organizations, the comparison is with wages in the whole economy.

[a] British Gas, Britoil.

[b] British Airways, British Airports Authority, National Freight, Associated British Ports.

[c] Jaguar, Rolls-Royce, British Aerospace.

end of the period than they were under public ownership. This we may partly attribute to changes in pay for individual employees and partly to a composition effect. In fact, workers with below-average wages disproportionately lost their jobs following the reorganization of privatized companies (as in other large firms in the United Kingdom). Dessy and Florio (2003) use panel data to control for the composition of the workforce in regard to skilled and unskilled workers and find clear evidence of individual pay increases in some privatized utilities above the average for the service sector. Their data refer to gas, electricity, and water, and interestingly, they show a relative pay increase after privatization for both manual and nonmanual (male) workers (see table 6.5).

The data I have cited contradict the prediction that the change of ownership of privatized British firms implies a removal of possible rents attributed to the workers. Either these rents did not exist, in the sense that high salaries somehow reflected differences in productivity when the firms were publicly owned, or the rents existed and have been perpetuated under private ownership, despite the weakening of the trade unions.

A separate point raised by Martin and Parker (1997) concerns the ratio of wages to turnover, or rather the relative position of wages, on the one hand, and profits and interests on the other. Here a tendency is observed for the share of wages in added value to fall, while the share of external inputs (i.e., goods and services purchased from suppliers) rises, and above all the remuneration of private companies' own and third-party capital rises as well.

I have discussed profitability trends in the privatized industries elsewhere (chapter 5). One aspect of the change in the structure of the income statement of the denationalized corporations was the increase in the ratio of external procurement to turnover. This change reflects a wide shift from "make" to "buy" that has been a major trend in all large British firms since the late 1970s. Privatization and diminished unionization probably reinforced this trend.

However, the fall in the wage bill as a share of value added has been slow and started well before divestiture or its announcement. For example, over more than fifteen years, the share of wages in value added at British Airways decreased only 3.7 points. It decreased 2.3 points at British Gas and 2.6 points at Rolls-Royce, and it increased at Jaguar. Where we observe a sharp decrease in the wage share after divestiture, for example, at British Telecom, Associated British Ports, and British

Table 6.5
Relative gross weekly earnings in selected privatized sectors, Great Britain, 1974–1996

Sector	Gas		Electricity		Water supply		Railways[a]		Air Transport	
	Preprivatization	Postprivatization	Preprivatization	Postprivatization	Preprivatization	Postprivatization	Preprivatization	Postprivatization	Preprivatization	Postprivatization
Number of years	12	10	16	6	15	7	7	6	13	9
Manual laborers										
Average number of observations per year	355	207	714	331	275	180	1,083	221	233	186
Relative earnings	115	129	112	127	102	114	114	139	125	145
Non–manual laborers										
Average number of observations per year	313	254	459	308	160	156	306	134	253	203
Relative earnings	101	106	113	119	99	99	94	94	127	141

Sources: Dessy and Florio 2003; author's calculations on data published in *New Earnings Survey Part C (1974 to 1996): Analyses by Industry* (ONS, various years).

Note: Relative percent earnings are calculated by dividing average gross weekly earnings for each sector by average gross weekly earnings in all industries and services. The New Earnings Survey is based on a panel of 1 percent sample of employees who are members of pay-as-you-earn (PAYE) income tax schemes. Individuals are selected by reference to the last two digits of their national insurance numbers, producing a random sample of those in the system. Questionnaires for each individual are completed by the relevant employer. The PAYE sample is supplemented by data provided by large employers, using extracts from their payroll systems. Current published data are based on returned information, and there is no grossing, weighting, or imputation undertaken for nonresponse or sample frame deficiencies. The survey concerns the earnings of employees in employment and is designed to represent all categories of employees in businesses of all kinds and sizes. The subsample considered in this table includes only full-time males whose pay for the survey pay period was not affected by absence.
[a] Since railways were privatized in 1996, for this sector the time period is 1988–2002.

Airports Authority (a ten-point decrease, on average), the main causal factor is technology change and liberalization, not ownership change.

6.2.4 Managers' Compensation

The salaries of 215 members of boards of U.K. utilities (British Telecom, British Gas, RECs, PowerGen, and National Grid) amounted to £5,267,000 before privatization and to £30,594,000 in 1996 (Boyfield 1997). This is a nominal increase of around 600 percent. According to Boyfield, however, this simply shows that the average preprivatization salary of £24,500 per year for each board member, according to the above data, was below market rewards. This point was made also by Cragg and Dyck (1999a, 1999b), who find convergence of top executive pay in the privatized companies and in a matching sample of publicly traded firms.

The boards of privatized U.K. companies were, however, largely composed of the same personnel that had been recruited under public ownership (at least for some years following divestiture). Therefore, the increase in compensation for board members does not reflect change in abilities. Nor it is just the reflection of higher salaries in the private sector. Probably, it is simply the result of the board members' moving into a different segment of an imperfect labor market.

According to Bishop and Kay (1988), between 1979 and 1988 the dynamics of management salaries were noticeably more marked in privatized U.K. firms than in the other U.K. companies. Just one year after privatization, the salaries of top management in privatized firms had increased sharply: in British Airports Authority, by +110 percent; in British Airways, by +126 percent; in British Gas, by +68 percent; and in British Telecom, by +32 percent. The average for eleven companies studied by Bishop and Kay was 78 percent after one year. This trend appears to be confirmed if we look at the period 1979–1988 (see table 6.6).

The figures show that top management did gain a lot from privatization in terms of increased wages. This may be only part of the story, however, because of generous stock options schemes (see Pendleton 1999; Cragg and Dyck 1999a, 1999b).

6.2.5 Industrial Relations

The coal miners' strike of 1974 in the United Kingdom led to the reduction of the working week to three days in many sectors and to the

Table 6.6
Compensation of top managers (percent nominal increase)

Privatized company	Top management
British Airports Authority	+308
British Airways	+462
British Gas	+276
Average privatized	+247
Average public sector	+111
Average private sector	+85

Source: Bishop and Kay 1988.

fall of the Heath government. When it won the general elections, the Conservative Party saw the trade unions in the public corporations as the adversary to defeat. Goods and services essential to the government were considered to be under threat from union action, and the regime of legal monopoly in some of these sectors made any alternative procurement impossible. The Conservatives hoped that, on the one hand, privatization, by cutting the umbilical cord to the Treasury, would lead the management of the privatized firms to resist pressure from the unions for pay increases. On the other hand, they hoped that liberalization would be able to create alternative sources for government supplies. Both strategies ought to have weakened the unions.

The change in industrial relations in Britain after privatization was considerable.[3] In 1948, 60 percent of the workers in nationalized firms were unionized, with a maximum of 90 percent in the railways (according to Pendleton and Winterton 1993). In 1979, the year in which Thatcher became prime minister, the entire sector of nationalized firms recorded a unionization rate of 90 percent, compared to 55 percent for the country's economic activities as a whole. For decades, however, strikes in the nationalized industries had been quite rare (with the notable exception of the coal industry), and disputes more often than not were settled by negotiation or arbitration procedures. The 1970s were a turning point that culminated in the "winter of discontent"[4] in 1978–1979 and in the anti-unionist shift that the Conservatives took advantage of in winning an electoral majority in 1979.[5]

Salama (1995) focuses on organizational change in Britain after privatization and its implications for industrial relations. He studies a number of cases (Jaguar, British Nuclear Fuels, British Airways, and British Airports Authority) and observes that the firms had totally different reactions to privatization according to their situations prior to privatization.

For example, in the case of British Nuclear Fuels (15,000 employees at divestiture) the historically prevailing company culture was oriented toward security, secrecy, and the hierarchy. There was rather slow career advancement, based on specialization in technical capacities and to a certain degree on conservatism. The climate within the firm was one of a short working day (8:30 A.M.–4 P.M., with long coffee breaks), salary increases based on length of service, a job for life, and so on. In the new climate since privatization, commercial objectives (the firm now exports a large part of its services) have overtaken those of security (which obviously, given the sector, are, however, still important). Career paths are faster, and the company culture has become more open to innovation.

In British Airways, the prevailing culture prior to privatization maintained some "military" aspects. The commercialization of the company wiped out this tradition. The changes in corporate culture appear to be less substantial in the case of British Airports Authority, since the management was already innovation-oriented under public ownership.

The case histories presented by Salama (1995) point to highly idiosyncratic organizational responses to the shock of divestiture. It is therefore difficult to draw general conclusions from them.

6.2.6 A Case Study in Perceptions: The Water Industry

We can see many of the issues previously discussed in studies of specific British industries. One research trend of some interest is the study of workers' and managers' perceptions of the change in ownership resulting from privatization of the firms that employed them. Authors of such studies are often economic sociologists, and economists should pay more attention to the results.

In this section, I discuss in detail a survey by Saunders and Harris (1994) of employees of the North West and the Southern Regional Water Authorities three months before privatization and eighteen months after. Their data are based on a small sample of interviews, and the time span is too limited for serious statistical analysis; they do allow us, however, to look into the firm's "black box." Moreover, the water industry is interesting because we can observe the impact of ownership change per se, without liberalization and with a rather lax regulatory environment (see chapter 7).

The high degree of unionization in the water sector under public ownership did not mean there was a high level of conflict. The prevailing company culture before privatization was predominantly conservative and consensual, partly a legacy of the system of municipalized firms (before 1974), partly because the sector's activity is actually carried out in small plants, and partly as result of the ethos of a public service supplying an essential commodity. Half of the water sector's workers in 1989 voted Conservative. Three-quarters of those interviewed by Saunders and Harris regarded managers and workers as part of a team rather than as opposing sides, and there was a clear acceptance of a trade-off between high wages and a secure job. In the sample as a whole before divestiture, 50 percent of employees disapproved of the impending privatization, 27 percent approved, and the rest were undecided. The proportions are reversed in the case of the sector's management (roughly half in favor and a quarter against). In 1991, a year and a half after privatization, the proportions were 44 percent in favor and 42 percent against, but the change in opinion was entirely due to a shift in the feelings of the managers, with workers in lower positions (blue and white collar) for the most part still against privatization. Only a quarter of these lower-level workers would have disapproved renationalization at the time.

Previous studies in the water sector (O'Connell Davidson 1993) had shown that the greatest concerns of sector employees were salaries, hours of work, duties, job security, and opportunities for promotion. Saunders and Harris's study offers some evidence that the main concern of the workers was the risk of losing their jobs after privatization. Before privatization, workers had some positive expectations about other aspects of labor conditions (for example, wages); this resulted in disappointment except among managers.

Actual data, however, do not confirm that there was factual ground for workers' disappointment with pay after denationalization. The wages of workers in the privatized water companies in fact grew more than those for the employees of the national river authorities (still public). Presumably, this disappointment with wages among workers in privatized water firms had more to do with reductions, after privatization, in overtime and weekend work, both of which are paid at a higher rate than work during the standard workweek.

On the other hand, there is no doubt that top management in the water industry gained a lot from privatization in terms of salaries. The average salary of the chairman in the ten privatized water companies thirty months after divestiture had risen by 166 percent. Added to this was the usual option to purchase shares in the privatized firms, which could have resulted in a bonus of £180,000 each, on average. The share purchase option benefited 33 executive directors in 1992 to the tune of £130,000 each and resulted in average gains of £30,000 each for a further 450 top managers. In eight of the firms, a performance-related pay (PRP) scheme was introduced for the managers.

From the point of view of job security, the water sector employees' preprivatization concerns turned out to be unfounded. Whereas in the case of telecommunications, technical progress saved labor, resulting in the need for fewer employees, this was not the case in the water sector. In fact, whereas employment fell from over 60,000 to slightly more than 40,000 between 1980 and 1988, before privatization, between 1989 and 1992 it increased by 15,000, because of the expansion of water sector companies into other diversified activities.

Thus, although there was no objective basis for concern about job security, Saunders and Harris's study, in agreement with other research, emphasizes the increase among water sector workers in the feeling of insecurity as a result of privatization of firms in the sector. The increase in the perception of job insecurity was also due to the employees' lack of information about company long-term strategies concerning sector diversification, mergers, and acquisitions. In general, the authors conclude, also by way of comparison with a control group of workers from the Scottish water authority, which remained state owned, that water sector privatization, although it only modestly affected the real conditions of the sector's employees, nevertheless created a marked polarization between the expectations of managers and workers. The former were enthusiastic supporters of privatization, from which they reaped substantial benefits; the latter were much more skeptical about the long-terms gains in their own personal conditions.

Another clear change in industrial relations as a result of privatization was the marginalization of the unions in the water sector. At the time of privatization 82 percent of manual laborers and 76 percent of white-collar workers were unionized. After privatization, the rate of unionization nearly halved. The weakening of water sector unions was the result of several concurrent factors. The companies diversified outside their regulated core business into new services (engineering design, laboratory analyses, etc.) in which the unions were not very well represented. Similarly, the reorganization of the water sector according to profit centers shattered any preexisting links between unions in different branches of the companies.

A third important trend in industrial relations in the water sector after privatization was the abandoning of national bargaining, based on a mechanism that involved all the public firms in the sector, in favor of a decentralized bargaining system. Although this made negotiations more efficient, it actually weakened the role of each union. Firm managers could refuse to recognize one union without ruining the table around which other unions continued to negotiate (this trend appears to have been underway as early as 1993–1994).

Moreover, the increasingly widespread adoption of PRP schemes shifted negotiations from a collective to an individual level. This has practically eliminated the unionization of managers. The less qualified workers remain tied to the unions as a defense element, and this confirms the thesis of a greater polarization between managers and laborers after divestiture.

I suggest that the history of privatization in Britain's water sector illustrates well several aspects of the overall privatization picture in the United Kingdom. Another interesting example is British Telecom (see chapter 9).

6.3 Discussion

The evidence presented in this chapter does not confirm the prediction of property rights theory (section 6.1) that the management of a privatized firm always has a greater incentive to squeeze labor costs than the management of a public firm. The wage bill in privatized British firms, as a share of value added, is observed to decrease over time. This decrease, however, is often small and slow, and it started well before privatization or its announcement. There was certainly some labor shedding in privatized firms after privatization, but there was huge downsizing in these firms under public ownership as well, twenty years or more before privatization and well before its announcement. Wages for the average employee increased more in the privatized industries after divestiture than elsewhere in the private sector (we do not, however, have data on wages paid by suppliers, which were probably lower than those in privatized companies). Thus, the decrease after privatization in the wage share in added value reflects higher markup of prices over costs and an increase of procurement from external suppliers.

I suggest that in the absence of competition or of incisive regulation, monopolistic rents enable the management of privatized firms to distribute part of the extra profits to the workers.[6] Firm managers might do this for various reasons, whether or not they are in agreement with the owner about this sort of corporate income policy. One reason could be to avoid internal conflicts that force the managers into costly efforts to control industrial relations. On the other hand, privatization could create an incentive for firm managers to increase discretionary expenses aimed at enhancing their own prestige and power, for example, in the field of external relations, advertising, legal services, and dealings with regulatory authorities.

One clear trend in the United Kingdom was the change in the role of firm managers after privatization. Top executives and probably the upper echelons of middle management appropriated a larger quota of monopolistic rents after privatization than could reasonably be expected from a company in the public sector. This restricted group also profited from the transformation of public corporations into companies quoted on the stock exchange, with a more widely dispersed ownership.

An interesting test regarding the position of management in the changeover from public firm to private firm involves managerial turnover. If the public sector had employed people who were not very efficient, who accepted salaries below the market rate for equivalent positions, one could have expected a considerable turnover in managerial staff upon privatization. On the contrary, however, we observe the retention of commanding positions by the same people for several years after privatization. Consequently, in the new situation, they obtain a windfall gain from privatization. This phenomenon appears to have happened on a large scale. (I discussed this point in chapter 5.)

A change can be observed after privatization in the role of the unions as stakeholders in corporate governance. The reasons why a higher rate of unionization is probable in the public sector and in state-owned enterprises than in private firms are well known. The weakness of the incentive to owners and management to minimize costs in the case of soft budget constraints, or more simply when they are faced with an objective different from maximizing profit, means that tolerating unionization is less costly in publicly owned firms. On the contrary, when public firms have additional objectives (in some cases even preeminent ones) regarding employment, unions may even be a useful

tool for company management. Unions may reduce the costs of transactions between management and various groups of workers or individual workers. The argument that unionization reduces transaction
costs may be true to some extent for large private firms as well. In the
case of private firms, however, management has less need than in
public firms for a consensual deal concerning pay, workloads, and
other aspects of labor conditions, so the union becomes a hindrance
and must be more forcefully contained. Furthermore, the greater risk
of disciplinary action or of firing to workers engaging themselves in
union activities may make membership in the union more costly. This
greater risk is perhaps more a result of a general anti-union offensive
by the British government than of any specific stimulus to managerial
efficiency resulting from private ownership.

If, therefore, it is likely that privatization means increased power
for firms' management and a decline in the power of the unions, we
should expect changes of some importance in labor conditions after
privatization. For example, a more flexible use of the workforce should
be possible, perhaps even in the form of greater commitment of individual workers to corporate targets, with a decrease, in the broadest
sense, of the worker's security, resulting in a different psychological attitude of the employees toward the corporate culture. Studies in this
regard, however, have not been conclusive in establishing that less
unionization implies greater worker consensus on the objectives of
owners and managers.

Increased insecurity for workers usually implies increased effort on
their part, but it is not at all certain that this immediately translates
into an increase in productivity. The Japanese corporation, with its
lifelong labor contracts, was leading the productivity league worldwide for decades before the crisis and stagnation of the economy in
the 1990s, whereas the U.S. corporation, before the advent of the New
Economy, showed slow changes in productivity despite a more mobile
workforce.

A fairly substantial amount of shares in privatized British firms was
reserved for employees. In this regard, two quite different methods for
involving employees in privatization should be distinguished: the
management buyout and the distribution of minority shares on favorable terms. The empirical evidence does not allow us to make any
clear-cut predictions concerning the change in corporate culture. One
school of thought claims that the effects of employee ownership of
shares in the firms that employ them are generally positive, given that

there is an increase in the sense of belonging to the firm that is believed to increase productivity. A more pessimistic view believes that the effects of such ownership are negative because of conflicts between the objective of maximizing profits and that of increasing the incomes of worker-owners. In addition, according to some authors, in a situation of diversification of risks, it is irrational for workers to invest a large proportion of their savings in the single asset on which their own current income is already highly dependent.

In the case of Britain, the evidence seems to suggest that the participation of workers in share capital has had little influence on their psychology and behavior. Results appear to have been better, in terms of overall productivity growth, in the case of management buyouts but such buyouts affected only a limited group of managers and higher-level staff.

Finally, I did not find any empirical evidence of indirect effects of privatization of public firms in a particular sector on workers in other sectors. It is possible that competitors and suppliers reabsorbed part of the excess labor force from privatized firms. Even more indirectly, one can conjecture that the increased competitiveness of privatized industries may have had a positive impact on other industries, which may in turn have thus benefited from lower costs, expanded their production, and created new jobs. Obviously, these are indirect effects not so much of privatization as of the potential reduction in relative prices, following divestitures, a reduction that may have different causes from case to case, as I discuss in chapter 7.

Summing up, my conclusions from the discussion presented in this chapter are the following. First, as a social group, the positions of less-skilled workers involved in British divestitures since 1979 may have worsened as a result of privatization. Many have lost their jobs; others have kept them, but with less protection provided by the unions and some uncertainty about their future, and occasionally with lower relative wages (including overtime pay). Most of the workers who remained with the privatized utilities, however, received larger wage increases than those recorded for the private sector: A reasonable explanation for this is the presence of monopolistic rents that survived privatization. Others may have found equivalent or better jobs elsewhere (this is perhaps more likely in the telecommunications industry than in steel). Some adverse effects of privatization on employees are, in fact, difficult to attribute to change in ownership as such: Company reorganization had often been launched by firm management before divestiture, and in any case greater subsequent effects were provoked by liberalization and other trends that have little to do directly with ownership.

Second, trade unions which were particularly strong in the public corporations, have clearly lost ground since privatization. Perhaps this trend toward diminishing union influence is more due to the general anti-union policy of the British government since the late 1970s, both inside and outside of the nationalized sector, than to a change in management incentives following privatization. Third, managers, on the other hand, gained a lot from privatization, both in terms of income and wealth (often becoming shareholders) and in terms of power, having succeeded in securing themselves a larger quota of income than in the past.

Fourth, the indirect effects of privatization on employment at the national level are rather inscrutable. Overall, the labor market underwent great changes during the period under study. On the one hand, official unemployment initially rose considerably under the Thatcher government. Subsequently, it fell, but on the other hand, the number of people receiving disability benefits exploded. Furthermore, inequalities in income have increased dramatically. It is possible to assume that privatization supported this social trend toward regressive income redistribution. For example, the explosion in disability pensions and other forms of assistance had something to do with the mass prepensioning (early retirement) of steelworkers, miners, railway workers, and the like. The overall decline in the social weight of the trade union, achieved also by means of privatization, may have had an influence on the increase in inequality of pay among categories of employees.[7]

My final assessment is that top management and the higher grades among white-collar workers clearly gained from privatization (even discounting their compensation for increased effort and increased risk profiles in terms of job security), and unskilled workers clearly lost. Those employees between the two levels who stayed with the privatized companies experienced a modest increase in their income and had to make some increase in their levels of effort.

When the fact that downsizing of privatized firms started under public ownership, several years before privatization or its announcement, is considered, the reasonable conclusion is that the overall welfare balance of privatization for employees was neutral. It perhaps becomes negative if a high weight is given to increases in inequality of pay and of family incomes.

6.4   Further Reading

There is a growing literature on the impact of privatization on labor, particularly at the International Labor Office (ILO) and at the World Bank (Kikeri 1998) (see also Peoples 1990). Chong and Lopez-de-Silanes (2002) study detailed labor force data from 308 divestitures in eighty-three countries (1982–2000). They find that there was downsizing before privatization in 80 percent of their sample and rehiring of employees fired in preparation for privatization in one-third of the sample. They suggest that governments should not restructure firms before divestiture because when they do, they tend to separate the wrong workers. A 5 percent reduction in employment before privatization, however, is found to increase the sale price by 6 percent (I do not find similar evidence for the United Kingdom).

On reform of British industrial legislation in 1979–1997, see Brown, Deakin, and Ryan 1997 and Oswald 1999. Pendleton (1999) offers a number of helpful references, including research on contracting out in public services and on other issues related to different aspects of privatization and commercialization in the public sector.

Very helpful are the essays included in Gregg 1997 and Gregg and Wadsworth 1999. Participation of workers and managers in shareholding is studied by Nejad (1987) and by Grout (1988, 1994), who deal with the subject of popular capitalism, a theme also examined by Saunders and Harris (1994). Wright, Thompson, and Robbie (1989, 1994) study management buyouts in particular. There were more than 150 management buyouts in the British privatization program. The most important were the National Freight Company and the National Bus Company. Some of the companies that originated from the splitting of British Rail were also acquired by former managers. Most of the management buyouts, however, were acquisitions of small operations, mainly in ancillary activities.

On contracting out, see Hartley 1990 and Talley 1998. On the compensation of chief executive officers and for a comparison between the United States and United Kingdom, see Conyon and Murphy 2000. Haskel and Szymanski 1993a suggests that market share does influence pay in privatized companies. Haskel and Szymanski 1992a is an attempt to add a theoretical dimension to the study of the labor market following privatization.[8] Haskel and Szymanski's conclusion, based on data for fourteen companies between 1972 and 1988, points, however, to a more general shift in objectives as an explanatory factor of employment change: "To summarize, our evidence suggests that the 'change-in-objectives effect' has served to reduce employment, controlling for other factors. Wages have not been greatly affected by this, but are significantly altered by market power. So our results support the following stylized general story: employment fell in many privatized firms as public-sector objectives became more commercial; wages of the remaining workers also fell somewhat and fell further where there was liberalization" (1993a, 176–177).

7   Consumers

7.1   Topics for Discussion

This chapter is about the change in the welfare of British consumers with and without privatization. The broad question I wish to discuss is how privatization of U.K. public firms changed consumers' welfare through changes in prices and consumption. This implies a series of related issues: definition of price indexes; direction, amount, and causes of changes in those indexes; price discrimination and redistribution; quality, information, and expectations; and sequence and interplay of privatization, regulation, and liberalization. This introductory section is in three parts: definitions and measurement, analysis of causation, and evaluation.

7.1.1   *Definitions and Measurement*

The nominal price of the goods produced by privatized firms can fall, but the price can increase in "real" terms. Real prices depend upon the deflator we use to calculate them. For example, as a deflator we can use the consumer price index or the index of input prices in the sector. The meaning is different depending on which we decide to use. The price of a firm's good can decrease in comparison to a broad GDP deflator or RPI and at same time increase relative to a basket of the firm's own input prices.

Particular caution would seem necessary in cases in which there is no single reference price for the firm's output, but weighted price indices. (An example of such a case is telephony.) In such cases, the effects of quantity, for different causes, can create movements in those price indices.

Changes in indirect taxes should also influence the extent and direction of the change in consumer prices. For example, the British government introduced an 8 percent VAT on domestic energy consumption in 1993 and reduced it to 5 percent in 1997.

7.1.2   Analysis of Causation

When we observe a change in pretax prices in real terms, the question of what has caused the change arises. Obviously, there may be explanations for such a change other than the transfer of ownership.

The relative prices of the privatized industries may have changed because of exogenous changes in their input costs. Prices can decrease as a result of increases in productivity determined by technological shocks or changes in demand conditions. In these cases, it would be wrong to attribute to privatization effects that would have happened (sooner or later, more or less) even had the firms involved remained public. Energy prices are one example. The advent of new technologies in the 1980s affected different sectors or subsectors in the United Kingdom in the field of public services, particularly telecommunications, but also the production of electricity (combustion of gas). The capacity of firms to adopt new technologies and to transfer the benefits of those technologies more or less integrally to consumers depends on a number of factors. A similar consideration applies to dynamic economies of scale and scope. The exogenous expansion of demand, determined by changes in the preferences of consumers (as perhaps happened in Britain in the case of air transport), can determine a decline in the cost per unit produced that may (or may not) be transferred to consumers.

Other important drivers of prices are market structure and regulation. For example, in the transition from a situation of statutory monopoly to one of oligopolistic competition, changes in observed prices may be wholly or partially attributable to increased competitive pressure and not to the change in firm ownership. In turn, the regulatory regime may shift from one that is quite lax or discretionary cost-plus to one that is high-powered one (e.g., the imposition of a price cap $RPI - X$). In some privatized industries in Britain (for example, telecommunications), all these changes can be observed, and it is important to try to disentangle the various factors in price changes. This is difficult, but feasible, if changes in ownership, technology, price regulation, and market structure do not happen at exactly the same time (or if we have a panel of firms and reforms in different countries).

Then under what circumstances can we say that privatization has lowered the price of a particular good? Clearly, we need to observe an increase in productivity in the sector, a reduction in the unit cost of the input, a decrease in the markup on the good, or a combination of these changes. We can attribute these changes to privatization when they occur following a change in the objective function of the firm and not because of other factors. For example, under property rights theory assumptions and in standard microeconomics, one can say that in some circumstance privatization *without* liberalization may deliver a lower price for a particular good than public monopoly.

Suppose a hypothetical public monopoly has the objective of achieving a required positive rate of return on capital. Because of weakly defined property rights, the managers of the monopoly firm do not deliver optimal effort but fix prices to satisfy the capital constraint. Privatization occurs. The firm's managers have now an incentive to deliver more effort. For a private monopoly, with the same demand curve as when it was public, under profit maximization, a decrease in marginal costs may lead to a lower sale price, not just to higher profit.

I discussed predictions of this type in chapters 1 and 4. When we turn to the empirical verification of such predictions, caution is necessary, as the results of such verification are sensitive to pricing rules. If the government-required rate of return is low enough, the gains in internal efficiency resulting from privatization may (or may not) offset any change in the markup of the good. Prices may increase with privatization, as has usually happened in transition economies and as happened in some industries in the United Kingdom. Nevertheless, in some sectors prices may decrease, as occurred in the gas and telecommunications industries in the United Kingdom. Therefore, we cannot say in general whether privatization per se will increase or decrease prices and consumers' welfare. One has to make a determination case by case, looking backward to the performances of the public-firm predecessors of the privatized firms under examination.

7.1.3 Evaluation

Suppose we have identified relevant data and controlled for other causal factors. How do we evaluate changes in the prices of goods following a public firm's privatization? One can argue that postprivatization prices are "right" on allocative efficiency grounds (i.e., they are cost-reflective), because they now support profit maximization.

Prices may be more or less "right," however, according to optimal-pricing rules, which in turn depend on the social-welfare function we adopt. On the other hand, from variations in observed prices we cannot immediately infer changes in consumers' welfare. Optimal prices, by definition, are the social-opportunity costs of goods around a general equilibrium. In fact, we can look at privatization as a way to generate a price reform, through changes in the markup of prices over marginal costs. Some contributions to the theory of reform of indirect taxes can be helpful in this context (see, e.g., Coady and Drèze 2002 or the references cited in chapter 2).

The important issue here is that "right" prices must take account of both distribution and efficiency issues. Again, there is no simple prediction that private ownership will generate less price distortion than public ownership.

It is also necessary to consider the possibility of changes in any rationing constraints on the demand and supply of goods. When rationing decreases, an increase in price for a public service will actually be of less importance in welfare terms than otherwise. Two examples of indirect ways of establishing rationing constraints on users' demand are the time taken to install a telephone and the waiting list at a public hospital. A rationed telephone user or a hospital inpatient may have a willingness to pay for the service that exceeds the actual price they need to pay. Consequently, when a reform lifts the ration, although the price does not change, there is a welfare net benefit that risks being ignored by welfare measures based on observed prices. These examples, however, do not imply that rationing is always inefficient.

Perhaps one of the most elusive effects to capture in the transition from public to private firm is the change in price discrimination on the part of utilities in regard to tariffs for their services. In the United Kingdom, following privatization the structure of tariffs changed dramatically. Different consumers now pay very different prices for almost the same service. Under public ownership, different consumers paid the same price for different services (e.g., electricity at peak and off-peak hours). It is not obvious that one price structure is more distorted than another, particularly when cost attribution is difficult, as in network-based industries.

Another issue to consider is output quality. For traditional analysis, different levels of quality are different goods. In fact, it may be useful to consider the quality of a particular service as another output dimension, although this does pose complex problems of measurement.

Closely linked to the issue of output quality is the question of the information given by prices and the existence of informative incompleteness or asymmetry. Privatized firms often provide services that are only imperfectly verifiable ex ante, and occasionally ex post (e.g., water quality), by the consumer. It is therefore necessary to observe whether variations in information occur with privatization, and if so, what consequences these have for the welfare of consumers. A related topic, and one that is definitely rather elusive since it has marked psychological connotations, is consumer perceptions of the implications of the change in ownership that comes with privatization of a firm.

This cursory identification of related issues shows that the study of the effects of a large-scale privatization policy involves formidable problems of empirical analysis. The possibility of addressing the problems posed far transcends the capacity of a single independent scholar. The evidence available is rather fragmentary. The rest of this chapter should therefore be considered simply an illustrative account of some problems raised in the preceding discussion, rather than an exhaustive attempt to answer all the questions. Having said this, I shall try to offer my overall evaluation.

The rest of the chapter has the following structure. The review of the empirical evidence in section 7.2 includes discussions of price trends before and after privatization; I consider in this context water, electricity, gas, coal for domestic use, telecommunications, railways, and buses. I then discuss the distributive impact of price changes and information and quality issues, and eventually I sketch an evaluation of the welfare impact of privatization on consumers. The discussion in section 7.3 comments on the evidence presented in the body of the chapter.

7.2   The Empirical Evidence

7.2.1   Price Trends before Privatization

This section discusses price trends between 1960 and 1975 in the following U.K. sectors: gas, electricity, coal, steel, railways, postal services, and telecommunications. For each sector, based on NEDO 1976,[1] the index number of three series of prices is considered: the prices of products sold to consumers, the prices of products sold to companies, and an aggregated index of the nationalized industries as a whole.

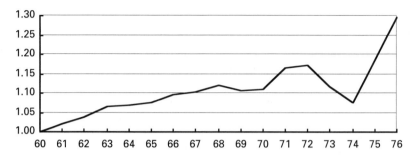

Figure 7.1
Ratio of nationalized component of retail price index to general retail price index
(1960 = 1).
Source: Author's elaboration on NEDO 1976.

These price indices are in turn compared with the relevant aggregated indices: the retail price index, an index of energy input acquired from the manufacturing sector, and the implicit GDP deflator. The principal results are as follows:

1. Between 1960 and 1972, retail prices in the nationalized industries considered increased at a faster rate than the RPI (see figure 7.1). In 1973–1974, because of the worldwide oil crisis, the British government froze prices in the nationalized sector in an attempt to contain inflation. Following the relaxation of the price controls imposed during the freeze, relative prices showed strong growth in 1975. Between 1960 and 1975 the logarithmic rate of growth of the price index for the nationalized industries was 8 percent, whereas that of the retail price index was 7.2 percent. Increases in prices in the nationalized sector accounted for 8.6 percent of the total increase in the aggregated index.

2. The trend of the price index for energy output sold by the nationalized sector to the manufacturing sector (see figure 7.2) is very different from that of the RPI. The comparison here is between the coal, gas, and electricity produced by the nationalized sector and the wholesale price index of all basic materials and fuel purchased by manufacturing (NEDO 1976). There was relative growth of the nationalized industries price index between 1960 and 1967, then a decline until 1972, and a subsequent recovery, within the framework of the increase in the prices of oil and derivatives as a result of the 1973–1974 oil crisis and the policy of price containment in the nationalized industries imposed in response. In any case, at the end of 1975, the price index of

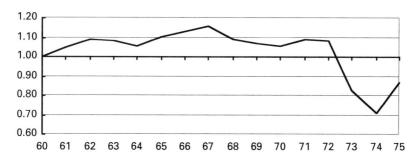

Figure 7.2
Ratio of wholesale price index of fuel to wholesale price index of basic materials and fuel (1960 = 1).
Source: Author's elaboration on NEDO 1976.

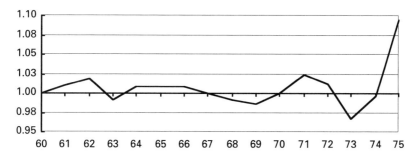

Figure 7.3
Ratio of price index for all nationalized industries to final expenditure price index (1960 = 1).
Source: Author's elaboration on NEDO 1976.

the nationalized industries rose less than the aggregated index. Because the aggregated index contains both energy and nonenergy inputs, my reading of this story is that overall prices of the nationalized industries tracked energy input prices.

3. A third important comparison is between the aggregated index of prices of output produced by the nationalized sector and the implicit GDP deflator. Between 1960 and 1974 the ratio of the nationalized industries price index to the GDP deflator shows little variation around an average unitary value. This stability of the unit ratio implies the same growth in prices in the nationalized sector and in the economy as a whole (see figure 7.3). An increase in the ratio was noticeable in 1975 after the easing of controls following the first oil crisis.

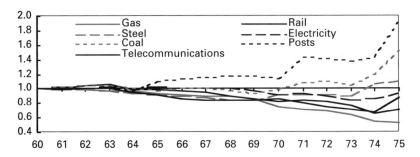

Figure 7.4
Ratio of individual prices to total final expenditure deflator (1960 = 1).
Source: Author's elaboration on NEDO 1976.

These trends, taken together, show that results of any empirical analysis of price trends are sensitive to the price benchmark index. If we consider RPI as the benchmark for analyzing relative price changes, the performance of the nationalized industries looks unfavorable. A substantial share of the output of those industries, however, went to other industries, and the GDP deflator may be more appropriate as a benchmark. In fact, when we consider the aggregate nationalized industries prices relative to the GDP deflator, they show remarkable stability before the first oil shock.

An analysis by individual industries shows considerable differences in price performance from sector to sector. In the case of gas, the ratio between sector prices and their relative aggregated indexes clearly decreases over the long run. For railways, the price increase was higher than that for aggregated retail prices (but lower than that for wholesale or deflator prices). In postal services and coal, the price trend was always one of relative growth. In telecommunications, the relative prices were clearly falling in the period under study. The prices of electricity and steel did not show any noticeable trend over the period 1960–1975 compared to the aggregated indexes (see figures 7.4 through 7.6).

Government controls played an important role in the determination of price trends in the nationalized industries. There was no stable regulatory mechanism for prices. Nationalized industries had to request increases in prices whenever their costs increased. The administrative authorities often resisted increasing the prices, postponing increases for a number of months and sometimes only granting them in part. Here are just a few examples:

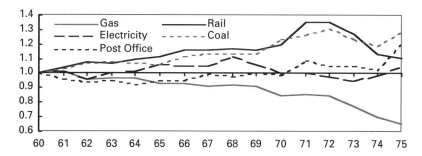

Figure 7.5
Ratio of retail component price to retail price index (1960 = 1).
Source: Author's elaboration on NEDO 1976.

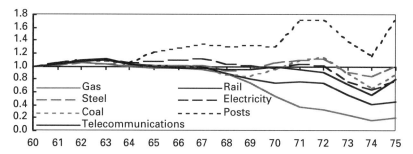

Figure 7.6
Ratio of industry component price to wholesale price index (1960 = 1).
Source: Author's elaboration on NEDO 1976.

• In 1965–1966 British Gas was forced by the National Board of Prices and Incomes (NBPI) to defer its requested price increase for three months; in 1966–1967 it adopted general measures to control prices; again in 1967–1968 and in 1969–1970 requests from British Gas to increase prices were deferred by the NBPI by as much as a year; in 1971–1972 an increase of 7.5 percent was requested, but one of only 5 percent was granted; in 1972–1973 there was a general price freeze; and in 1973–1974 any increase whatsoever in retail prices was postponed until January 1974.

• In the case of electricity the NBPI intervened with deferrals or limitations to tariff increases in 1965–1966 (London Electricity Board) and in 1967–1968 (CEGB bulk supply tariff); in 1970–1971 the government intervened directly and froze prices; similar measures continued until 1975.

• Similar cases were documented for the Post Office, British Steel, and British Railways. For example, for the last, the NBPI intervened to prevent the increase in tariffs requested in 1966 and approved by the Transport Tribunal from being implemented until 1967. For British Steel the price increase requested in December 1968 was granted only in November 1969.

The NEDO (1976) report reached the following conclusion as to the effects of this policy of price control: "It is clear that government policies of price restraint have kept down price increases in the nationalised industries covered, at times in the 1960s but more strongly in the early 1970s. Often the industries have been requested to keep down prices when there has not been any official policy and they have been subject to more stringent price controls than the private sector. Although the government has subsidised these industries, they believe that subsidies have been inadequate and not full compensation for revenue loss" (Background paper 5, p. 21).

In fact, a detailed examination of the relative performance of prices and costs in some nationalized industries (NEDO 1976, Background paper 5, pp. 43ff) shows how contradictory the regulatory policies covering these industries were. On the one hand, the government defined targets of economic return (generally in the form of various types of required return rates). On the other hand, it rendered those targets quite difficult to attain by controlling prices (and sometimes imposing additional social obligations on the industries).

Thus, for example, for the five years 1962–1963 through 1966–1967, the government fixed the required gross return on capital for the gas industry (before interest and depreciation) at 10.2 percent. The ex post result was 9.8 percent. The difference between the two rates of return was entirely due to the delays in implementing price adjustments that resulted from the previously mentioned interventions of the NBPI. When a tariff adjustment in the desired amount was granted (e.g., in 1968–1969), the rate-of-return target was exceeded (the rate of return for that year was 10.9 percent). The same pattern can be observed later, when the requested rate of return was redefined as the rate net of depreciation (but still including profits and interest). The new target of 7 percent fixed in the 1970s was often not reached, with ex post results in the region of 6.5 percent. Following the financial losses resulting from the government-imposed price freeze of 1973–1974, in 1975–1976 considerable price increases were granted, and the rate of return rose to 8.6 percent.

In 1962, the government required an overall gross return on net assets in Britain's electricity sector of 12.5 percent for the subsequent five-year period, and this target was accepted by the sector board. With practically no limitations on prices, the ex post result was very nearly on target—12 percent on average over five years—and it continued so until 1969–1970. Later, the same net rate was fixed as for gas, 7 percent. For four consecutive years (until 1975) prices were subject to stringent control. Ex post results were decidedly lower, on average 4.9 percent over five years.

These examples show the contradictory nature of regulation for the nationalized industries. The government simultaneously regulated prices and returns, in an apparently inconsistent way. On the other hand, the average real return (including interest on public capital) was low but still positive. I document this point in the next chapter, in which I discuss the impact of privatization on taxpayers. In a broad sense, the tariff revenues of the nationalized industries on average covered costs, when the public-sector accounts are consolidated.

7.2.2   Price Trends after Privatization

According to the British government, the $RPI - X$ system used to regulate prices by the regulators has delivered lower real prices in the privatized industries (see, e.g., H.M. Treasury 1995). This is true, with certain exceptions. If we extend our field of observation backward, however, to include the nationalization period, we have a more complex picture. In what follows I consider price trends in individual industries.

On this subject, a number of studies examine specific sectors, and for some of them, there are statistical data from official sources (e.g., Department of Energy, ONS, and regulatory offices). In the discussion here, in addition to data on prices, for each sector I briefly discuss the system of controls put into place at the same time as privatization. A detailed analysis of the regulatory mechanisms for U.K. public utilities is, however, beyond the scope of this study. There is already abundant literature on this subject. (In section 7.4, I suggest selected bibliographical references.) My interest here is to consider evidence relevant for the assessment of changes in consumers' welfare as a result of privatization.

7.2.2.1 Water

The British government proposed water industry privatization in 1986. When the industry was fully privatized in 1989 in England and Wales (Water Act), it supplied drinking water to and maintained the sewerage system for about twenty million users. Ten large operators that currently offer an integrated service (drinking water and sewerage) owe their origins to privatization: Their share was over 75 percent of the market in the regions they served. At that time, the other twenty-one (initially twenty-eight) preexisting privately owned companies operated exclusively in the supply of water.

The licensing act for the privatized water utilities contemplated a system of local monopoly, with the obligation to supply water of a quality that conforms to current regulations, to suitably maintain infrastructures, and to satisfy the demand for connections (obligation of universal service). The Office of the Water Regulator (OFWAT) used the following formula for capping prices (i.e., to determine the maximum permitted price increase):

$$RPI + K + U$$

where K is a factor of cost recovery, especially recovery of capital costs, including financial ones, and it is fixed (and subsequently modified) for every company by the regulator. Initially it was set between 0.03 and 0.07 for the privatized firms, between 0.03 and 0.025 for private water suppliers. The U component is the amount of K not used in the previous year. Firms have three years to use their K factors to pass their investment costs on to consumers. For years 1995–2000, the K range was from -0.02 up to 0.04.

The formula applies to a basket of tariffs that includes metered and unmetered[2] water, metered and unmetered sewerage, and trade effluent (sewage from business users), as well as a charge for infrastructure. It should be noted that the formula contains no explicit mechanism for passing on to consumers the increase in productivity (as with the $RPI - X$ used in other sectors), even though in principle the K factor could be modulated in that sense.

In 1991, an OFWAT initiative led to firms' voluntarily reducing prices. Starting in 1992, OFWAT reduced the K factor for some firms. The following year, the same regulator set up the National Customer Council, a consultative body intended to express consumers' complaints about service. Progressively, the price cap regime administered by OFWAT became more stringent, particularly in 1995. The press and

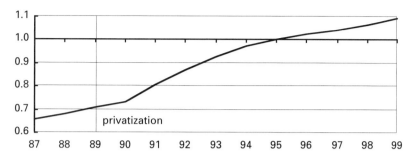

Figure 7.7
Water: Retail prices, relative to RPI (index 1995 = 1).
Source: Author's calculations on ONS data.

the consumer lobbies also expressed some concern about continuity of service in light of the many processes of mergers and acquisitions in the sector and about the frequent interruptions of water distribution during a season of drought.

After privatization the price to consumers of water and sewerage services increased sharply (see figure 7.7), at least until the price cap became more stringent toward the end of the period: For the ten privatized water firms in the United Kingdom, the average charge for domestic users between 1989–1990 and 1993–1994 increased by 55 percent, compared to an increase of 39 percent between 1985–1986 and 1989–1990. This increase was considerably higher than that of the RPI.

The variance in tariffs among the regions served by each water company increased noticeably as well after privatization, by as much as 76 percent between the two extreme cases (it was 39 percent in 1985). The average bill in the region served by South West rose by 187 percent between 1989 and 1994, whereas, for example, the increase was only 30 percent for that served by Thames and 24 percent for that served by North West over the same period (Buller 1996) (see table 7.1).

The water companies argued that these price increases were necessary to finance the investment program they had undertaken to improve water quality and to meet European Community (EC) environmental standards. The extent of this price cap mechanism, however, was very generous to the companies (see section 7.2.5). In reality, water prices increased partly because of the implicit environmental tax element related to EC directives and embodied in the K factor, and partly simply because of unchecked monopoly profits (see chapter 5). Construction costs, the most important component of capital expenditure

Table 7.1
Average household bill for unmetered water and sewerage across the ten water and sewerage companies, 1985–1994

Year	Average bill (pounds)
1985–1986	85.62
1986–1987	92.49
1987–1988	104.06
1988–1989	113.35
1989–1990	118.84
1990–1991	133.93
1991–1992	154.23
1992–1993	168.85
1993–1994	183.68[a]

Source: NCC 1993.
[a] In the same year the average metered bill was estimated to be in the region of £203.

for water companies, decreased for many years in real terms and in 1991–1992 were 15 percent of the level expected in 1989 (OFWAT, cited in Ernst 1994, 116–117).[3] The high profits the water companies were earning attracted foreign capital, particularly from France. In recent years, price regulation in the water industry has become more aggressive, and some water companies have run into financial troubles.

7.2.2.2 Electricity

The twelve RECs in England and Wales were privatized in 1990 and the two Scottish companies in 1991. In 1990, the British government abolished the CEGB, the public body responsible for generating power. In its place three companies were set up: National Power, PowerGen, and Nuclear Electric, with the majority of shares in these companies placed on the stock exchange the following year. Transmission of electricity was entrusted to the National Grid Company, owned by the regional electricity companies through a holding company. Each REC operated in a predetermined area, inherited from its ancestor public structure.

The Office of the Electricity Regulator (OFFER), the regulator for the electricity industry in the United Kingdom, controlled both supply and distribution prices. For the whole of the period that interests us, monopoly powers in sales to customers below a certain size, which included domestic users, were guaranteed. After 1990, consumers of electricity had to pay a price broken down into five components: gen-

Table 7.2
Components of consumers' electricity bill (percent)

Type	Low (£415 per year)	Medium (£45,000 per year)	Large (£500,000 per year)
Generation	54	64	68
Distribution	25	19	15
Fossil fuel levy	10	10	10
Transmission	5	6	6
Supply	6	1	1
Total	100	100	100

Source: Thomas 2000.

eration, transmission, distribution, supply, and a subsidy for the nuclear industry (the fossil fuel levy). Table 7.2 shows the breakdown for type of user at 1992–1993 prices.

OFFER applied different formulas to control prices in different periods and for different segments of the electricity industry (excluding power generation, for which there was no price control). Between 1990 and 1993, companies were allowed to increase the supply price to consumers in a franchise regime (mostly domestic users) by the full RPI index. The formula was

$$RPI - X + Y,$$

where X was set to zero and Y was an index of the costs of purchasing electricity (e.g., transmission costs paid to National Grid, distribution costs). Subsequently, X increased to 0.02 for 1993–1997 period and to 0.04 for 1997–2001. Since 1999, there has been full liberalization of the domestic market and since 2002, there has been no cap on the supply price of electricity.

Between 1990 and 1997–1998 the average annual tariff reduction was 2 percent; prices were increased by 7 percent, however, in the year before privatization. As I noted in chapter 5, this allowed the companies to earn big profits.

For electricity distribution, OFFER's price control formula until 1994 was

$$RPI + X,$$

where the term X was fixed (at between 0 and 2.5 percent) for each REC. In fact, OFFER allowed all the companies to increase their bills more than inflation. Subsequently the regulator set tougher targets. Some companies were required to make one-time price cuts (in some cases, of more than 10 percent), and X was set at -0.02 in 1994 and -0.03 in 1995, thus reversing the sign of the control mechanism.

For the control of the transmission price, National Grid had to use a formula:

$RPI - X$,

with X set to 0 initially for 1990–1992; it was then increased to 0.03 in 1993–1997 and 0.04 in 1997–2001. Moreover, OFFER imposed a one-time cut in transmission prices of 20 percent in 1997–1998.

The fossil fuel levy initially was set at 10 percent of producer price, and the proceeds given to Nuclear Electric, whose income was subsidized up to one half of revenues by this transfer. The British government privatized most of the country's nuclear plants in 1996 and the nuclear element of the fossil fuel levy was phased out. The levy decreased to 3.7 percent in 1996, 2.2 percent in 1997, 0.9 percent in 1998.

According to NCC (1993) estimates, a typical family in the United Kingdom consumes 3,300 kilowatt-hours (kWh) of electricity per year. In April 1985, the cost of this amount of electricity was estimated to have been £203.56, and in April 1993 it was estimated at £289.24. The cost thus increased by 42 percent over those eight years, whereas the increase in the RPI over the same period was 48 percent. In 1990 the bill in nominal terms (excluding the value-added tax, but including the quartely standing charge) for 3,300 kWh per year was £258; in 1997 it was again £258, corresponding to a real decrease over the period of around 18 percent (see table 7.3).[4]

We should read these data in relationship to the trends in the determinants of electricity price, especially the costs of raw materials and transmission and distribution costs. Four sources accounted for 90 percent of raw material costs in 1990–1998: coal; combined cycle gas turbines (CCGTs); the independent power producers, that is, those other than National Power and PowerGen (basically the RECs); and nuclear power. (In Scotland hydroelectric power was also of some importance.) Let us examine each of these inputs in detail.

Coal accounted at privatization for 70 percent of power generation in the United Kingdom, because of government protection of domestic mining. At divestiture, generators were obligated to buy coal from British Coal, at a declining rate of procurement year to year, until 1993.

Table 7.3
Electricity bill for a typical U.K. user

Year	Nominal bill (current pounds)	RPI	1990 pounds	1990 = 100
1990	258	130.3	258	100.0
1991	286	135.1	276	107.0
1992	291	139.9	271	105.0
1993	291	141.8	267	103.5
1994	281	145.2	252	97.7
1995	266	149.8	231	89.5
1996	266	153.8	225	87.2
1997	258	159.0	211	81.8

Source: Thomas 2000.

Between 1990 and 1997 the price of coal mined in Britain decreased 30 percent in real terms, and its share in inputs to generation decreased as much as 35 percent. The lower cost of coal was largely appropriated as extra profits by generators until 1993. In 1994–1997, the cost savings from the lower coal prices were shared somewhat with the RECs and marginally with consumers. Until 1993, the cost of coal represented around 22 percent of the unit cost of electricity distributed to domestic consumers; thus ceteris paribus, tariffs would have had to fall by 8 percent in real terms to pass on to consumers the benefit of lower input costs, instead of increasing by 7.8 percent, again in real terms, as actually occurred.

The wide diffusion of CCGTs among power generators initially was a response to government regulations that obliged the country's electricity generators to reduce emissions of acid gases after 1990. CCGT plants in 2000 supplied 15 percent of the country's generation capacity, and an additional 15 percent is supplied by the RECs. Although the price of gas fell 40 percent, in real terms, between 1990 and 1997, consumers benefited little from the decrease; in fact, the cost of old contracts at higher prices was passed on to consumers.

Nuclear plants at divestiture increased their output by 50 percent, and their market share increased from 17 to 25 percent. Some benefit accrued to consumers through the phasing out of the fossil fuel levy.

According to George Yarrow, a leading British expert in the field, "electricity prices for domestic consumers were, by 1991, higher than would have been expected on the basis of pre-privatisation trends" (quoted in NCC 1993, 36). The retail price of electricity grew at a rate

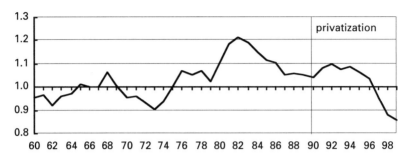

Figure 7.8
Electricity: Retail prices, relative to RPI (index 1975 = 1).
Source: Author's elaboration on NEDO 1976 and ONS.

that was generally below inflation between 1980 and privatization (see figure 7.8). The year before flotation on the stock exchange of the shares of the electricity companies, there were sizable increases in electricity tariffs, higher than inflation, which were hardly motivated by cost dynamics. In the opinion of various observers the permitted price increase in 1989–1990 in particular was a dowry that made the shares of the firms more attractive to potential purchasers at privatization. As of 1993, the system of price control for electricity in the United Kingdom was more incisive.

To explain the impact of electricity industry reform on consumers, three facts are particularly salient. First, trends in electricity output in the United Kingdom since privatization show a decrease in the rate of growth. Second, in spite of stable production and demand, electricity prices for residential consumers in the United Kingdom increased between 1990 and 1995. This increase was not justified by the price trends for oil, gas, or coal over the same period (see figures 7.9 and 7.10 for real price trends for gas and coal).[5] Third, industrial users of electricity in the United Kingdom enjoyed a price reduction of around 25 percent between 1985 and 1995. The trend toward decreasing electricity prices for industrial users is evident both before and after privatization and is similar in magnitude to the trend observed in France, whereas in Italy, electricity prices for the industrial sector decreased even more than in Britain and France.

One possible explanation for the inverse correlation between costs and prices for domestic consumers of electricity is that generators and distributors differentiated the benefits of cost decreases across customers. They offered discounts in the more competitive market for large

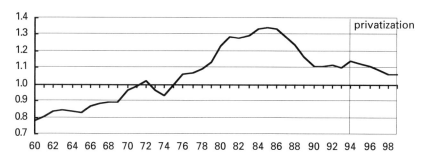

Figure 7.9
Coal: Retail prices, relative to RPI (index 1975 = 1).
Source: Author's elaboration on NEDO 1976 and ONS.

customers (above one megawatt) and financed this policy by charging more to the more inelastic and captive residential market (Ernst 1994). According to Thomas (2000):

In the light of dramatic reductions in generation and fuel costs, a reduction in the prices paid by consumers for generation of about 2 percent and the removal of the nuclear subsidy looks a poor return. There have been dramatic falls in gas and coal prices, massive improvements in nuclear performance and a dynamic new technology, the CCGT, was unexpectedly available. In addition, there have been steep reductions in employment in the generation companies, with National Power and PowerGen employing only about 25 percent as many as staff as in 1990.... If we look at the profits of the two large fossil fuel generating companies, it becomes much clearer where some of the rent from improved labour productivity and lower fossil fuel price has gone. (17–18)

Summing up: Privatized utilities in the British electricity industry did not pass on to consumers the cost savings they realized after privatization, largely as a result of exogenous shocks. Although National Power's revenues decreased between 1990 and 1997, from £3,948 million to £2,658 million, its profit/turnover ratio increased from 5.9 to 17 percent over the same period. PowerGen's turnover decreased from £2,412 million (in 1990) to £2,105 million (in 1996), its profit/turnover ratio increased from 4.8 to 21.4 percent.[6]

There has also been noticeable regional variability in electricity prices since privatization (in net contrast to the uniformity of tariffs in continental European countries such as France and Italy, where supply is predominantly in a regime of national public monopoly). Before privatization, in 1985, the average (unweighted) tariff for a typical domestic user of the 12 RECs and the two Scottish companies was 6.17 pence per kWh. The minimum tariff was 5.59 (Scotland), and the maximum was 6.47 (South Wales). Three years after privatization, in 1993, the average tariff was 8.76 pence per kWh, with a minimum of 8.35 (Scottish Power) and a maximum of 9.58 pence (South Western). These data could underestimate the differences for the single users.

7.2.2.3 Gas

The Gas Act (1986) established the Office of the Gas Regulator (OFGAS) and gave a consultative role to the Gas Consumer Council (established in 1972). The latter was independent of the former, a unique case in the 1980s of a separate institution's being set up to protect the interests of consumers. At the end of the same year, British Gas was privatized, with the quasi monopoly in production, and the integral monopoly in transmission and local distribution to about eighteen million domestic consumers maintained intact.[7] At the time of privatization, British Gas was required to open to competition the market for the larger consumers (those that used over 25,000 therms per year). This threshold was subsequently reduced to 2,500 therms in 1992, allowing an additional 200,000 medium-sized consumers to choose their gas supplier. Further liberalization of the gas market came at the end of the period under study (its effects exceed the time span of this study, so I shall limit myself to a few references later).

The sector regulator, OFGAS, managed a system of price caps on average revenue per term based originally on the formula

$$RPI - X + CPT,$$

where CPT was a "cost-pass-through" mechanism, with $X = 0.02$. In 1992 the following formula was adopted:

$$RPI - X + (GPI - Z) + E + K,$$

where

- X was 0.05 (reduced to 0.04 in 1994)
- GPI is an index of the cost of procurement of gas
- Z was fixed at a cumulative level of 0.01 per year
- E was defined as the cost of energy savings
- K is a factor of correction

The X value was fixed at 0.02 in 1987–1992, 0.05 in 1992–1994, and 0.04 in 1994–1997.

This formula is noticeably more complex than the one used to regulate prices in other privatized sectors. In addition to the X factor, it took into account a second control (an incentive) and a Z factor that deducts 1 percent from the increase in the cost of procurement. Though X and Z are factors that limit British Gas's ability to transfer cost to consumers, the E coefficient allows it to recuperate the cost of energy-saving projects, and the K factor allows it to correct mistakes in forecasting costs. There was also a price cap on transportation charges, again of the form $RPI - X$, with $X = 0.05$ in 1994–1997, then reduced to 0.02 thereafter.

Periodic crises and controversies shake the regulatory system for the gas industry. Back in 1988, the Office of Free Trade (OFT) referred British Gas to the Monopoly and Mergers Commission (MMC) in regard to its monopolist power in the nonregulated market, and as a consequence, the British Gas license was later modified. In 1992, OFGAS referred British Gas to the MMC in regard to the running of the branch of the company dealing with transmission (TransCo). This led in 1993 to the MMC's most famous inquiry, which concluded unfavorably for British Gas (see MMC 1997).[8] Since 1996, even domestic consumers have been able to choose their gas suppliers, and the system is totally liberalized. In 1997, British Gas broke up into different regional companies, and there was broad liberalization. In the space of a year, 20 percent of consumers changed their gas suppliers.

In 1999, OFGAS and OFFER merged to create the Office of Gas and Electricity Markets (OFGEM). Here I concentrate exclusively on the effects of the British regulatory system for the gas industry on retail prices before the liberalization of the domestic market, which were mostly felt beyond the period that we are studying (cf. section 7.4).

Between 1985 and 1993 gas tariffs in Britain increased by 17 percent, well below the rate of inflation. In real terms, the resulting reduction in spending for the typical consumer was 24–27 percent. For the industrial user the drop in real prices was about 50 percent (Stern 1997).

If we look in detail, however, at data on prices and costs, the picture that emerges is less favorable to users. It is interesting to focus on the first five years after privatization, before the industry regulators changed their attitude toward the incumbent. Between 1987 (divestiture year) and 1991, BG's nominal prices for domestic consumers rose by 19.5 percent, whereas the RPI rose 31.6 percent. This means that prices decreased in real terms over the period, when we use the RPI as deflator. In the same years, however, the average price of natural gas (including indirect tax) purchased by BG increased by just 5 percent. Because gas costs represent around 40 percent of BG's total costs, OFGAS calculated that in retrospect consumers paid 3 percent more for gas than what would have been possible if BG had passed on to consumers the benefit of lower costs. Therefore, when we use an index of input prices rather than the RPI as deflator, gas prices actually increased, rather than decreased, in real terms over the period.

Moreover, prices differed widely among various type of users. Between 1988 and 1991, real prices (RPI deflator) to domestic users decreased just 3 percent; those for small industrial users (less than 50,000 therms per year) decreased 13 percent; and those for other industrial users decreased 31 percent. Because the good supplied is the same, and differences in costs by type of users cannot be so marked as to justify such a wide variance in prices, this is plain price discrimination that amounts to expropriating part of the consumer surplus under monopoly conditions.

In 1991, OFGAS began to recognize what was happening and imposed more binding constraints on gas prices. At the end of the 1990s, BG's monopoly on gas was eliminated—not less than ten years after divestiture, however. During this long period between divestiture and the loss of monopoly status, the benefits for consumers were modest when prices are compared with costs and not different from the long-run trend of RPI-deflated real price (shown in figure 7.10 for the period since 1960).

7.2.2.4 Telecommunications

I discuss in detail British Telecom, which was divested in 1984, as a case history in chapter 9. Here I briefly mention salient aspects about

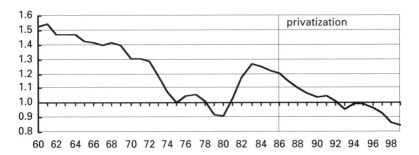

Figure 7.10
Gas: Retail prices, relative to RPI (index 1975 = 1).
Source: Author's elaboration on NEDO 1976 and ONS.

the formation of prices for roughly twenty million domestic users of telephone service. The market regime for much of the period studied was one of almost integral monopoly, with the exception of limited fields of action initially granted to a second operator, Mercury, and subsequently to a number of local operators.

OFTEL, the sector regulator, controlled prices for telephone service using a variety of formulas. Those in force between 1993 and 1997 were as follows:

• $RPI - X$, for the so-called basket of services (that is, a list of activities subject to control in an aggregated form), with X fixed at 7.5 percent for the period; originally it had been 3 percent, subsequently 4.5 percent (1989–1991), and then 6.25 percent (1991–1993)

• RPI, for single items in the basket, except for the rental of exchange lines

• $RPI + X$, for exchange line rentals, with $X = 0.02$

• RPI, for connection tariffs.

Note that this regulatory mechanism allows prices of single services included in the basket to be modified freely, as long as price changes for each service are within the limits of the RPI change for each and the price cap $RPI - X$ for the basket as a whole.

The contents of the basket changed over time, with the inclusion of new items, such as tariffs for international calls and for local and national calls, line rentals, and information services for telephone numbers. It is difficult to study the tariffs actually paid by consumers over time because of the variety of contracts available, the changes over time in the pricing methods used (from a unit system to time), and the difficulty in obtaining disaggregated data for each category of user. Rebalancing of the tariffs in this period, compared to the period before privatization, was generally unfavorable to domestic users and to the users of public telephones.[9]

In the period 1985–1993 a typical domestic user in the United Kingdom would have seen his telephone bill rise by 24 percent. On the other hand, a business customer, without considering international calls and on the hypothetical basis of a reverse symmetrical structure compared to the domestic user (predominance of national rather than local calls), would have seen a reduction of 20 percent (according to NCC 1993).

Figure 7.11 shows strong decrease in real prices for telephone service after divestiture. This trend started before divestiture, however,

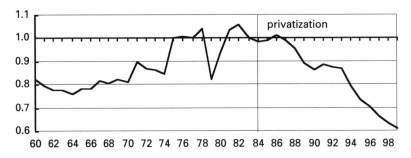

Figure 7.11
Telephone: Retail prices, relative to RPI (index 1975 = 1).
Source: Author's elaboration on NEDO 1976 and ONS.

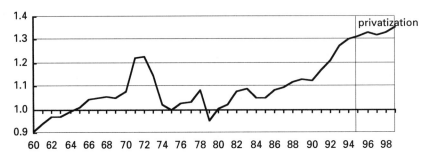

Figure 7.12
Railways: Retail prices, relative to RPI (index 1975 = 1).
Source: Author's elaboration on NEDO 1976 and ONS.

and the decrease in real prices was less than the decrease in technical costs.

7.2.2.5 Transport Services

In this section, I briefly examine some privatized transport services: railways, buses, airports, and airlines. The most important divestiture in the transport sector was obviously that of the railways, which occurred too recently for the trend in prices to be analyzed with any validity (see, however, figure 7.12, showing long-term increases in rail transport prices before and after divestiture).[10]

British Rail is beyond doubt also the most controversial of all the privatizations that have taken place in Britain over the last quarter century. According to the *Economist* (1999): "The privatisation of British Rail has proved a disastrous failure ... a catalogue of political cynicism, managerial incompetence, and financial opportunism. It has cost taxpayers billion of pounds and bought rail travelers countless hours of delay" (67).

Here I simply note a few facts about the privatization. The British government unbundled British Rail, a state-owned monopoly, into over a hundred companies, through an array of management buyouts, direct sales, tenders, and one flotation: that of Railtrack in 1996. Three leasing companies (rolling stock companies, or ROSCOs) acquired the rolling stock by tender. Six companies acquired the freight business. For passengers service there was franchising to twenty-five train operating companies (TOCs). Separate companies inherited maintenance and other ancillary activities. There were then hundreds of subcontractors and sub-subcontractors.

The Office of the Rail Regulator (ORR), the Railtrack regulator, concerned itself with controlling access prices for tracks, stations, and depots. The X element in the $RPI - X$ formula that ORR used was 0.08 in 1995–1996; it was subsequently reduced to 0.02 in 1997–2001.

ORR's monitoring effort went well beyond that of other regulators. It involved a very detailed assessment of investment plans, efficiency targets and a definition of output (see, e.g., ORR 1999b). This painstaking oversight did not prevent wide criticism of the operations of the company and eventually its financial meltdown. Currently, Railtrack operates under the status of quasi renationalization.

The regulator in charge of the TOCs was the Office of Passenger Rail Franchising (OPRAF). OPRAF focused its attention on franchises for lines for passenger transport and imposed controls on the prices of some types of tickets ("savers," weekly, and some commuter fares for metropolitan areas). The X element in OPRAF's $RPI - X$ formula was set at zero in 1996–1998, then at 0.01 in 1999–2001. For some commuter fares, however, X varied between $+0.02$ and -0.02 according to improvements in the quality of service.

The Strategic Rail Authority inherited OPRAF's duties in 1999.[11] It plans to replace the existing franchises for lines with longer-term contracts and service targets. This restructuring of the regulatory framework is the response of the U.K.'s New Labour government to wide criticism of the privatized railways (despite, or perhaps because of, increases in the number of trains, passenger miles, and other output indicators since privatization). The level of service provided by the industry is, however, now carefully monitored by the regulator, which also regularly prints a bulletin, *Rail Complaints* (in the year 1998–1999 alone there were 1,072,958 such complaints).[12]

The privatization of local bus services in Britain is also interesting. In the 1970s, local public monopolists provided these bus services, under the concession of exclusive lines by the traffic commissioners. There were two large national public bus companies and seventy local subsidiaries, as well as companies owned by local public authorities. The subsidies provided to these companies were often in the region of 20 percent of costs, but in the larger urban areas they could be as much as 50 percent. The situation changed radically with the Transport Act (1985), which deregulated the bus lines (and abolished concessions of exclusivity). For a particular company to gain or retain the right to operate a loss-making line, the subsidy for the line had to be based on bids following call for tenders.

Between 1986 and 1991 there was a total divestiture of bus transportation firms dependent on the central government. For the metropolitan area of London, a special system was established that created a central company with planning responsibilities and a number of public subsidiaries operating in competition with private firms for three-year concessions for lines.

Contrary to expectations, this system did not create a highly competitive market, except for in the case of lines with the highest density of traffic. Nevertheless, the surviving public firms and incumbent privatized firms found themselves exposed to a dose of competition. The main consequences of deregulation and privatization (which are difficult to separate in this case) are the following (Savage 1993):

• Costs fell sharply, basically because of the collapse of collective bargaining. Between 1986 and 1989 wages in Britain's bus industry declined by 15 percent compared to other sectors, whereas the number of vehicle kilometers per worker increased by 26 percent (but only by 4 percent per vehicle). Some authors refer to a total reduction in the cost per vehicle kilometer of 20 percent.

• Subsidies per vehicle kilometer decreased by about 20 percent in the large cities (excluding London) and by 10 percent elsewhere.

• Tariffs increased by an average of 25 percent in the metropolitan areas in the three-year period following the reform (in extreme cases of high subsidies, e.g., in Sheffield and Liverpool, by as much as 200 percent). Elsewhere the increase in real terms was 2 percent (see figure 7.13).

• The number of vehicles per kilometer increased, but with some negative effects of traffic congestion in some cities and with a drop in the

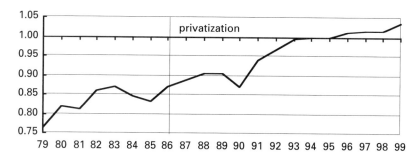

Figure 7.13
Buses: Retail prices, relative to RPI (index 1995 = 1).
Source: Author's elaboration on NEDO 1976 and ONS (various years).

occupancy rate of vehicles (even though smaller buses were often introduced).

• The total drop in demand for bus service exceeded what could be expected as a result of the increase in tariffs, probably because of the confusion created by frequent changes in timetables and routes, lack of information, and so on.

White (1990) examines transfers in income from bus system workers to bus passengers (through lower wages), then from passengers to tax-payers (through lower subsidies). Taking into account the decrease in bus traffic attributable to the loss of an integrated bus network, he finds an aggregated social benefit of £10 million in metropolitan areas, but a net loss of £63 million in other areas. Even considering a shadow price greater than one (Savage 1993) for the taxes saved thanks to reduced subsidies, the impact of privatization on users appears to be negative because of the loss of organization in bus services. The welfare impact seems to be better for London. Here, as noted previously, a scheme à la Demsetz preserved the integrity of the system, including a competitive role for public firms, with considerable improvements in costs and an increase in service and the rate of occupancy of vehicles.

I mention, finally, the privatization of the British Airports Authority (BAA). The regulator for the BAA is the Civil Aviation Authority, which looked particularly at airport charges at airports in southeast England, with an $RPI - X$ formula and frequent changes in X values:

1987–1992 $X = 0.01$
1992–1993 $X = 0.08$

1994 $X = 0.04$

1995–1996 $X = 0.01$

1997–2002 $X = 0.03$ for Heathrow and Gatwick Airports

              $X = -0.01$ for Stanstead Airport

The regulated price index was the average revenue per passenger. Retail and parking revenues at the airports were unregulated.

According to Jones and Jones (1993) the average revenue per passenger in the four airports under the BAA fell significantly in real terms during the early 1980s, but there was a small increase after privatization. A tightened regulatory regime then stopped the trend of increasing prices.

The government announced the intention to privatize British Airways as early as 1979, and in 1981–1983 new top executives were appointed, and the staff was reduced by 30 percent.[13] In the case of BA, the government operated to make competition difficult and to protect the privatized firm, contrary to the concerns of the Civil Aviation Authority (which wanted a "second force" in the sector). The MMC and the European Commission allowed a merger with British Caledonian whereby the dominant position of BA in the domestic market increased in comparison to its position during the period of public ownership. International competition, however, had an impact in lowering prices.

7.2.3 Distributive Impact

The price trends observed in the various sectors following privatization in some cases had a considerable distributive impact. Hancock and Waddams Price (1998) study three sectors (gas, electricity, and telecommunications) with Family Expenditure Survey (FES) data. They measure the change in welfare resulting from privatization simply as the product of estimated consumption at the time of the FES and the difference between prices at privatization and prices in 1996. The authors find that as a result of privatization the average consumers gained £240 per year (at 1996 prices), equal to less than 3 percent of income, or 0.32 percent of income (net of housing costs) for telephony, 1.61 percent for gas, and 0.66 percent for electricity. The relative positions among social groups in terms of expenditure and welfare distribution changed, however, and some consumers were net losers from privatization. On average pensioners suffered a net welfare loss of 25 percent compared to preprivatization levels. In general, the two lowest income quintiles found themselves in a worse relative position after privatization in terms of the gap between them and the top income quintiles. Again in relative terms, the greatest gainers from privatization were consumers in the top income quintile (+20 percent above par). Hancock and Waddams Price also analyzed the effects of tariff rebalancing for individual services and types of users and found evidence of regressive redistribution effects of privatization.

The distributive impact for single sectors is worth examining. I start with the water industry, which Waddams Price and Hancock do not study, then turn to the electric, gas, and telephone industries.

Because of the new tariff regime for water after privatization, the number of families who were not able to pay for water service increased. In 1990–1991, there were 7,673 disconnections of water service in the United Kingdom; in 1991–1992, there were 21,286; the following year there were 18,636. According to NCC (1993), 55,000 U.K. citizens per year came to the National Association of Citizens Advice Bureaux for assistance with their debts to companies supplying water. This problem of unpaid bills in arrears came about partly because of the gap created between the amount charged by the water companies and a new system of income support instituted in 1988. Previously families dependent on state assistance benefited from a mechanism that automatically paid water bills. Beginning in 1988, families had to pay their water bills using the subsidy provided, which calculated a theoretical charge for water of £1.65 per week, compared with the water companies' effective charge of £2 per week. OFWAT observed the emergence of a problem of "water poverty": "Bills are becoming substantial in relation to the income of some households. About 25 percent of households have income of less than half the average and water and sewerage bill already represent 2 percent or more of household income for them. Customer debt is rising and there has been a significant increase in the rate of disconnections for non-payment of bills" (quoted in NCC 1993, 70).

One aspect of privatization of the water industry that affected domestic consumers significantly was a system of different standing charges for measured and unmeasured water service. Water bills in the United Kingdom include a fixed charge that is a substantial part of the bill, and this fixed charge increased more for unmetered households after privatization than for metered ones, which accounted for just 3 percent of total households with water service in England and Wales in

1993. The cost per meter was around £200, and metered consumers in the early 1990s paid a bill 21 percent higher than unmetered ones for the same amount of consumption.

A study commissioned by OFWAT (Atkins 1992) showed that because of the diffusion of metering (i.e., because of the increasing number of households with a meter installed by the utilities in their homes), 18 percent of the families interviewed for the study (and 62 percent of those with disabilities and requiring specific health assistance) used an amount of water inferior to their needs. Eight percent of the families had problems involving debts to the water companies. (This would correspond to 1.5 million families in England and Wales.) Of these "more than one third [that is, roughly 500,000 families] said their hygiene had been affected, largely through flushing the toilet less often and taking fewer baths" (NCC 1993, 71). More than 50 percent of the people dependent on public assistance (roughly five million people) had even reduced their household laundry schedules in response to the increase in water bills.[14]

According to OFWAT data (quoted in Boyfield 1997), the weekly average cost of water and sewerage services to unmeasured domestic customers in England and Wales in 1982 was £1.29, and it had increased to £4.19 in 1996–1997. Whereas in 1989, 1 percent of families were in arrears on their water bills, in 1994 this figure had risen to 9 percent.

The water companies responded to the problem by introducing systems of advance payment, for example, cards to be used with computerized water meters. This solution may reduce the incidence of arrears, but it definitely aggravates the problem of water poverty, as it results in demands for advance payment from the more needy segments of the population.[15]

There is also evidence of the emergence of "fuel poverty" in the United Kingdom after privatization. Fuel poverty refers to the impossibility of obtaining adequate domestic heating and lighting (opportunely defined) without spending a disproportionate share of income, a phenomenon probably unknown to in other EU countries to the extent it is found in Britain. Conventionally the threshold amount of income that can be affordably devoted to energy expenditure is 10 percent. According to this definition, in 1996 in England alone five million households (8.5 percent of families in the United Kingdom) were in a state of fuel poverty. These five million households have energy requirements that would cost them between 10 and 20 percent of their incomes if their requirements were fulfilled; another 5 percent are in conditions of extreme fuel poverty, with an energy requirement of between 20 and 30 percent of their incomes. Obviously, many families in this situation must reduce their consumption to below the minimum necessary to meet sanitary and functional standards.

Between 1970 and 1997–1998, expenditure for energy as a percentage of total income generally decreased for all income quartiles in the United Kingdom, but these figures need to be looked at carefully. In the twenty years before privatization, despite the oil crises, all four quartiles of income showed a reduction in expenditures for energy as a percentage of total income (and as a ratio to expenditures for food). Between 1990 and 1996–1997 expenditures for energy remained constant or increased for the three highest quartiles, but for the lowest quartile they decreased. This does not necessarily mean that fuel poverty decreased: It could simply mean that people on lower incomes cut their energy consumption. Only the following year, with the liberalization of the domestic market, was there an evidence of a sag in prices (see DTI 1999).

Privatization was not solely responsible for fuel poverty: It was part of the more general trend of increased social hardship in the country (see chapters 1 and 3). Privatization exacerbated the problem, however, with tariffs discriminating between users who paid by direct debit (on higher incomes) and those who paid in advance. The privatized energy companies in the United Kingdom operate as commercial entities and have no specific social responsibilities except those laid down in their respective licenses. Industry regulators see themselves as organisms for promoting efficiency in production and in consumption and not as managers of welfare policies. The sector ministries, in turn, tend not to consider themselves responsible for problems of assistance to the poor. In this game of refusing to accept social responsibility, the fuel poverty phenomenon assumed huge proportions, until recently, when the government increased cash transfers to some social groups (e.g., a winter fuel bonus).

Among the fuel poor in Britain, there are 2.5 million households in which methods of prepayment for fuel (cards or tokens) have been introduced. According to some estimates, winter temperatures in almost two million homes in England are below the World Health Organization minimum of eighteen degrees centigrade (and in fact, a temperature two to three degrees higher is necessary for older people and children). If a household's electric meter is operated by coins, tokens, or prepaid cards, the price for the service can be 70 percent higher than that for those who pay by debit.

In the year following privatization there were 48,000 disconnections for nonpayment of the electric bill (decreasing to 18,000 in 1992); in the same year there were 19,000 disconnections for nonpayment of the gas bill (16,000 the following year). The decrease in the number of disconnections after the first wave following divestiture has been linked to the introduction of systems of prepayment: 2.3 million in 1992 for electricity, 780,000 for gas.

Such a widespread use of prepayment meters disguises the problem of disconnection. Service to households with prepayment meters is not actually interrupted, per se, but if the users are not in a position to pay, they are forced into periodic self-disconnection. According to a study by the Rowntree Foundation (quoted in NCC 1993), in Bristol and Birmingham, the introduction of prepayment meters had a dramatic effect in reducing fuel consumption in the households interviewed. This was achieved for instance by cutting the number of cooked meals and minimizing the use of hot water.

A similar problem in the case of water was compounded by an increase in tariffs, but in the case of gas, in which tariffs dropped, and electricity, in which the increase was moderate, the problem nevertheless manifested itself. Prior to privatization, the tariff policy for these industries had offered a cross-subsidy to the poorest customers.[16] Some companies continued for a time to voluntarily offer some coverage of service provision to the most needy users, but this approach was inadequate.

According to Waddams Price (2002), metering per se should not carry the blame for the regressive impact of tariff changes following privatization. There is evidence that self-disconnection affects only one-quarter of consumers on the prepayment method, and most of them only once, because they have forgotten to charge the meter. Those who disconnect several times in a year, however, are more likely to be experiencing true social hardship. Those who disconnect more than six times per year constitute less than 1 percent of the consumer base. Nevertheless, I would suggest considering three disconnections per year as a threshold to distinguish between those who simply forget to pay and those who cannot pay. Then the total number of users who experience service disconnection because of social hardship could be more than one million users. In principle a feasible remedy would have been was a compensatory subsidy from public assistance, with a spe-

Table 7.4
Changes in electricity prices, 1989–1991, by type of user

Domestic	+26%
Small business	+23%
Medium industrial	+1%
Moderately large	−6%
Extra large	+18%
RPI	+18%

Source: Ernst 1994.

cial fund or office to manage the problem, but this did not happen until recently.

Moreover, in the early years following privatization, there was also evidence of marked differences in price increases among different types of consumers (see table 7.4). The system moved toward an elaborate policy of regressive price discrimination, as opposed to the progressive implicit discrimination concealed by uniform tariffs under public ownership.

Although telephone service is not apparently in the same league as water or energy as a necessary good, it is important for some of the weaker sections of the population, especially the disabled and the aged. For the poor, the telephone means less social exclusion through more opportunities of communication.

According to OFTEL data for 1994, domestic user telephone coverage in the United Kingdom was 90 percent, which means that two million families at the time were without a telephone. Coverage rose to 96 percent for those who owned their homes and was 80 percent for those in rented homes. It was 78 percent for households whose head was unemployed. It was 65 percent for single parents with one or more children, and it fell to 60 percent for people on an income of less than £50 per week.

Two-thirds of those who lacked a telephone did not have one because of the bill,[17] especially because of the increase after privatization in the charge for the first connection in a household and in the deposit required. The principal concern that lack of a telephone raised for these people, especially for old people or the disabled, was the inability to make emergency calls if the need arose.

The problem was not solved by schemes such as "Support-Line," operated by BT to reduce costs for users with minimal traffic. These schemes in fact helped only those who already had a telephone.

Moreover, the tariffs on public telephones had risen most among all those for telephone services.

The concentration of people with no in-home telephone connection (or very low consumption levels of telephone services) is obviously highest in the lowest income quintile. Paradoxically, they have suffered the impact of tariff rebalancing less than those in the second-lowest quintile, mostly pensioners (Waddams Price 2002).

7.2.4 Consumer Information and Perceptions

Prices are signals firms send to consumers. When price elasticity is low, probably because goods have no economic substitutes and they are necessities, it is quite interesting to see the consumers' perception of prices they have to pay.

The results of a mid-1990s MORI survey (approximately 2,000 interviewees in a representative sample) of consumers' assessment of prices for services such as water, electricity, gas and telephone[18] seemed to indicate a progressive worsening in perceptions of the fairness of those prices. Of consumers surveyed, 25 percent of consumers felt that water prices were totally unreasonable, and a similar proportion felt the same way about telephone tariffs.

In July 1994 a MORI survey the question "Have the goals of privatization been achieved?" obtained an affirmative response from 39 percent of respondents for British Steel and just 10 percent for water (cited in Boyfield 1997). In November 1995 another MORI study reached the following conclusions: For BT, only 20 percent of interviewees felt that privatization had improved the service (more than ten years after divestiture). This was the *highest* percentage among all utilities; the percentage expressing the perception of an improvement was lower for all of the others.

In chapter 1, I mentioned a 1995 editorial in *The Economist* on this subject. The editorial stated that all surveys show privatization to have a surprisingly low popularity rating among the British public. The interpretation of this respected British magazine was that consumers' perceptions were mistaken, based on scanty information and on an incurable skepticism on the part of the majority of the population toward the free market and capitalism. This interpretation appears to be unconvincing when the electoral orientation of Britain in the 1980s and most of the 1990s is considered.

To evaluate the results of the opinion polls to which *The Economist* was referring, we must remember that British consumers were the target of enormous amounts of communication from privatizing companies, usually during the period of stock flotation, but also subsequently. For example, at the time of BT's privatization, 42.5 million units of advertising material were distributed, including video clips (see Newman 1986). This was one of the most massive company communication campaigns ever carried out in Europe. Its aim in fact was not merely to induce savers to purchase shares in the privatizing companies: There was little need for that, given the level of underpricing, the size of the minimum lot, and the availability of an installment purchase plan. It was in fact advertising not so much of stock availability, but of the government's policy of large-scale privatization. These advertising campaigns, although they had investors as their primary targets, probably raised consumers' expectations that privatization would have been able to deliver greater efficiency, improved service, and lower prices than the former nationalized industries.

Newman (1986) refers to a series of MORI studies ("Attitude to Nationalisation Trends" for the period 1973–1983, before the campaign for BT). Those who favored "more nationalization" totaled about 30 percent in 1973–1974; this total fell to 25 percent in 1975 and remained stable in the region of 20 percent between 1976 and 1983, during the years of gestation of the Thatcher privatization policy. On the other hand those who favored "denationalization" amounted to 27 percent in 1973 and 24 percent in 1974, and the total leapt to 35 percent the following year, reaching 39–40 percent in 1979–1983.

There is therefore consistency between electoral trends and attitude toward the policy of denationalization. Thus, British consumers' dissatisfaction with prices charged by the privatized utilities does not seem a widespread anticapitalist feeling, as suggested by *The Economist*. More likely, many consumers perceived that there was something wrong with the prices they paid, or that those prices did not live up to expectations.

The phenomenon of dissatisfaction with the outcome of British privatization appears to be persistent over time. To the question "There is a talk at the moment of privatizing the London Underground. Do you think that the London Underground should be privatized or not?" on a Gallup poll in March 1997, 20 percent of respondents replied that it should, 9 percent indicated they did not know or did not care, and an overwhelming majority, 71 percent, said it should not.[19] These data worried some commentators. According to Vass (1997), the lack of public confidence in the private provision of essential public services because of a perceived abuse of monopoly power puts in doubt the continuity and stability of the regulatory system.

The available evidence confirms that most U.K. consumers do not think they are paying fair prices to the privatized utilities, and there has been widespread dissatisfaction with the level of service provided. It is not plausible simply to dismiss this evidence and consider consumers to be irrational.[20]

7.2.5 Quality

The subject of changes in the output quality of privatized British utilities is a very complex one. Systematic evidence is scant (Spence 1975; for a review of the evidence, see NERA 1996).

The mechanism adopted for regulating the privatized industries was decisive in respect to the quality levels achieved, and there is some consensus that it generally contributed to higher quality through definitions of standards. Cave (1993) maintain, however, that although the required-rate-of-return approach probably increases quality because it is biased toward capital intensity, the price cap method may reduce it. Pegging price increases to an $RPI - X$ formula could generate an incentive for the regulated utility to offer lower quality, because it appropriates quality-related cost savings. This probably happened in the earlier privatizations, and then industry regulators intervened to preclude it.

Regulators may find it difficult to define standards for multiattribute goods. Empirical methods based on willingness to pay (WTP) for quality, as revealed during interviews with consumers, may largely underestimate the subjective value of goods. Furthermore, how does one add up the individual contingent evaluations obtained in such methods? In the method of the simple algebraic sum, the WTP for those in higher income brackets counts for more than that among those in lower income brackets, and this can distort judgments about what level of quality of a particular good or service is considered by consumers to be desirable.

Finally, under a monopoly regime, consumers have poor information on quality, because they have no shopping options. Saunders and Harris (1994) found considerable suspicion on the part of consumers about the quality of water after water industry privatization, but also very little information that was verifiable by the users.

In the 1990s the solution to British consumers' lack of adequate information about public services was to define verifiable standards of service and to ask the regulator, and other bodies, to monitor quality (Rovizzi and Thompson 1992).[21] The link between quality regulation and privatization per se, however, is not very strong.

In fact, as NERA (1996) points out, the regulatory frameworks put in place to govern the earliest of the privatizations, those of BT, BAA and BG, did not consider quality or service issues. In 1987, following criticism by the NCC about the declining quality of BT services, the sector regulator, OFTEL, launched an investigation and required BT to publish quality-of-service information, to introduce standards of customer service, and to compensate consumers for performance that did not meet those standards. The subsequent Water Act (1989), Electricity Act (1988), and Railways Act (1993) established quality performance as a requirement for the license granted to privatized utilities.

Quality regulation may also have counterintuitive implications, however. Glaister (1996) discusses water industry regulation and observes that it asks consumers to contribute to the financing of infrastructure investments in the sector, partly as a result of legislation concerning environmental quality. The weakness in the British regulatory mechanism is that the regulator for the water industry, OFWAT, unlike government authorities, lack democratic legitimization. Fundamental market failures (externalities, public goods, increasing scale returns) are a permanent feature of the industry. In this framework, there is no market discipline in fixing prices, investments, and quality, but there is an administrative discipline that is controlled by OFWAT and other public institutions (e.g., the European Commission). The consumer participates in the mechanism through the tariffs he pays. Regulation offers companies an incentive to expand capital (in a modified form of Averch-Johnson effect), and paradoxically, the request from environmental movements and the requirement through legislation to raise the standard of environmental quality in the industry offers profit opportunities. For example, the desire to insure the population in general against the risk of drought prompts an increase in fixed investments. Glaister shows, however, that if one introduces distributive weights into the evaluation of the costs and benefits of the investments, the effects are counterintuitive. Users of greater amounts of water are often the richest ones, and at the same time, those who contribute the least to the cost of service in proportion to their income. The result may be an excessive virtual demand for quality, with adverse distribution impact.[22]

I conclude that the quality of the services provided by U.K. privatized utilities improved in the late 1980s and 1990s, but more because of the change of attitude of policymakers toward consumers than because of the change of ownership. Quality increased in several nonprivatized public services as well (including the now financially troubled Post Office). Obviously, the shift in market structures toward an increase of competition focused companies' attention on their customers, but most of the actual improvements in the level of service were in fact consequences of customer dissatisfaction and the reaction of the regulator.

7.2.6   Consumer Protection after the Conservative Era

At the end of the 1990s, the subject of consumer protection came back into fashion under Britain's New Labour government, with the widespread perception that privatization and regulation in the United Kingdom had not had the desired effects in various sectors.[23] The issue of consumer protection has a long history in the United Kingdom. The National Consumer Council was established in 1975 as a government-funded independent advisory body. The NCC opposed some privatizations in the 1980s but in general focused more on regulatory issues than on ownership. I have cited the NCC's 1993 report *Paying the Price*, which revealed that in three sectors out of the four studied (water, telecommunications, and electricity, with gas being the exception) the representative consumer paid more after privatization than before for the services offered. The report was part of an ample campaign to influence regulators and probably contributed to changing their lax attitude toward the utilities. This campaign also raised the issue of the most appropriate way to give a voice to consumers in the regulatory framework of utilities. Consumer representation under the nationalized industries framework was offered by the National Consumer Council and by some sector bodies established by the government in the 1970s. These consultative bodies were financed by the Treasury, but formally independent of the government. The current pattern of consumer representation in the context of regulation of privatized industries is still fragmented and still evolving.

OFTEL has regional advisory committees on consumer issues, plus specialist committees on issues involving disabled people and small business. There are also 169 local telecommunication advisory committees, funded directly by the government. The New Labour government proposed the establishment of a new Communications Consumer Council outside the OFTEL structure (with OFTEL itself to be reformed). This proposal, however, was not included in the Utility Bill of 2000.

The Gas Consumer Council was set up in 1972, financed by a levy on the industry, and in later years, it remained independent of both the government and the sector regulator, OFGAS. It probably played an important role in pushing OFGAS to take a hard line with British Gas regarding the price cap.

The Utility Bill confirms the independent role of the Gas Consumer Council. In the water sector, there are ten regional customer services committees, one for each of the former authorities, and they handle complaints. OFWAT appoints their chairpersons (for a detailed discussion, see Ogden and Anderson 1995). A proposal by OFWAT to separate the committees from the regulator's office was not included in the Utility Bill. A similar existing arrangement for electricity (twelve consumer committees in England and Wales, plus two in Scotland, whose chairpersons are appointed by OFFER) has changed with the passage of the Utility Bill, and an independent consumer council established.

Simpson (2000) suggests that better representation for consumers in regard to privatized U.K. utilities would require bodies independent of both regulators and the government. These bodies should, according to Simpson, have authority to deal with domestic consumers' issues, prices, quality, and complaints. They should have an appropriate geographical coverage, their own research capacity, access to information, and adequate budgetary resources. Moreover, and crucially, they need to have the right to appeal the decisions of the sector regulators, as the industry has the right to appeal to the newly established Competition Commission (formerly the MMC).[24]

In recent years, there has been more emphasis, on the one hand, on liberalization, and on the other, on procompetitive legislation. A new Competition Bill introduces market structure regulation based on the European Union approach to antitrust policy. The government has also reformed the institutions that regulate the industries, with the objective of increasing consumer protection (see DTI 1999). The Utility Bill of 2000 also addresses consumer protection:

The principal objective of the Secretary of State and the Gas and Electricity Markets Authority ... is to protect the interest of consumers in relation to gas conveyed through pipes, whenever appropriate by promoting competition ... having regard (a) to the need to secure that, so far, all reasonable demands ... are met; and (b) the need to secure that license holders are able to finance the activities. In performing that duty the Secretary of State or the Authority shall have regard to the interests of (a) individuals who are disabled or chronically sick; (b) individuals of pensionable age; (c) individual with low incomes; (d) individuals residing in rural areas; but that is not to be taken as implying that regard may not be had to the interests of other description of consumer.

The bill also contains articles concerning the new Gas and Electricity Consumer Council, established by the government but independent of both the government and the regulator. The council will have the duty of publishing statistical information about complaints, quality of service, and the like in the gas and electricity industries.

It is clear that the Utility Bill tries to reinforce the consumer's voice in the framework for regulating U.K. utilities. The reforms proposed in the bill do not seem radical departures from the framework established by the preceding, Conservative governments. They do, however, reveal a widespread concern about impact privatization and previous regulation have had on consumers, as well as the perception that their voice must be strengthened.

7.2.7   Welfare Changes

I conclude my overview of the empirical evidence regarding the effects of privatization on consumers with a crude conjectural calculation of the resulting changes in the welfare of consumers (see Brau and Florio 2002 for details on other approximated welfare measures). First, because of data availability, I focus here on seven sectors between 1974 and 1999, in both their nationalized and their privatized forms: telephone, rail, bus, electricity, gas, water, and coal. During this twenty-five-year period, the overall share of expenditures for goods and services provided by these sectors in total household expenditures showed limited oscillations, between 7 and 9 percent. The share of such expenditures in total expenditures was 7.8 percent in 1992, a median postprivatization year between 1984 and 1999, the last year we consider. Therefore, given that total private consumption in 1992 was about £380 billion, expenditures for the goods and services of privatized was around £30 billion for that year.

Second, I consider price indexes for these seven sectors to estimate an aggregate change in Marshallian gross surplus for each sector (the ratio between expenditures and a price index for that sector). Between 1987 and 1999, the cumulated average decrease in prices in the seven sectors was 16 percent relative to the RPI. A very simple formula for a Marshallian surplus is

$$M = E^*(p_1 - p_2)/p^*,$$

where E^* is expenditure in a median year; and $p_1, p_2,$ and p^* are, respectively, price indexes at the privatization year, at the latest year, and at a median year.[25] All data employed in the current analysis are in 1995 prices. The result is a change in the Marshallian gross surplus over the period 1987–1999 of around £3.2 billion (see table 7.5).

A similar way to calculate the Marshallian gross surplus is to consider for each sector long-run average price elasticities. We use the following formula:

$$\Delta CS = (E_1 - E_2)/(2\eta),$$

where ΔCS is the change in the consumer surplus over the period 1987–1999, E_1 and E_2 are expenditures in constant sterling, and η is average price elasticity (I estimated -0.62 for our group of sectors). The result of calculations using this formula is a change in the Marshallian gross surplus over the period 1987–1999 of around £4 billion.

The net present value of a perpetual welfare increase, with a 5 percent discount rate, would thus be between £64 billion and £80 billion. Brau and Florio (2002) offer a wider discussion and a different estimation strategy, in which they also consider the actual years in which each sector was privatized and an industry-by-industry calculation of welfare change. Using distributional characteristics of goods,[26] based on Newbery 1995, they obtain a coefficient to allow for the distributional impact of price change of 0.805. With a 5 percent discount rate, the resulting net present value of the gross welfare change (socially weighted) generated by privatization price reforms is between £97 billion and £101 billion (with first- or second-order approximations of welfare changes) (see table 7.6).

I consider here a median value of the estimates of tables 7.5 and 7.6. Let us say that for these seven privatized sectors, the price change following privatization was worth £80 billion in perpetuity welfare terms, with an adjustment for intersector distributional characteristics. There

Table 7.5
Welfare changes by privatized industry, 1984–1999 (millions of 1994 constant pounds, at median year's expenditure)

	Privatized utilities							Total
	Phone	Rail	Bus	Electricity	Gas	Water	Coal	
Privatization year	1,984	1,995	1,989	1,990	1,986	1,990	1,995	
Median year	1,991	1,997	1,994	1,994	1,992	1,994	1,997	
E^*	6,842	3,144	2,808	8,082	5,684	4,014	499	
P^*	0.88	1.19	1.14	1.01	0.85	1.52	0.82	
P^1	0.98	1.18	1.04	0.97	1.02	1.14	0.85	
P^2	0.6	1.22	1.19	0.8	0.71	1.7	0.8	
η_{X_i,q_i}	0.6	0.8	0.9	0.5	0.7	0.5	0.2	
$\bar{d}_i$	0.875	0.573	0.756	0.893	0.9	0.938	0.992	
Welfare measures								
First-order approximations								
Marshallian surplus: $M = E^*(P^1 - P^2)/P^*$	2,779.243	−113.960	−417.030	1,360.337	1,815.768	−2,225.584	22.609	3,221.382
Socially weighted: $dW \equiv -d_i X_i dq_i$	2,431.837	−65.299	−315.274	1,214.781	1,634.191	−2,087.598	22.428	2,835.065
Distributive correction	−12.50%	−42.70%	−24.40%	−10.70%	−10.00%	−6.20%	−0.80%	−11.99%
Second-order approximations								
Unweighted: $\Delta W \approx -X_i\left[1 + \frac{\Delta q_i}{2q_i}\eta_{X_i,q_i}\right]\Delta q_i$	3,092.939	−112.155	−389.159	1,417.579	2,010.828	−1,917.087	22.721	4,125.666
Socially weighted (linear or quadratic-in-logs Engel curves) $\Delta W = -\bar{d}_i X_i\left[1 + \frac{\Delta q_i}{2q_i}\eta_{X_i,q_i}\right]\Delta q_i$	2,706.322	−64.265	−294.204	1,265.898	1,809.745	−1,798.228	22.539	3,647.807
First-order "error"	11.29%	−1.58%	−6.68%	4.21%	10.74%	−13.86%	0.50%	28.67%

Source: Brau and Florio 2002.
Note: E: expenditures; P: price index (real); M_{X_i,q_i}: price elasticity; d_i: distributive characteristics; dW: welfare change. Variables marked with an asterisk represent median-year values.

Table 7.6
Welfare changes by privatized industry, 1984–1999 (millions of 1994 constant pounds, cumulated yearly changes)

Welfare measures	Privatized utilities							Total
	Phone	Rail	Bus	Electricity	Gas	Water	Coal	
First-order approximations								
Laspeyres index: $M = X_i(p^t - p^{t+1})$	4,211.055	−132.640	−411.214	1,438.416	2,072.856	−1,701.746	33.601	5,510.329
Socially weighted: $dW \equiv -d_i X_i dq_i$	3,684.673	−76.003	−310.878	1,284.506	1,865.570	−1,596.238	33.332	4,884.963
Distributive correction	−12.50%	−42.70%	−24.40%	−10.70%	−10.00%	−6.20%	−0.80%	−11.35%
Second-order approximations								
Unweighted $\Delta W \approx -X_i\left[1 + \dfrac{\Delta q_i}{2q_i}\eta_{X_i,q_i}\right]\Delta q_i$	4,290.320	−133.820	−397.713	1,469.587	2,111.365	−1,675.905	33.674	5,697.508
Socially weighted (linear or quadratic-in-logs Engel curves) $\Delta W = -\bar{d}_i X_i\left[1 + \dfrac{\Delta q_i}{2q_i}\eta_{X_i,q_i}\right]\Delta q_i$	3,754.030	−76.679	−300.671	1,312.341	1,900.229	−1,571.999	33.405	5,050.655
First-order "error"	1.88%	0.89%	−3.28%	2.17%	1.86%	−1.52%	0.22%	3.39%

Source: Brau and Florio 2002.

is, however, a residual intrasector distributive impact of price change, that is, the redistribution of welfare because of rebalancing of tariffs within each sector.

Most important, observed price changes in privatized industries depend on a number of factors, as explained in section 7.1. Ownership change is one such factor. Regulation, demand trends, technical progress, prices of inputs, and changes in preferences are others. The question arises as to how much privatization or ownership change per se contributed to the observed price trends in the privatized industries. This is an important question that I cannot answer here in a precise way. In fact, answering this question would require a natural experiment in which public and private corporations were observed simultaneously and other factors were controlled for. International comparisons may be helpful, but they are difficult and in fact often inconclusive (see Florio 2003a for a discussion of electricity prices in Europe and Boylaud and Nicoletti 2000 for telecommunications).

Because we do not have such a natural experiment, we can formulate an ideal experiment and build a range of counterfactuals. As a starting point, we can then examine two extreme counterfactuals: First, that under continued public ownership of the privatized utilities, no change at all in welfare from that under nationalization would have occurred; and second, that the welfare change that would have occurred under continued public ownership is equal to the observed change in gross welfare. In the former case, 100 percent of the observed change in gross welfare can be attributed to privatization. In the latter case, the net change in gross welfare is zero, because nothing changes for the consumer. One can think of even more extreme cases, but under any scenario envisioned, the actual welfare worth of privatization would be expected to be anywhere between zero and £80 billion (in constant 1995 pounds). This defines the range for sensitivity analysis.

All of this is more a mental exercise than an actual estimation, but it offers a benchmark for further analysis. The maximum amount we get for the perpetual net present value of average consumers' welfare change per capita, under our counterfactuals, is around £1,400, or £70 per year. The minimum, before considering distributive issues, is zero. As noted previously, the true value may lie anywhere in between.

As a third option, we can look at industry-by-industry information and guess counterfactual trends under different hypotheses, of which there potentially are a huge number (through various combinations of sectors, regulatory regimes, and other factors). We can test some intermediate cases that amount to saying that a given percentage of price changes (increases or decreases) would have occurred anyway, without privatization, as a result of productivity increases, better regulation, and some liberalization.

Based on the previous discussion, I consider it reasonable to suppose that under continued public ownership, consumer prices in energy (electricity, gas, and coal) would have *decreased*, and transport prices (bus, rail) *increased*, at the same pace as observed trends. I think this is a crude but plausible assumption, looking at long-term price and productivity trends of the nationalized industries and considering the role of fuel costs in prices of energy services. In fact, I think that the reduction of prices for gas and electricity under continued public ownership could have been something more than what was observed before wider liberalization in 1997. Later, the European Union gas and electricity market directives would have forced competition in these industries, even if somewhat later than the actual date of privatization.

The important industries, of the seven considered, for the counterfactual are therefore telecommunications and water. I think that under continued public ownership, the price decrease in telecommunications would have been somewhat smaller than that which was actually observed, and in water, the price increase would have been somewhat smaller. BT was a net contributor to the Exchequer before privatization; thus OFTEL would have to fight on two fronts for a stringent price cap. On the other hand, under public ownership the water tariff was too politically sensitive, so the regulator would have an ally to contain price.

It is important to remark that the gross impact of the decrease in telecommunications prices on welfare is more than two-thirds of the total welfare change. This justifies a close examination of this sector, as I shall conduct in chapter 9, in which I analyze BT performance over forty years. In the meantime, let us attribute to ownership change most, but not all, of the benefit of lower telecommunications prices under privatization. Suppose, for example, that 20 percent of the price decrease in telecommunications would have happened *anyway*, even without privatization of the sector. Moreover, let us say that water tariffs under continued public ownership would have increased exactly as observed after privatization.

Under these assumptions, we are very likely to overestimate the net benefit of privatization to the consumer. What we get per capita is around a net benefit of £38 per year for each consumer. When the distributional impact of tariff rebalancing not yet accounted for (among each utility user group) is considered, as well as the nature of the assumptions made, I suggest that the overall value of privatization's benefits to consumers is most likely even below this figure.[27]

7.3   Discussion

In section 7.1, I listed some topics for discussion. I now briefly return to these in light of the empirical evidence presented in the previous section.

A comparison of the trends in nominal utility prices before and after privatization in the United Kingdom shows no clear structural break in those prices, at least until the end of the 1990s. In the case of electricity, prices had been falling for over a decade under public ownership; they increased in preparation for privatization and in the years that followed it, especially prices for residential users. Subsequently they started falling again in a manner not too different from their long-term trend since the 1960s. There is a clear structural correlation between electricity prices and fuel input prices. Privatization seems to be responsible for the temporary increase in prices before and following it. In the case of gas, there was a net drop in prices after privatization, but prices fell sharply even when British Gas was a nationalized industry. Trends in the price of coal for domestic use have only a marginal impact on my calculations of the welfare change of consumers. The coal industry was restructured under public ownership, and the price of coal started to decrease ten years before divestiture.

In the case of water, tariffs rose considerably after privatization. Part of the price increase would probably have happened anyway, even under continued public ownership. Buses and rail prices increased after privatization as well, and again it is difficult to see a break with past price trends.

The construction of a price index for telecommunications is particularly difficult. Data suggest that after privatization, there was a big cut in tariffs for business users and for some years an increase in the unit cost for domestic users. Subsequently, there was a general reduction of prices, following a change in the regulatory constraint and increased competition. Telecommunications prices in fact do show a structural break around privatization, but tariff decreases started some years before divestiture and are no more than what we can observe in state-owned telecommunications companies in the same years in various EU countries.

If ownership change does not explain the price trends in these industries very well, other factors must be at work. For regulated utilities, an important factor in prices is simply the signal given by the price cap imposed by industry regulators. As we have seen, the price cap formula was different from sector to sector, variable over time, and differed in regard to what outputs were covered. In the case of water, the increase in prices after privatization was in fact interpretable as an almost integral transfer to consumers of the cost of infrastructure investments, even when the benefit (for example, to the environment) affected taxpayers in general. In the case of gas, the price cap imposed was more stringent than that imposed on the water sector, in the face of a prolonged conflict between the regulatory body and the incumbent firm.

The price cap mechanisms in telecommunications allowed for the rebalancing of tariffs within a basket of services. This enabled British Telecom to raise tariffs for some services (domestic use, less exposed to competition and less price elastic) and to reduce them for others (international calls, business users).

Historically, this utility regulatory framework was born in the United Kingdom with privatization, probably as a way to make privatization more acceptable. According to some of its earlier proponents, particularly Stephen Littlechild, the framework had to be a transitory feature, in preparation of a full development of competition. The historical association in Britain between one specific kind of regulation $(RPI - X)$ and privatization does not, however, imply that other solutions for the restructuring of utilities were not feasible. We have no opportunity to observe a natural experiment with continued public ownership, or with restructured public and private-public ownership, plus regulatory reform. Careful observation of price trends, however, shows that industry regulators had a leading role in actual price determinations. Without regulation, and in some industries without increasingly tough price caps, privatized utilities would not have delivered lower prices. Actual prices closely tracked permitted maximum prices.

In some sectors, the empirical evidence shows that changes in costs, as observed by the companies and the regulator, explain a large part of the changes in price. These are often exogenous input costs. In the case of electricity and gas, both before and after privatization, there was a spectacular crash in the price of fuel. In the case of telephony, a cycle of technological innovation provoked a sizable increase in productivity. In other sectors (e.g., water), the change in costs was due to changes in environmental or sanitary norms. Different sectors were in different phases of their technological cycles when privatization occurred, and only a detailed analysis case by case can disentangle the effect on prices of new regulations from that of new technologies or other exogenous factors.

The case of electricity is particularly revealing. A number of elements are essential for comprehending the restructuring of the industry after (but not necessarily as a result of) privatization: the abolition of the CEGB's obligation to use British Coal as a supplier; the end to European Union restrictions on the use of gas as a fuel in power generation. And more restrictive EU norms regarding sulfurous emissions.

At privatization of Britain's electricity sector (1990), the CEGB used the following mix of fuels: coal, 92 percent; oil, 7 percent; and gas, 1 percent. By 1998, the sector as a whole used a rather different mix: oil, 5 percent; coal (and others), 63 percent; and gas, 32 percent. At the time of the great coal miners' strike in 1984, there were 250,000 miners; ten years later there were just 7,000. There was also a large increase in imports of electricity (especially from France). It is therefore evident that a large part of the reduction in generation costs in this sector was due to three simultaneous changes in public policy.

One can speculate as to whether the continuation of a nationalized CEGB would have allowed a restructuring in the sector of this scale. Newbery and Pollitt (1997) think it doubtful. I suspect that the process would have been delayed, but—as in the case of steel and other sectors, including coal—in the end, it would nevertheless have happened in a regime of public ownership as well, driven by pressure to comply with EU environmental norms and convenience for the Exchequer. The same can be said for the reduction in employment in the CEGB. It could have been delayed, but not indefinitely. I observed in my discussion of employment trends in chapter 6 that public corporations' downsizing started well before privatization.

On the other hand, as Newbury and Pollitt themselves observe, until 1997, very little of the saving in production costs resulting from privatization had been transferred to consumers through reductions in prices. I feel that this clarifies my discussion. Regulation and liberalization had a clear direct impact on prices and costs. Ownership change had a limited or negligible direct impact.

One might argue, however, that privatization was a prerequisite of other policy reforms that took place, and that one therefore has to show that effective price regulation and market liberalization were impossible without ownership change. Proving such a contention is, however, difficult. In the 1990s, in other countries, at least those in the European Union, there was restructuring, regulation, and eventually liberalization of many industries with only limited privatization. Price trends were decreasing, as in the United Kingdom, sometimes even more. The case of electricity is perhaps an extreme one, but it is not isolated (and it is in itself important).

Moreover, British privatization did not uniformly feature widespread liberalization. The association between privatization and liberalization policies is not terribly strong in the United Kingdom. The monopolistic regime of British Gas remained intact for over a decade after privatization (until it was eliminated by the 1995 Parliamentary Act). Divestiture in the electricity industry initially safeguarded an oligopoly in production, regional monopolies in distribution, a "corporatist" solution for the control of National Grid, and a spot market in the electricity pool that probably led to collusive practices. With the exception of some profitable routes, the deregulation of the buses in Britain did not lead to a competitive system but to the rise of lots of small local monopolies or duopolies. The water sector consists of a system of regional monopolies. The government and the industry regulator allowed British Airways to take over its only inland private competitor, British Caledonian. British Telecom enjoyed for many years a monopoly on some services and an asymmetric duopoly on others.

Liberalization policies in the United Kingdom were fully implemented only in the late 1990s or later, many years after the great privatization design. For example, prices in the electricity sector were fully deregulated in 2002. The price trends we observe to the present have been the result often of privatization and regulation, with limited liberalization until very recently. This sequence of privatization followed by liberalization only after a significant delay offers an approximate substitute for a natural experiment.

In summary: We observe a variety of trends before and after privatization, but no structural break is attributable to it, even though there were some changes in the contemporary environment, including those in costs of input, regulation of prices, technology, and market structure. It is difficult to find indisputable evidence of reductions in prices linked exclusively to the change in the objective function of a company with its transition to private ownership, and thus automatically to the change in productivity and endogenous costs. The changes in the exogenous scenario would appear to largely overshadow the change in ownership regime.

There is a small but important group of empirical studies available for the United Kingdom that enable us to pass from the changes observed in prices after privatization, whether or not actually attributable to privatization, to the welfare of consumers over the period considered. Galal et al. 1994 deals with BT, British Airways, and National Freight. There is one study of the bus sector (White 1990). Newbery and Pollitt (1997) discuss the case of the CEGB with a methodology derived from that of Galal et al. Other cost-benefit studies on electricity are Pollitt 1995; Pollitt 1997; and Pollitt 2000 as well as Hancock and Waddams Price 1998 for gas, electricity, and telecommunications.

In the case of BT, Galal et al. arrive at a positive overall evaluation of the welfare changes resulting from privatization, but at a negative welfare balance for domestic users, especially because of the increase in prices for a number of years following tariff rebalancing. White evaluates the privatization's effect on the welfare of bus users as negative, especially in regard to the effect on demand, which goes beyond the forecast based on price elasticity in the sector.

In the case of the CEGB, Newbery and Pollitt conduct a detailed cost-benefit analysis and resort to various alternative scenarios, using various social discount rates and various welfare weights. Their conclusion is that the final evaluation of social welfare following privatization depends on how one sums the gains and losses of the various subjects, especially shareholders, taxpayers, and consumers. In all of Newbery and Pollitt's scenarios, however, consumers suffered a net loss of welfare.

Overall, the message of these studies is that, at least until around 1997, the social welfare gains resulting from the ownership change at privatization are modest. Benefits to consumers had to arrive later, with liberalization and/or tougher regulation. Some studies are more optimistic about the impact of privatization on costs, and of regulation on prices. I find some evidence to support the latter proposition, less to support the former (see chapters 4 and 6).

An essential step in making conjectures in this regard is to formulate hypotheses about the courses other than those taken that would have been practicable in the period studied. Counterfactual scenarios can include very different policies; for example:

1. continuation and restructuring of public monopoly, with the inter-position of the regulator between the government and public corpo-rations' executive boards, to define the system of price control in a more stable manner (in section 7.2.1, I showed the destabilizing effect of occasional interference by the government in the running of nation-alized enterprises)

2. public ownership of some companies or networks and the radical liberalization of the remainder of the sector (as happened to a certain extent in the electricity sector in Norway, for example)

3. regional breakup of public corporations and liberalization

4. experimentation with mixed formulas for both ownership and mar-ket regimes, including mutualization.

I return to policy counterfactuals in chapter 10.

Turning now to distribution issues, the empirical evidence shows that the price trends following privatization created distributive effects that were not negligible. For some consumers in the lower income brackets, family spending for the acquisition of a decent level of elec-tricity, gas, water, public transport, and telephone services could exceed 20 percent of the family's income and be, in practice, unafford-able. The increases in the prices of these services that took place fol-lowing privatization were due to the abolition of price cross-subsidies from heavy users to light users or to the introduction of regressive dis-crimination into pricing schemes. Those affected were not marginal fringe groups, but millions of people, most of them aged, disabled, sin-gle parents, long-term unemployed, or the working poor.

The social hardship that these price increases created was unneces-sary for an improvement in allocative efficiency. A price system that makes marginal users pay in advance and pay more than those whose consume a lot, and at the same time shows a big wedge between unit average costs and revenues, may be profitable, but it is not necessarily efficient. The standard theory of optimal taxation and tariffs shows that welfare weights should enter in pricing rules if the government is even moderately averse to inequality.

Alternatively, adequate monetary lump-sum subsidies could have compensated for the regressive effects of these pricing policies. A special tax on extra profits of utilities or appropriate license modifications (e.g., with a provision for universal service transfers from the Exchequer) could finance such subsidies. The British government and regulators, however, until recently did not design such a comprehensive subsidization scheme. Consequently, privatization contributed to increasing economic inequality in Britain.

There were however, improvements in other aspects of the provision of public services. To account for consumers' welfare changes, the prices of the industries providing public services should be virtually adjusted for any change in the quality of the service, and there is no doubt that after privatization, there were important qualitative improvements in various services provided by the utilities. Perhaps not all services improved after privatization, and the improvements may not always have been socially desirable, because the quality improvement was only an excuse to charge high tariffs (as Glaister's discussion of the case of water shows). Having said this, however, regulation played an increasingly important role through defining performance standards.

Admittedly, I have not been able to document in this chapter the indirect effects on British consumers of price changes in services provided by privatized utilities to business users. The most obvious cases are those of the telecommunications, gas, and electricity sectors. In those sectors, the reduction in prices after privatization was more marked for business users than for residential users. There was therefore a reduction in costs to companies, which to some extent may have been transferred to their customers. In the information available so far, however, no effects of this sort are discernible. The trend of the aggregated price indexes examined in chapter 3 does not offer any reason for particular optimism that such effects occurred.

It is possible that there has been since privatization an attenuation of preexisting rationing constraints, for example, in waiting times to have a telephone line installed. In general, however, price discrimination has increased in the privatized industries. A sophisticated system of fine-tuned tariffs and consumer exploitation has replaced old systems of cross-subsidies and uniform tariffs.

From the point of view of markets' informative completeness, privatization as such has not been effective in resolving the considerable information asymmetries and imperfections of some markets. On the other hand, regulation and liberalization may have contributed to greater transparency. There has also been abundant noise in information concerning service contracts between utilities and consumers. In later postprivatization years, after the full liberalization of domestic energy markets, regulators were concerned with the increasing difficulty that consumers were having in interpreting the contracts proposed them by aggressive door-to-door salesmen. In any case, these matters are quite independent of the change in regime of ownership that occurred with privatization. Public corporations could have been subject to the same kinds of quality standards and obligations to provide information to consumers as privatized companies are. Some British companies that have remained public have experienced this change of orientation toward the consumer (e.g., the Post Office). Although the postal service in the United Kingdom was recently in financial trouble because of managerial errors, postal services in several European countries have undergone sizable performance improvements, through standards definition, benchmarking, and exposure to a dose of competition.

I have provided in this chapter an illustrative calculation of the welfare impact of privatization on the consumer, based on changes in prices and expenditures in seven privatized industries. Under different calculation methods, a median estimate of the gross welfare change resulting from privatization, partially adjusted for distribution effects, is around £4 billion per year (in 1995 constant pounds). This is around £70 per capita per year, or £1,400 of perpetual value.

To estimate the net welfare change resulting from privatization, one has to forecast under a counterfactual that assumes continued public ownership. As an example, I have suggested assuming that under continued public ownership, consumers' prices in energy (electricity, gas, and coal) would have decreased, and transport prices (bus, rail) increased, at the same pace as in the actual observed trends under privatization. I think this is a rather crude assumption, but a reasonable one, and one that is more or less justified when one examines long-term trends in prices, fuel costs, and productivity.

In contrast, I do not think that water prices would have increased and telecommunications prices decreased to the same extent under continued public ownership as they did under privatization. If, however, most (80 percent) of the merit of lower telecommunications tariffs is attributed to the ownership change, and nothing of the blame for higher water tariffs, the maximum net welfare benefit of privatization works out to be less than £40 per person per year. Consumers in the two bottom income quintiles probably had no net benefit at all, and around one million households probably suffered a negative welfare change.

Overall, these figures are small and uncertain. Moreover, they critically depend on the performance of one single company, British Telecom, which is taken to account for two-thirds of the overall impact of privatization. This suggests the need to study more in depth the impact of telecommunications sector privatization. I return to such a study in chapter 9.

7.4   Further Reading

Books on utilities regulation in the United Kingdom (and elsewhere) include Prosser 1997; Graham and Prosser 1991; Newbery 2000; Baldwin and Cave 1999; Helm and Jenkinson 1998; Vickers and Yarrow 1988a; and Alison 2001. The bibliographies in these books provide many helpful additional references. For a year-by-year update on the development of utilities regulation in the United Kingdom, see the *Regulatory Review* published annually by the Centre for Regulated Industries (CIPFA). This literature is often critical of the regulatory bodies governing U.K. industries. At the end of the Conservative government term, an independent official commission proposed a wide reform of the regulatory system (Flemming 1996). One of the recommendations in the commission's report was to create bodies to represent consumers that would be independent of regulators. The model for such bodies was the Gas Consumer Council, financed by a tax on producers. The proposal in itself revealed the increasing perception that regulation did not sufficiently protect consumers. I have already mentioned the Utility Bill of 2000 in this context. See Markou and Waddams Price 1999 for a discussion on utilities legislation reform.

Helm (1994, 1995) maintains that the British regulatory system led to arbitrage between different regulators, each of which followed its own line of intervention; capture of the regulators, shown by the unjustified level of prices in the industries they regulated; high administrative costs; distortion in investments because of games between regulator and regulatee in regard to the cost of capital; and political instability as a result of the low level public consensus about the functioning of the regulatory framework. See also Parker 1997a, 1997b; Thompson

1987; Vickers and Yarrow 1988a, 1988b, 1990; Button and Weyman-Jones 1993, 1994; Cave 1993; and Ogden and Watson 1999.

Lowe (1998) puts the subject of regulation in a historical perspective and concludes that regulation of privatized utilities may be an inefficient solution to the provision of public services. According to Lowe, there is a case for public ownership of the monopoly elements of the utilities, and he thinks that this arrangement may, in the long run, return to the forefront of political debate in the United Kingdom. This view is shared by a minority of authors: Sawyer and O'Donnell (1999); for telecom, Harper (1997); for rail, Salveson (1989). In fact, Railtrack and the National Air Traffic Control are now again under public control, but not officially renationalized.

An important approach to research on industry reform is international comparison. There are some countries in which we can observe privatization without liberalization and without effective regulation, others with liberalization and without regulation, and so on (Simpson 2002; NCC 1994). There is currently a research program with this focus at the OECD, as discussed in OECD 1997. In the specific case of electricity, no clear pattern across countries correlates ownership regime, industrial structure, and prices. In a liberalized European market, one of the "winners" is the state-owned French monopoly EDF, which now has thirty million users in France and seventeen million abroad and is now the owner of London Electricity, the company that illuminates 10 Downing Street. A comparative analysis is Midttun and Thomas 1998, which compares the electricity markets in the United Kingdom and in Norway, the latter based on municipal public ownership of companies and extensive competition, and the former on private ownership and oligopoly. For the case of distribution in Sweden (three hundred companies, with 65 percent of the market controlled by municipal companies, 25 percent by private companies, and 10 percent by public-private companies), see Kumbhakar and Hjalmarsson 1998. Other useful readings on the electricity sector include OFFER 1995; Yarrow 1992; Newbery 2000; APIS 1995; Thomas 2000; Brower 1997; Pollitt 1995, 1997, 2000; Surrey 1996; Steiner 2000; DTI 1999; Collier 1995; and Fells 1991.

On price discrimination and distributional issues in the United Kingdom, see Burns 1994; Waddams Price 1997; and Waddams Price 2002. Waddams Price suggests that uniformity in prices of public services under public ownership was not cost reflective and in a sense, then, a form of discrimination. Under privatized monopolies, there was less rebalancing than expected in regard to rural versus urban users and peak and off-peak tariffs. These tariff structure changes arrived more with liberalization. Otero and Waddams Price (2001a) study the pricing policy of unregulated entrants, as opposed to incumbents, in the retail (supply) electricity market after the 1998 liberalization of the electricity sector. They consider average consumers using direct-debit and prepayment methods and test whether price differences across regions, companies, and types of customer reveal discrimination (i.e., charging different markups over costs for the same service). They find evidence of price discrimination and show a trade-off between regulation to protect low-income consumers using the prepayment method, who are prevented from switching from that payment method because of standing debt, and the benefits of deregulation. Otero and Waddams Price (2001b) study a similar issue for gas retailing. On the impact of recent price reforms on the fuel poor, see Bennett, Cook, and Waddams Price 2002; DTI 1998; Piachaud and Sutherland 2000.

On transport regulation, see Thompson 2000; DETRA 1993a, 1993b, 1994, 1997, 1998a; DOT, Civil Aviation Division 1994; Kennedy, Glaister, and Travers 1995; Murray 2001; and NCC 1992. On social attitudes, see MORI 1998a, 1998b, 1995; and Morgan 1995. Some helpful regulators' reports include OFFER 1998, 1999; OFWAT 1991; OFGAS 1998; OFGEM 1999, 2000; OPRAF 2000; SSRA 2000a, 2000b; ORR 1994, 1995, 1997, 1998, 1999a, and 1999b. For OFTEL, see chapter 9.

On water privatization and its impact on the environment, see Rees 1989. For a neoliberal critique of regulation in the United Kingdom, see Veljanovski 1991 and Veljanovski 1993.

8   Taxpayers

8.1   Topics for Discussion

H.M. Treasury 1995 summarizes the benefits of privatization for British taxpayers as follows: "The taxpayer has benefited from the £60 billion of proceeds the programme has raised; and from the substantial fall in the annual charge nationalized industries' financing makes on the Exchequer. This charge has reduced by about £4.3 billion in real terms since 1979–1980. In 1994–1995 the privatised companies paid the Exchequer £55 million a week, mainly in corporation tax" (4). There are several flaws in this way of presenting the privatization story. First, the taxpayer receives a benefit from divestiture proceeds only if the sale prices of the privatized firms reflect their asset value. Second, Exchequer disbursement to finance the nationalized industries is a loss only if there is no matching acquisition of assets. Third, corporation tax revenues are a net benefit only if they exceed the future gross profits (interests, dividends, and retained profits) that the industries would have reaped had they remained nationalized. Fourth, in an intertemporal setting, there are complex relationships between public finance and macroeconomic variables, and their sign is ambiguous.

As mentioned in chapter 2, one way to look at changes in taxpayer welfare is through the public-sector net worth (PSNW) at shadow prices. When the latter are simply the producer prices, the PSNW is the sum of the financial and real assets and liabilities owned by the state and thus jointly by the taxpayers.

In the case of underpricing of companies being privatized, which I have documented in detail elsewhere, the taxpayer suffers a loss. The government has in such a case sold on his or her behalf an asset at a discount. The price of an asset that should leave the taxpayer unaffected after transfer is the net present value of future returns deriving from the ownership of the asset itself.

There may be a systematic divergence between the return on privately and publicly owned capital. Such a divergence exists if there is an expectation that the private manager is technically more efficient than the public manager. Hence, the maximum price at which the private investor is prepared to buy and the minimum price below which the public sector should not sell may diverge.

However, the value of an asset is its opportunity cost. If the state negotiates efficiently the price for companies it is privatizing, the taxpayer succeeds in appropriating future profits from the private sector (for example, through competitive bidding).

For the buyer of an asset, the right price to pay is the present value of profits net of taxes. The seller should add future tax revenues to the sale price. If private ownership is more efficient than public, then corporate and capital income taxes will recover part of the difference in profitability.

This reasoning implies that at any time PSNW depends on several variables: the stock of public capital and debt, the marginal rate of return on public and private capital before tax, and the tax rate. When ratios of various quantities to GDP over time are examined, GDP rate of growth and its relation to fiscal variables should also be considered. The ratio between financial liability and GDP in the simpler macroeconomic models depends solely on the primary surplus, the interest rate, and the rate of growth in GDP. When the existence of public capital is also considered, however, it becomes crucial to know the difference between the returns on private and on public capital, the rate of investment, and the taxation of profits.

Therefore, without an appropriate fiscal model, we cannot predict the impact of divestitures on the PSNW. Neither can we predict the interplay between privatization and macroeconomic conditions. In general, however, when the Exchequer uses the receipts from privatization to reduce government debts, the PSNW improves only if the sale price equals the asset value. When an asset is underpriced, the PSNW decreases, unless the state subsequently appropriates profits through taxation.

In this chapter, I focus on the PSNW at actual prices as a crude proxy for my welfare measure for taxpayers. I postpone a discussion of appropriate shadow prices for evaluating the welfare impact of privatization on the taxpayer, including the shadow price of public funds, until chapter 10.

This chapter starts with a broad overview of some public-finance real variables in the United Kingdom since 1970, including public investment, current expenditures, debt and taxation, and net worth. Then I consider the role of nationalized industries in the country's public finances. I consider constant-price data since 1963 on borrowing requirements, payment of interest and dividends, financial surplus and deficits, and investment. Then the chapter offers a discussion of the definition of PSNW, the relationship between tax reforms and privatization before 1997, cash flows between the public sector and nationalized/privatized firms, the windfall tax imposed by the New Labour government, and the Private Finance Initiative launched in the 1990s. I conclude with an assessment of the dramatic decrease in the net worth of the public sector in the United Kingdom over the last twenty years.

8.2 Empirical Evidence

8.2.1 British Public Finances: An Overview, 1970–1997

In this section, I give a quick overview of the main fiscal variables in the United Kingdom since 1970, and particularly over the 1979–1997 period. This allows me to put the discussion of the effects of privatization on the taxpayer in a broader perspective. I consider yearly data at constant prices on public current expenditures, gross fixed capital formation, revenues, net debt, and net wealth (see table 8.1).

In the decade before the arrival of the Thatcher government, public current expenditures as a percentage of GDP increased considerably, from 32 percent at the beginning of the 1970s to almost 40 percent in 1976. This increase was due mainly to the slowdown in GDP growth. In the early Thatcher years, this percentage continued to increase. In 1984, BT stock was being floated, public current expenditures were 42.5 percent of GDP. Subsequently, expenditures were frozen, and in some years they even decreased in absolute terms (in constant pounds), returning to around 36 percent in 1990. Later, under the Major government, the expenditure/GDP ratio increased again to around 40 percent. Therefore, after eighteen years of Tory government, the ratio of current expenditures to GDP was unchanged (see figure 8.1).

Table 8.1
Public finance in the United Kingdom, 1980–1997

	1980	1985	1990	1995	1997
A. Structure of public expenditures and taxation (Percentage of GDP)					
Expenditures (total)	43.0	44.0	39.9	43.0	39.7
Current consumption	21.6	21.1	20.5	21.2	20.1
Transfers to households	10.6	12.7	10.7	13.7	13.0
Subsidies	2.5	2.0	1.1	1.1	1.0
Fixed investments	2.5	2.1	2.3	1.8	1.0
Other	5.9	6.2	5.3	5.3	4.7
Tax receipts (total)	39.6	41.2	38.7	37.4	37.8
Income tax	13.4	14.5	13.9	12.9	13.2
of which:					
Personal income tax	11.1	10.6	11.2	10.5	10.1
Corporate profits tax	2.3	3.9	2.8	2.3	3.1
Social security contributions	10.5	10.9	10.5	9.8	9.6
Taxes on goods and services	15.7	15.9	14.2	14.7	15.0
Memorandum item					
Net lending	−3.4	−2.8	−1.2	−5.6	−1.9
B. Tax rates (Percentage)					
Personal income tax					
Lowest marginal tax rate	30	30	25	20	20
Highest marginal tax rate	60	60	40	40	40
Number of brackets[a]	6	6	2	3	3
Marginal income tax (for single average production worker)	30	30	25	25	—
Social security contributions					
Marginal contribution rate (for single average production worker)	20.5	19.5	19.4	20.2	—
of which:					
Employees' contribution rate	6.75	9	9	10	—
Employers' contribution rate	13.75	10.5	10.4	10.2	—
Corporate income tax rate	52	40	34	33	32
VAT standard rate[b]	15.0	15.0	15.0	17.5	17.5

Source: OECD 1998.
[a] There were two brackets from April 1988 to March 1992.
[b] VAT standard rate was increased to 17.5 percent on April 1, 1991.

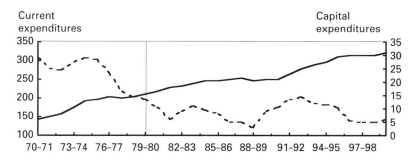

Figure 8.1
Public-sector current expenditures (solid line) and capital expenditures (broken line)
(millions of 1998–1999 pounds).
Source: H.M. Treasury 1999.

On the other hand, the composition of current expenditures changed over the period of Tory rule. Whereas current public consumption remained stable, at around 21 percent, and subsidies to producers decreased, transfers to families increased. I briefly discussed changes in the welfare state in Britain during this period in chapter 1. From a public-finance perspective, these changes were modest or marginal.

Unlike current expenditures, fixed capital expenditures did show a marked trend of decline over the period of Conservative governance. A decline was already in evidence in the pre-Thatcher era; for example, between 1970 and 1979, the public investment/GDP ratio fell dramatically, from 6.4 percent to 2.7 percent. The ratio fell below 2 percent in subsequent years. In some years it was even below 1 percent, and in the early years of the Blair government, it remained in the region of 0.6 percent, probably one of the lowest values internationally.

The reasons for this dramatic decline are relatively easy to explain. First, privatization transferred outside the public sector some of the most capital-intensive nationalized industries. Second, budget restraints cut public works. Third, in recent years, forms of project finance have also emerged that switch the expenditures necessary for running certain services (prisons, schools, and hospitals) from the capital account to the current account. This trend contributes to a decrease in levels of public investment.

Against expectations of tax cuts, in the first years of the Thatcher government, the overall tax burden on British taxpayers increased by five percentage points in proportion to GDP and then began falling again, following swings in the business cycle. By the end of the Major

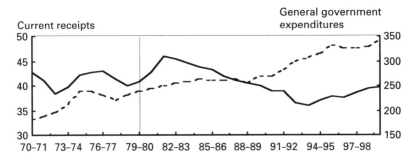

Figure 8.2
Public-sector current receipts (solid line) (percentage of GDP) and general government
expenditures (broken line) (millions of 1998–1999 pounds).
Source: H.M. Treasury 1999.

government, the tax burden had risen once more and was not much
lower than during the Labour government that had preceded Thatcher
and Major (see figure 8.2).

Perhaps the most important structural reform under Conservative
governance was the reduction in the progressiveness of the personal
income tax. The maximum marginal rate under Labour was at 83 percent; it fell in the Conservative era to 60 percent, then to 40 percent,
and the minimum declined from 30 percent to 20 percent. There were
eleven tax rate bands before reform, then six and later three (they were
initially reduced to just two). Social security contributions by employees rose from 6.75 percent to 10 percent, and those by employers
fell from 13.75 percent to 10.2 percent.

The value-added tax rose from 8 to 15 percent and then again to 17.5
percent. These changes offset the decline, from 33 to 30 percent, of the
basic personal income tax rate for the vast majority of taxpayers. Consequently, whereas for the latter, the reform of Britain's tax system had
a negligible impact, for top-income taxpayers, it was a bonanza, which
increased posttax income inequality in the country. The statutory corporate income tax rate fell from 52 to 32 percent (there was, however, a
change in the allowances for fiscal deductions that diminished the fiscal impact of the lower rate).

There were big reductions in taxes on investments as well. At the
time of the placement of the first BT tranche, the government abolished
the 15 percent surcharge on investment income. The top marginal tax
rate on personal income including the surcharge decreased from 98

to 60 percent. At the same time, there was a broad change in capital taxation, marking a reversal of the traditional U.K. policy of tax breaks for pensions, life insurance, and owner-occupied housing. During the 1980s, the British government raised taxation on these forms of savings, which were particularly important for wide categories of savers, including low-income ones.

Leape (1993, 2002) documents how, in contrast, there was simultaneously a substantial reduction of the effective tax rate on equity investments in individual companies, the kind of investment more relevant for privatization of public offerings. Particularly, in 1986, personal equity plans were introduced that exempted from tax the returns on equity in individual companies. These tax reforms were clearly linked to mass privatization through share placements.

I consider now trends in the public-sector borrowing requirement (PSBR). In the 1970s the country's annual budget deficit increased rapidly; it reached a peak in 1975, then shrank under Labour governments and negotiations with the IMF. The Thatcher government in its early years was committed to a rigid monetary policy and actively tried to reduce government borrowing. In fact, the Exchequer achieved a modest surplus in those years. This result was unsustainable, because it was followed by a noticeable slowdown in GDP growth. In the 1990s, there was a reversal in the trend toward declining annual deficits, when the Major government recorded an absolute maximum deficit of 7.8 percent of GDP for two consecutive years. Subsequently, economic recovery enabled a reduction in the deficit and led to a surplus in the first years of the Blair government.

Finally, with regard to trends in public debt and in public-sector net worth, in the ten years that preceded the Thatcher government, the stock of net debt in the United Kingdom fell from 69 percent of GDP at the beginning of the 1970s to 47.3 percent in the last Labour budget. Subsequently, until 1985, there was no noticeable reduction in the debt in proportion to GDP. There was a large reduction after the launch of the major divestitures and at the end of the 1980s, leading to an all-time debt/GDP low of 26.3 percent in 1994. The Major government again reversed the trend, and the debt increased again to 44 percent in 1996.

In the end, the policies implemented by the Thatcher and Major governments brought the national debt to a level that was only slightly lower than when they started. Under the Thatcher government,

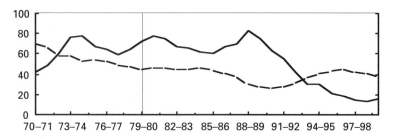

Figure 8.3
Public-sector net worth (solid line) and net debt (dashed line) (percentage of GDP).
Source: H.M. Treasury 1999.

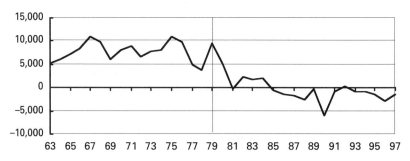

Figure 8.4
Public corporations: Borrowing requirements, 1963–1997 (millions of 1995 pounds).
Source: Author's elaboration on ONS data.

however, the overall increase in the tax burden, the control of current expenditures, the cuts in spending for investments, and large-scale privatization achieved a considerable drop in the public debt that was probably politically unsustainable.[1] The Major government, in fact, had to change the government's fiscal stance.

Figure 8.3, based on official Treasury data, shows PSNW in the United Kingdom from 1970 through 1998. The PSNW was more than 60 percent of GDP in the 1970s, increased slightly in the 1980s, and eventually fell dramatically, to well below 20 percent in the second half of the 1990s. I discuss this surprisingly strong decrease in section 8.2.3.

8.2.2 Public Corporations: Finance and Investment

I now discuss the financial performance of U.K. public corporations between 1965 and 1998. The time-series data presented in figures 8.4

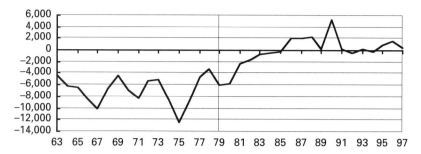

Figure 8.5
Public corporations: Financial surplus or deficit, 1963–1997 (millions of 1995 pounds).
Source: Author's elaboration on ONS data.

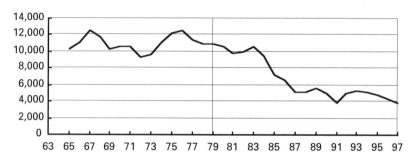

Figure 8.6
Public corporations: Gross domestic fixed capital formation, 1963–1997 (millions of 1995 pounds).
Source: Author's elaboration on ONS data.

and 8.5 may help us understand the element of fiscal illusion that arises in regard to privatization because of incomplete public-finance accounting.

Thatcher's government actually reduced the financial deficits and borrowing requirements of the nationalized industries to around zero in the aggregate. The borrowing requirements were between five and ten billion constant 1995 pounds until 1979, around the same magnitude as the financial deficits.

Some may interpret these data as an indication of financial disarray of the nationalized industries, or at least as an indication of a substantial burden for the Exchequer (see, e.g., the quotation from H.M. Treasury that begins the chapter). Figure 8.6 shows, however, that in the 1960s and the 1970s, the nationalized industries were able to implement a huge fixed investment program, between ten and twelve billion

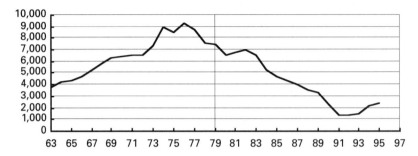

Figure 8.7
Public corporations: Payment of interest and dividends, 1963–1997 (millions of 1995 pounds).
Source: Author's elaboration on ONS data.

pounds per year, which sharply decreased to four to five billion pounds per year in the 1990s. Thus, before privatization, borrowing in these industries broadly matched investment. In fact, a large part of the investment was self-financed, as the British Telecom case history presented in chapter 9 confirms.

To a government committed to tight monetary policy and to curbing the overall public-sector borrowing requirement, the nationalized industries were a burden. Nevertheless, in accounting terms, against Exchequer disbursements there was fixed capital formation in the public sector.

Moreover, in considering borrowing requirements, it should be remembered that the Treasury acted as the main financier for the corporations and cashed interest and dividends. Thus the difference between the borrowing requirement and cash inflows into the Treasury for interest and dividends offers a useful additional view of the net burden public corporations imposed on taxpayers. Figure 8.7 shows that in the 1960s and 1970s, the nationalized industries paid the Treasury a substantial return on capital, around eight billion pounds per year (constant prices) on average in the 1970s. In some years, this flow of funds to the Treasury from the nationalized industries exceeded the borrowing requirement.

At the end the 1970s, the net financial burden of the nationalized industries for the Treasury in yearly cash flow terms was probably in the region of 1.5 percent of general government expenditures. Against this, there was substantial asset accumulation. The value of the latter, in the same years, was around 4.8 percent of government expenditures.

The balance implied an increasing contribution of the nationalized industries to the net worth of the public sector.

8.2.3   Public-Sector Net Worth

In this section, I evaluate the role of privatization in the subsequent decline in the PSNW in the United Kingdom. Vickers and Yarrow (1988a) contend that privatization impoverished the government's wealth by an amount equal to the undervaluation plus the related transaction costs, and in fact worsened the government's financial position in the long run.

Since the early 1980s, independent studies have observed how the selling of the "family silver" in the end worsened the balance sheet in the public sector (cf. in particular Hills 1989). Hills (1989) reconstructs the balance sheet for the public sector in the United Kingdom between 1957 and 1987 at constant 1987 prices (using the implicit GDP deflator). He shows that public-sector net wealth, which was still negative in 1957 because of war debts, continually increased in the 1960s and 1970s, reaching £364 billion by the time the Thatcher government came into power in 1979. Between 1979 and 1987, however, there was a net reversal of this trend toward increase.

Some delicate problems are involved in this analysis. For example:

• Would it be more appropriate to evaluate public real estate at the market price for empty or occupied council houses?

• Is it possible to compare with previous values the stock exchange values at which the shares of partially privatized firms that remained in public hands were charged to the balance sheet?

• How should the still-unexploited state-owned oil reserves in the North Sea be evaluated?

According to Hills, between 1957 and 1979 public net assets in Britain increased by £120 billion, thanks to the revenue from oil reserves in the North Sea. After 1979, in the space of just eight years, these assets decreased by £150 billion, bringing the net assets of the state back to the position of thirty years before. Contributing to this decrease in assets were declines in the price of oil, the accrual of the pension fund for civil servants, a decrease in public investments in proportion to GDP, and privatization. Privatization would have contributed to a considerable extent in the years considered by Hills, especially the

Table 8.2
Stock of dwellings by housing tenure, Great Britain (percentage)

Year	Owner occupied	Rented by local authorities	Others
1974	53.0	30.7	16.3
1979	54.7	31.4	13.9
1984	59.6	27.4	13.0
1989	65.2	22.8	12.0
1993	66.4	20.1	13.5

Source: Department of Environment, housing construction statistics.

divestitures related to real estate. This point is worth studying in detail because it illustrates fiscal illusion.

I mentioned in chapter 1 that local public housing has been an important feature of the British welfare state over several decades, under the responsibility of local councils. Sales of public housing were, however, limited. Between 1960 and 1967 the number of council houses sold varied between 3,000 and 5,000 per year. In the three-year period 1968–1970 this number rose to about 8,000 per year. Over the next three years, a massive sales campaign resulted in the sale of over 100,000 homes. There followed three years of stagnation in 1974–1976, when sales fell to again to 4,000 per year. After 1977, there was a clear increase, but it was under the Thatcher's government that sales of council houses boomed. The average number of sales per year in 1980–1990 was around 130,000.

The policy of mass transfer of ownership of council houses from local authorities to tenants had a profound effect on the structure of real estate ownership in the United Kingdom (see table 8.2). Whereas in the mid-1970s, slightly more than half of all dwellings were occupied by their owners, by the mid-1990s, the proportion had increased to more than two-thirds.

This policy was indeed very popular. The average sales price of council houses in Britain in 1986 was £13,800, but only one-fifth of the proceeds from the sale of council houses could be spent by local councils; the remaining four-fifths had to go toward paying off debts (Neubeurger 1987). The sale price of public residential property was well below the market value, which meant that a transfer was realized in favor of the buyers, usually in the working classes (see figure 3.2). Braddon and Foster (1996) observed that the British privatization with the greatest social impact was actually that of public housing, not popular capitalism.

In fact, the average British taxpayer subsidized the purchases of over 1,500,000 family units between 1979 and 1997. The discount often exceeded 30 percent of the value of the assets. It was a progressive transfer, because the average taxpayer has a higher income than the average buyer of council houses does (the very poor, however, may have been unable to participate in the sales). The social impact of the transfer overall had the sign opposite to that of the underpricing of the shares and may have played a positive role in poverty reduction (Leape 2002). Nevertheless, both contributed to a decreasing net wealth of the public sector.

An analysis of the impact of privatization on the accounts of the public sector would require, in addition to the cash accounting of the cash proceeds from privatization, (1) the construction of a historic series of assets and liabilities, and (2) a verification of the effects specifically attributable to privatization. As to the first requirement, an official accounting of this type was not available for the years considered, but one was produced as an experiment for the first budgets presented by the New Labour governments (H.M. Treasury 1997a, 1998a).[2] This new official series of the PSNW distances itself considerably from the estimates of Hills and is worth commenting on in detail.

The PSNW aims to provide a counterpart to public financial accounting, mostly based on cash flows. The context for this accounting was a shift of emphasis by the New Labour government from the PSBR to the two general criteria of conduct of public finance:

• the so-called golden rule of public finance: "over the economic cycle the government will only borrow to invest and not to fund current expenditure"

• the stabilization of the ratio between public debt and national income.

The golden rule implies that taxation should finance current expenditures and that borrowing should finance public investments only. This implies a better calculation of the two types of spending on a yearly basis and the recording of the cumulative effects of the process of investment and divestment. Under the golden rule, the PSNW remains constant even if there is a deficit, given that the increase in financial debt exactly offsets the value of the investment assets acquired.

Construction of a balance sheet for the public sector involves listing and consolidating assets (real and financial) and liabilities at various levels (central government, local authorities, and public corporations).[3] One step in this direction is the publication of the National Asset Register, probably the greatest effort ever made to account for the size of public property holdings in a country. The register draws from a census of all the tangible and intangible property assets of the departments of central government, their executive agencies, the organisms of the NHS, other public corporations, and nationalized industries.[4]

According to a survey by the Office for National Statistics at the end of 1996, the public sector had tangible assets of £405 billion and net financial liabilities of £340 billion. The balance left when the liabilities are subtracted from the assets gives a PSNW of £65 billion. The principal tangible assets are civil engineering works (including roads), housing, and industrial and commercial real estate;[5] the principal items of financial debt are Treasury bonds and national savings.

Before the balance sheet results are discussed in detail, I suggest looking again at figure 8.3 and at table 8.3, based on data from H.M. Treasury 1999a. The table shows the levels of net public sector debt since 1970 and the PSNW as a percentage of GDP. The debt/GDP ratio, after a substantial decrease in the Thatcher years (thanks in some part to privatization proceeds), returned exactly to its starting point in the subsequent decade. Alongside this U-shaped trend, there was a steep decline in PSNW, from 71.8 percent in 1979–1980 to 14.7 percent in 1997–1998.

H.M. Treasury (1998a) offers two possible explanations:

• an increase in financial liabilities as a result of the deterioration of public finance following the recession in the early 1990s

• a decrease in tangible assets following a drop in the value of land and the effect of privatization that transferred public corporations' assets from the public sector to the private sector.

The first explanation, however, is valid only for the early 1990s. In those years, there was an increase in the public debt as a proportion of GDP. It is obviously not applicable for the entire period since the Thatcher government came to power, given that the debt as a whole has been stable or slightly declined over that period. The other explanation appears to be more consistent with the available data.

Table 8.3
Public-finance data

	Public-sector current expenditure[a]	Public-sector net capital expenditure[a]	General government expenditure[a]	Public-sector current receipts[b]	Public-sector net debt[b]	Public-sector net worth[b]
1970–1971	143.5	29.0	183.3	42.7	69.6	41.7
1971–1972	150.1	25.2	188.6	41.1	65.2	48.1
1972–1973	157.6	24.5	196.7	38.5	58.5	60.0
1973–1974	173.5	27.5	211.8	39.7	58.4	76.8
1974–1975	192.0	28.8	238.0	42.2	52.4	78.0
1975–1976	196.3	28.5	238.1	42.7	54.2	66.5
1976–1977	202.0	23.4	232.1	43.0	52.6	63.9
1977–1978	198.8	16.4	221.2	41.3	49.2	58.6
1978–1979	204.7	14.3	231.7	40.1	47.3	64.9
1979–1980	210.9	13.6	237.9	40.8	44.1	71.8
1980–1981	217.7	10.6	245.4	42.6	46.2	77.1
1981–1982	226.9	5.9	248.8	45.9	46.4	74.7
1982–1983	232.7	9.2	254.7	45.4	44.9	67.1
1983–1984	239.5	10.9	257.6	44.5	45.2	65.5
1984–1985	245.9	9.6	262.9	43.8	45.4	61.4
1985–1986	246.6	8.0	261.8	43.2	43.6	61.0
1986–1987	250.5	5.0	261.3	41.8	41.2	66.6
1987–1988	253.8	5.0	262.5	41.0	36.9	69.1
1988–1989	247.7	2.9	255.8	40.6	30.7	82.4
1989–1990	248.9	9.2	268.0	39.9	27.9	74.5
1990–1991	250.3	10.5	268.8	39.0	26.3	62.8
1991–1992	265.3	13.3	281.4	38.8	27.6	55.3
1992–1993	279.3	14.6	297.3	36.5	32.2	42.4
1993–1994	287.8	12.0	306.4	35.9	37.5	30.2
1994–1995	298.0	11.3	314.7	36.9	41.1	29.7
1995–1996	311.3	10.5	331.0	37.9	43.2	21.6
1996–1997	313.5	5.4	325.5	37.6	44.1	17.8
1997–1998	312.7	4.9	326.6	38.7	42.2	14.7
1998–1999	312.5	5.0	327.7	39.4	40.3	13.7
1999–2000	321.6	6.2	340.8	39.6	38.2	15.6

Source: H.M. Treasury 1999b.
[a] Millions of 1998–1999 pounds.
[b] Percentage of GDP.

H.M. Treasury 1997a explains some other important methodological issues:

1. The stock of public securities is recorded at its market value. It is therefore sensitive to changes in the interest rate: A decline in the interest rate increases the value of the public-sector debt.

2. The appropriate evaluation of tangible assets is not obvious when a market price is lacking: For roads, the value of land at market prices is used, which introduces a considerable variability into road values over time. The question of how to evaluate tangible assets is a particularly delicate one. The method used for public accounting is that of a permanent inventory. This method requires assumptions as to the average life of each type of asset or other methods based on timely evaluations that use the price indexes for categories of assets (cf. Florio 2001a).

3. If accounting at market prices, the PSNW changes with inflation.

4. The definition of PSNW adopted by H.M. Treasury excludes future debts, in particular, those related to unfunded pension schemes.

As for the impact of privatization, H.M. Treasury (1997a) acknowledges that "privatisations may have had an effect on net wealth insofar as the balance sheet valuation of the underlying asset was different from the privatisation proceeds received; in some cases the differences seem to have been significant and we think that this would mainly reflect inaccurate valuation in the balance sheet data (or perhaps valuation on a different basis)" (6).

8.2.4   The NERA Report: On Cash Flow Accounting

This section evaluates the findings of a particularly data rich study by NERA, a consulting firm, for the Center for Policy Studies (NERA 1996, vol. 2, *Finance*). The report analyzes cash flows between the public and private sectors in the United Kingdom between 1980 and 1999 for thirty-three companies that were originally nationalized and later privatized, representing around 75 percent of total U.K. divestiture proceeds. The sample comprises the water and sewerage companies, the electricity generation and distribution companies, British Gas, Associated British Ports, British Airports Authority, British Airways, British Gas, British Telecom, and British Steel. An individual company analysis of cash flows is provided as well, based on annual reports and other official sources. Although based on a large sample and very detailed, the data from the NERA study are less comprehensive than the series I presented in section 8.2. For example, NERA's report does not consider investments. Its focus is exclusively on certain cash flow items.

The NERA report, including its statistical annex, is worth specific mention here for two reasons. First, it is probably unique in the literature on the fiscal impact of privatization in its scope and detail. Second, it offers a good example of the reasons why cash flow analysis requires careful interpretation. Table 8.4, based on NERA data, shows the yearly flows between the public sector and the thirty-three companies NERA studied, and between those companies and the rest of the rest of the private sector. Although the original data were in current pounds, I prefer here to express everything in constant 1995 pounds to make comparison easier. This manipulation of the NERA data does not change ratios in nominal terms.

The flows in table 8.4 include, for the public-sector companies,

• Cash proceeds to the Exchequer from privatization, net of underwriting costs, selling, distribution and brokers' commissions, banks' printing costs, marketing costs, and advisers' fees, without considering the internal cost of government departments. I discussed these transaction costs in chapter 5.

• External-financing repayments. These are the net repayments of government, foreign, or short-term debt (or net borrowings, if the sign is negative sign) by public-sector companies.

• Debt repayments and share redemption. These are repayments of public-sector debt by privatized companies (including debt bought back by BT and some of the electricity companies).

• Interest received by the Exchequer on debt owed to the government by the nationalized industries. This debt was negotiated between H.M. Treasury and the public corporations within the so-called external financial limits (EFLs). These were ceilings on the amount of external finance that the public corporations were authorized to use. The financial transfers from the government to the corporations were in the form of drawing agreements from the National Loans Fund or public dividend capital. The required rate of return on the latter was at least equivalent to the rate of interest charged for the former. In bad years public dividends decreased or were not paid at all. Privatized companies continued to pay National Loans Fund interest.

Table 8.4
Cash flows between the public and private sector, thirty-three nationalized/privatized companies, 1980–1995 (constant 1995 millions of pounds)

Year end (31 March)	1980	1981	1982	1983	1984	1985
Public-sector flows[a]						
Net privatization proceeds				81		2,093
Other flows to public sector						
External-financing repayments[c]	−3,143	−3,157	−2,695	−426	17	−1,341
Debt repayments and share redemptions				46		73
Interest received on government debt	1,743	2,397	2,123	2,100	1,956	1,801
Corporation tax received	97	55	359	395	422	228
Dividends received	39	15			2	18
Other						
Total other flows	−1,266	−689	−211	2,114	2,397	781
Total flows to public sector	−1,266	−689	−211	2,195	2,395	2,874
Private-sector flows[b]						
Share (and debt) purchases				−84		−2,350
Other flows to private sector						
External-financing repayments[c]				−46	17	180
Interest received	1,717	1,991	1,813	1,684	1,492	1,326
Dividends received					2	3
Total other flows	1,743	1,991	1,813	1,639	1,512	1,508
Total flows to private sector	1,717	1,991	1,813	1,554	1,512	−842

Source: Author's calculations based on NERA 1996, vol. 2, *Finance*, table 5.1: Combined Financial Flows for All 33 Companies.
Note: The thirty-three companies are associated British Ports, British Airports Authority, British Airways, British Gas, British Steel, British Telecom, National Power, PowerGen, National Grid, Eastern Electricity, East Midlands Electricity, London Electricity, MAN-WEB, Midlands Electricity, Northern Electricity, NORWEB, SEEBOARD, Southern Electricity, SWALEC, SWEB, Yorkshire Electricity, Scottish Hydro-Electric, Scottish Power, Anglian Water, Northumbrian Water, North West Water, Severn Trent Water, Southern Water, South West Water, Thames Water, Welsh Water, Wessex Water, Yorkshire Water.
[a] Cash flows from the companies to (the rest of) the public sector. Negative entries indicate that the companies were net recipients of public-sector funds.
[b] Cash flows from the companies to (the rest of) the private sector. Negative entries indicate that the companies were net recipients of funds from the rest of the private sector.
[c] A negative entry indicates that the companies were net recipients of financing from either the public sector (this would be shown in government statistics as positive external financial limits) or the private sector.

1986	1987	1988	1989	1990	1991	1992	1993	1994	1995
1,967	4,783	4,041	4,561	2,229	5,547	7,098	6,402	4,675	3,422
128	2,676	2,026	2,776	1,754	376	50			
96	1,620	396	800	1,135	532	1,344	1,501	849	2,195
1,735	1,831	1,810	1,665	1,113	841	771	619	412	230
619	1,419	2,229	2,229	1,835	2,639	2,350	2,935	2,054	2,679
425	458	468	447	429	449	449	339	97	98
							538	1	−0,41
3,002	8,006	6,930	7,917	6,266	4,838	4,964	5,929	3,413	5,203
4,969	12,789	10,969	12,478	8,494	10,385	12,062	12,332	8,089	8,625
−1,967	−5,095	−4,100	−4,623	−2,395	−5,839	−7,315	−6,940	−4,775	−3,481
−204	415	−1,595	−1,797	−2,260	−4,558	−3,094	−2,001	−1,946	−74
1,256	1,019	857	908	1,015	1,009	1,420	1,632	1,568	1,760
335	377	866	1,005	1,273	1,844	2,603	2,555	2,904	3,775
1,387	1,811	128	115	29	−1,704	928	2,184	2,526	5,461
−579	−3,284	−3,972	−4,508	−2,366	−7,545	−6,387	−4,755	−2,249	1,981

• Corporation tax received. All privatized companies pay advance corporation tax, and some nationalized companies do as well.

• Dividends received on the government's residual shareholdings in privatized corporations whose stock was placed in tranches.

• Other flows, particularly proceeds from the sale to the private sector of debt owned by BT and received from electricity companies in respect to property income claw-back arrangements.

Table 8.4 also reports cash flows between the thirty-three companies and the rest of the private sector:

• Purchases of shares and debt, gross of transaction costs.

• Financing repayments. These are the net repayments (or borrowing, if the sign is negative) from the privatized companies to the private sector.

• Interest received. This consists of payments of interest by the companies to private lenders. Before privatization, lenders other than the
government included the European Investment Bank and other foreign
or domestic financiers (usually for short term loans).

• Dividends received. These are dividends paid by the companies to
private shareholders (thus they exclude dividends paid on any remaining shares owned by the British government).

The NERA report had a number of interesting findings. The sale of
shares in the thirty-three companies generated average (nominal) proceeds for the government of £3.5 billion per year in 1985–1995. In addition, from 1987 onward, the government received further net inflows
of between £3.3 billion and £5.8 billion per year from the privatized
companies. Taken as a whole, these same companies were net recipients of government funds in the early 1980s. Additional inflows to the
Exchequer from these companies in 1985–1995 included the corporation tax, dividends from residual government shareholding, and con-
tinuing interest on and repayments of government debt.

The report acknowledges that the analysis performed cannot give a
complete picture of the impact of privatization on public finances in
Britain. First, the original NERA figures are in current pounds, and this
is not appropriate for comparisons before and after privatization or for
averages across years, like those mentioned above. (As noted, I prefer
to consider constant pounds in table 8.4.) Second, and most important,
obviously against cash proceeds there are assets transferred to the private sector. Cash flow accounting considers only one side of the coin.
Third, in some cases, the time horizon of the analysis does not seem
appropriate for a comprehensive evaluation of the fiscal impact of privatization, because of substantial residual debt. Net present values of
economic flows would give a more comprehensive view of the long-
term position of the Exchequer following the divestitures of public corporations. Fourth, the analysis does not consider public debts written
off or created at divestiture (for example, the government wrote off
£1.5 billion in debt of the water companies). Fifth, there is not a counterfactual; neither is there any provision for the cost to public finances
of unemployment and other welfare benefits disbursed to displaced
workers of privatized companies.

In fact, the NERA report mentions most of these points and carefully
states the nature of the exercise. One might think, however, that the
results suggest that privatization was beneficial to the Exchequer and
the taxpayer, because before divestiture, "these 33 companies ... taken

as a whole, were net recipients of public sector funds in the early 1980s" (NERA 1996, i), whereas after privatization, they were transferring funds to the public sector.

A closer look at table 8.4 confirms that in 1980–1983, the thirty-three companies were net borrowers from the government. The yearly amount was decreasing over time, however, and was apparently low when compared with the substantial investment of the public corporations (not reported in the NERA study, but see my discussion in section 8.2.2). Figure 8.4 shows that before the beginning of substantial divestitures in 1984, the net borrowing requirement of the nationalized industries was negligible or small. In fact, the thirty-three companies, even before the start of privatization, were positively contributing to public finances. They were no longer net borrowers and instead generated a cash surplus for the Exchequer in 1983 and 1984. In the following years, some of the thirty-three companies were still owned, totally or partially, by the government. Therefore, the net cash flow we observe in these years comes from a mixture of privatized and still nationalized industries (for example, the electricity companies). The net flow toward the public sector is clearly positive and increasing. Moreover, privatization proceeds obviously match asset sales, exactly as asset acquisitions match government finance before divestiture. Therefore, in the first instance, those flows do not influence the taxpayers' financial position, and I prefer to consider them neutral (I disregard here underpricing of assets in the privatized firms).

Second, a substantial part of the cash flows transferred to government by the companies after 1986 were debt repayments to the Exchequer. In particular, companies still owned by the state were paying back their debt to the Exchequer in years 1986–1992. The Exchequer continued to cash debt repayment by the privatized firms until the end of the time series and probably beyond it. Again, these flows are neutral: The public sector gets back its loans, and standing credit becomes cash.

Third, the cash flows that are most worth our attention here are the interest on government debt and corporation tax. The NERA data actually show that the corporation tax gradually substitutes for interest and dividends previously paid by companies to the Exchequer. At the end of our time horizon, the annual corporation tax cash flow to the Exchequer is £2.6 billion. This is the flow that we should compare with interest and dividends paid to the Exchequer before privatization.

In the long term, therefore, privatization proceeds match asset sales, debt repayment matches standing government loans, and corporate taxes take the place of interest and dividends to the public sector.

Moreover, the observed flow of interest and dividends underestimates the potential interest and dividends to the Exchequer under continued public ownership. In fact, as time series and company case histories may show, there is evidence that in the 1980s, the organizational and financial restructuring of public corporations was successful at reducing the need for external finance, even before the announcement of privatization. Therefore, the NERA data do not support the view that divestitures improved the long-term position of the Exchequer or of the taxpayer. What they say instead is that in the short term, the Exchequer exchanged fixed assets, credits, and its current and future quasi rents for cash and for future corporate taxes. In other words, the Exchequer became more liquid, not necessarily more rich.

My interpretation has a counterpart in the cash flows between the privatized companies and the private sector. Before privatization, the private sector received positive cash flows from the nationalized industries, mainly through interest on short-term loans. The private sector then paid for shares in the privatized companies and purchases of debt. Suppose, again, despite the evidence of asset underpricing at privatization, that against these outflows there was an exact acquisition of assets. This operation would then be neutral in terms of the overall value of asset holding. Nevertheless, when we focus, in table 8.4, on "Other flows to the private sector," the negative external-financing repayments imply that the privatized companies became net borrowers again over the period studied, as their nationalized predecessors were.

There is, of course, a striking generation of cash flows to pay dividends and interest to the private debt owners and shareholders. This reflects the dramatically increased profitability of the privatized companies. I discussed profitability in detail in chapters 4 and 5, where I observed that increased profits do not strongly correlate with an increase in productivity performance after ownership change but do correlate with other factors.

To sum up, it would be meaningless to say that the taxpayers benefited from privatization because the Exchequer shifted from assets to liquidity or from negative total cash flows to positive ones. In the same vein, it would be unreasonable to say that the private sector got a bad deal because it received positive cash flows from nationalized industries and negative ones when those industries were privatized.

The NERA report does not actually say this, however. It is carefully worded and a good data source as a starting point for more structured analysis. Accurate interpretation of the report's data requires an understanding of cash flow accounting, of the report's internal logic, and of its limitations. A comprehensive discounted cash flow analysis would consider any individual privatization as a project, forecast cash flows until the relevant distant time horizon, and compare the project scenarios with and without privatization.

8.2.5   The Windfall Tax

With the arrival of the Labour government in 1997 there was a sort of official acknowledgment that privatized firms had been sold at too low a price and that the initial regulation was too lax (Vass 1997). The new government decided to introduce a new tax, the so-called windfall tax, that aimed to capture at least a part of the excess profits of privatized firms and to fund a New Deal for Britain's unemployed. The tax base was "to tax, at a rate of 23 percent, the difference between the value of the company at privatization and a 'more realistic' valuation based upon that company's after-tax profits for up to the first four years after privatization. That more realistic value was found by averaging profits for the first four years, as set out in the company accounts, and by multiplying that annual average profit figure by a price-earnings ratio, set at nine" (Baldwin and Cave 1999, 234). The total receipts from the tax amounted to £5.2 billion, with 28 percent coming from the RECs, 12.5 percent from electricity-generating firms, 31.7 percent from firms in the water sector, and the remainder from all of the others, including telecommunications companies (Chennells 1997).

The windfall tax has been criticized from various points of view. Some have observed that it did not hit the shareholders that benefited from the excess profits that resulted from the original underpricing of the privatized firms. These were the buyers at placement, who could have resold their shares and paid only those taxes required under the ordinary tax regime. It was also said that the tax constituted a breach of "regulatory contract," weakening the future credibility of the government.

I can subscribe to both of these critiques to a certain degree, but here it is only worthwhile commenting on the first one. Excess profits arise because of a prolonged difference between the return on capital in a privatized sector and a benchmark index of returns in the financial markets. This difference originates from expectations of the sector's continued market power. At stake here is the whole system for regulating privatized firms, not only the initial underpricing of those firms.

In chapter 5, I documented the extent of abnormal returns in the long term. The amount of the windfall tax is probably equal to one-third of the value I estimated for the initial underpricing of the privatized U.K. firms (£14–17 billion) or the immediate return for buyers at placement. Long-term excess profits are a different story. Their value is the discounted sum of additional returns to shareholders after the initial underpricing. I develop this point in section 8.3.

The question arises as to how to consider this tax in calculations of taxpayer and shareholder welfare. When evaluating the relative impact of privatization on the welfare of shareholders and taxpayers, one has to make a decision about the time horizon to be considered. If the time horizon is from 1979 until now, the tax should be included in the evaluation, like several other things, including the deflation of stock values in recent years. I think, however, that the appropriate time horizon for our purposes is 1979–1997, the years of Conservative governments. We want to assess the results of a rather coherent policy experiment, and it is very unlikely that a continued Conservative cabinet would have introduced a windfall tax. Having said this, in the final chapter I test the overall evaluation by including the tax in my analysis of privatization's welfare impacts.

8.2.6 The Private Finance Initiative

The Private Finance Initiative (PFI) was launched at the beginning of the 1990s. Whereas with privatization the state sells the assets it owns, with the PFI the state acquires the capital goods it needs in a new form. In fact, the government makes a contract with private companies that implement purchases the government is planning and are responsible for managing the goods purchased on behalf of the state. The sectors in which this type of contract is now most common in Great Britain are health, prisons, transport, and defense. The contracts can be divided into three types (Pollitt 2000):

• purchase of services from the private sector, which is the most common form; in this case the private contractor is responsible for the investment and for managing it and receives a payment for the services effectively supplied to the public sector (this is how privately managed prisons, e.g., were financed)

• concessions to private-sector operators for the construction and running of financially free-standing infrastructures, in which the investment is recovered through tariffs (e.g., toll bridges)

• joint ventures, which are essentially cases falling between the first two types

The contracts can provide for long-term payments, payments according to the service supplied, or payments according to the availability of the asset, and the type of payment specified determines different risk and incentive structures for the supplier of the services.

At the beginning of 2000, about 250 public projects were financed using PFI methods, with an investment by private companies of around £15 billion and with a cut in capital account public spending of between 20 and 30 percent for the year.[6] This method of financing public infrastructures started in 1992 with the Major government and has continued under the Blair government. There were two modifications to the initiative following official policy reviews: the launch of initiatives called public-private partnerships, and the constitution of a company of mixed capital, Partnership U.K. (see Privatisation International 1999, 2000).

Again, PFI risks creating some financial illusion. Against a decrease in capital account spending in a given year, there is a contractual commitment for the future, sometimes long term. For roughly two hundred contracts, it is estimated that future payments over the space of twenty-five years will be £84 billion (1997 National Housing Federation data, quoted in Pollitt 2000).

A number of surveys by the National Audit Office concluded that although the results of PFI projects were very good in some cases, in others they were poor, because of the excessive future cost. Pollitt (2000) concludes his review of the initiative with this analysis: "At its best however the PFI provides finance for cash strapped departments, saves time and money, stimulates innovation and efficiently allocates risk. At its worst it leads to unreasonable future claims, costs money and time and ineffectively and expensively allocates risk. It remains to be seen how the balance between the best and the worst scenario will alter over time as experience with the PFI grows and as projects mature" (35).

One politically delicate aspect of the initiative is that through the PFI (and the same is true of privatization), a present-day government can at a low cost make choices that backfire in the (even distant) future. In this respect, an accounting issue related to the PFI is worth mentioning. In business practice (rules of the Accounting Standards Board), future payments for contracts between private firms similar to those between the government and private firms under the PFI should not be capitalized unless the supplier carries any contractual risk. If, on the other hand, the contract is a lease, accountants should capitalize future costs at their net present value. If the government followed these accounting rules in regard to PFI contracts, today's reductions in capital account spending would clearly be measured against future expenditure. From what I can see, the argument that privatization allowed the government to avoid expenses for considerable investments in various sectors must be qualified as follows. Present avoided expenditure should be assessed as a counterpart of the net present value of future receipts.

The PFI illustrates the accounting confusion that one encounters when future flows are ignored in investment and divestment decisions. I am not implying that the public infrastructures financed through PFI have always been a bad deal for the government, as I do not imply that privatization has always been bad. The way in which the British government has presented data in regard to both, however, has often been inadequate for evaluating their long-term public-finance impact. In a sense, the same element of fiscal illusion affects the government's accounting practices with regard to both privatization and the PFI.

8.3 Discussion

Empirical evidence on the impact of privatization on the British taxpayer is neither very extensive nor very reliable. Only recently has an official estimate been available of the public-sector net worth, and without more comprehensive accounting, the cash flow data on privatization proceeds and their role in reducing Britain's public debt have little meaning.

The available figures seem to tell a clear story, however. When the Tory government took office, it was committed to tight money and a reduction of the borrowing requirement. A major reason for the divestitures of public companies was to avoid future investments, particularly in the telecommunications and water sectors. Treasury accounting considered these investments (mistakenly) simply as liabilities (whereas they were in actuality asset acquisitions). The divestitures generated a substantial amount of receipts for the Exchequer. At first the combination of privatization, a regressive increase in the tax burden, stabilization of current expenditures, and reduction of capital expenditures brought the national debt down. Subsequently, this policy mix became unsustainable. There was a wide discontent among the

British population on fiscal issues, particularly with the poll tax. After Thatcher's resignation, the Major government oversaw sizable budget deficits, despite further privatization of national industries. The net worth of the public sector collapsed.

Moreover, although the sale at a discount of council houses had progressive redistribution effects, there was a wider regressive redistribution of posttax income as a complement of the placements of the shares of the privatized firms. According to Leape (2002):

> The nature and timing of the reforms to capital income taxation thus suggest that tax policy in the 1980s was, to a significant extent, driven by the perceived need to create a larger investing population in order to secure the success of the privatisation programme. As these tax changes clearly had major welfare effects, and were undoubtedly strongly regressive in their impact, a comprehensive assessment of the welfare impact of privatisation must also take into account the impact of these tax changes over the period. (8)

In what follows I therefore disregard the opposite redistribution effects of council housing sales (benefits for around 1.5 million low-income households) and of regressive tax reforms (substantial benefits for around two million top-income earners and an increased burden for several million in lower income brackets). Consequently, I refer subsequently to effects on a median taxpayer. (I return to redistribution issues in chapter 10.)

The median taxpayer initially suffered a substantial loss in the capital account from privatization, because of underpricing of firms being privatized, to the benefit of the purchasers, including the foreign sector. Such underpricing occurs in any initial placement of firm shares. Nevertheless, I have shown that privatization IPOs in the United Kingdom were particularly cheap. While the ratios of current spending and tax pressure to GDP did not record any fundamental changes between 1979 and 1997, public investments decreased dramatically over the period.

It is too early to say whether the British taxpayer will have to offset this reduction in the stock of public capital with an increase in taxes or with a decrease in growth and welfare. It is in fact difficult to say what the optimum proportion is between public and private capital in a particular country. Recourse to methods of private finance for public infrastructures may mask the effective expenditure on such infrastructures in the capital account. There is now the perception, however, that infrastructure investment in Britain is largely inadequate and that national productivity may suffer as a result.

One example of investment gap is the railway sector, in which the capital expenditures by Railtrack and the companies running train services are probably not sufficient to guarantee, in the long run, the standard of service required by the sector regulator. Moreover, whereas many other European countries have been able to finance a new network of high-speed train lines, Britain has not built any new line in decades other than the Channel Tunnel.

These are controversial subjects. Nevertheless, I suggest that the taxpayer did not recover the initial loss resulting from underpricing of privatized firms through an increased fiscal dividend. To make calculations simpler, suppose that all privatization occurs in 1995, near the end of the observation period. Suppose also that the social discount rate is 5 percent. (All figures are in constant 1995 pounds). I use rounded figures, near my best estimates, based on available data. I disregard here council house sales and direct sales of some firms; thus the calculation at this stage is purely illustrative, but realistic.

The government cashes £70 billion as privatization proceeds plus the perpetual value of corporate taxes. Let us say that, based on H.M. Treasury estimates reported previously or on NERA data, revenue from the latter is £2.8 billion per year (starting around 1995) or £56 billion in perpetual value. Therefore, taxpayers are entitled through privatization to around £126 billion of net present value of corporate taxes, under an infinite time horizon.

Suppose then the average effective corporate income tax rate to be 30 percent for privatized companies, slightly less the statutory rate (because of some exemptions, and so on). Thus, the gross-of-tax profit for the privatized companies may be around £9.3 billion per year. This is a conservative estimate: NERA reports for 1995, and for 75 percent of the privatized assets, £2.6 billion in corporation tax plus £3.9 billion in dividends, and one has to add to those figures retained profits, not shown in the NERA data. If dividends were as high as 50 percent of profits, and we extrapolate from the NERA sample, the gross profit for privatized companies would be £13.8 billion. (I suspect that in reality, around 1995, the actual gross profit of privatized companies exceeded that amount, but I prefer here to use the more conservative estimate.) The perpetual value of net profits for the shareholders of the privatized firms was then £186 billion − £56 billion = £130 billion.

Turning now to taxpayers, from the mid-1970s until the mid-1980s, the nationalized industries paid yearly to the exchequer, as interest and dividends, more than £7 billion (in constant 1995 pounds). Because the trend was toward diminishing interest and dividends, and again to be conservative, £6.5 billion would seem a reasonable counterfactual estimate of the cash transfers from the restructured nationalized industries to the Exchequer over the same period. (Moreover, again to be conservative, I ignore here possible retained profits within the public corporations.)

Under these assumptions, the net present value of future cash flows for the Exchequer originating from interest and dividends of the nationalized industries is £130 billion. In this illustrative example, the latter value is the same as the value of net profits to private shareholders, simply because the effective tax rate in this example is the same as the ratio of excess to normal returns.

Because the Exchequer cashed £70 billion + £56 billion = £126 billion from privatization, the British taxpayers lost £4 billion. If we apply a shadow price of 1.3 to public funds (see, e.g., Laffont and Tirole 2000), taxpayers lost, in welfare terms, around £5 billion. With different assumptions, the result may change and may look slightly better for the taxpayer. For example, if we include the proceeds from the windfall tax (around £5.2 billion), there is a slightly positive balance for the taxpayer (but I view that tax as an aspect of a different policy regime).

However, in terms of opportunity cost, the loss was much higher. The reservation price for the private investors in privatized firms was £130 billion (or even more, as previously noted). They paid 70 billion for their shares in the firms. There clearly was ample room for a better deal for the taxpayer, even if the private discount rate is higher than the public one (more on this in chapter 10).

Two points need to be stressed in regard to this illustrative example. First, the widely held view that the nationalized industries were a burden for the Exchequer is the result of improper, unilateral accounting. The Exchequer was the owner of the nationalized industries. Borrowing from the private sector was limited, and in any case, it entered in the external-financing limits. Therefore, the nationalized industries largely had to borrow from their owner. The interest they paid on these loans was sizable. Actually, it represented most of the Exchequer's return on its own capital.

I have shown that the borrowing requirement of the nationalized industries was the counterpart of their deficit after the payment of interest to the owner, or the public sector. Investment matched the deficit. When we consolidate everything, assets and liabilities, real investment and deficits, the taxpayer had a potential profit in real terms.

The nationalized industries were in fact managing a net accumulation of capital. The profit for the taxpayer was embodied in the new infrastructure and the other fixed assets of the nationalized industries. On yearly average, this was two-thirds of public investment. The Treasury's obsession with short-term cash disbursement, on one hand, and its disregard of real asset acquisition and long-term returns, on the other, was illogical. Moreover, at the beginning of the 1980s, even before any grand privatization plans or their announcement, the nationalized industries as an aggregate were paying back in cash to the Exchequer more than they received. The trend was clearly toward further improvement in the financial conditions of most public corporations.

Second, an element in this analysis of the fiscal impact of divestiture is the counterfactual scenario: how much profit would the firms have made if they had remained public? In the calculation in this section, I have supposed that the returns (inclusive of interest to their owner) of the nationalized industries showed zero excess profit. It is likely, however, that some corporations (e.g., BT) could have been able to earn monopoly profits, whereas British Rail operated at a loss. Clearly, the counterfactual depends, inter alia, on the effectiveness of industry restructuring of the latter, and price regulation under continued public ownership. It can be conjectured that if the same regulatory régime applied under continued public ownership as the one observed after privatization, the nationalized industries might have accumulated large extra profits. One has to remember that the nationalized industries never enjoyed a stable price regulation framework. Under $RPI - X$ price cap regulation, a clear set of rules about retained profits, and appropriate incentives for managers and workers, I think many public enterprises would have performed financially not very differently from their observable privatized counterparts.

I return to the discussion of the counterfactual in chapter 10. Here, however, I have been conservative. My illustrative calculations are based on official figures on financial trends in the nationalized industries. These show why the net worth of the public sector decreased with divestiture and why the claim that the underpricing of the privatized firms at sale was recovered through the fiscal dividend (i.e., through payment of future corporate [and other] taxes to the Exchequer) is unconvincing.

I conclude that the British taxpayer received no net benefit from privatization. An improvement of the fiscal balance was possible if there was a wide gap between the expectations of profit under public and private management, and taxation or placements through auctions recouped to the Exchequer a large share of these profits. With widespread underpricing at flotation and lower corporate tax and capital income tax rates, such an improvement did not take place.

Moreover, whatever the counterfactual returns under continued public ownership, in terms of the opportunity cost of assets, privatization largely failed to extract all the possible income from purchasers of shares in the privatized firms. The cash proceeds from divestitures were not reinvested. In Newbery's (2002) words: "If we ask what happened to privatization proceeds ... the implication is that Britain has eaten the capital that was in the public sector" (8).

8.4   Further Reading

Buiter (1985) proposed a more general public-sector "comprehensive net worth," but calculating it raises considerable methodological and practical problems (cf. Odling-Smee and Riley 1985). Mayer and Meadowcroft (1986) advance some public-finance topics related to privatization (see also Vickers and Yarrow 1988a). Among other things, they propose an example to illustrate the financial illusion created accounting practices in regard to the placement of the second tranche of BT shares, contrasting receipts with the loss of gross profits (net of investments) and the interest paid by BT to the government.

The *Budget Report*, released yearly in March by H.M. Treasury, updates public-finance data for the United Kingdom. A useful source for international comparisons of United Kingdom public-finance data are the OECD surveys (1998, 2000). There are some considerable problems in such cross-country comparisons, however, particularly because the definition of public investment across countries is not homogeneous (see, for detailed discussion, Florio 2001).

Sawyer (2003) expresses several convincing criticisms of PFI. Bertero (2002) discusses mechanisms that can increase the financial discipline of state-owned enterprises and observes that some of these mechanisms were potentially available for the U.K. public sector as an alternative to privatization.

9   The British Telecom Case History

9.1   Topics for Discussion

This chapter offers a discussion of the performance of British Telecom before and after privatization. I use a data set based on company accounts over forty years (1960–1999) and additional company information on several variables. The analysis focuses particularly on output, prices, revenues, costs, employment, productivity, profits, investments, and welfare impact on consumers. Therefore I reconsider some of the issues discussed in previous chapters in the context of the BT case history.

First, I explore whether there is a change in real output and productivity trends after divestiture as compared with the nationalization period and whether it is possible to detect any change in the rate of growth of labor productivity, of capital productivity, and of TFP, and to try to understand the determinants of any such change discovered.

Second, I break down revenues into their output and price components and search for any major changes over time in the different services offered by BT. After divestiture, OFTEL regulated most BT prices: thus, it is interesting to determine the correlation between effective and permitted tariff trends.

Third, I turn to costs and ask whether there was a change in staff costs after privatization. Any such change might be a consequence of changes in employment, in wages, or in both. The share of wages in company income depends also upon changes in procurement. One reason put forward for privatizing various British industries was the difficulty the Exchequer had in financing huge investment programs in nationalized industries. Therefore, I wish to observe the investment performance and self-financing ratio of BT. I am interested in the expenditures for both fixed assets and research and development, because both influence the long-run performance of the company.

Finally, I ask how divestiture changed the company's profitability and how its operative profits were split between taxes, interest, dividends, and retained net profits. I want to explore how different agents shared the social costs and benefits of privatization.

For many reasons a reconsideration of the performance of British Telecom (now BT plc) before and after divestiture may offer an interesting case study in the broader debate on the economics of privatization. As Megginson and Netter (2001) observe, the placement of BT shares in November 1984 (Kleinwort Benson Ltd. 1984) was the turning point for privatization policy. Privatization was proposed (Beesley 1981) in a key industry whose services are relevant for millions of domestic and business users, one in which technology has been impressively progressing and demand rapidly expanding, and one that displays a complex combination of natural monopoly and potentially competitive activities. The BT initial public offering of around 51 percent of total shares attracted hundreds of thousands of individual investors, excited the City, and captured the interest of the public at large. Governments and other telecommunications firms immediately perceived its relevance for the industry worldwide. Thus BT divestiture provided a crucial experience for the wider policy of privatization and regulation of network utilities. This puts the British Telecom case history in a class of its own in the huge existing empirical literature on privatization. Moreover, because the divestiture of British Telecom took place more than twenty years ago, and because we can go back with data for the company at least to the 1960s, British Telecom offers longer time series than any other privatization. Therefore, there is less risk of a bias as a result of a small sample of observations.

Unlike AT&T in the United States, British Telecom was not broken up, and until the end of the 1990s, it owned more than 90 percent of local lines in the United Kingdom. Only in 1991 was its duopoly with a small competitor, Mercury, ended, new licenses issued, and the access charges structure modified. In fact only after six years beyond divestiture was the company to wider market liberalization and tough price cap regulation. The case of BT thus offers some ingredients for a natural experiment in regard to the question "Does ownership matter?"

The rest of the chapter is organized in the following manner. First, I present a brief historical background and some results of previous study on British Telecom. Second, I offer my reading of the firm's performance over forty years. Third, I turn to the welfare impact of BT privatization and discuss the results of previous research. I conclude by summing up and evaluating my findings.

9.2 Empirical Evidence

9.2.1 Historical Background

Until 1980, British Telecom was part of the Post Office. The origins of the Post Office date back as far as the seventeenth century with the introduction of the Postmaster General. In the middle of the nineteenth century, the General Post Office (GPO) was part of the civil service. Its managers in the Victorian era belonged to the elite of public administration, with their own traditions and a proud sense of belonging.

The telegraph service had begun in the private sector in the first half of the nineteenth century. The British government established public monopoly for the Post Office in 1869, both to safeguard the traditional postal service and because of the dissatisfaction with the poor quality of the private service. In 1870, the telephone was introduced, and the GPO was responsible only for the "trunk service," that is, the links between cities, whereas the local service was managed by private companies. In 1912 the government set up a telephone public monopoly that was to last for almost seventy years, until 1981 (with the curious exception of the city of Kingston-upon-Hull, in which the telephone service provider was municipally owned).

In the 1930s, dissatisfaction with the management of the GPO was already apparent (Bridgeman Committee).[1] In the 1950s the waiting list for connection was half a million, compared to three million subscribers. This highly unsatisfactory situation was probably due to the Post Office's status of departmental enterprise, with a exceedingly bureaucratic internal organization. A series of mainly accounting reforms began in 1961 that did not prove to be conclusive. The company became then a nationalized industry. One internal witness recalls: "Despite the 1961 Act the GPO was quite profoundly unsuited to the tasks it had to face. Its atmosphere still wore the imprint of the Edwardian Civil Service and of the discipline called forth by two World Wars. It was staffed by hierarchies fated to conflict and led by officials wrestling with their own system. On the telecommunications side it was sitting on a bomb of technology and growth. The situation could not be allowed to go on" (Harper 1997, 61).

A first breakthrough in the organization of the industry came with the Labour government and the nomination of Tony Benn as Postmaster General, who proposed studying the possibility of granting the GPO the status of public corporation. In 1967, a government White Paper proposed the creation a public corporation with separate branches for post and telecommunications. With the 1969 Telecommunications Act—after exactly a century—Parliament transferred to the new corporation the privileges provided for in the 1869 Post Act and several subsequent acts (a veritable jungle of laws and special regulations).

The decisive step in the privatization process was taken in 1981 with the constitution, as part of the Telecommunications Act, of the British Telecommunications Corporation. Up to 1984, BT was under the responsibility of the Secretary of State for Telecommunications. November 1984 saw the placement on the stock exchange of 51 percent of the ordinary shares in the new corporation. This first placement was wholly a fixed-price public offering, with a small part of the stock reserved for employees. In December 1991, the British government started to place on the stock exchange roughly half of the shares it still held. The remaining 22 percent of the shares in the firm were then sold in 1993. The quota on nonordinary shares owned by the state was reduced to one (the golden share) in 1993.

From the point of view of market regime, up until 1981 the company operated as a statutory monopoly, except for a small number of services for the private networks within companies or their networks. In 1982, the government granted another firm, Mercury, a license to operate telephony. This established a duopoly, with the incumbent in a strong dominant position. There was subsequent liberalization in 1991 (with sixty new licenses issued). At the end of 1996, there were 126 cable operators in the United Kingdom authorized to deal directly with the public. In 1995, for the first time ever, there was a decline in the number of domestic subscribers to BT; competition was even more ruthless in the business sector and for international calls. Even so, in 1997 British Telecom still had about 90 percent of the telecommunications market and twenty million subscribers (Mercury had 375,000, and many of the other licenses were not operative).

Parliament delegated to OFTEL the regulation of prices and other aspects of the services BT provided. Initially about 50 percent of the company's turnover was subject to an $RPI - X$ price cap, with X initially set at 3 percent. In 1997, this portion rose to 60 percent and X increased to 7.5 percent, while the RPI dropped. Between 1997 and

2001, X decreased again to 4.5 percent and applied to only a quarter of the business (domestic users with low traffic). In a situation of increasingly stringent price caps (and, since 1992, also stagnation in the demand for some services) company strategy concentrated on inputs and restructuring of costs. There was a huge downsizing in 1993.

In the first ten years following privatization, the major technological innovation in the company was the change from electromechanical to digital switching (from 20 percent at the end of the 1980s to 100 percent by the late 1990s). In fact, an investment cycle started long before divestiture (for more details, see Harper 1997; OFTEL 1995; and OFTEL 2000).

9.2.2   Earlier Studies: Output and Productivity

I first briefly look at some earlier studies of British Telecom's productivity performance. Table 9.1 presents some findings in this area.

Between 1960–1961 and 1975–1976, the growth rate of BT's output at 1970 prices was in the region of 10 percent annually, whereas employment was growing at about 2.1 percent annually. Consequently, there was a very large increase in per capita product, of around 7.7 percent annually (NEDO 1976). Gross fixed capital in turn grew by 10 percent annually in real terms, which is the equivalent of a growth in capital stock of about 6 percent. The average annual changes in product per capital unit and in per capita capital were 3.6 percent and 3.9 percent, respectively. TFP, using official aggregated data for the shares of capital and labor in the telecommunications sector (67.9 percent for labor and 32.1 percent for capital in 1970) shows a rate of growth of 6.4 percent annually. The picture that emerges from these data is one of steady growth in both product and productivity for British Telecom under a regime of public ownership.

Harper (1997, appendix 2)[2] says that the firm's rate of productivity growth (1970–1995) was about 7.5 percent annually up to 1989, with the firm showing exponential growth. There was a break in the pattern of growth at the beginning of the 1990s because of the economic recession at the time, and then a return to the previous trend.

According to Foreman-Peck and Manning (1988) and Foreman-Peck (1989), British Telecom's TFP increased after privatization. This increase, however, was in line with that of similar companies elsewhere in Europe. Consequently, one cannot attribute any specific TFP effect to privatization during the first years of the new regime.

Table 9.1
Selected earlier studies on BT productivity performance

Author	Period considered	Some variables considered	Main results
NEDO 1976	1960–1975	Output, employment, labor productivity, investment, TFP	Yearly average increase in output was 10%, employment 2.1%, labor productivity 7.7%, investment 6%, TFP 6.4%.
Foreman-Peck and Manning 1988	1985–1986	Tornqvist TFP index, labor productivity, lines per employee, international comparison	BT performance not better than that of its state-owned, monopolistic counterparts in continental Europe.
Kwoka 1993	1965–1987	TFP (compared BT and AT&T)	"Scale economies continue to play the principal role in productivity gains." Privatization responsible for 17% of productivity growth at BT.
Bishop and Thompson 1992b	1970–1990	TFP, labor productivity	Labor productivity average yearly increase: 4.3%, 1970–1979, 7.2%, 1980–1990. But TFP drops from 4.6% to 3.2%.
Parker 1994	1979–1994	Profitability, R&D, labor productivity, TFP	Finds increase of labor productivity and decrease of TFP, profitability increases after divestiture.
NERA 1995 and NERA 2000	1990–1994 1995–1998	Comparison with U.S. operators of unit costs and other service indicators, various estimation techniques	BT cost per switched line £341, better than most U.S. operators, but less than state-owned France Telecom (£315), Deutsche Telekom (£308). Cost per minute: All companies, except France Telecom, do better than BT. Other techniques show an estimated inefficiency 1.5–4% of a "target level."
Harper 1997	1970–1995	Productivity growth	Yearly average increase 7.5%, with small effect of privatization
Martin and Parker 1997	1977–1995	Labor productivity, TFP, profitability	TFP yearly average increase under public ownership 2.9%, postprivatization profitability increases.
Durant, Legge, and Moussios 1998	1982–1993	Labor productivity, profitability, investment (time series modeling)	Increased private ownership had no impact on any of the dependent variables.
Boylaud and Nicoletti 2000	1991–1998	Labor productivity, OECD countries panel data	No clear evidence of effects of ownership structure on performance.

Bishop and Kay (1988) show that BT's average rate of growth in TFP over the period 1979–1988 was 1.9 percent, with a rate of 1.6 percent before privatization and 2.2 percent after. Their results are not comparable with those of other authors because of the time period considered and computation methods. Bishop and Thompson (1992b) found that the average rate of increase of labor productivity in British Telecom was 4.3 percent in the 1970s and 7.2 percent in the 1980s, but TFP dropped from 4.6 to 3.2 over the period.

Martin and Parker (1997, 100–101, 108–109) study BT's labor productivity and TFP from 1977 to 1995.[3] They do not find a clear pattern in labor productivity or TFP. For example, the average yearly increase in TFP was 7.1 percent in the nationalization (1977–1981) period and decreased to 2.9 percent in the postprivatization (1985–1989) years. Labor productivity increased 15 percent in the latest period (1992–1995) (following wide cuts in the price of labor) but was higher in the preprivatization (1981–1985) years than in the postprivatization period.

It is clear that the greatest changes in labor productivity occurred following the stiffening of price cap regulation (1991), with a drastic reduction in the firm's staff. According to Martin and Parker, the gap between labor productivity and total productivity in the latest period suggests that "there was either exceptional slack in the use of labor inputs or that there is still considerable scope to improve the utilization of non-labor inputs" (104).

As a counterfactual proxy, the same authors deduce the growth in productivity of the economy from the above company productivity trends. The productivity change for BT is always higher than that for the economy as a whole, for both labor and TFP. For TFP, the best results were obtained during the period of nationalization, and for labor productivity in the latest period. The authors comment that the higher-than-average increase in productivity for BT is not surprising for a high-tech sector.

Summing up, previous studies concur in observing that BT's output trend did not dramatically change following privatization. The firm's productivity trend increased after privatization, probably because of the substitution of capital for labor and because of technological change. Nevertheless, comparison with the previous performance of the nationalized industry and international comparison with other companies, some of them state-owned, does not support evidence of a structural break in productivity at privatization.

Unfortunately, several productivity studies consider a limited number of years. In particular, they do not fully consider the BT experience

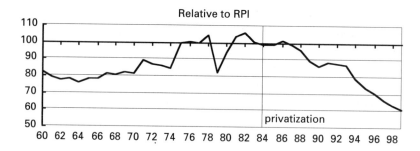

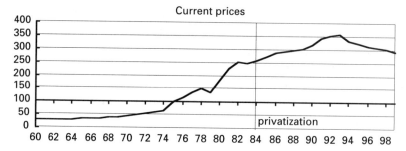

Figure 9.1
Telephone price index (1975 = 100).
Sources: Author's elaboration on NEDO 1976, and ONS, various years.

since nationalization, but just some years before divestiture. The 1970s were, however, particularly troubled by demand shocks. A more comprehensive analysis of the company's productivity should go back at least to include the 1960s.

9.2.3 Earlier Studies: Prices, Wages, and Profits

Figure 9.1 shows the trend of real prices for telephony services (relative to the RPI) between 1960 and 1999. The ratio of price to RPI is stationary (less than one) between 1960 and 1970, then there were sizable increases between 1970 and 1982, and subsequently a decline. For comparison the figure shows nominal prices trends as well. As I show in section 9.2.8, understanding these aggregate data requires detailed analysis for each of the single services provided and categories of users served, and we should not understand them as evidence of a price decrease caused by privatization.

Harper (1997) presents a different series of adjusted prices for 1967–1995, based on BT internal data. Harper's series shows that the huge increase in BT's prices in 1976 resulted from the government's imposition of nonremunerative tariffs during the years of recession prior to 1976, which caused considerable losses. In the same year, there was a radical reform of the budgeting system. Tariffs were similarly adjusted in 1981–1982. Before divestiture, between 1976 and 1984, the average annual reduction in real prices was 3.9%, whereas in the period 1985–1995, it was 4.5 percent. According to Harper, "This is a remarkably small difference, bearing in mind that in marked contrast to the 1970s the national economy was stable from 1984 right up to the 1990 recession, and how rigidly the national industrial relations climate and the incidence of pay disputes had improved" (227). Harper notes that in the twenty-five years between 1970 and 1995, there were two drivers of price reductions: increased volume (which brought down unit costs given the characteristics of increasing returns from the industry) and technical progress. "At no time in the period since 1984," he asserts, "have there been any detectable effects on the overall price envelope attributable to privatisation or competition as such" (228).

Finally, I discuss some previous studies concerning added value, profits, and wages. Martin and Parker (1997), again for 1977–1995, with the same subperiods previously noted, report data on BT's annual rate of return on capital and the value added per worker of the economy as a whole. For each subperiod, they compare BT's annual rate of return on capital with the average return of the industrial and commercial company sector (using the pretax rate of return on capital stock at replacement cost). For BT, the return fluctuates between 14.7 and 22.8 percent, which is between two and three times higher than the average for the economy. Even the added value per worker for BT shows a better performance than that of the rest of the economy.

Martin and Parker also analyze the distribution of business income among production factors, again for the subperiods. Here I deal with only the figures for the nationalization and latest periods for selected components of company accounts, in percentages of turnover. They find that the share of wages was 43.7 percent of turnover during the nationalization period, whereas the share for the latest period was 29.4 percent, and the share of turnover accounted for by purchase of other inputs rose from 19.6 to 34.6 percent over the same period. The share of other items, such as profit and depreciation, did not show much change across time. Martin and Parker comment that the decline in the share of wages in turnover favored profits and capital returns, although more recently, stiffer regulation has reduced profitability. The drop in the share of wages in turnover was mainly to the benefit of other inputs.

Also interesting is Martin and Parker's analysis of relative wages. Wages at BT were 141 percent of the average for the economy in the period of nationalization and were 154 percent in the latest period. Stability of or even increases in wages relative to the average for the economy were observable in all cases considered by Martin and Parker.

Summing up: the existing literature[4] does not support the view that BT's privatization was responsible for a productivity shock. Nor does it support the view that major changes in wages and prices in the firm can be attributed to divestiture per se. There is ample evidence of an increase in net-of-interest profitability, but not of a similar increase in operative profits.

Again, a serious problem with the existing literature on BT performance is that it does not consider the long-run data and fails to compare adequately the nationalization period with the subsequent regime. Moreover, in some cases it fails to take into account the change in the composition of services offered by BT over time.

9.2.4 Sources of Data

This chapter analyzes in detail the performance of BT in the period from 1960 to the advent of the Thatcher government and until 1999–2000. The original data employed in my analysis are taken from the company's *Annual Reports and Accounts* for 1982–1999, the *Extracts from Post Office Accounts and Report of British Telecom for the Year Ended 31 March 1981*, and additional British Telecom publications (see the References) for earlier years. Some additional information on volumes and prices was supplied on request to the author by OFTEL and BT.

Whenever possible I thus offer forty years of data. For more recent data, I am able to offer a detailed reading. Because of changes in definitions and classifications of individual items over time, and particularly after divestiture, in some cases I have had to recur to some ad hoc treatment of data (explained in detail in Florio 2001b). For example, I have reconstructed output data for some years starting from turnover and prices. In turn, I have computed prices as averages for different kinds of tariffs and so on.

I consider yearly data of the following nominal variables, as well as their growth rates and relevant ratios: turnover, prices or unit revenues, output, labor costs, other operating costs, depreciation, profits (gross and net), interest, taxes, retained profits and dividends, investment, and research and development (R&D) expenditures. For the first three of these items, I have also reconstructed the breakdown for specific services (local, national, regional, and international calls; rentals and others) and up to ten types of tariffs.

The presentation of data in this chapter is selective. Some yearly data series are presented in figures or in tables in which I have averaged yearly data in two public-ownership decades and in three post-Thatcher subperiods:

1. nationalization period I: the 1960s

2. nationalization period II: the 1970s

3. preprivatization years: 1979–1984

4. postprivatization years: 1985–1990

5. regulatory change years: 1991–1999

The last of these periods, as noted previously, sees a hardening of the $RPI - X$ regime, a step forward in liberalization, and the end of the investment cycle in new switching technologies. Table 9.2 offers a first overview of the data; an item by item commentary is offered in subsequent sections.

9.2.5 Turnover

British Telecom is a complex organization providing a number of services. I focus on the services outlined in the following classification:

• Calls: The provision of telephone lines for residential and business users, which allows them to make local, national, and international telephone calls and to use data transmission and other services.

• Rentals: Access to the service is through exchange lines, for which a quarterly rental fee is charged. Moreover, the customer may need to pay a quarterly rental fee for rented equipment used to connect to the line, including telephones, faxes, and modems (customer premises equipment). "Rentals" in table 9.3 includes both the fee for the line and that for the equipment.[5]

• Other: The other services provided by BT include public telephones, more high-tech services such as videoconferences (other sales), the rental of lines to other operators (receipts from U.K. operators), mobile telephony (mobile communications), and the Yellow Pages and other

Table 9.2
Summary of BT financial data, 1960–1999 (percentage of turnover)

	National-ization period I 1960–1969	National-ization period II 1970–1979	Prepriva-tization 1980–1984	Postpriva-tization 1985–1990	Regulatory change 1991–1999
Turnover (yearly percentage change)[a]	+11%	+20%	+16%	+10%	+4%
Turnover[b]	100.0	100.0	100.0	100.0	100.0
Labor costs[b,d]	44.5	38.4	42.5	35.1	28.3
Other operating costs[b]	13.7	25.8	20.8	26.9	35.1
Depreciation[b]	20.6	23.0	12.2	13.8	15.3
Gross profit[b]	21.2	20.6	24.4	24.1	21.2
Interest[b]	12.7	15.6	10.5	3.5	1.8
Other items[b]	0.1	−2.1	−0.6	−0.2	−1.4
Tax[b]	n.a.	n.a.	n.a.	7.7	7.3
Net profit[b]	8.4	7.0	14.5	13.2	13.5
Dividend[b]	n.a.	n.a.	n.a.	5.6	9.2
Retained profit (deficits) of the financial year[b]	8.4	7.0	14.5	7.6	4.3
Cash flow/investment ratio[c]	52.9[e]	72.0	106.5	88.7	106.3

Source: Author's elaboration on Post Office and BT data. See table 9.12.
Note: n.a. = not available.
[a] Yearly average increase for the period at current prices.
[b] Yearly percentage average share of turnover for the period.
[c] Cash flow/investment ratio data start from 1966.
[d] Labor cost is calculated only for 1970–1977.
[e] 1966–1969.

directories; it also receives income from other operators for using BT lines (private circuits) or so-called dedicated lines.

Table 9.3 shows a breakdown of turnover over time for these broad items. I focus here on data for the last twenty years, which show some important changes in the structure of BT businesses (in the previous twenty years, the "other" component was very small and rentals were simply correlated with calls).

Between 1980 and 1999 calls accounted for an increasingly smaller share of the company's total turnover. The business of providing a national and international telephone service, which accounted for 60.9 percent of turnover in 1980, progressively became less important over the years. The share of other services in total turnover increased, par-

Table 9.3
BT turnover breakdown

	National-ization period I 1960–1969	National-ization period II 1970–1979	Prepriva-tization years 1980–1984	Postpriva-tization years 1985–1990	Regulatory change 1991–1999
Percentage yearly average increase for the period					
Calls			14.2	10.3	0.1
Rentals	n.a.	n.a.	21.1	4.7	3.8
Others			33.4	23.1	9.9
Total	11.0	20.0	16.0	10.0	4.0
Percentage share of the turnover average for the period					
Calls			56.8	53.5	48.1
Rentals	n.a.	n.a.	34.6	27.8	25.6
Others			8.7	18.7	26.3

Sources: Author's elaboration on BT 1983; BT 1990; BT 1994; and BT 1999.
Note: n.a. = not available.

ticularly that of mobile phone services, which started booming in the second half of the 1980s (after privatization). Growth rates for calls were over 20 percent up to 1984; they progressively fell through the 1980s to below 10 percent in 1990, and then subsequently fell to zero or even below.

The two other categories of turnover recorded quite different dynamics. Rentals showed continuous, if fluctuating, growth and stayed at between 20 and 30 percent of turnover over the period. The turnover from the provision of goods and services[6] carried less weight, especially after 1993, because of the sales of BT-owned shares in Mitel Corporation.

Items classed as other services, such as mobile telephony activities, services linked to the Internet, and private circuits, recorded the fastest growth rates and claimed increasingly larger shares of turnover. The number of cellular telephones (Cellnet, the mobile phones operator owned by BT) increased from 64,000 in 1986 to 4,552,000 in 1998. The share of revenues for this category increased from 8 to 36 percent of total turnover between 1979 and 1999.

The changing structure of the revenues of British Telecom over time should be carefully considered in any analysis of the firm's productivity. Clearly, the boom in cellular telephones was driven by a new technology and was only marginally influenced by privatization. In fact, in

Table 9.4
BT output growth and unit revenue, 1960–1999 (percentage average yearly change)

	National-ization period I 1960–1969	National-ization period II 1970–1979	Prepriva-tization years 1980–1984	Postpriva-tization years 1985–1990	Regulatory change 1991–1999
Inland calls volume[a]	24.6	10.1	4.1	8.6	5.3
International calls volume[a]	118.2	27.2	14.3	12.7	7.0
Inland calls revenues[b]	n.a.	21.7	13.0	10.1	0.7
International calls revenues[b]	n.a.	24.6	10.8	11.0	−1.8
Unit revenues inland calls	n.a.	13.7	8.8	1.5	−4.2
Unit revenues international calls	n.a.	14.2	8.1	1.6	−4.8

Sources: Author's elaboration on BT 1983; BT 1990; BT 1994; and BT 1999.
Note: n.a. = not available.
[a] For the period 1960–1969, the average is based on data for 1960, 1965, and 1967 only.
[b] Average is calculated starting from 1971.

the same years, quite similar or greater growth rates for cellular telephones were recorded by state-owned operators in continental Europe.

9.2.6   Output

The trend in turnover reflects nominal values and should be analyzed by breaking turnover down into the dynamics of output and unit revenues. As table 9.4 and figure 9.2 show, the volume of international calls increased at rates of more than 100 percent yearly in the 1960s and of 27 percent in the 1970s, then increased at a lower rate until 1990 and continued at around 7 percent in the 1990s. At that time, international calls were the object of intense competition. Other operators effectively challenged BT in this business.

Before privatization, the volume of national calls rose considerably more than thereafter, and in the 1990s the rate of growth seems to converge with that of international traffic. There was a noticeable increase in the volume of international calls, which in 1999 was six times that in 1980, whereas for inland calls, the increase was to less than three times the volume of traffic in 1980.

In fact, the growth in volumes partially compensates for the decrease in unit revenues from international calls resulting from competition.

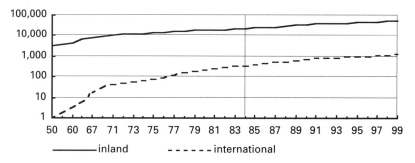

Figure 9.2
BT output trends, log scale, 1950–1999.
Source: Author's elaboration on BT data.

Table 9.5
BT exchange line connections, 1971–1999 (percentage average yearly increase in number of connections)

	National-ization period II 1970–1979	Prepriva-tization years 1980–1984	Postpriva-tization years 1985–1990	Regulatory change 1991–1999
Percentage average yearly increase for the period				
Exchange line connections				
Business	3.1	3.1	7.2	4.1
Residential	9.1	4.3	3.0	0.5
Total exchange lines per employee	7.3	4.0	2.9	9.5

Sources: Author's elaboration on BT 1983; BT 1990; BT 1994; and BT 2000.

In terms of unit revenue (pence per call), there is a greater decrease over time for international calls than for national calls. As far as inland calls are concerned, we find that the share of turnover has not changed very much since 1990, although there has been a significant increase in volume.

As regards the turnover for rentals, the underlying dynamics of output (see table 9.5) show a constant increase in business connections and slower growth in the residential area. The table also provides a crude productivity indicator frequently used in the industry: exchange lines per employee.

I suggest that a careful consideration of these trends may explain the difficulties BT experienced in the 1960s and 1970s. In fact, in the nationalized period, BT had to respond to booming demand with a huge increase in supply and investment effort, financed through tariffs and by the Exchequer in some years.

9.2.7   Price Regulation

I have already (figure 9.1) shown some data on nominal and real price trends in BT since 1960. I have also mentioned, in section 9.2.6, changes in unit revenues against changes in output. Before presenting a more detailed analysis of BT price trends, I need to touch again on the change in the regulatory regime for BT after privatization. Before divestiture, price regulation of telecommunications was in principle based on a required rate of return for the nationalized industries. In actuality, it was the result of complex negotiations between the company and different government bodies. At privatization, the price regulation mechanism chosen by the government and Parliament was the price cap, $RPI - X$.

Control of current prices is carried out at both the retail and network levels. The retail price for some tariffs and for public rentals can reach the maximum level of $RPI - X$, whereas for some dedicated lines, the price ceiling is RPI.

The average prices of the basket of services subject to price control must not exceed the $RPI - X$ control defined by OFTEL to reflect the long-term reduction in costs resulting from improvements in technology. The limits on the increases and decreases must, in addition, be applied to all users.

Figure 9.3 shows the changes over time in the RPI, in X, in $RPI - X$, in the permitted increase in prices (which may slightly differ from $RPI - X$ because of time lags and other technical aspects), and the actual price change as a weighted average for the individual components of the basket.

Over the years both the basket of goods subject to price controls and the X factor have changed. OFTEL modified the sample basket of services periodically to include new emerging services. X increased continuously, especially from 1990 onward. In the first price cap formula, the sample basket was based on the tariffs charged for the principal inland telephony services (subscriptions and inland telephone). Revenues from telephone directories were included from 1990 until August 1, 1997. International calls were also included in 1990, and in 1991, the regulatory basket was extended to include "private circuits," for which increases in tariffs were limited to the level of the RPI. As far as

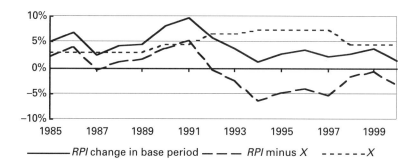

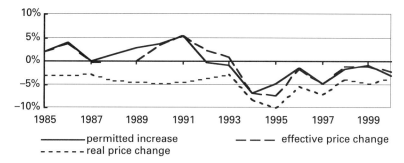

Figure 9.3
BT price trends, *RPI*, and *X*, 1985–2000 (percent yearly change).
Sources: Author's elaboration on BT and OFTEL data.

network charge control is concerned, some tariffs for connection are controlled by $RPI - 8$: These are services that are not very competitive. Similarly, some tariffs for services designated as prospectively competitive are controlled by *RPI* (that is, $X = 0$). In principle, tariffs for competitive services are not subject to price control.

Up until 1990 the price control mechanism for telecommunications services had allowed nominal price increases, as shown by the price trends in figure 9.3. In 1989 a lively debate changed the price control regulation; in fact, *X* rose from 3.0 (1984–1989) to 4.5 (1990–1991) to 6.6 (1992–1993) to 7.5 (1994–1997), then returned to 4.5 in 1997. Furthermore, the sample basket after 1989 was also modified to include international calls, and the price increase on such calls could not exceed $RPI - 4.5$. This extension of the basket increased the percentage of total turnover that was subject to price regulation.

In 1997, the composition of the basket changed again. Under the 1997 modification, the basket of services that was the base for the calculation of the RPI formula included the principal telephony services provided for the bottom 80 percent of residential subscribers classified according to the size of their bills.

The most significant point in this complex story is that X increased gradually but steadily between 1984 and 1997, without a clear link with observed inflation and productivity change. In fact, until 1991, OFTEL granted BT positive nominal average price increases year by year, but there was then a change of regime. Whereas in 1984–1990, the average yearly *real* price change (effective price change less the RPI) was around −3.8 percent, between 1991 and 1997, it was −6.6 percent (see figure 9.3). This "regulatory squeeze" occurred at the same time as a wide review of the entry conditions in the industry and liberalization in some businesses. The change in the regulatory and market environment had far-reaching consequences for BT productivity performance.

9.2.8   Price Trends for Individual Services

My main interest in this section is to examine how tariffs in telecommunications were rebalanced over time. As I show subsequently, beyond the average price change inside and outside the regulated basket, there are important differences in the price performances of individual services (see table 9.6).

Telephony tariffs in the United Kingdom differ for national and international calls, according to distance, length of call, and time of day. Tariffs have changed progressively because of different methods of calculation of the tariff level and because of the new competitive context and the regulation imposed upon BT. I have reconstructed here[7] tariffs per minute of conversation in local, national, and international telephony for calls to western Europe and North America.

Charges for local calls in Britain were originally divided into three types: peak, daytime, and evening/nighttime; a weekend tariff was introduced on July 31, 1995, following the abolition of the peak tariff. As figure 9.4a shows, there were increases in the tariffs for all types of calls between 1984 and 1987; the peak tariff in particular increased by 40 percent between 1984 and 1987. The peak tariff followed a constant trend between 1987 and 1993, when BT significantly reduced it, and then abolished it the following year. The other two types of tariff showed a growth trend between 1987 and 1995 and greater stability in subsequent years.

National calls were billed according to three types of tariff: The A-rate applied for calls within the same region; the B1-rate and B-rate ap-

Table 9.6
BT price trends 1985–1999 (change since start of price control August 1984)

		Cumulative change (percent)	In real terms (percent)
Exchange line rentals	Residential (exclusive)	123.4	19.5
	Business (exclusive)	96.0	4.9
	Wholesale lines	104.8	9.6
Connection charges	Residential	−14.4	−24.9
	Business	−33.1	−41.3
Local calls	Peak	−16.0	−55.0
	Standard/daytime	2.5	−45.1
	Cheap/evening&night	7.6	−42.4
	Weekend	−9.8	−51.7
Regional (A-rate) calls	Peak	−36.5	−66.0
	Standard	−8.8	−51.2
	Cheap	34.1	−28.2
	Weekend cheap	1.9	−45.5
National (B1-rate) calls	Peak	−66.9	−82.3
	Standard	−56.8	−76.9
	Cheap	−32.7	−64.0
	Weekend cheap	−51.5	−74.1
National (B-rate) calls	Peak	−73.2	−85.7
	Standard	−64.9	−81.2
	Cheap	−44.9	−70.5
	Weekend cheap	−60.2	−78.7
International calls		−44.2	−53.5
Directory inquiries		−40.5	−51.2
Weighted average		−6.8	−50.1
RPI: All items index		86.9	—

Source: Author's elaboration of OFTEL data.

plied for national calls outside the region. The B-rate tariff, the higher of the two was greatly reduced as of 1984 and was eliminated in 1997. The B1-rate was also reduced noticeably (see figure 9.4b) thanks to the introduction in 1993 of the weekend tariff (a separate one for national calls, not to be confused with that for local calls, discussed previously). This is a clear example of how regulation has led to a more significant reduction in national tariffs than in local ones, which constitute the most commonly used component of the telephone service for the population. The A-rate tariff increased for all times of the day until 1990; it

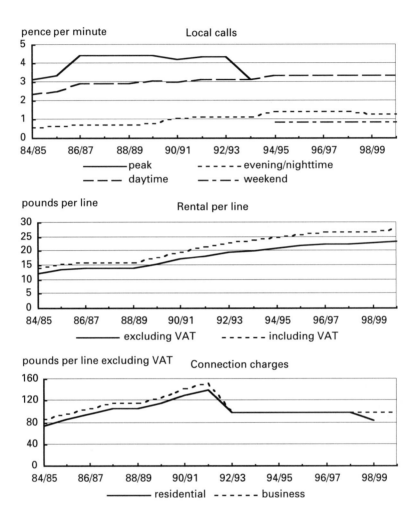

Figure 9.4
BT prices: (a) local calls, rentals, connection charges; (b) national and international calls
(selected categories).
Source: Author's elaboration on BT data.

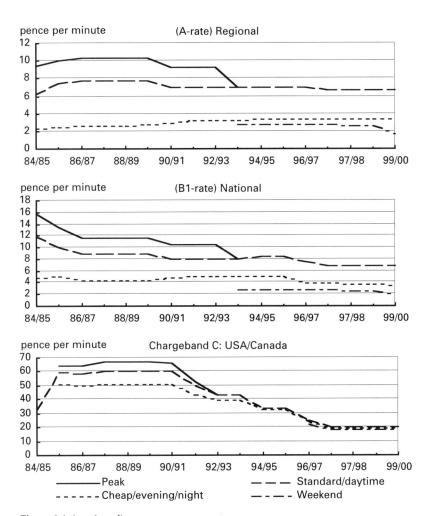

Figure 9.4 (continued)

was then reduced slightly, and a small rate of growth was maintained in both standard and cheap tariffs (the latter being applied mainly over nights and weekends). The weekend tariff dropped significantly as of 1996.

Tariffs for international telephony were based on the zone to which the country of destination belonged. For the purpose of my analysis, I chose to study the trends in tariffs to northern Europe (chargeband A-1A), southern Europe (chargeband A2-1) and North America (charge-band C). The tariffs for calls to northern Europe declined considerably between 1992 and 1996 and then stabilized in 1996. Tariffs for southern Europe increased slightly until 1990 and then decreased until 1993, remaining constant thereafter, with the only novelty being the introduction of a weekend tariff for calls to southern Europe in 1996. The tariffs for calls to Canada and the United States decreased significantly as of 1990. Between 1990 and 1997, the daytime tariff for calls to the United States and Canada was cut by 67 percent (figure 9.4b).

Tariffs for connection differ for domestic and business users, with the domestic tariff lower than that for business. As figure 9.4a shows, connection charges increased significantly until 1992, with an annual growth of roughly 10 percent as of 1984, for a cumulative percentage of 85.8 percent. There were two sharp reductions in the domestic connection tariff in 1993 and in 1999, which brought the cumulative increase since 1984 down to only 12.3 percent. These reductions were linked to the introduction of the connection component into the basket of services subject to regulation as of 1993. The tariffs for business connections were included in the regulation basket between 1993 and 1997. The tariffs charged to corporate users also show significant growth, 90 percent on a cumulative annual basis between 1985 and 1990. After 1990 there was a sharp decrease, followed by stability between 1993 and 2000. Another type of tariff, one charged for rental of the telephone line, showed noticeable growth, again about 90 percent on a cumulative basis between 1984 and 1999, as can be seen in figure 9.4a.

To sum up: When we standardize prices and consider some individual services, between 1984–1985 and 1999–2000 we observe the following:

• Residential rental charges per line nearly doubled: They increased (excluding VAT) from £12.5 to more than £22.

• Connection charges increased from £80 to £100 per line (£140 in 1991–1992).

• Local daytime calls increased from around 2.5 pence per minute to 3 pence.

• Regional calls slightly increased over their starting level of 6 pence per minute.

• National daytime calls decreased from 12 pence to below 8 pence.

• International calls to Europe decreased from around 40 pence to 25 pence.

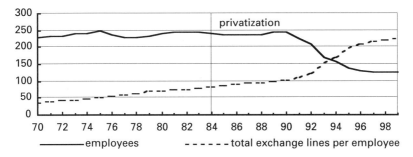

Figure 9.5
Number of BT employees (thousands) and number of exchange lines per employee.
Source: Author's elaboration on BT data.

• International calls to the United States initially increased from 30 to 60 pence until 1990–1991, then decreased dramatically to 20 pence or less under some contracts.

This complex pattern of changes shows how BT adapted its price strategy to the changing regulatory and market environment. Unit costs or productivity trends are poor explanatory variables for these evolving price structures.

9.2.9   Labor Cost Trends

Having presented data on output and prices, I turn now to costs. My cost analysis focuses on personnel and operating costs (discussed in this section) and on fixed investment and research and development costs (discussed in section 9.2.10).

My first observation is that the increasing regulatory pressure after the duopoly review[8] and the increase in X in the 1990s caused a sharp decrease in BT's employment. The number of people employed by BT was remarkably constant in postprivatization years (figure 9.5 and table 9.7). Data from the company's balance sheets show the first signs of restructuring in fiscal year 1990–1991, with an extraordinary provision for layoff costs of £390 million, equal to 12 percent of the company's operating profit. BT's workforce in 1990 amounted to 245,700, a slight increase over the preprivatization and nationalization years. If there was overstaffing in the nationalized industry, change in ownership per se did little or nothing in the first six or seven years to rectify this problem. Over the next five years, however, BT employment dropped

Table 9.7
BT employment and labor costs

	National- ization period I 1960–1969	National- ization period II 1970–1979	Prepriva- tization years 1980–1984	Postpriva- tization years 1985–1990	Regulatory change 1991–1999
Average number of employees	n.a.	235	242	239	157
Percentage yearly average increase					
Labor costs[a]	8.8	19.7	14.4	7.6	−0.8
Number of employees	n.a.	0.3	0.2	0.8	−7.1
Labor cost as					
Percentage turnover[a]	44.5	38.4	42.5	35.1	28.3
Percentage operating costs without depreciation[a]	76.5	66.7	67.2	56.6	44.7

Sources: Author's elaboration on BT 1990; BT 1994; and BT 1999.
Note: n.a. = not available.
[a] Averages calculated through 1977.

dramatically, by 40 percent. This sudden downsizing effort was very effective, and it cannot be just by chance that it happened at the same time as the more demanding regulatory regime, including the granting of a number of licenses to new telephone operators, took effect.

In 1993, restructuring costs created a "layoff costs" component of labor costs equivalent to 15.3 percent of total operating costs and 42 percent of the operating profit. The number of jobs lost that year in BT was 39,800. In subsequent years the restructuring process led to the layoff of a further 10,000 workers, at a cost of 15 percent of the operating profit. Overall the process was managed with little opposition by the workforce, which was given rather generous severance compensation.

Personnel costs in fact decreased much less than employment in the period under consideration. Probably many of those sacked were in the lower salary grades, and at the same time those remaining in BT enjoyed pay increases, reflective of the company's higher productivity. As I show in section 9.2.11, the downsizing policy was essential to maintaining a satisfactory return on capital for BT shareholders, who were totally unaffected by the change in the regulatory and market regime.

Table 9.8
BT investment and research and development expenditure (percentage of turnover average for the period)

	National-ization period II 1970–1979	Prepriva-tization years 1980–1984	Postpriva-tization years 1985–1990	Regulatory change 1991–1999
Research and development	1.5	2.7	2.0	1.9
Capital expenditure	47.6	25.4	24.2	18.5
Transmission equipment	n.a.	7.0	8.4	7.9
Exchange equipment	n.a.	10.8	7.8	4.0
Land and buildings	n.a.	2.7	1.9	0.8
Other[a]	n.a.	4.9	6.2	6.1
Detailed as follows after 1985				
Other network equipment	n.a.	n.a.	2.4	2.8
Computers and office equipment	n.a.	n.a.	2.1	1.9
Motor vehicles and other	n.a.	n.a.	0.8	1.3

Sources: Author's elaboration on BT 1983; BT 1990; BT 1994; and BT 1999.
Note: n.a. = not available.
[a] Average of the period 1985–1990 starting from 1986.

9.2.10 Procurement, Investment, and Research and Development Expenditures

Purchases of goods and services from third parties increased steadily in the period I consider. In fact, "other operating costs" (i.e., operating costs other than personnel) were 20 percent of turnover in 1979 and had risen to 40 percent twenty years later (table 9.12). This increase reflects a drastic change in the procurement policy that probably follows an overall trend in large firms, and it is interesting that it had already started in the 1970s, under public ownership.

Capital expenditures amounted to 140 percent of the company's operating profit in 1980 and then progressively diminished to about 100 percent of the operating profit until 1990, to settle in the region of 80 percent in the 1990s. As a percentage of turnover (table 9.8), capital expenditures drop from a peak of 47.6 percent in the 1970s to only 18.5 percent in the 1990s.

Expenditure for research and development exceeded 15 percent of the operating profit until 1983 and dropped to 12 percent in 1984, then to 10 percent in 1985. It held steady between 7 and 8 percent of

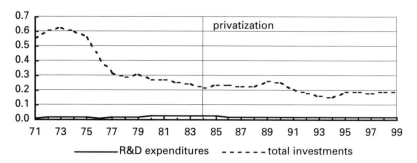

Figure 9.6
BT investments and R&D expenditures (ratio to turnover).
Source: BT 1999.

the operating profit until 1992, increased to 10 percent in 1993 and decreased to 7 percent in 1999. BT spent relatively little on research and development, probably because it increasingly bought technology from its suppliers. It is also possible that investment and R&D were somewhat excessive under public ownership, but clearly one cannot think that they were simultaneously constrained and excessive.

Overall I think these figures offer very little support for the view that privatization was essential to the relaxation of an investment constraint on BT. The company's investment performance after privatization was not so different from its investment performance before. Actually, the level of investment in BT changed dramatically in the 1990s, but it was rather downward, probably again as a short-term response to increasing regulation and competition. In the following years, investment recouped the previous trend. Figure 9.6 and table 9.8 show that research and development expenditure in absolute terms or relative to turnover did not change dramatically over the period under study, being higher in preprivatization years than in previous or following years.

9.2.11   Gross Profits, Interests, Taxes, and Net Profits

As I have shown in section 9.2.2, the rate of growth of BT's nominal revenues was very high in the nationalization years. The annual increase was still over 20 percent in 1981 and 1982 and was around 10 percent until 1990, then fell to below 5 percent until 1999.

Operating costs changed significantly over the years studied. Whereas before divestiture, personnel costs accounted for more than

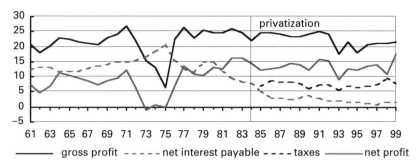

Figure 9.7
BT gross and net profits (percentage of turnover).
Source: Author's elaboration of BT data.

40 percent of operating costs, the restructuring process that began in 1990–1991 led to the reduction of personnel costs to less than 30 percent of the total operating costs by the end of the 1990s. These trends in personnel and operating costs jointly determine the performance of operative profits.

A striking observation from table 9.2 is that operative profitability (before interest and taxes, "gross profit" in the table), measured as a percentage of turnover, was stable for over 40 years beginning in 1960, with modest oscillations between 20 and 25 percent. In 1991–1999 it was exactly 21.2 percent, just as it was in 1960–1969 (figure 9.7).

Operative profits in a sense are "social profits" (Galal et al. 1994). They show how much the company capital contributes to national income, before the division of this income among holders of equity, holders of debt, and the state, at a given set of prices of input (including labor) and output. The stability of BT's operative profits before and after privatization is thus quite interesting, and I comment on it further in section 9.3.

Net interest payable, measured as a percentage of the company's operating profit, was obviously reduced significantly as of 1984, the year of the first BT stock placement. Before 1984, financing costs accounted for 30 percent of operating profit. Subsequently, in the second half of the 1980s, they claimed between 12 percent and 15 percent of operating profit and fell to below 10 percent in the 1990s, or just 1.8 percent of turnover.

The decrease in interest payable, however, simply reflects the change in the source of finance for the firm (and in some years, the diminishing rate of investment). It is important to note that under public ownership, BT paid interest to the Exchequer, which was at the same time a holder of equity and a financier. Thus, in a sense, it would be reasonable to sum British Telecom's interests and profits before privatization. Both were returns to the taxpayer for public investment in the corporation.

The state-owned BT did not pay taxes on its profits. Taxation, included in company accounts since 1985, was on average around 32 percent over the period considered, with a high incidence on the operating profit in 1986 (a year of recession) and in 1998 (because of the burden imposed by the windfall tax). The minimum tax incidence was 24 percent in 1990, and the maximum was 40 percent in 1997 (which coincided with the windfall tax).

Dividends after divestiture were in the region of 6 percent of turnover in the 1980s and were closer to 8 percent during the 1990s, with the exception of 1997, when the company paid out an extraordinary special dividend. Dividends averaged 25 percent of operating profit until 1992, shot up to 40 percent in 1993, and were over 35 percent in 1994. The 1997 special dividend amounted to 108 percent of the company's operating profit for the year.

The percentage of the company's operating profit claimed by net financing costs started at 77 percent in 1980 progressively fell over the period until it was below 10 percent as of 1994. There is clear evidence of a financial problem until 1977, matched by a corresponding level of debt. Subsequently, however, there is no evidence that BT had difficulty in self-financing its investment expenditures, either in the nationalization and preprivatization years (1977–1984) or in the post-privatization years (see figure 9.8). The company's self-financing ratio

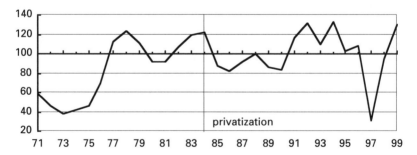

Figure 9.8
Cash flow as a percentage of investment, 1971–1999.
Source: BT 1999.

(the ratio of cash flow to investment) changed dramatically in the more recent years of the period studied, following acquisitions and other structural changes. These changes, and related BT financial troubles, however, are beyond the scope of my analysis.

The company had to make significant investments in new technology to carry on its business, thus its asset composition was mainly fixed investments, but BT had great liquidity, which allowed the cash management of large investments. It also had sufficient liquidity to pay out a large special dividend, as noted previously, in 1997.

Net profits showed a positive trend over the period under study, with a stable growth trend and only two significant variations. One was in 1984, the year of privatization, in which the ratio of net profits to turnover was 14.4 percent, almost double that of previous years and of later ones up until 1992. In fact, for many years, net profit was stable in the region of 7–8 percent of turnover. The other fluctuation out of line with the trend was in 1997, with a negative result of £1,422 million, equivalent to 9.6 percent of turnover.

Apparently, the company was managed and regulated in such a way as to allow shareholders to earn a stable return on sales. Its ROS ratio was twice as high under private ownership as under public ownership, but only because private finance was substituted for public finance. The sum of interest and net profit (gross profit), as previously noted, was unchanged. The sum of gross profit and depreciation decreased slightly after divestiture.

9.2.12 Effects on Aggregate Welfare

I turn now to consideration of how this company performance trend influenced the welfare of consumers of BT's products and services and other agents. In chapter 7, I simply attributed to privatization most of the benefit of lower prices for telecommunications services. In this chapter, I try to prove or disprove this attribution.

To do this, I evaluate the results obtained by Vogelsang, Jones, and Tandon (VJT) (in Galal et al. 1994).[9] Their study is one of the most extensive attempts ever made to analyze privatization's welfare effects comprehensively. It shows that the privatization experiment in the United Kingdom and elsewhere was a success not only for one section of society, but for society as a whole, a Pareto-improving reform.

The methodology of Galal et al. (1994) is, in the authors' own words, the following: "The approach we adopt is to compare the performance of the enterprise after divestiture with what that performance would have been had the enterprise not been divested. Thus we construct for each enterprise a counterfactual scenario that serves as our control. The welfare gain (or loss) from divestiture that we report is then the difference between the level of welfare under divestiture and the level of welfare in our counterfactual scenario" (19). The change in welfare of privatization is measured as the difference between the social value of the firm in the actual and counterfactual scenarios.[10] This social value in turn depends on the welfare of the groups potentially affected by the change in regime: the consumers, the government and any other shareholders before privatization, the buyers, employees, competitors, and the taxpayers. This has all been summarized by VJT in a *basic divestiture equation*:

$$\Delta W = \Delta S + \Delta p + \Delta L + \Delta C.$$

Here ΔS is the change in surplus of the consumer, and the subsequent addends refer, respectively, to the change in company profits (including the effects on the government, the shareholders, and the buyer), the change in effects on suppliers of input (especially workers), and the change in effects on competitors.

The basic equation can be extended by introducing a welfare weight for the increase in the welfare of the rest of the world, in cases in which the net beneficiaries are foreign subjects. VJT do not feel it is appropriate in the case of the United Kingdom to apply a shadow price to public revenue or to other items. (I return to this methodological choice in section 9.3.) For the moment, I follow the authors in their own approach; I make a test with a simple set of shadow prices in section 9.3.

VJT assess the consumer's surplus very simply. First, they assume that the demand curves are linear; second, they estimate or guess the elasticity of demand; and third, they define the consumer's surplus as the area between the demand curve and the price.[11] The assumption of linearity is arbitrary, but quite harmless. What matters is the difference between the surpluses of the consumer in the two scenarios (with and without privatization).

The assessment of profits implies the observation of the prices, quantities, and costs of both the privatized firm and its competitors. The assessment of costs includes those for employment and wages. VJT contrast private profit with a notion of "public profit" or net quasi rents, calculated as the difference between revenue and the cost of intermediate products, wages, leases, and the opportunity cost of working capital. In practice, public profits are gross of taxes, interest, and depreciation.

In general, I find the VJT method of analysis to be acceptable under partial equilibrium. I have an important reservation as to the use of shadow prices and welfare weights, as I explain in section 9.3, when the method is applied under general equilibrium.

I now show that VJT's results are optimistic and not robust when certain assumptions are examined. My demonstration requires a careful assessment of a number of individual components: consumer surplus, profits, and employees and taxpayers. I examine each of these components in turn.

9.2.12.1 Consumer Surplus

VJT present an estimate of the changes in consumer surplus for ten different types of BT product, 1980–1990 (see Galal et al. 1994, table 4.4), observing that generally there was a deterioration in the first two years and then a constant improvement. This is, however, the result of quite different changes for the various categories of users: "In sum, to the extent that consumer surplus can be used as a measure of consumer welfare, consumers in the aggregate have done better every year since the announcement of BT's divestiture, but consumers of long distance services have done considerably better, whereas consumers of local and other services have barely broken even over the period" (73).

The analysis is then carried out with projections for the period 1990–1996 in which different hypotheses are made about the mechanism of price adjustment. Based on the hypothesis that under state control, changes in prices would have been slower, VJT arrive at an estimated welfare difference of £4,151 billion (time-discounted at 1985 prices) in favor of the privatization scenario until 2010. However, they acknowledge that the increase in rental charges (see section 9.2.8), if considered as the price paid for a specific service (as it should be, I think), would reduce this amount by around £3 billion.

The authors believe that if privatization had not taken place, then probably neither would the changes in regulation that have been made since privatization. Therefore, to understand the attitude of the government toward the price of telephone services, they look back (at the ten to fifteen increases in price recorded between 1960 and 1984): "price changes were generally made when achieved rates of return were getting substantially out of line with target returns" (81). The new form of sector regulation under privatization differs from the preceding one in the type of indicator chosen (from a bland rate of return to a bland—at least initially—price cap) and in the frequency with which it is revised. Furthermore, the authors think it is probable that the shakeup in the price structure that came about with privatization was efficient (raising the prices of services with a more rigid demand). In fact, BT increased local call rates and installation charges (more rigid demand services), kept monthly rentals and calls of intermediate length constant, and substantially reduced rates on long distance and international calls.

This restructuring of prices, not observed in any other country at the time, could be attributed to privatization. VJT observe, however, that the competition with Mercury and international trends would probably have had the same effects, whereas the government would have opposed an increase in tariffs and rental charges for domestic users. Thus, in the counterfactual scenario, consumer lobbies would have succeeded in limiting the price increases that affected them to 7 percent annually, but for the rest, the trend would have been the same as under privatization. For all the other prices in the basket regulated by the price cap, VJT hypothesize a reduction in prices if the rate of return had exceeded 20 percent and an increase if it had fallen below 16 percent. Finally, in the counterfactual scenario, the restructuring of prices for basic services is excluded: "BT's actual price restructuring resulted in consumer outrage, which is easier for a divested enterprise to deal with than for the government as owner of a public enterprise" (83). Furthermore, the counterfactual scenario assumes that for some services, the market share of BT would have contracted more than it actually did under privatization.

9.2.12.2 Profits
An examination of BT's balance sheets for 1980–1990 shows that annual profits in the usual sense (dividends plus retained profits) doubled in 1982, stayed the same until 1985 at around £1 billion, then grew steadily until they almost doubled again (£1.9 billion) in 1990. On the other hand, "public profit" shows a different trend: "public profit tells a quite different story, showing essentially a continuous linear trend with no pronounced flattening across the pre- and postdivestiture period ... the total size of the pie (public profit or quasi rent) has grown fairly smoothly, but its distribution has not" (59).

According to VJT, in 1982, before privatization, but after it had been announced, there was nevertheless already a noticeable increase in public profit. This increase seems to be basically due to an increase in labor productivity in real terms. This public profit performance continued until 1990, whereas the trends in the price of the product and in the cost of intermediate goods remained linear. In substance, whereas output and intermediate input grew at the same rate, the quantity of labor input stayed more or less constant. Over the same period, the discontinuity was even more pronounced for investments: Stable in the years before privatization, they grew at an annual rate of 16 percent following it.

A closer examination of the trends in terms of prices and quantities would show that "both before and after divestiture BT generated substantial additional revenues from sales each year, and it used those funds for roughly equal increments in intermediate inputs, labor, and profits. The major difference was that, before the announcement of divestiture, the revenue boost came primarily from raising prices; thereafter it came primarily from increasing output" (67). One of the reasons for this discontinuity in behavior seems to be the removal of the external-financing limits, which encouraged greater investments that enabled labor productivity to increase. Examination of the productivity trend and international comparisons lead VJT to conclude that there is therefore no difference between the effective scenario and the counterfactual one. There is no evidence that privatization caused productivity growth up to 1990, given that increases in productivity can also be found in the period preceding privatization and in other countries. For the years 1991–1996, however, VJT, acknowledging that in 1991 BT announced the layoff of 30,000 employees, assume that in the effective scenario, the downsizing operation is feasible without reductions in output, whereas they believe that in the counterfactual scenario, the layoffs would not have occurred.

The justification for this assumption (which the authors themselves admit is rather extreme) is that before privatization, the company's management had not succeeded in coming to an agreement with the unions regarding the reduction of the workforce, whereas subsequently it did.

9.2.12.3   Employees and Taxpayers

VJT do not believe that there are any differences in welfare for the workers under the two scenarios: This point could be justified by admitting the nonexistence of unemployment, whereby laid-off or early-retired workers would not be involuntarily unemployed. Perhaps the BT employees whose jobs were eliminated were well qualified and had no difficulty in finding new jobs. In fact, the downsizing process was rather consensual.

The net welfare equation benefit mentioned in section 9.2.12 includes the position of the government, given that the company's increase in profits is gross of taxes. The accounting proposed by VJT is the following. The government collects £3,750 billion as a sale price, and this is a benefit for the government and a loss for the private sector. For that price, however, the latter acquires an asset worth £7,471 billion in profits after taxes. Thus, it realizes a net time-discounted profit of £3,721 billion, of which £999 billion go to foreign investors. The government sustains a capital loss of £3,348 billion, having also had to bear the transaction costs of privatization, but obtains £2,004 billion in additional taxes. That means an additional share in the profit of 61 percent for the private sector and 39 percent for the government.

9.2.12.4 Aggregation

The net impact of BT privatization on the aggregate welfare of the citizens of the United Kingdom is estimated by VJT to have had an actual value of £10 billion (at 1985 prices, 1985–2010). This is 2 percent of the total welfare generated for society by the firm. For the consumers, the corresponding welfare gain would be 0.8 percent of their time-discounted surplus, or £175 per capita in constant 1985 pounds. This is perhaps equivalent to around £325 in 1995 pounds, around one-third of my own preliminary estimate of *gross* welfare change in chapter 7. The difference between my previous result and VJT's is explained by the fact that VJT's estimates are of *net* welfare change. Moreover, they use a higher discount rate (9 percent, compared to my 5 percent) and a shorter horizon (twenty-five years, compared to my perpetuity), and they do not consider the increase in benefits of the years 1996–1999 and of lower prices of BT competitors (in chapter 7, I used sector price indexes).

Nevertheless, Galal et al. (1994) consider these welfare gains significant, although they admit that they are quite small: "Welfare gains from our three UK divestitures are comparatively small because, at the same time, performance of the remaining state-owned enterprises in the United Kingdom during the 1980s improved considerably. Thus, the very fact that we have found consistent gains is remarkable" (177). I comment on these results in the next section.

9.3 Discussion

My analysis of BT accounts over forty years shows major changes in the company's performance over time. Divestiture, however, does not mark a radical departure from some long-term trends. Other factors play a leading role in explaining BT performance.

The rate of growth of turnover from telephone services was higher in preprivatization years, then decreased, and eventually became negative after 1992. Call revenues decreased from 60 to 40 percent of the total revenues between 1979 and 1999.

Revenue growth from rentals and from the supply of equipment was also very high in preprivatization years, then slowed. As for other services, including mobile phones, the trend of revenues was U-shaped, with slow growth in 1992–1995 and higher growth before and after those years. My estimate of output trend shows that the volume of inland services provided increased by about three times over twenty years, whereas that of international calls increased by about six times. The higher growth in volumes compensated for the greater decrease in prices for the latter type of service.

Since privatization, the weighted average of tariffs (1984–1999) has been halved in real terms. The drivers of this sustained decrease in tariffs have been the introduction of new technologies (electronic switching and mobile phone), the end of duopoly, stringent regulatory pressure after 1991, and competition in the market for international calls. There has been a real increase in rental charges (which have more than doubled in current prices for residential users). The structure of price changes has been such that the top gainers were business and users of international calls. The losers, or the least gainers, have been residential users who make mainly local calls and who make low numbers of calls.

Against these trends for revenues, output, and prices, I have shown that personnel costs remained a stable share of turnover until 1990, when the regulatory regime changed and employment decreased suddenly by 40 percent. Wages for the surviving employees increased in real terms and increased more than the average for British industry in general. Investment, particularly in transmission equipment and networks, widely substituted for labor, whereas R&D expenditures decreased as a percentage of turnover.

BT's gross profit was 21 percent of turnover on average in the nationalization period (1960–1979), increased to 24 percent in preprivatization years (1980–1984), and remained at that level after divestiture. Then it returned to 20 percent after the regulatory squeeze in the 1990s. Profit net of interest increased from around 12 percent to more than 20 percent after privatization. The Exchequer at divestiture lost any future interest on debt and claim to BT surplus. The Exchequer recouped around 35 percent of these lost profits on average through corporate taxation (other than the windfall tax), whereas shareholders captured around 40 percent as dividends, with the rest being retained as profits. Self-financing was critically low until 1975, then exceeded 100 percent, several years before any privatization plan.

The sharp increase in net-of-interest profits was not based on a change in operative profits or productivity, but on conversion of debt owed to the previous owner, the Exchequer, into equity of the new shareholders. Nothing changed in terms of economic efficiency.

In conclusion, it is difficult to attribute to privatization substantial changes in BT's operating profits, prices, and costs. Most of the changes in these areas resulted either from new financial arrangements or from liberalization and regulation.

I suggest that the missing productivity shock may have something to do with the peculiar nature of private ownership of BT after divestiture and of the new regulatory environment. Property rights theory suggests that private ownership is superior to public because private owners have an incentive to require managers to promote efficiency. Who, however, are actually the new owners of BT? Tables 9.9 and 9.10 may suggest an answer. At divestiture, in 1984, there were almost 1.7 million shareholders. In 1992, there were half that number. In 1993, following the final placement, the number of shareholders had risen to almost 2.3 million; it peaked at 2.7 million in 1994 and then dropped again.

These are impressive figures, but 98 percent of BT's shareholders in 1985 held fewer than 1,600 shares. In 1999 a little less than 92 percent of the shareholders held less than 1,600 shares. Almost all had fewer than 10,000.

Actually, the new BT owners in 1999 were a small group of ten financial institutions, who between them owned 20 percent of the company's stock. About 600 shareholders held more than one million

Table 9.9
BT shareholders

	Number of shareholders at March 31			
	1985	1989	1993	1999
1–399 shares	481,896	363,519	1,241,871	859,404
400–799 shares	814,994	574,116	675,662	550,734
800–1,599 shares	368,826	240,121	288,686	332,355
1,600–9,999 shares	23,536	22,490	87,270	154,331
10,000–99,999 shares	2,283	1,687	2,382	3,589
100,000–999,999 shares	1,083	977	1,341	1,291
1,000,000–4,999,999 shares	360	332	484	393
5,000,000 shares and above				175
Above 1,000,000 shares (government)	1	1	1	
Total	1,692,979	1,203,243	2,297,697	1,902,272

Sources: Author's elaboration on BT 1983; BT 1990; BT 1994; BT 1999.

shares each, including the top institutions, and they controlled 80 percent of the company's capital. The vast number of "popular capitalists" with less than ten thousand shares, 2.5 million, owned just 20 percent of BT, and their influence on the company was accordingly limited or perhaps best described as negligible. This ownership structure, similar to that of other British public companies, says something about the specific form of capitalism and private governance that has substituted for government control.

It may be the case that the new ownership and governance structure implicitly has been more interested in achieving a "satisfactory" rate of return on capital than in maximizing returns. Perhaps old theories of the "managerial firm," combined with a peculiar regulatory environment, may be helpful in explaining the observed company performance. Whatever the explanation of the missing productivity shock, any simplistic view of the efficiency impact of ownership change seems to be inconsistent with the BT privatization case history.

Turning now to the welfare impact of BT privatization, I suggest, with the benefit of hindsight, that the VJT result, although interesting and based on a sensible approach, and admittedly small, actually may exaggerate the net benefits of BT privatization. A good half of the result depends on the assumption that labor productivity makes a leap in 1991 in the privatization scenario. To make this assumption, one must allow that BT can lay off 30,000 workers (in fact it was to be

Table 9.10
Main BT shareholders at March 31, 2000

Name of shareholder	Number of ordinary shares held	Ratio of number of ordinary shares to total number of issued ordinary shares
Chase Nominees Limited	312,906,820	4.81%
RBSTB Nominees Limited	170,847,151	2.63%
Prudential Client (MSS) Nominees Limited	160,369,396	2.46%
Stanlife Nominees Limited	144,652,210	2.22%
Nutraco Nominees Limited	133,952,862	2.06%
MSBC Global Custody Nominee (UK) Limited	113,416,245	1.74%
Guaranty Nominees Limited	90,137,527	1.39%
The Bank of New York Nominees Limited	74,515,436	1.15%
BNY Norwich Union Nominees Limited	72,347,800	1.11%
Schroder Nominees Limited	71,276,558	1.10%
Total	1,344,422,005	20.67%
Other (less than 1% of the issued ordinary shares)	5,159,796,694	79.33%
Total issues ordinary shares	6,504,218,699	100.00%

Sources: Information provided to the author by BT.

many more), whereas this would not have been allowed for a publicly owned BT. The authors themselves consider this an extreme hypothesis. Nevertheless, they accept it. The downsizing at BT can be compared with that of British state-owned enterprises. I observed in chapter 6 that there were drastic reductions in personnel in steel, coal, railways, the postal service, and other British industries under public ownership. VJT acknowledge that labor productivity has a decisive impact on their result. Just one percentage point more (an increase in productivity from 1.05 to 1.06) in the private scenario leads to an increase of 80 percent in the net additional benefit. The same variation in the public scenario determines a change in the sign of the net benefit: in that case, privatization determines a *loss* in aggregate welfare.

The other half of the VJT result depends on the variation in the welfare of consumers, which in turn depends on the decrease in prices. Here there are two crucial steps. First, one attributes *all* the benefits of price regulation to privatization, a disputable assumption, I think. Second, losses and gains for different categories of users, presumably of different income levels, are aggregated with the same welfare weight. This is cost-benefit analysis that totally ignores privatization's redistribution impact. Ignoring the distributive considerations in social welfare implies choosing a particular type of social-welfare function, totally indifferent to considerations of equity. As noted previously, for example, if an increase in rental prices is computed explicitly, VJT find a *decrease* in the consumer surplus difference of £3 billion. I also cited evidence in chapter 7 that the rebalancing of BT tariffs provoked net losses to some users.

The authors themselves are conscious of this problem: "The average residential consumer is quite possibly a net loser from divestiture. In this light, the decision by the Thatcher government to widen share ownership to all sections of society could be seen as a mechanism to compensate consumers and encourage their acquiescence in the divestiture and the price changes that resulted" (99). This view of share sales as compensation is implausible. The net losers from BT privatization are the largest social group, that is, the subscribers with telephones for domestic use, over which BT has a monopoly. This group overlaps only very partially with the purchasers of BT shares, as I showed in chapter 5.

Moreover, VJT's analysis of the fiscal position of the government is rather debatable. The authors estimate that privatization was based on enormous underpricing of the firm, which made a gift to the private sector, foreigners included, of over 50 percent of the option value of BT. However, they believe that the account balances, thanks to the taxes obtained subsequently. In turn, it all depends on the hypothesis of a difference in the global productivity trend, a disputable assumption in view of long-term productivity trends. It is easy to show that under constant gross profits before and after privatization, taxation covers only a part of the initial underpricing.

In table 9.11, I show the VJT results together with those under two alternative scenarios. I cannot compare directly the figures in this table with my welfare impact calculation elsewhere in this book, because of different discount rates and numeraire. In scenario A, I use the same baseline projections as VJT, but I use a set of shadow prices: 1.3 for public funds (a value often given in the literature, e.g., Laffont and Tirole 2000, and tested by VJT as well) 0.5 for private domestic profits (because I would consider 50 percent of these profits to be extra profits), and 0 for foreign shareholders' profits (because their wealth increase adds nothing to national income). The result is still positive

Table 9.11
BT welfare impact: Sensitivity analysis (billions of constant 1985 pounds)

	VJT	Shadow prices	Scenario A	Scenario B
Government				
Taxes	2.0	1.3	2.6	2.6
Net quasi rents	−3.3	1.3	−4.3	−12.2
Net sales proceeds	3.6	1.3	4.7	4.7
Employees	0.0	0.0	0.0	0.0
Private domestic shareholders				
Diverse	2.7	0.5	1.4	1.4
Concentrated	0.0	0.5	—	
Foreign shareholders	1.0	0.0	0.0	0.0
Competitors	−0.1	0.5	0.0	0.0
Consumers	4.1	1.0	4.1	4.1
Distributional impact	—		—	−3.0
Total	10.0		8.5	−2.4

Source: Author's calculations based on Galal et al. 1994.

but is reduced to £8.5 billion (at 1985 prices, in net present value, at 9 percent social discount rate, as used by VJT).

In scenario B, in the last column of table 9.11, I introduce two further corrections:

• I add £6.1 billion to profits in the VJT public scenario by assuming that productivity trends are not different under continued public ownership (i.e., I assume that employment would have been reduced by the public corporation as it was by the privatized BT).

• I use the estimate of £3 billion proposed by VJT for the loss of consumer surplus following the increase in rental charges.

The result of these corrections is that BT divestiture would have a net social cost, rather than a net social benefit.

I consider these corrections to be no more than a simple sensitivity analysis. Some readers may want to explore different combinations of assumptions, but the overall result does not change dramatically.

To the best of my understanding, based on the foregoing discussion, the net social benefit from privatization of BT was modest. The net benefit would, however, largely be canceled, and probably of a reversed sign, if one takes into account:

• the adverse redistributive effects that would result from applying even a moderate welfare weight to different classes of income (and of income transferred to foreign shareholders)

• a scenario in which a restructured BT under public ownership is capable of sustaining investments and increasing productivity, in line with the other corporations that remained in the public sector or with state-owned telecommunications firms in continental Europe in the same period

• a more careful consideration of the effects of welfare deriving from the position of the taxpayers, as would result from the application of a shadow price of public funds.

This last point merits clarification. In fact, the VJT study aggregates a pound of private profit after taxes and a pound of taxes in the same way. This neglects the distortional effect of taxes. In contrast, attributing a shadow price to public funds is customary in cost-benefit analysis (see the discussion in chapter 2). Perhaps more importantly, however, the existence of a sizable monopoly profit in the sector is totally ignored by VJT in the case of both public and private ownership.

The return on capital in BT during the 1980s was far higher than that for the economy as a whole or in other competitive sectors. For a number of services, the market share of BT, both when public and when privatized, remained well over 90 percent for the whole period studied. It therefore seems very likely that part of the profit observed is monopoly profit. This we cannot simply add to social welfare. The most sensible treatment of monopoly profit in a general equilibrium framework is to consider it a social cost rather than a social benefit. In general equilibrium, monopoly profit is a pure transfer. There is no valuable output behind it. Equivalently, one could use a shadow price near long-run marginal costs for BT revenues.

In conclusion, my reading of the available evidence points to a relatively small social benefit of BT privatization or perhaps even to a small net social cost, if distributional and allocative efficiency considerations are accounted for. Obviously, if one conjectures that divestiture was the necessary prerequisite for changes in finance, regulation, and market structure, one might reach different conclusions. There might have also been more intangible, long-term effects (Bell 2002; Turk 2002) that I have not considered. In other European countries, however, such as Germany and France, a different pattern of reform is observed, with similar or better measurable results, for example, with lower prices for most services (OFTEL 2000). The main conclusion of this chapter is thus that BT ownership change per se, until the end of the 1990s, had only a small measurable impact on social welfare, whereas regulation and liberalization of the sector had a dramatic impact. This result is important, I think, because chapter 7 shows that two-thirds of the overall net welfare impact of privatizations on British consumers depends on the evolution of the divestiture of BT.

9.4   Further Reading

Armstrong 1998 offers a general discussion of regulation of telecommunications in the United Kingdom; see also Armstrong, Cowan, and Vickers 1994. For an international comparison, see Boylaud and Nicoletti 2000. On telecommunications industry regulatory models in the framework of incentive theory, see Laffont and Tirole 2000a. On BT, see also OFTEL 1995; OFTEL 2000; and Parker 1994.

Table 9.12
BT financial data, 1961–1999 (current pounds)

For year ended March 31	Sales (A)	Labor costs (B)	Other operating costs (C)	Depreciation (D)	Gross profit (E = A – B – C – D)	Net interest payable (F)	Other items (G)	Tax (H)	Net profit (I = E – F – G – H)	Dividend (L)	Retained profit (deficits) for the financial year
1961	245.6	116.5	24.3	53.6	51.2	30.3	2.5		18.4		18.4
1962	262.3	129.2	28.5	57.5	47.1	34.5			12.6		12.6
1963	288.8	138.0	32.1	60.5	58.2	38			20.2		20.2
1964	342.7	148.8	48.4	66.7	78.8	40.3			38.5		38.5
1965	372.9	161.4	53.2	74.9	83.4	43.7			39.7		39.7
1966	404	175.7	58.4	82.1	87.8	48.5			39.3		39.3
1967	441.8	190.3	67.7	90.6	93.2	55.5			37.7		37.7
1968	485.0	206.9	77.6	99.5	101.0	65.8			35.2		35.2
1969	568.2	228.9	97.4	111.3	130.6	80.5			50.1		50.1
1970	652.1	248.3	113.5	131.6	158.7	97.4			61.3		61.3
1971	771.3	268.9	139.5	156.5	206.4	116.8	-3.9		93.5		93.5
1972	883.1	323.3	176.4	188.3	195.1	137.1			58.0		58.0
1973	1,001.4	385.9	211.1	248.9	155.5	165.2			-9.7		-9.7
1974[a]	1,159.5	455.9	264.6	286.0	153.0	214.4	-71.1		9.7		9.7
1975[a]	1,386.2	616.6	311.8	365.8	92.0	286.6	-194.6		-0.0		-0.0
1976	2,166.8	869.8	331.9	480.6	484.5	329.8			154.7		154.7
1977	2,658.0	930.0	450.6	573.9	703.5	338.1			365.4		365.4
1978[b]	2,924.0		(1,546.2)	713.2	664.6	338.0			326.6		326.6
1979[b]	3,243.9		(1,643.0)	776.4	824.5	488.1			336.4		336.4
1980[c]	3,601.0	1,609.0	658.0	441.0	893.0	533.8	-107		466.2		466.2

Year											
1981[c]	4,570.0	2,110.0	770.0	566.0	1,124.0	538.7			585.3		585.3
1982[c]	5,708.0	2,394.0	1,197.0	632.0	1,485.0	548.7			936.3		936.3
1983[c]	6,377.0	2,571.0	1,410.0	825.0	1,571.0	540.0			1,031.0		1,031.0
1984[c]	6,876.0	2,715.0	1,773.0	866.0	1,522.0	532.0			990.0		990.0
1985	7,653.0	2,807.0	2,038.0	933.0	1,875.0	395.0		535.0	945.0	275.0	670.0
1986	8,387.0	2,998.0	2,244.0	1,068.0	2,077.0	267.0		743.0	1,067.0	513.0	554.0
1987[d]	9,339.0	3,164.0	2,600.0	1,311.0	2,264.0	282.0	−1.0	754.0	1,229.0	565.0	664.0
1988[d]	10,185.0	3,530.0	2,743.0	1,525.0	2,387.0	279.0	−180.0	833.0	1,455.0	609.0	846.0
1989[d]	11,071.0	3,944.0	2,920.0	1,610.0	2,597.0	340.0	−167.0	858.0	1,566.0	636.0	930.0
1990[d,e]	12,315.0	4,209.0	3,329.0	1,791.0	2,986.0	484.0	226.0	767.0	1,509.0	720.0	789.0
1991[d]	13,154.0	4,393.0	3,498.0	1,935.0	3,328.0	417.0	−164.0	995.0	2,080.0	818.0	1,262.0
1992[d]	13,337.0	4,458.0	3,585.0	2,056.0	3,238.0	304.0	−109.0	999.0	2,044.0	888.0	1,156.0
1993[d]	13,242.0	4,095.0	4,688.0	2,116.0	2,343.0	256.0	143.0	724.0	1,220.0	967.0	253.0
1994[d]	13,675.0	4,085.0	4,505.0	2,156.0	2,929.0	230.0	−19.0	951.0	1,767.0	1,039.0	728.0
1995[d]	13,893.0	3,912.0	5,310.0	2,137.0	2,534.0	259.0	−382.0	926.0	1,731.0	1,108.0	623.0
1996[d]	14,446.0	3,680.0	5,580.0	2,189.0	2,997.0	170.0	−186.0	1,027.0	1,986.0	1,184.0	802.0
1997[d]	14,935.0	3,778.0	5,753.0	2,265.0	3,139.0	129.0	−169.0	1,102.0	2,077.0	3,510.0	−1,433.0
1998[d]	15,640.0	3,917.0	6,043.0	2,395.0	3,285.0	249.0	−158.0	1,488.0	1,706.0	1,220.0	486.0
1999[d,f]	16,953.0	3,881.0	6,843.0	2,581.0	3,648.0	286.0	−914	1,293.0	2,983.0	1,322.0	1,661.0

Sources: Author's elaboration on BT annual reports. 1961–1975 figures based on Post Office data. 1976–1979 figures based on BT *Report and Account*, 1981–1982, except for labor costs, which are based on Post Office, *Report and Account*, 1976–1977. 1980–1999 figures based on BT *Annual Reports and Accounts.*

a "Other items" includes government compensation for price restraint.

b For 1978–1979, "Other operating costs" includes labor costs.

c For 1980–1984, "Depreciation" does not include supplementary depreciation according to Post Office rules.

d Amount of "Other items" for 1987–1999 includes profit and loss on investment undertakings, minority interests, and exceptional charges.

e "Other items" includes a special provision for restructuring costs of £390 million.

f "Other items" includes a profit on sale of fixed asset investments of £1,107 million.

10   Epilogue: A State without Ownership

10.1   Introduction

The privatization policy pursued in the United Kingdom in the 1980s and 1990s is the largest experiment in public divestiture ever undertaken among capitalist economies. It had a deep impact on economic policymaking worldwide. Governments in western Europe, in the former planned economies, and in a number of less-developed countries imitated Britain. Privatization is now an accepted paradigm. In economics, it marks a wide shift in opinion about the role of the state.

From this angle, the British experience is particularly relevant for several reasons. The historical background of nationalization was country-specific, but the British experience was not entirely different from that of other western European countries. Thus, we have a yardstick for international comparisons. The time span was long enough to study some long-run effects. The British governments at the time enjoyed (at least until their last term) a comfortable majority in Parliament, so they were able to implement their policy in a consistent way. Finally, there is now a wide body of scholarly literature and reliable data sources on company performance, on price trends, and on other relevant variables in regard to the British privatization experience. These opportunities, in combination, offer Britain as a unique case study of the privatization phenomenon.

I have considered in this volume the impact of British privatization on five types of agents: firms, employees, shareholders, consumers, and taxpayers. The main conclusion of my study is that privatization had more modest effects on efficiency than the theory of property rights and other orthodox privatization theories may have expected. On the other hand, privatization did have substantial regressive effects on the distribution of incomes and wealth in the United Kingdom.

In most cases, I have considered the joint effects of the broad policy reform undertaken in regard to the formerly nationalized industries in the United Kingdom. As far as possible and reasonable, however, I have tried to disentangle the impacts of ownership change, of regulatory shocks, and of liberalization. I sum up my main results in the remainder of this chapter.

10.2 Productivity Trends: The Missing Shock

From a broad macroeconomic angle, a large-scale privatization can be considered a supply-side shock. If the ownership change resulting from privatization raises firms' productivity, aggregate output and productivity time series should show some evidence of a structural break—perhaps not exactly on the day of divestiture, but after the privatization announcement, or after a reasonable time lag. Underpricing of the privatizing firms may add a demand shock.

Chapter 3 has offered some simple tests to detect the macroeconomic impact of privatization. The empirical modeling approach uses quarterly data on privatization proceeds at constant 1995 prices, controls for other macroeconomic variables, and tests for cointegration. The aggregate impact of privatization on output is found to be either not statistically significant or, if significant, very small. Probably, the change is too small relative to the economy to enable it to be recorded against noise. Nevertheless, the size of British divestiture was not small in terms of public finance. Proceeds in some years were as high as some GDP points, an equivalent size, for example, to that of a tax reform. Moreover, substantial divestitures happened over a twelve-year period from 1984 to 1996, and their cumulative impact should be detectable. The small results obtained suggest that privatization per se had a very modest impact on the long-term growth pattern of the British economy. This macroeconomic evidence is consistent with the results of microeconomic analysis, which is the preferred approach in the volume.

Turning to the performance of individual privatized industries in the United Kingdom, I have reviewed previous research and presented time series (since the 1960s) of per capita output for electricity, gas, coal, telecommunications, and railways. An advantage of looking at long-run time series is that we can avoid considering the performance of nationalized industries only in the late 1970s, prior to privatization, when they faced adverse shocks.

I find mixed evidence among the industries I consider. In the electricity industry, we observe a clear increase of output per capita. The most convincing explanation of this increase is a change in technology, with the substitution of gas for coal as fuel. This technology substitution was possible because of related energy policy changes by the British government (the end of coal protection), not necessarily because of privatization. In industries in which there was no change in technology, such as the gas industry, privatization had a limited impact on long-term productivity trends.

I have examined detailed BT output data for over forty years (1960–2000) and apparently, the change in the company's ownership at privatization had a negligible impact on productivity trends. In fact, BT's productivity changed dramatically only in the 1990s—no less than seven years after divestiture—as a response to a more demanding regulatory policy.

I have tested company data provided by Martin and Parker (1997). These data comprise eleven firms and six subperiods (the duration varies from company to company), for a total of sixty-six observations. According to my simple test, dummy variables for subperiods generally have an estimated coefficient not statistically different from zero, with the following (reasonable) exceptions:

· TFP decline in recession years: This is compatible with faster slowdown of output than of production factors.

· Return on capital: Postannouncement there is an increase, probably to make privatization shares more appealing.

· Added value: There is a positive impact of the dummies for the last period and a negative one for the recession period.

These results confirm the overall conclusion of previous studies that although the business cycle (and restructuring, while the company is under public ownership) has a discernible effect on a company's performance, privatization per se has no visible impact.

In conclusion, I have been unable to find sufficient statistical macro or micro evidence that output, labor, capital, and TFP productivity in the United Kingdom increased substantially as a consequence of ownership change at privatization compared to the long-term trend. There are exceptions for some firms and some periods, but overall a significant productivity shock is lacking. I suggest that if one occurred, it was small.

10.3 Employees: Losers and Winners

The counterpart of the missing productivity shock is a corresponding lack of structural breaks in time series of employment and/or investment at the company level. I have found that privatized companies actually cut personnel, but the nationalized industries recorded huge decreases in employment as well. For example, British Rail, well before privatization, decreased employment by more than 50 percent, around 120,000 employees. British Steel and British Coal are other obvious examples. British Gas, NFC, and the water and electricity companies also recorded substantial downsizing under public ownership. In contrast, BT did not cut its staff for many years after privatization, until a change in the regulatory regime governing the company forced it to undertake a huge downsizing.

The overall picture appears to be clear. For the sample of firms examined, privatization does not denote a break in employment trends, except in specific cases. In general, whenever there are drastic changes in a firm's employment patterns, these are the result of external factors, such as changes in regulations (e.g., British Telecom, British Gas, Associated British Ports), demand conditions, or industrial organization (e.g., Britoil, British Steel).

At the end of the privatization period, in about 1996, employment in a large sample of previously nationalized industries was roughly 517,000. In the same firms, employment in 1979 stood at around 1,320,000. There was thus tremendous downsizing in these firms over the period, with more than 800,000 jobs lost. Nevertheless, at the time of divestiture (which varied from firm to firm, and therefore the total has a purely indicative significance), employment had fallen to 638,000. Consequently, seven-eighths of the total jobs lost in these privatized firms had already been lost prior to privatization, under state ownership.

I constructed a data series on the annual growth rate of employment for fifteen corporations, covering the period 1960–1997. Estimation results lead to the conclusion that there was no significant change in employment with respect to any of the subperiods before and after divestiture, except for the latest one, which showed a remarkable decrease in employment, in a new regulatory environment.

Turning now to wages, between 1970 and 1983, wage increases in nationalized firms were higher than in the private sector. This trend does not change, however, after divestiture.

Company data on wage levels in the periods before and after privatization show that privatization usually did not alter the position of the average wages of workers employed in the firms considered relative to the economy. Industry data can be standardized with the wages of the manufacturing sector or those for the economy as a whole. Interestingly, real wages in several privatized industries are higher at the end of the observed period under privatization than they were under public ownership. This can be attributed partly to a reshuffling of positions (of which there is some evidence) among different sections of the workforce. I have tested these data by broad types (manual, nonmanual) as well, however, and found similar results.

The data I have cited seem to contradict the prediction by orthodox privatization theories that the change of ownership resulting from privatization implies a removal of possible rents attributed to workers. Either these rents did not exist, in the sense that high salaries somehow reflected differences in productivity when the firm was under state ownership, or alternatively, the rents existed and continued under private ownership, despite the weakening of the trade unions.

In conclusion, and perhaps contrary to widespread expectations and perceptions, the average surviving employee in privatized firms did not incur major costs specifically attributable to ownership change. The clear employee gainers from privatization were the top managers. There is some evidence of convergence of top executive pay in the privatized companies and in a matching sample of publicly traded firms. The boards of privatized companies were largely formed (at least for some years following privatization) from the same personnel who had been recruited under public ownership. There is some evidence that the rate of turnover of firm managers changed after divestiture, but not dramatically. Employees' ownership of shares in the firms that employed them had negligible effects on their behavior at work, on their wealth, and on corporate governance.

There were indeed changes in industrial relations as a result of privatization, and these changes were unfavorable to trade unions. Among less-skilled workers, there was greater job insecurity than prior to privatization. Probably in some industries, there was a reduction in relative pay for positions filled by unskilled workers, and perhaps in safety at work, particularly for those whose positions were transferred to subcontractors of the original firms.

10.4   Shareholders: A Not-So-Popular Capitalism

One of the constitutive elements of government policy during the Conservatives' eighteen years office was the maximum possible diffusion of shareholding in British firms, presumably seen as a way to make capitalism popular and especially to increase support for privatization. According the evidence I have reviewed, however, privatization did not stop the decline in individual ownership of shares in British companies that was underway before privatization was undertaken. In 1957, individuals owned shares in British firms listed on the London stock exchange totaling almost two-thirds of the value of all shares owned. Between 1963 and 1997, the value of the stocks owned by individuals has fallen from over half to just over one-sixth of the total. Ownership of British firms became an indirect phenomenon, with ownership shares managed by insurance companies, pension funds, and other financial institutions. Furthermore, beginning in the 1980s, the foreign sector became the largest owner of shares of British firms, in relative terms, with ownership reaching a quarter of the value of the securities.

Figures on individual shareholding may look impressive (more than ten million Britons became shareholders in British firms in the postprivatization period). Nevertheless, the phenomenon was not truly popular. Of the over forty million adults in the United Kingdom, I estimate that at the end of 1997, less than two million (or less than 5 percent of the total) were participating more or less actively in "popular capitalism." The others became shareholders in firms through initial issues, inheritance, or distribution of shares to employees, with a negligible or very small amount of value involved in these transactions. The demutualization of the building societies had the same effect.

By far more relevant to a discussion of trends in shareholding was the growth in the weight of the foreign sector, fund managers, insurance companies, and pension funds in total ownership. Thus, the direct beneficiaries of the initial underpricing of shares of privatized firms are a thin minority of the British population and a group of large financing institutions, both national and international.

As for the dimension of that underpricing, my own findings on short-term data, based on a sample of fifty-five privatization operations, are in keeping with some previous studies on this topic. When seasoned offerings and some minor transactions are excluded, there is evidence of first-day abnormal returns to purchases of stock in privatized companies of around 20 percent. This was certainly much larger than the returns to underpricing for typical private initial public offerings.

More important, I think, is the long-term performance of the British privatization shares. International empirical literature shows that with ordinary IPOs, subsequent negative abnormal returns correct the excessive reaction of the market to the IPO. Previous studies on the United Kingdom suggest that for U.K. privatized companies, the abnormal positive returns may instead continue in the long run.

Chapter 5 tested the abnormal returns for a large sample of privatized firms, extending the analysis to different periods: one year, five years, and ten years. The results confirm that there is clear evidence of abnormal returns in the long run (using the FTA index as a benchmark, and using as share prices the monthly values corrected by dividends and other operations), at least until 1996–1997. Cumulative abnormal returns of 21 percent at one year; 30 percent at two years; 57 percent at five years; and 38 percent at 10 years (for a smaller sample) were found. These results were also tested by subsamples, particularly by industry, and by the time of the public offering and other variables, with comparable results.

The values found are statistically significant, and they appear to confirm that the returns of U.K. privatized firms, after the initial underpricing, were much higher than for the rest of the companies examined. This result might look different if the price fluctuations after the 2001 stock exchange worldwide crisis were factored in, but this fluctuation is beyond the time horizon considered and has other explanations. The empirical evidence thus suggests that beyond the initial underpricing dowry, the market appreciated the protection of the monopolistic position granted by the U.K. government to most of the country's privatized firms. It is no coincidence that sectors such as electricity and water showed particularly high abnormal returns.

Summing up: The initial purchasers of shares in privatized firms obtained a substantial transfer from the Exchequer thanks to the policy of underpricing. In addition to this one-time effect, shareholders benefited from a total return on capital invested that was significantly higher than the average for other sectors. This high profitability is the other side of the lost benefit for consumers: reductions in costs not transferred to prices. In addition, it is proof of the fundamentally non-competitive nature of many of the markets in which privatized firms operate.

10.5 Consumers: A Matter of Price

Was denationalization beneficial to the British consumer? I have considered long-term trends (1960–1998) in prices, nominal and real, for several sectors: electricity, gas, and coal for domestic use (i.e., the essential energy inputs for households), as well as water, telephone, and two transport modes (railways and buses).

Electricity tariffs had been falling for over a decade when industry was nationalized. Prices for residential users increased shortly before divestiture and in some of the subsequent years, then they started falling again. In the case of gas, there was a clear price decrease after privatization, but the trend was similar in the previous decade, when British Gas was state owned. For coal, there was a decrease in prices following restructuring, but before divestiture. Observation of past trends and international comparison confirms that energy industries, public or private, use a markup over fuel costs as an essential element in price determination.

In the case of water, prices increased considerably after privatization. There was an implicit environmental tax element in these price increases, compounded with lax regulation that allowed for substantial monopoly profits. In the case of Britain's buses and railways, the price of the services increased after privatization, but the trend toward increases started well before any announcement of denationalization.

We have then three sectors with price increases after privatization, and three sectors with price decreases.

In telecommunications, the data presented in chapter 9 suggest that after denationalization, there was a reduction in the unit cost for business users, and for a number of years, an increase in the unit cost for domestic users. Subsequently, there was a generalized reduction, following a change in the regulatory constraints imposed on the industry and increased competition.

There is also mixed evidence for several other sectors. In any case, I find no structural break in long-run time series or real prices clearly associated with the timing of divestiture.

Other factors explain price changes better than ownership change. For the regulated utilities, one such factor is a progressive hardening of the price cap. This may have been the result of a learning-by-watching process by the regulators. More likely, however, it was the result of mounting public discontent with excessive profits reaped by the utilities. In some sectors, including those without price controls, such as steel, coal, and the airways, the empirical evidence shows that restructuring under public ownership and movements in exogenous input costs explain a large part of the change in prices.

In the case of electricity and gas, there was a spectacular crash both before and after privatization in the cost of input. In the case of telephony, a cycle of technological innovation provoked a sizable increase in productivity. In other sectors, the change in consumer prices resulted from changes in taxation or safety and environmental regulation.

Changes in market structures were a third important driver of price changes in the privatized companies. The degree of competition at divestiture varied from sector to sector, usually from pure monopoly to duopoly and oligopoly. In the space of the twenty years examined, the conditions of competition changed. There was increased liberalization, and the markup on the costs charged by the companies was sensitive to liberalization (or lack of it).

The Monopoly and Merger Commission, the sector regulators, and the government intervened frequently in the market structures in which the privatized firms operated. The regulatory contract proved to be a vague notion. The system for regulating the privatized industries was in a state of flux over the twenty years studied (and still is). In comparison with industries that remained nationalized, however, the privatized companies had a more clear understanding of their opportunities and administrative constraints. This was a clear advantage.

In summary: Several price patterns are observed before and after privatization, but no structural break is clearly attributable to the new ownership pattern. The most important drivers of prices were exogenous changes in costs, regulation, and market structure. Together, as a causal factor of the trend in postprivatization prices, they largely overshadow the shift in ownership regime. Some of these changes have nothing to do with private ownership and can be observed in other countries without privatization.

In turn, to assess the net welfare impact of privatization, we must rely on the observation of actual price and expenditure performances and on counterfactuals: "What if ..." This is not an exact science. My preferred approach in chapter 7 was to consider three simple possibilities. The indifference or pessimistic scenario is one in which the price performance of the industries under continued nationalization is assumed to mimic the actual observed trends in the privatized industries. The optimistic scenario is symmetric: All observed price changes are attributed to privatization and closely related reforms. This sets a range of values (there may be more extreme cases, but I consider them unlikely).

Clearly, something in between these two extreme cases is needed, if we do not want just to toss a coin. A closer look to the seven industries studied may help in formulating a crude, but reasonable, "median" scenario.

First, I have observed price increases in transport, namely, the railways and buses. For both services, postprivatization fare increases are on their long-term track since the 1960s. Labor productivity in the railways increased sharply in the 1980s, before denationalization, but this was insufficient to contain prices. Consequently, I suggest that it would be wrong to say that privatization *increased* transport prices in the United Kingdom. Thus, I adopt a scenario of indifference for these two sectors.

Second, I have looked at real energy prices. The observation of past trends and international comparisons suggest a strong correlation of energy prices with fuel costs. Costs for gas, coal, and oil decreased sharply in the years under study. Moreover, gas prices after privatization decreased at the same pace as before, in line with the observed long-term productivity increase in the sector. Coal for domestic use is a small component of household expenditures. Its price increased, and productivity growth was flat, for many years under state ownership, but wide restructuring of the industry achieved positive price and productivity results several years before privatization. Electricity prices after privatization show an increase that is hard to justify in terms of input costs, which again follow a decreasing trend that started eight years before privatization. My conclusion here is that there is no reason to credit ownership change (and regulation), until the end of the 1990s and wider liberalization, with any influence on price *decreases*. Consequently, my preferred option is again the indifference scenario.

One might like to go more in depth for each of these sectors and differentiate more the counterfactuals among them. The aggregate result of such fine tuning is likely to be modest.

In contrast, I do not think that water prices would have *increased* and telecommunications prices *decreased* to the same extent under public ownership as they did under private. The nationalized water and sewerage industry was in need of considerable investment to respond to new EU regulations on quality standards. Tariffs would have had to increase anyway under continued public ownership. The price cap formula for the sector, however, allowed the privatized industry to pass on to the consumers all (and probably excessive) costs of the required infrastructure investment, with a high return to the investors. I suggest that under public ownership, constraints on water prices would have been tougher, for political reasons.

The telecommunications industry experienced high productivity increases under public ownership, but also increasing prices in real terms, because of the necessity of self-financing big investments and because of monopoly profits. In fact, British Telecom was a net contributor under nationalization to the Exchequer. Privatization enabled the Treasury to avoid increasing borrowing requirements in preparation for further investments, but historically BT was not a true burden for public finance. I documented in chapter 9 that regulation and later liberalization were the drivers of decreases in telecommunications prices, in combination with technology change. Privatization may have accelerated a policy change that historically considered acceptable higher returns in telecommunication than, for example, in water or gas.

On the basis of previous discussion of the water and telecommunications industries, I prefer to adopt a prudent and optimistic option. I attribute to ownership change and related reforms most of the merit of lower telecommunications tariffs and *nothing* of the blame for higher water tariffs. This is generous to privatization, because the decrease in telecommunications tariffs accounts for two-thirds of the overall welfare impact of privatization. With a Marshallian measure of consumer surplus, or with a range of other welfare measures, the maximum net welfare benefit per capita I calculate is £38 per year in constant 1995 pounds. In fact, the nature of the counterfactual probably exaggerates the impact of privatization.

By any standard, this is a small welfare change, and it critically depends on the evaluation of the performance of one company, British Telecom. Chapter 9 shows, however, that ownership change at privatization per se had little impact on BT's productivity or gross profitability performance.

Moreover, the small welfare gain from privatization was not evenly distributed among users. Consumers in the two bottom income quintiles probably received no net benefit at all, and perhaps one million households actually suffered a negative welfare change from privatization.

For some consumers in the lower income brackets, family spending for the acquisition of a decent level of electricity, gas, water, public transport, and telephone service could now exceed 20 percent of their income and be, in practice, unaffordable. Increases in the prices of public services, particularly for water and energy, since privatization as result of the abolition of cross-subsidies or of the introduction of regressive discrimination in prices have had considerable effects on consumers with lower incomes. Welfare redistribution also had an impact on telephone users. Those affected were not marginal fringe groups, but a substantial share of the aged, the disabled, children of single parents, the long-term unemployed, and the working poor. I think privatization contributed to the hardship these groups suffered, because it is unlikely that nationalized industries would have been allowed to rebalance their tariffs in a regressive way, or at least not to the extent that the privatized industries did.

In principle, the government could have compensated for these regressive effects with adequate monetary lump-sum subsidies (financed, for example, by a capital gains tax for shareholders in privatized firms or by other means). Such compensation in practice never happened. In terms of standard welfare economics, only actual compensation is relevant for estimates of actual welfare changes. I propose to apply to the measures used to assess the welfare impact of privatization a welfare weight that considers the welfare of the bottom income quintile as the numeraire, and taxes away 30 percent of the welfare changes accruing to the top income quintile. My best estimate of the maximum welfare change, after this correction for redistribution, is around £30 per capita per year. My minimum nonnegative estimation lies somewhere between zero and this value.[1]

Consequently, my conclusion is that privatization per se probably had little overall impact on the welfare of British consumers. Other reforms, particularly increasingly tough regulation and liberalization, played a more important role in changes in British consumers' welfare.

10.6 Taxpayers: How Much Was the Family Silver Worth?

At the beginning of the Tory era, in 1979, public debt in the United Kingdom was around 44 percent of GDP. It reached an all-time low of around 26 percent at the beginning of the 1990s. At the end of the period we consider here, it was again around 40 percent. Alongside this U-turn there was a steep decline in public-sector net worth, which plummeted from over 70 percent of GDP to less than 15 percent over the same period.

Initially, the British divestitures generated a substantial amount of cash receipts, and this contributed to debt repayment. At first the combination of privatization, increase in tax pressure, and expenditure reduction brought the debt down. Subsequently this policy mix could not be maintained. The Major government oversaw substantial budget deficits. Although the trends in current spending and tax pressure did not record any fundamental changes between 1979 and 1997, public investments sharply decreased. Further privatization did not counterbalance the debt increase and the huge asset decumulation resulting from privatization, and the public-sector net worth collapsed.

I have analyzed detailed company data on cash flows between the public sector and thirty-three nationalized companies that were later privatized (excluding British Rail) and official time series data since the 1960s. In constant 1995 pounds, around 1982–1983, *before privatization*, these companies started to transfer a positive cash flow to the Exchequer, through repayment, interest, corporation tax, and dividends. In real terms, when we consolidate the public-sector budget including the nationalized industries, fixed capital formation matched Exchequer financing, and these industries imposed no real economic burden on the taxpayer.

Most of the financial problem attributed to nationalized industries by the Treasury was the consequence of mistaken or partial accounting (liabilities without corresponding asset accounting). Between 1985 and 1995 the Exchequer cashed from the nationalized/privatized industries between £2 billion and £4 billion per year (constant 1995 pounds) for interest, debt repayment, and repayment of capital, in addition to privatization proceeds and corporation tax.

I suggest that in the second half of the 1980s and in the 1990s, without privatization but allowing the same new price regulations as those that governed the privatized industries, the counterfactual nationalized industries (excluding railways) would have been able to finance their investment programs and still provide cash to the Exchequer. In a more conservative scenario, of less generous price cap regulations, there may have been a limited cash outflow from the Treasury, matched by asset accumulation.

I propose a simple illustrative calculation. All figures are at constant 1995 pounds, and I use a social discount rate at 5 percent. The average effective corporate income tax rate for privatized companies was around 30 percent. Their gross-of-tax profit was around £9.3 billion per year (BT alone had £3 billion in pretax profits in 1997). The net-of-tax profit was then £6.5 billion. The perpetual value of the net-of-tax profits to the shareholders in the privated firms was £186 billion − £56 billion = £130 billion. Because they had the opportunity to buy the nationalized industries at £70 billion (I do not consider here debt placement and other operations), they made a good deal, under my conservative estimate of gross profits and of the discount rate. One has to discount future private flows at around real 9.3 percent to find that shareholders paid the "right" price. This is perhaps nearly twice a reasonable social discount rate in real terms. In chapter 2, I argued that there can be a wedge between the private (after-tax) and public discount rate, but I do not think it can be quite so wide.

On the other hand, taxpayers did not receive a benefit, but probably a loss, from the sale of the privatized firms. One has to consider the long-term trends of interest and dividends for the Treasury, plus retained profits within the public corporations. I suggest that the net present value of future cash flows for the Exchequer from the privatized industries, excluding new finance for investment, had they remained nationalized, could have been £6.5 billion per year or £130 billion in perpetuity.

The Exchequer net present value of cash from the sale of the denationalized companies was £126 billion (£70 billion in sale proceeds plus £56 billion tax perpetuity), and the net present value of future cash flows under continued public ownership was £130 billion. With a shadow price of 1.3 to public funds, the taxpayer lost more than £5 billion (or if we include the proceeds from the windfall tax, there is perhaps a very small positive net balance for the taxpayer).

Thus it would be fair to say that privatization had a slightly negative or neutral impact on the welfare of the average taxpayer in accounting terms. In terms of opportunity cost, however, there was probably a substantial loss. I have guessed in chapter 8 that if the private discount rate is 7.5 percent and the public-sector discount rate is 5 percent (with the difference explained by tax rates, risk aversion, and greater investment opportunities for the private investors), the loss for the taxpayer because of underpricing is £17 billion. This figure may seem very high, but it is interesting to observe that it is close to the return, after the first trading day, to initial shareholders (i.e., those who bought shares at the IPOs). I have estimated this return to be around £14 billion. The market's valuation of the privatized firms' assets was then rational or simply more reasonable than the Treasury's (and its City's advisors') assessment.

A crucial point in this reasoning is the counterfactual scenario: How much gross profit would the firms have made if they had remained public? There are many possible alternatives related to the counterfactuals for prices and for changes in consumers' welfare (see above). I have adopted here one that is consistent with continued public ownership under consumer prices similar to those under privatization, except for telecommunications and water prices, and with higher production costs (by some percentage points) than under privatization.

In the early 1980s, *before privatization*, after the financial troubles in the 1970s, the public corporations (excluding the railways) were *net cash givers* to the Treasury. In a counterfactual scenario in which some of the most profitable firms remained in public hands and enjoyed the same conditions that the regulators granted to the privatized firms, the Treasury would have had considerable benefits in terms of dividends from the public corporations. With the windfall tax, the damage to the Exchequer was limited. However, it does not seem consistent to include that tax in my calculations, because it happened in a different policy framework. Therefore, I conclude that privatization did not improve taxpayers' position and probably worsened it.

10.7 Overall Welfare Balance: Some Conjectural Calculations

In this section, I make a bold attempt to guess the overall welfare impact of British privatization. I am very far from thinking that what follows is anything more than a crude guess and a starting point for further research on the United Kingdom and on other countries. The assumptions I employ are very simple:

1. I focus on four agents: consumers, workers, shareholders, and taxpayers. I try to evaluate the actual welfare change for each group, then I sum the values. The balance is the gross welfare change for the society. I define the net welfare change as the actual gross value less a virtual value for a counterfactual scenario of continued public ownership.

2. All values are expressed in constant 1995 pounds.

3. The social discount rate I use is real 5 percent. There is no particular justification for this rate; I simply consider it a realistic benchmark. I use real 7.5 percent for the private discount rate.

4. To simplify different time horizons and possible counterfactuals, I suppose that the welfare changes are all observed at the end of the period 1979–1997 and then stay unchanged with an infinite time horizon. I convert all yearly values in their net present value in the form of perpetuity.

5. I offer two calculations: one that does not employ shadow prices, which is mistaken but less controversial, and another with a very simple set of shadow prices. I take the average consumer's welfare, expressed in constant pounds, as the numeraire, with shadow price 1. I assign a 1.3 conversion factor to public funds, because of the excess burden of distortionary taxation (a benchmark value frequently used in public-economics literature). I assign a 1.3 weight also to the welfare of the poorest consumers (those in the 20th income percentile or lower) and a 0.7 weight to the welfare of the average shareholders (including the foreign investors), typically those in the top 20 percent of the income distribution. These welfare weights are simple benchmarks for a plausible social-welfare function with aversion to inequality (equivalent to marginal taxation of income around 42 percent). All these shadow prices and the discount rate we can easily test by simple sensitivity analysis.

I turn now to consider the results for each agent. My estimations of consumers' welfare change because of prices changes under different measures are between £3.8 billion and £4.8 billion. This would give us a gross welfare change between £76 billion and £96 billion. Here I consider a baseline value of between £80 billion and £88 billion as an estimate of the gross welfare change.

To this should be added reductions in prices of other consumer goods as an indirect effect of cost reductions in other industries. These indirect effects are very difficult to estimate. I therefore ignore these effects here, because I think they may be small.

Obviously attributing all price reductions (or increases) to privatization is surely overestimating. Under my "midway" counterfactual, the maximum privatization benefit to the consumer is £38 per year. This allows for 80 percent of the benefit of the observed British Telecom price decrease under privatization, none of the price increases in water and transport, and none as well of the price decrease in energy. One can test these figures using sensitivity analysis and refine the scenarios for individual industries, but overall the welfare impact of different reasonable counterfactuals is limited.

Finally, a further correction for the distributive impact of privatization should be introduced. The distributive characteristics of goods have already been considered, but tariff rebalancing has not been. I propose here that around 20 percent of the overall direct welfare change brought about by price decrease should be canceled out because of the regressive nature of the rebalancing of tariffs. My final estimation of the net welfare change for consumers is thus around £32 billion, or less than £30 per capita per year.

Shareholders' welfare is influenced by privatization in several ways: first, they pay to buy shares; second, they enjoy capital gains as a result of underpricing of firms and extra profits earned by firms; and third, they pay corporate taxes through the firms they own.

I showed in section 10.6 that under the assumption that the private discount rate is 50 percent higher than the social discount rate, shareholders received a net benefit from privatization of around £17 billion, near the 24-hour correction of the initial underpricing by financial markets. Since this gain was transferred either to the richer sections of the population or abroad, I suggest that it should be discounted by a distributive welfare weight of 0.7. This leaves a net welfare benefit of around £12 billion for the shareholders in the privatized firms.

Conversely, the loss suffered by taxpayers is only £4 billion if the opportunity cost is disregarded, and it potentially equals the amount by which the privatized firms were underpriced (i.e., £17 billion) if the opportunity cost is considered. I prefer to be conservative here and consider the smaller figure. Because public funds have a shadow price as a result of distortionary taxation, with a 0.3 correction, the net loss to the taxpayer (with opportunity cost disregarded) is around £5 billion. I exclude proceeds from the windfall tax from this calculation, our time horizon being the Conservative governments' privatization policy.

The impact of the change in workers' welfare may be neglected at this stage, because I found (section 10.3) no clear evidence that employment and pay under the counterfactual would have differed much from the actual trend under private ownership. There is some evidence, however, that blue-collar workers suffered a welfare loss and that top managers and some white-collar workers enjoyed increased rents. The evidence so far is not sufficient to hazard a guess for the change in workers' welfare from privatization. Presumably, there was here again a regressive redistribution of income, but I am unable to quantify it.

My overall result, under my benchmark scenario and without the use of any shadow price, is as follows. Taxpayers suffered a net loss of £4 billion from privatization; shareholders enjoyed a £17 billion bonus; workers' welfare was probably negatively affected, but overall this impact is difficult to quantify; and consumers enjoyed a perpetual discount on prices worth £44 billion. Taken together, these figures yield a net benefit of £57 billion, less than £1,000 per capita in perpetuity, or £50 per year. When the regressive impact of distribution and the shadow price of public funds are accounted for, the resulting social value of the taxpayers' loss is £5 billion, the shareholders' benefit is reduced to £12 billion, the consumers' benefit to £35 billion, and the overall net benefit per capita per year to £30. Table 10.1 summarizes the calculations.

This is a small benefit, based inter alia on the assumption of a private discount rate 50 percent higher than the private one, a cost counterfactual rather adverse to nationalized industry, and a price counterfactual that says that privatization has to be credited with most of the decrease in telecom tariffs since privatization and carries no blame for price increases in water and transport.

Three important aspects of privatization have not yet been considered: indirect impacts, the role of foreign ownership, and how to consider extra profits in general equilibrium. The overall impact of these aspects is probably to reduce further the welfare impact of privatization. The corrections associated with the first two aspects have opposite signs: There were indirect benefits to consumers thanks to reduced telecommunications prices to business users, and there were rents transferred abroad because of the increased role of foreign ownership. If these cancel out each other, we are left with social accounting for extra profits.

First, in general equilibrium, there is a unique social discount rate. This makes the opportunity cost of underpricing very high. Moreover, whereas in partial equilibrium analysis we can simply add one pound of monopoly profit to one pound of consumer surplus, in a general equilibrium perspective, the accounting is different. The social value of any project, including privatization, is worth the change in net output at shadow prices. Social cost-benefit analysis wipes out monopoly profits from financial values because there is no real output or opportunity cost involved. In other words, monopoly profits are pure transfers. For example, the H.M. Treasury (1997b) guidelines for publicinvestment appraisal suggest considering marginal costs and not prices when there are market distortions. Monopoly profit is a form of "private tax" that consumers pay, and it has an associated deadweight loss. I suspect that if an increase in extra profits in the U.K. economy, against the small decrease in real prices and compared with the continued nationalization counterfactual, is attributed to privatization or to lax regulation, the net benefits of denationalization may disappear or even become slightly negative.[2] I do not want to propose here, however, a further and controversial correction to my previous calculations.

I admit that these are very crude conjectures. They may offer a starting point, however, for a more detailed welfare analysis. They can be tested using sensitivity analysis for the values of the various parameters involved in the calculation. Only an in-depth, industry-by-industry analysis and a set of general equilibrium shadow prices would give us welfare estimates that are more precise. Such an analysis is beyond the scope of my research, and others may try to undertake it.

The most surprising aspect of my calculations is that the measurable welfare impact of British privatization is so low. If costs and benefits in general equilibrium are considered, the welfare impact is even smaller, because excess profits are then mere transfers. With greater aversion to inequality and shadow pricing, the impact may be zero or even marginally negative. Apparently, far from being a revolution, the great divestiture was more a reshuffling of relative positions of various agents, probably a regressive one, with a modest impact on aggregate economic efficiency.

10.8 Concluding Remarks

In this final section, I offer some more personal remarks, discuss policy implications, and examine indications for further research. My assessment of British privatization starts with the missing productivity shock. The lack of a clear increase in productivity causally linked to ownership change at privatization per se belies any simplistic theory of property rights. Private versus public ownership is a vague distinction for a wide range of institutions. In the United Kingdom, the governance of the denationalized industries was often a complex game

Table 10.1
Conjectures on the overall costs and benefits of British privatization (constant 1995 billion pounds, net present perpetual values at the end period)

	Without shadow prices	With shadow prices	Assumptions
Consumers			
Price changes for public services	+44	+35	Real discount rate: 0.05 Distributive correction: 0.20
Indirect effects (intermediate goods)	positive, not quantified	positive, not quantified	Counterfactual scenario: see chapter 7
Extra-profits correction	—	negative,[a] not quantified	
Balance	+44	+35	
Taxpayers			
Privatization proceeds	+70	+91	
Gross profit foregone	−130	−169	Shadow premium on public funds: 0.30 Real discount rate: 0.05
Taxes on profits	+56	+73	
(Opportunity cost)[b]	negative	negative	
(Windfall tax)[c]	(+5)	(+6.5)	
Balance	−4	−5	
Shareholders			
Payments to H. M. Treasury	−70	−49	
Pretax profits[d]	+124	+87	Distributive correction: 0.30 Tax rate: 0.30
Taxes on profits	−37	−26	Windfall tax not considered
Balance	+17	+12	
Workers			
Employment impact	negative, small	—	900,000 jobs lost, mostly under public ownership
Wage impact	neutral or slightly positive	neutral	No evidence of significant change in relative wages — shadow wage
Employees' share ownership impact	positive, small	neutral	Mostly a transfer from taxpayers
Distributive impact	—	negative, not quantified	Increase in pay dispersion, loser: some unskilled, contracting out, gainer: managers

Table 10.1
(continued)

	Without shadow prices	With shadow prices	Assumptions
Balance	neutral	small negative	
Society			
Consumers	+44	+35	
Taxpayers	−4	−5	
Shareholders	±0	+12	
Workers	+17	(−)	
Balance	+57	+42[e]	

[a] The net present value of the difference between gross profit under private and public ownership (see below) corresponds to the excess return of privatized industries.
[b] Opportunity cost to taxpayers of potential rent extraction at sale. This equals the balance to the shareholders, that is, up to £17 billion.
[c] Under a different policy regime.
[d] Private discount rate: 0.075.
[e] Without corrections for extra profits; otherwise probably zero or slightly negative.

among small control groups of financial investors, executive directors, and regulators. Dispersed individual shareholders (i.e., the majority of formal owners) played virtually no role. My reading suggests that such coalition ownership may not provide firms' executive directors with a strong incentive to exploit all the possible strategies to save on production factors. Productivity and profitability data tell two different stories.

Under such coalition ownership, firms' executive directors will probably be more interested in guaranteeing satisfactory profitability to shareholders, and good personal incomes to themselves, than in increasing productivity or reducing production costs as much as possible. The best option for top managers is probably to influence the sector regulator so that it allows comfortable profit margins. Conversely, under price cap regulation, subject to periodic revision, an excess of managerial effort to reduce investments or personnel costs could even be counterproductive. It could create undesired tensions with employees, suppliers, and customers and make the regulator think that there may be further margins for increases in productivity.

There are interesting parallels between the governance structures of nationalized and denationalized industries. The ownership of the British public corporation was also a coalition, with its specific agents and objectives. The Treasury had mainly a financial perspective on the role of the nationalized industries: the achievement of a required rate of return, or later minimization of the borrowing requirement. Ministries, directors, and trade unions had, in turn, other goals: a combination of national growth ambitions, social concerns, political agendas, and eventually self-interest. The proportions of the ingredients in the blend varied over time, but this last element, self-interest, was never dominant. The boards of public corporations may have not been "the high custodians of public interest," in Morrison's words, but neither were they just self-interested bureaucrats. In retrospect, the resulting productivity record of most public corporations in Great Britain over forty years was honorable. The British public corporations were not the result of a socialist plot. They were the outcome of the century-long interplay of social and economic factors in a highly developed economy with a decent public administration.

Privatization did not deliver miracles in regard to the privatized firms' efficiency, partly because the starting point was not abysmally low, and partly because the new ownership pattern did not offer terribly strong incentives for innovation, productivity growth, or endogenous cost savings. There was an obvious incentive to increase profitability, and increases in this area occurred on a wide scale, until the end of the 1990s, thanks to undemanding regulation. Most of the decreases in firms' costs after privatization were exogenous, such as the decrease in some input prices, technical progress, and dynamic scale economies. Price cap regulation, designed to increase efficiency, for many years offered a protection to monopoly rents, not a strong incentive to squeeze costs.

In contrast, public corporations never enjoyed the benefits of a relatively stable regulatory framework. They had to cope with a minimum required rate of return and permitted price increases that contradicted the rate-of-return requirement. There are few doubts that some public corporations, particularly British Telecom, under a lax price cap system, would have been able to increase their profitability, had they remained nationalized, more or less as their privatized counterparts did.

When regulators hardened the price cap constraints or competition started to bite (or both), company performance changed. I return in the following to sequencing and causation of privatization-regulation-liberalization reforms.

Looking beyond microeconomic efficiency in production and considering social-welfare changes, the privatization game had various stakes, which canceled each other out. As noted previously, I have been unable to detect a substantial impact of divestitures on aggregate growth. I find no evidence of big macroeconomic externalities. In turn, privatization's impacts on employment, inflation, and income distribution (the remaining macroeconomic welfare variables) were respectively neutral, modestly favorable, and unfavorable. This limited aggregate impact happened because, I suggest, benefits for buyers were losses for sellers; excess profits for shareholders were losses for consumers; high salaries for managers were costs for the firms; and so on. When all the calculations have been made in terms of costs and benefits, the outcome of the big privatization game is less than expected.

On the other hand, privatization's redistributive effects were not negligible. It is beyond dispute that the net beneficiaries of privatization often belonged to the wealthiest 10–20 percent of the population. They obtained a transfer from the Exchequer as purchasers of underpriced shares, additional capital incomes from monopoly profits for many years, and enjoyed a discount on capital income taxes. They enjoyed the benefits of regressive tariff rebalancing and price discrimination in favor of high users. Managers increased their salaries and associated benefits relative to others employees.

The reform did have some progressive aspects as well. Former tenants of council houses were able to buy property at a discount, and there were millions of winners at the lottery of initial public offerings.

Those who bore the net welfare costs of privatization, however, belong to the poorest 10–20 percent of the population. For many years, they had to pay increased tariffs or fixed charges for some essential public services; some lost their jobs or faced greater job insecurity. This added to social hardship and the increase in inequality. In this sense, privatization was an integral part of a series of policies that created a social rift unequaled anywhere else in Europe. In some ways, this rift has distanced the United Kingdom from the social model of its European partners. No government in the European Union would have considered acceptable a doubling of the percentage of people living in conditions of poverty in less than two decades. This process of regressive reshuffling of welfare has also brought into dispute the secular coevolution, since the Victorian era, of state and market in British society, as discussed in chapter 1. Britain's economic system is now closer to the U.S. form of capitalism than to the European pattern, without the benefits of American technological leadership, entrepreunerialism, and international hegemony.

These conclusions may seem too severe, as well as far from the conventional wisdom, according to which privatization must generate growth and welfare for all by removing the great inefficiency associated with public ownership. Unlike a few years ago, however, many professional economists now seem prepared to acknowledge that the benefits of privatization were exaggerated by the "Washington consensus" advocated by the IMF and by other international financial institutions. According to one prominent Washington consensus dissenter, Joseph Stiglitz, liberalization and good governance should be given more emphasis in structural reform packages than ownership change (Florio 2002).

I suggest, however, that it is not just a matter of priorities or sequencing. The important issue here is the extent of government responsibility in the provision of public services.

In the case of the United Kingdom, the great majority of privatized industries were trapped in a regulatory framework that was often admired abroad, but much less so in the United Kingdom itself. Regulation, stripped of verbal trimmings, evolved in the United Kingdom in a penetrating and often discretionary control of prices, quantities, and property rights exercised by a small group of people nominated by the government. These people usually had academic or other types of qualifications acquired outside the civil service and were commissioned to carry out their role for a number of years in conditions of formal independence from the government. This system became a permanent element of the functioning of some important industries. It is definitely no longer a transitory expedient, as it was in the initial aspirations of some protagonists of the U.K. experiment, including perhaps Thatcher.

Because this system represents a new form of government, we need to ascertain its superiority over other arrangements. Public monopoly, public-private ownership, or coexistence of different ownership patterns were, and still are, rather common in continental Europe, and their performance has been and is comparable to or often better than that of some British privatized and regulated industries. International comparisons of prices, output trends, and welfare changes following policy reforms are difficult to study, and I would need another book even to begin the task. Even if the focus is narrowed to the European Union, there are still a variety of patterns of ownership structures, regulatory frameworks, market organization.

It is not just that one has to stress more regulation and liberalization, nor is it a matter of sequencing along a unique path. There are different combinations. Variations in ownership structures are often a response to country-specific social and governance issues.

Ownership, public or private, is not just a bundle of rights. In a perfect assets market there is indifference between ownership and lease of production factors. Assets markets in reality, however, are far from perfect. For good reasons, we often prefer to own our house and car, even though we can afford to rent them. As early as the mid-nineteenth century, many British municipalities decided to own gas, water, tramways, and later electricity firms. They could have made contracts with private suppliers, but they decided otherwise. The Victorian gentlemen who governed those municipalities were not usually socialists, and they were not irrational. They simply did not consider public procurement and regulation a good substitute for ownership.

Nowadays in Germany or Norway a large proportion of the facilities for electricity generation are still owned by local government, and this is not necessarily because these countries are lagging behind in a reform pattern. When France defends its national tradition of large, vertically integrated public monopolies, such as the railways or electricity, it proposes a model that evolved over two centuries, performed reasonably well, and is now an integral part of a social consensus. All of this may conflict with the aspiration to a European market for public services, but we cannot dismiss it as the rusty remnants of old-fashioned ideologies.

Perhaps we should regard the new regulatory experiment in Britain, not privatization, as the most important legacy and contribution of the British reform in the Thatcher years. The reinvention or reshuffling of regulation in Britain during the last twenty years was perhaps misguided and unstable, and it did not really protect consumers from monopoly. It was, however, an original experiment on a wide scale. For example, it made the licensees' obligations to consumers, which had been very much a gray area even for the predecessor public firms, much clearer.

With these obligations and independent control systems having been defined, one might now wonder whether, in some sectors, a public enterprise with a clear status of autonomy from the government, adequately regulated and possibly exposed to a certain degree of internal or international competition, would not have been an equally

convenient or even better solution to the provision of public services than a regulated private firm. This might well have been the case
in regard to the railways, the water industry, the electricity and telecommunications networks, and everywhere where there is an obligation to provide public service and exit is socially too costly.

Thus, we are back to a key question: What actually went wrong
with the nationalized industries in Britain? At the end of the 1970s, the
British public corporations had reached a critical point, for three basic
reasons: stringent price control for sporadic curbing of inflation, limits
in some cases on investments in the corporations, and industrial relations that slowed down (but did not impede) restructuring processes,
including the agonizing but necessary cuts in employment in certain
sectors. Superficially, there were budgetary problems. At a deeper
level the crisis was a political one: The sense of a well-defined public-
service mission had been lost, and the government's public-service
planning framework was increasingly patchy (Alford 1993).

Privatization and regulation did away with these three limitations.
First, firms could often raise prices in real terms (in relation to their
own costs) and increase self-financing. Second, they had free recourse
to the capital markets. Third, they could restructure more rapidly in
response to changes in market regime and regulation. None of these
reforms was impossible, however, in a regime of restructured public
ownership.

The crisis of the public firm, which practically eradicated it not only
in the United Kingdom, but worldwide, although occasionally a financial crisis, in reality was above all a political crisis, arising from the in-
capacity or unwillingness of governments at the end of the twentieth
century to assume certain social responsibilities. The solution, in turn,
was a political one that consisted of shifting the responsibility to deliver certain public services to the private sector.

But this "divestiture of responsibility" option had a limit, and that
limit was reached when it was clear that policymakers' refusal to provide some public services directly was in the end only apparent. After
all, independent regulators are just another public-sector office. Why
should an exclusively private but regulated sector that controls a substantial share of GDP work any better than a public sector, appropriately regulated and/or liberalized? There is no compelling reason to
renounce public provision forever.

Paradoxically, privatization more clearly poses the problem of the
agenda of public policies concerning certain services. The painstak-

ingly elaborated licenses granted to the regulatees in Britain reflected an increasing awareness of specific policy objectives (consumer protection, social obligations, environmental sustainability, safety, etc.) for certain industries.

The weak part of British privatization, ironically, was private ownership. The new owners of the privatized firms were not entrepreneurs, but a coalition of regulators, top managers, and financial investors. Moreover, the "free" markets in which the privatized firms operated were rather an array of constrained forms of collusive oligopoly, with transitory episodes of destructive competition. This was not always the case, and not for all sectors; some businesses were successfully deregulated, but certainly too often this did not occur.

In some industries, the regulated and privatized sector looks increasingly like a form of public procurement. The key test in regard to this was the inability of the British government to allow privatized Railtrack or the traffic control agency to go bankrupt in 2001–2002. Mutualization (i.e., not-for-profit ownership) has now begun in the water sector.

That the net economic benefits of British privatization were probably modest, and that the social effect was one of regressive redistribution, is obviously not in itself an argument in favor of the traditional public monopoly. I am not nostalgic for the old nationalized industries. They were a failure, but not because their alleged inefficiency, or because they were a burden to the Treasury. The nationalized industries collapsed because many did not feel they were there for a valuable social purpose, like, for example, the National Health Service. Therefore, the public corporation was the victim of a too-narrow economic policy framework and incentives structure.

In a certain sense the U.K. experience permanently succeeded in changing our way of thinking about public intervention in some services. Today, it is perhaps clearer that property rights, far from being natural rights, can be defined by the state in different ways and transferred conditionally to different subjects, with adequate controls and incentives.

The crucial question was, and still is, whether or not there should be a public policy, and a planning framework, for water, energy, telecommunications, and transport, as there is for health and education, and what the objectives and tools of such a policy ought to be, or whether the state should have no policy and targets for these sectors, leaving the market to determine the amount and the characteristics of supply and demand. A discussion of the agenda for public policies is thus needed before one of property rights. Without it, privatization, regulation, liberalization are "empty boxes."

Nationalization in Britain collapsed when public firms and their boards and employees lost sight of their social mission, because of a lack of a suitable planning framework. The privatized and regulated utilities that followed, divested of the rhetoric about free enterprise, do not appear to be the solution to this lack of a framework. They still require the government or legislators to define a clear public mandate for their regulators.

Unless the market is really given a full chance (and this—despite the most far-fetched and contrived experiments—does not appear to be possible, or even desirable, in some crucial sectors), it will be necessary to envisage public policies for public-service provision. An appropriate public-policy framework, in attributing property rights and regulatory obligations to private or public subjects, according to the circumstances, should find creative solutions to give the users of public services (that is, of those services for which a policy is worth having) an institutionally well-defined role. It should give those who have ideas on how to introduce innovations in these services, both private entrepreneurs or entrepreunerial public managers, a way to realize them.

Ownership and property rights are thus instrumental to a policy framework for the provision of public services. If one thinks that government has to offer this framework for water or health provision, one cannot say that ownership of some assets is out of the question, always and everywhere. One has to say instead that ownership is one governance option, among others, to be assessed against feasible alternatives, in terms of social net benefits.

Periodical privatization of less-efficient state-owned enterprises could be an effective threat to inefficient management. One needs to own something, however, to be able to sell it. When one is stripped of assets, it is time to think again to buy, if one wants to play this game. The game here is government's responsibility for social integration through public services. The contents change over time and country by country, but there is a core that does not change.

The reasons for the public's mistrust of the governments' ability to plan and manage policies for public services are very serious; the crucial issue, however, is not inferior efficiency. It is the functioning of democratic political systems. Privatization policies quite often defer the problems inherent in achieving a broad consensus on public-service provision by trying to reduce state institutions' responsibility toward society. It is a reversal of the process of coevolution and core-sponsibility between the state and the market that the United Kingdom, like other European countries, has pursued for almost two centuries. That process was not driven solely by ideology. It was a collective response to social and economic problems. On the other hand, where should one stop this process of deconstruction of government? How "minimal" must the state be before the community ceases to be a polis? And how large must the recourse to repression and to the principle of authority be before the state will be reduced to safeguarding order (and redistributing incomes), if this order is not based on the well-defined right of access to certain goods as basic as water and energy or as complex as education and health? In other words, what is citizenship, and what is the state without a collective responsibility for ensuring universal access to some essential goods (whatever they are, according to specific national conditions in a given time period)?

There may be various solutions to granting this access. State-owned enterprises, often under statutory monopoly, have historically been one solution. Privatized and regulated utilities are another solution, not entirely new. Neither seems to be without difficulties. Efficiency considerations alone do not solve the access problem. The answer for the future may imply a wider reconsideration of the economic scope of public institutions (including public ownership, regulation of private ownership, and public procurement of services), their functioning in a progressive environment, and their responsiveness to social needs. Critical assessment of the British experience will help us to understand from where we have to start this rethinking.

Notes

Chapter 1 Historical Background

1. The internal rate of return (IRR) is an interest rate that zeroes the net present value of cash inflows and outflows. The TDR is a benchmark value. For example, if the TDR is 8 percent, any project with an IRR of 7 percent should be rejected.

2. Under this system, in fact only rarely implemented, the nationalized industry could calculate its revenues and net returns with a mix of actual and accounting prices, the latter based on marginal costs, when it had an obligation to provide services below their cost.

3. The external financial limits were appropriations of funds in the Treasury budget to cover the borrowing requirements of the nationalized industries to finance capital expenditures or to cover losses. (The nationalized industries usually had no right to recur to borrowing through commercial banks or through the issue of corporate bonds.) In this way the Treasury had a firm control on the finance of the nationalized industries, whereas the other ministries (e.g., those for transport and energy) had no powers in this respect.

4. The Heath government (1970–1974), although initially inclined to free-market policy, reacted to the recession following the first oil shock in 1973 with an expansive fiscal policy and the abandoning of the fixed exchange rate, and it approved measures to support shipyards, aerospace, and other sectors with public subsidies.

5. Many years later, in 1998, when Pinochet was arrested in Great Britain at the request of the Spanish judiciary, Thatcher spoke up loudly in defense of the Chilean dictator.

6. According to Lord (Derek) Ezra, a Liberal Democrat member of Parliament who has experienced over two decades of debates on privatization and regulation bills, at the time of privatization the regulatory issue was not a major topic of discussion (Vass 1997). The objective was privatization in itself, with financial return in second place, and promoting competition only in third place.

7. In the United Kingdom, building societies are mutual organizations, similar to cooperatives, that accept investment at interest and lend to persons buying houses.

8. For a summary of available data, see ONS 2000a.

Chapter 2   Privatization Theories and Cost-Benefit Analysis

1. See Tanzi and Schucknecht 1995 for such an attempt.

2. For a review of the literature, see, for example, Vickers and Yarrow 1988a or the 1996 work by Polish economic sociologist Jacek Tittenbrun. More recently, see Shirley and Walsh 2000, which has a strong proprivatization bias.

3. In this framework, however, full competition with other firms may constrain public firms to behave efficiently, and thus market structure dominates ownership structure as an explanatory variable for the industry's performance (Beato and Mas-Coleil 1984; Kay, Mayer, and Thompson 1986).

4. Cf. Alchian 1965, 1997; Alchian and Demsetz 1972; Demsetz 1988; and Hart and Moore 1988. For a review article, see Furubotn and Pejovich 1972. An excellent restatement is Barzel 1997.

5. At an empirical level see, for example, De Alessi 1974. De Alessi finds greater stability of public management compared to private and infers inefficiency of the public firm; see also De Alessi 1969 and De Alessi 1980.

6. For a recent review, see Schleifer and Vishny 1997; see also Tirole 2001.

7. The political economy of privatization can be seen as a reformulation of public choice theory; see Shapiro and Willig 1990; Boycko, Schleifer, and Vishny 1996; and Schleifer 1998.

8. Two contributions that deal explicitly with the cost-benefit analysis of privatization are Galal, Tandon, and Vogelsang 1990 and Galal et al. 1994, to which I return later.

9. For an update on the state of the debate, see Bös 1994 and Laffont and Tirole 2000a.

10. For this transformation, cf. Drèze and Stern 1987, 425 ff.; and Florio 1990b; for a more general decomposition, see Starrett 1988.

11. As noted, monopoly profit in itself generally shows a situation of price distortion and should not therefore be included in welfare calculations.

12. For a general theoretical treatment, see Bös 1991 and other references cited within this chapter.

Chapter 3   Macroeconomic Trends

1. The IS-LM framework represents the macroeconomic equilibrium in terms of income and interest by simultaneous equilibrium in the investment-saving market (i.e., in the market for consumption and investment goods) and in the market for money (i.e., in the supply and demand of money and liquid assets). Prices are considered exogenous, and the model is then limited to the analysis of short-run equilibria.

2. The AS-AD (Aggregate Supply-Aggregate Demand) framework is a model of macroeconomic equilibrium in terms of prices and income. The AD function relates the IS-LM equilibria for different price levels; the AS function is a relationship between prices, labor market, and pricing mechanisms by firms. Prices are endogenous in this model, and technology is exogenous.

3. The OECD data, on the other hand, are not in full agreement with the picture that emerges from H.M. Treasury (1998a, 131), which, at 1995 prices, shows growth in the ratio of nonresidential investments to GDP between 1982 and 1989, then a drop off until 1994, and subsequently a noticeable recovery.

4. The inflationary impact of cuts in capital account public spending was studied by Buiter (1990) in a different context. He shows, applying a model of a small open economy, that cuts in public investment have four separate effects: (a) a direct effect on spending, which presumes a reduction of the budget deficit of exactly the same size as the investment cut; (b) a direct effect on budget revenues, equal to the variation in cash flows from the management of public capital; (c) an indirect effect on tax revenue, as a consequence of the influence of lower investments on aggregate demand and thus on fiscal receipts; and (d) an effect on the demand for money that, given a certain rate of real interest and of inflation, operates through the income (or wealth) of the agents. Although it is clear, also intuitively, that ceteris paribus effect (a) is deflationary and that effect (b) is ambiguous, the last two effects are unambiguously inflationary. It is therefore possible that the two groups of effects balance each other out.

Chapter 4   Firms

1. Hamilton (1971) on British Airways and private airlines in the 1960s; Polanyi (1968; Polanyi and Polanyi 1972, 1974) on the return on capital in the nationalized sector compared to the private sector over the same period; Pryke (1971, 1981, 1982) for the 1970s, among others.

2. Initial controls prevented mergers in the first five years after divestiture. On water, see also the results by Parker and Saal (2001).

3. Background Paper 3, "Output, Investment and Productivity," of NEDO 1976 gives detailed data for 1960–1975.

4. But a noticeable one at that: British Steel (−6.9 percent annually!).

5. In terms of yearly percentage increase, against +2.3 percent for the manufacturing sector, three out of five nationalized industries for which we have data show greater TFP growth.

6. Since the weight to be assigned to capital in the index of TFP is given by the share of profits, as wages are used to weigh the contribution of labor, when public firms are structurally running at a loss, one must resort to an estimated weight, for example, a social discount rate, such as the official test discount rate. Cf. NEDO 1976, Background paper 3, p. 28.
    As in most other studies there is no quality adjustment for these indicators.

Chapter 5   Shareholders

1. On the basis of the efficient-market hypothesis, the divergence in price from a firm's intrinsic value, represented by the expected present value of future dividends, conditioned by the information available at any given moment, should not be systematic.

2. Hayri and Yilmaz (1997) use a simple methodology to test their data: the variance ratio test and the Box-Pierce Q test.

3. Vickers and Yarrows' references are the offer-for-sale price and the one recorded twenty-four hours later, at the end of the first day of trading.

4. On the contrary, there were two cases of overpricing.

5. Other indications of the difference in price after the first day can be found in Hayri and Yilmaz 1997, tables 1–2; see also the appendix to this chapter.

6. The cases examined include British Aerospace, Cable and Wireless, Amersham, ABP, Jaguar, BT, BG, BA, Rolls-Royce, and British Airports Authority.

7. Cf. the international comparisons and interpretation given by Perotti and Guney (1993).

8. This is not so in other countries: For a recent review of international evidence, see Megginson and Netter 2001.

9. Information on some minor privatized companies was not available.

10. The long-term returns are sensitive to the benchmark used. In addition to the FTA (Financial Times Actuaries All Share Index) (which is a value-weighted index covering 650 stocks accounting for 90 percent of the value of the stock market), the author also uses another index (Extended Hoare Govett Smaller Companies) that includes smaller companies than those in the FTA. A third index (All Share Equally Weighted) is also used. This index moved much faster than the FTA and the Hoare Govett Smaller Companies in 1980–1988.

11. The hypothesis that the "beta" coefficient is in the region of one for the shares of U.K. privatized firms seems realistic.

12. For a smaller sample, I still find a 38 percent abnormal return after ten years.

13. Underpricing implies that after the IPO, the share outperforms the market over a short initial period of time. Then to restore equilibrium, it should underperform the market over a subsequent period of time. See Megginson and Netter 2001 for a discussion and the evidence on outperformance of privatization IPOs in other countries.

14. According to OFWAT (1992), in the water sector, despite slow demand dynamics, and notwithstanding the great investments necessary to tackle the qualitative adjustments in service standards required by community norms, among other things, the sustained price dynamics (+50 percent in ten years) should have guaranteed a 20 percent pretax profit, compared to a return on equity in the seventy years prior to World War I of less than 7 percent in real terms (while bonds provided 1 percent real profit). It seems difficult to say that, at least in this case, the regulators were surprised by the profits from the utilities. In any case, except for momentary fluctuations, the financial market did not really take into serious consideration the capacity or desire of the regulators to create competitive conditions in the industries, or at any rate to keep prices at the lowest levels compatible with the financial sustainability of the firms, until the end of the 1990s.

15. See, for example, the discussion carried on by Coffee (1999), which shows how legal systems can be extremely important not only in the formal protection of the rights of a firm's minority shareholders, but also in determining the basic power structure of the firm.

16. Individuals owning shares of one privatized company may own shares of other companies as well. Thus obviously it would be wrong simply to sum the numbers of shareholders of each company to guess the total number of individuals in the United Kingdom who own shares.

17. Florio and Manzoni 2002, reports more-detailed results.

18. Prices at the first and at the last trading day of the first trading month have been downloaded from Datastream International as unadjusted prices. In this case, the closing price has not been historically adjusted for bonus and rights issues, and it therefore represents the actual or "raw" price as recorded on the day. All the other prices, that is, the monthly closing prices from the second trading month on, have instead been collected as adjusted prices; that is, they have been adjusted for the factors mentioned above.

19. See note 18.

Chapter 6   Employees

1. Secondary picketing is picketing conducted at firms other than the primary target to induce a solidarity strike.

2. A simple linear regression test, not reported here, shows that employment changes explained by subperiod dummies are very limited, except for the latest years. This result broadly confirms the findings of the survey by Pendleton (1999).

3. There are a number of sectoral studies dealing with the decline of the unions in privatized firms: For example, Parry, Waddington, and Critcher (1997) study the coal industry, and Ogden (1994) examines the case of the water authorities.

4. The winter of 1978–1979 was a period of extraordinary labor unrest in the United Kingdom. A number of major trade unions went on strike. Particularly disturbing were the strikes in some essential public services, such as burials and garbage collection.

5. Pendleton and Winterton 1993 includes a broad outline of the subject in the introductory chapter, along with case studies concerning the Post Office, railways, coal, electricity, water, steel, docks, and buses.

6. Here and elsewhere the terms "extra profits" or "excess profits" are used as sustained corporate profits above the "normal" profit level, as empirically observed from the average returns on capital (or returns on sales) (see discussion in chapter 5).

7. On the question of the flexibility of labor conditions, see Sanchis 1997, which concludes, on the basis of data taken from the 1990 U.K. Workplace Employee Relations Survey, which covers over 2,000 companies, that privatization coincided with an increased effort from workers. The survey includes questions like "During the last three years has management introduced any changes in working practice that have reduced job demarcation or increased the flexibility of working at this establishment?"

8. Other works by the same authors include Haskel and Szymanski 1993b and Haskel and Szymanski 1994.

Chapter 7   Consumers

1. Cf. "Background paper 5: Price Behaviour."

2. "Metered" users pay their bills on the basis of a record of quantity supplied by the utility, as measured by a meter installed in the household. "Unmetered" users pay a lump sum proportional to some household characteristics or house parameters.

3. See also OFWAT 1999. Dean, Carlisle, and Baden-Fuller 1999 discusses aspects of organizational discontinuity in water companies and their performance. One documented critical work on the privatization of water is Shaoul 1997, which concludes, "this analysis has refuted the claim that all would benefit [from the privatization of the water companies]. Consumers found that prices rose by more than 50 percent, workers lost their jobs, and the nation, meaning the taxpayers past and present, in effect made a huge loss on the sale and gained nothing from tax revenues despite the profits" (504).

4. Thomas (2000) gives more data that are more up to date but limited to the typical bill for the residential consumer of one company.

5. Bunn and Vlahos (1989) examined forecasts that could have been made before privatization about the long-term trends in energy. The authors used a model of linear programming with horizons 1994–2037, based on data relative to the single plants managed by the CEGB. The central point in their analysis is that the transition to the private sector implies a sharp increase in the real required rate of return, from the 5 percent required within the public sector to the 10–12 percent required by the private investor. The article is notable in that it is one of the few examples of forecasts of costs and prices in the scenario with and without privatization.

6. In 1997, Power Gen recorded a huge loss for financial reasons, and the profit/turnover ratio was negative, at −12.6 percent.

7. The regulation of energy utilities is still a controversial topic in the United Kingdom. Robinson (1992) believes that privatization of energy utilities was designed to support some interests, especially that of the City, but also for electoral reasons. Hammond, Helm, and Thompson (1985) observed that the Lawson energy doctrine (named after Nigel Lawson, the chancellor of the Exchequer under Thatcher) in the energy sector consisted of abandoning the idea that the government should have an energy policy in favor of the following approach: "Our task is to set a framework which will ensure that the market operates in the energy sector with a minimum of distortion and that energy is produced and consumed efficiently" (1). The privatization of British Gas, however, followed a different path: "Where competition is impractical privatisation policies have been developed to such an extent that regulated private ownership of natural monopolies is preferable to nationalisation" (John Moore, minister for privatisations in the Thatcher government, quoted in Hammond, Helm, and Thompson 1985, 2). Hammond, Helm, and Thompson indicate that the evidence may not support Moore's assertion: "[E]xperience in other countries (in particular the United States) indicates that regulated private monopolies may frequently be less efficient than corresponding public enterprises.... Changes in the level and structure of prices will also have distributional consequences. It could be argued that a general government transfer to the poor is preferable to an artificially low particular price (though this argument is premised on the assumption that such compensation takes place)" (13). Beginning in 1997, the market for domestic users of gas was fully liberalized. The Office of Gas and Electricity Markets launched a large and effective campaign in the media that aimed to explain to consumers that they could switch to the most convenient gas supplier. Under liberalization, each user of gas in the United Kingdom would be able to choose among different supply contracts. For the debate on the privatization of the coal industry, see Bailey 1989, which poses the question in a European context, examining in particular the German protectionist policy for the sector. Energy policy has national and political dimensions that we have not discussed here but that are obviously important in the context of EU market integration.

8. The broad debate on the matter is quite technical. The recommendations of the MMC, now renamed the Competition Commission, are weighty document on the running of the industry, based on examination from the point of view of the parties and on the opinions

of associations and even of the single users. See the Commission's Web site at ⟨http://www.competition-commission.org.uk⟩.

9. This conclusion is confirmed both by the analysis in the best study available so far (Galal et al. 1994) and by my own study of the data from official sources (see chapter 9).

10. Pollitt and Smith (2001), however, show that more recently there has been some decrease in real prices in rail transport.

11. These include the release of detailed information on the record of the franchisees (see SSRA 2000b). The data are updated on the Strategic Rail Authority Web site ⟨http://www.sra.gov.uk/publications⟩.

12. Nash (1993) summarizes the debate that preceded privatization and the creation of the 100-plus companies into which British Railways was broken up. Else and James (1994) employ a model to forecast an increase in demand and a decrease in demand after privatization. They examine various market structures with a simple model and explain how a monopoly chain can be worse than a vertically integrated monopoly. On the other hand, the model Else and James use considers only prices and costs, without examining quality and the possibility of price discrimination (or of tariff structures that can mitigate the monopoly chain problem). In reality, demand unexpectedly increased after privatization. One possible explanation is that the privatization of bus services (discussed later in the section) created some disarray in the routes, leading users to choose rail service over bus service. Moreover, the congestion on roads gave users no alternatives other than to go back to the rail. Gibb, Shaw, and Charlton (1998) confirm that in fact the situation that developed in regard to the British rail system can be defined as a type of monopoly, in spite of the plurality of companies operating in the industry. The idea of maintaining public ownership of the network, but learning from the experience of twenty years of regulation, is found in a work on the financing of the road system (Newbery and Santos 1999), which proposes the institution of a public Roadtrack company.

13. Vogelsang and Green (in Galal et al. 1994) offer a cost-benefit analysis of the case of British Airways (privatized in 1986).

14. A subsequent independent study, Marvin, Graham, and Guy 1996, documents the development of water poverty following privatization and the subsequent realignment of tariffs.

15. With the advent of the New Labour government there was a change in the political climate surrounding consumer issues. Greater attention to consumers was visible in DETRA 1998b, a consultation paper, "Water Charging in England and Wales." The document, having established that every year since privatization it had been necessary to ration water because of droughts and so on and that at the same time the time taken to pay arrears had increased, takes a stand against the water company's unilateral right to disconnect. As stated in a DETRA press release (DETRA 1998c):

We also propose to remove the powers of water companies to disconnect domestic water supplies in the event of non-payment. This will be particularly reassuring to those who are most vulnerable. Access to water is essential to the maintenance of general good health and well being, and the water charging arrangements need to reflect that. Of course, water companies are entitled to be paid for the services they provide, but other debt recovery procedures are available to them. Our concern about public health demands that we maintain the flow of water supplies to households in all circumstances.

See section 7.4 for recent policy changes in the sector.

16. Under the typical cross-subsidy mechanism in the nationalized industries, the tariffs for business users or for residential users with high consumption were higher than long-run marginal costs. The profit from this markup over costs covered the losses from reduced tariffs applied to users with low consumption levels, usually the poor.

17. Data referred to by the NCC (1993), based on a 1991 study by the Association for Consumer Research ("The Telephone System and the Domestic Market—Subscription Levels and the Effect of Cost."

18. See NCC 1993. Similar studies were commissioned by the NCC in 1987 and 1990.

19. The survey was based on 1,000 telephone interviews between February 28 and March 4, 1997. In contrast, in another Gallup survey (1998), with regard to the National Health Service (NHS), 91 percent of respondents declared they were satisfied with the treatment they had received (1,006 interviews between June 25 and July 1, 1998); the comparable figure was 92 percent in 1948. Thus there is a surprising stability in the perceptions of the most popular and emblematic British public service, the NHS.

20. Hicks (1993) offers some contributions on the relationship between privatized utilities and consumers. The National Consumer Council, should have been consulting consumers since 1975 about the level of the service provided by utilities. The Citizen's Charter of 1991 dealt with standards, information and openness, choice and consultations, courtesy and helpfulness, redressing mistakes, and the like. Judging by the opinion polls, however, British consumers do not appear to be very impressed by these measures.

21. Thus, for example, even in apparently modest questions: The Scottish Office of the Department of Environment, Transport, and the Regions (1992) deregulated motorway service areas in Scotland. This raised the problem of which services should be offered to the motorist in these service areas in addition to fuel supply. The problem of evaluating the quality of services from the point of view of consumers raises interesting legal issues. According to Graham and Prosser (1991), the privatized companies cannot be seen in any simple sense as private companies because they have an obligation to provide a universal service and because they are regulated. Neither are they public, because their shareholders are private. This is therefore a borderline case, in which the rights of the consumers play an important role in defining the nature of the industry. Articles in the *Utilities Law Review* frequently debate the rights of consumers in this field. Regulators can ask the utilities to systematically gather data from consumers. In the case of gas, I mentioned the existence of a sector consumer council that communicates to the regulator the problems raised by users; there is a Post Office Users National Council; and similar mechanisms are in place for the railways and other utilities. A detailed account on these arrangements and their limitations is given by Ernst (1994).

22. Buller (1996) also deals with this subject in a comparison between France and the United Kingdom.

23. For an account on the role of consumer representation in the regulatory process, see Simpson 2000; Simpson 2002; and Ernst 1994.

24. There are proposals that are more radical. Holtham (1998) proposes a mutualistic or cooperative model (the consumers elect the board of directors for the industry). Sawyer and O'Donnell (1999) propose a new role for public enterprises and discuss different solutions (I return to this subject in the concluding chapter). Renationalization in any form is not, however, an option being considered by the New Labour government.

25. This formula is an extension of the approach by Hancock and Waddams Price (1998).

26. Distributional characteristics of a good are defined in the appendix to chapter 2.

27. One has to consider, for example, that the net welfare loss for one-quarter of telephone users, usually those on low income, was £24 yearly (Waddams Price 2002).

Chapter 8   Taypayers

1. It is perhaps worth remembering the role played by reforms in local finance (the poll tax) in causing a huge wave of government unpopularity at the time.

2. Methodological details of this exercise can be found in a subsequent Treasury paper (H.M. Treasury 1998b). More recent data can be found in H.M. Treasury 1999b (p. 142 and table B20).

3. Currently the only country to have officially adopted public-wealth accounting is New Zealand.

4. The first edition of the register was published in November 1997.

5. Military assets are considered public consumption, although the ESA95, the new European System of Accounts, allows for separate accounting of assets with a dual use (for example, military hospitals).

6. These figures were supplied by Helen Dell, Treasury Taskforce, at a London School of Economics seminar in March 2000. Updates on the British government's Private Finance Initiative are available at ⟨http://www.pfi.ogc.gov.uk/publications⟩.

Chapter 9   The British Telecom Case History

1. The government appointed the Bridgeman Committee in 1932 following increasing dissatisfaction with the management of the Post Office. The findings and recommendations of this committee were the starting point for a process of restructuring of the service (see Harper 1997 for a detailed BT history).

2. Harper's appendix 2 is a graph, based on the estimates of a sector expert (J. J. Wheatley, ex–chief economist of British Telecom), and obtained by deflating the data values by constant company prices.

3. Martin and Parker divide their data into subperiods as follows: nationalization period (1977–1981), preprivatization (1981–1985), postannouncement (1983–1985), postprivatization (1985–1989), recession (1988–1992), and latest (1992–1995).

4. Other interesting research strands on BT performance that I cannot discuss here but are worth mentioning involve international comparisons of the telecommunications industry (e.g., Foreman-Peck and Manning 1988; Kwoka 1993; Curwen 1997; Hulsink 1999; Boylaud and Nicoletti 2000; and Newbery 2000); political economy and regulatory issues (e.g., Moon, Richardson, and Smart 1986; Pitt 1990; Doyle 1997; Cruickshank 1998; Durant, Legge, and Moussios 1998); and accounting and management issues (e.g., Penn 1988; Antoniou and Pescetto 1997; Puxty 1997).

5. Given that prior to 1987 the BT annual reports carried only the data for rentals, but later reports broke these data down into a number of items, we needed to use some proxies. The greatest detail is provided in the balance sheet for the year ending March 1988. In this we find the turnover per division and the rentals components under the

items "Telephone Exchange Line Rentals," "Other Network," and "Customers' Premises Equipment Supply." For details on assumptions made in the disaggregation of company data, see Florio 2003b.

6. Equipment supply is included in "Rentals."

7. The standard method of calculation used for all tariffs until July 31, 1995, was based on a sum in pence per unit consumed. This unit consisted of seconds of conversation which varied according to the type of call: local, national or international; and to the time the call was made. For international calls the distance was measured in charge bands made up of a number of countries of a similar distance. There were 10 bands up until 1991 subsequently they become 19 and a tariff is specified for every country in the world. There was also often a minimum cost per conversation with variations according the type of contract signed by the subscriber which includes various types of discounts. For details see Florio 2002.

8. In the early 1980s a duopoly was established in which only two companies, BT and Mercury, had the right to establish interarea fixed links. The government ended this duopoly in 1991, and thereafter new entrants were allowed to establish their own links and exchanges.

9. VJT also propose the case studies of National Freight and British Airways.

10. VJT use data from 1980 to 1990, with projections to 2025. In previous sections, I have considered longer time series than that which VJT use.

11. If the price is regulated, the price observed will not be on the demand curve, because of rationing.

Chapter 10   Epilogue: A State without Ownership

1. Under some less optimistic assumptions concerning the counterfactual trends of productivity and prices under continued nationalized industries and more inequality-adverse social-welfare functions, I cannot entirely rule out a small net welfare loss for the British consumer. I do not want to explore here the entire range of possible scenarios, and I focus instead on a reasonable combination of assumptions.

2. In my scenario, the wedge between counterfactual public profits and actual private profits implies around £2.8 billion in extra profits per year. To this figure, one should add the excess burden of the monopoly profits for the consumer.

References

Alchian, A. A. 1965. "Some Economics of Property Rights." *Il politico* 30, no. 4:816–829.

Alchian, A. A. 1997. *Economic Forces at Work*. Indianapolis: Liberty Press.

Alchian, A. A., and H. Demsetz. 1973. "The Property Rights Paradigm." *Journal of Economic History* 33:16–27.

Alchian, A. A., and H. Demsetz. 1972. "Production, Information Costs and Economic Organization." *American Economic Review* 62:777–795.

Alford, B. W. E. 1993. *British Economic Performance 1945–1975*. Cambridge: Cambridge University Press.

Alison, Y. 2001. *The Politics of Regulation: Privatised Utilities in Britain*. Basingstoke, U.K.: Palgrave.

Antoniou, A., and G. Pescetto. 1997. "The Effect of Regulatory Announcements on the Cost of Equity Capital of British Telecom." *Journal of Business Finance and Accounting* 24, no. 1:1–24.

APIS (Conseil en Politique Industrielle). 1995. "Le système électrique Britannique: Expérience ou modèle?" Paris. Photocopy.

Armstrong, M. 1998. "Telecommunications." In *Competition in Regulated Industries*, ed. D. Helm and T. Jenkinson. Oxford: Oxford University Press.

Armstrong, M., S. Cowan, and J. Vickers. 1994. *Regulatory Reform, Economic Analysis, and British Experience*. Cambridge: MIT Press.

Ashworth, W. 1991. *The State in Business: 1945 to the Mid '80s*. London: Macmillan.

Ashworth, W., and P. Forsyth. 1984. *Civil Aviation Policy and the Privatisation of British Airways*. Report no. 12. London: Institute for Fiscal Studies.

Atkins, W. S. 1992. *The Social Impact of Metering*. London: W. S. Atkins and Partners.

Atkinson, A., and J. Stiglitz. 1980. *Lectures on Public Economics*. New York: McGraw Hill.

Aylen, J. 1988. "Privatisation of the British Steel Corporation." *Fiscal Studies* 9, no. 3: 1–25.

Bacon, N., P. Blyton, and J. Morris. 1991. "Steel, State and Industry Relations: Restructuring Work and Employee Relations in the Steel Industry." Paper presented at the International Privatisation Strategies and Practices Conference, University of St. Andrew, September 12–14.

Bailey, R. 1989. "Coal—The Ultimate Privatisation." *National Westminster Bank Quarterly Review* 8:2–17.

Bailey, R., and R. Baldwin. 1990. "Privatisation and Regulation: The Case of British Airways." In *Privatisation and Deregulation in Canada and Britain*, ed. J. J. Richardson, 93–107. Aldershot, U.K.: Institute for Research on Public Policy.

Bairoch, P. 1989. "European Trade Policy, 1815–1914." In *The Cambridge Economic History of Europe*, ed. P. Mathias and S. Pollard, vol. 8, 1–160. Cambridge: Cambridge University Press.

Baldwin, R., and M. Cave. 1999. *Understanding Regulation: Theory, Strategy and Practice.* Oxford: Oxford University Press.

Barnett, S. 2000. "Evidence on the Fiscal and Macroeconomic Impact of Privatisation." Working paper no. 00/130, International Monetary Fund, Washington, D.C.

Barzel, Y. 1997. *Economic Analysis of Property Rights.* 2nd ed. Cambridge: Cambridge University Press.

Beato, P., and A. Mas-Colell. 1984. "On the Theory of Perfect Competition." Schwartz Lecture, Northwestern University, Evanston, IL.

Beesley, M. E. 1981. "The Liberalisation of British Telecom." *Journal of Economic Affairs* 2 (October): 19–27.

Beesley, M. E., ed. 1996. *Regulated Utilities: A Time for Change.* London: Institute of Economic Affairs and London Business School.

Beesley, M. E. 1997. *Privatization, Regulation and Deregulation.* London: Routledge.

Beesley, M. E., and S. C. Littlechild. 1989. "The Regulation of Privatized Monopolies in the United Kingdom." *RAND Journal of Economics* 20:454–472.

Bell, A. 2002. "Some Reflections on the British Telecom Case-History." Paper presented at the First Milan European Economy Workshop, University of Milan, Milan, June.

Bennett, M., D. Cook, and C. Waddams Price. 2002. "Left out in the Cold? The Impact of the New Energy Tariffs on the Fuel Poor and Low Income Households." *Fiscal Studies* 23, no. 2:167–194.

Bennett, J., S. Estrin, J. Maw, and G. Urga. 2003. "Privatisation Methods and Economic Growth in Transition Economies." Paper presented at the 59th IIPF Congress, Prague, August.

Berle, A. A., and G. C. Means. 1993. *The Modern Corporation and Private Property.* New York: Macmillan.

Berlin, I. 1969. *Four Essays on Liberty.* Oxford: Oxford University Press.

Bertero, E. 2002. "Does a Change in the Ownership of Firms, from Public to Private, Make a Difference?" Paper presented at the First Milan European Economy Workshop, University of Milan, Milan, June.

Biais, B., and E. C. Perotti. 2002. "Machiavellian Privatization." *American Economic Review* 92, no. 1:240–258.

Bishop, M., and R. Green. 1995. "Privatization and Recession: The Miracle Tested." Discussion paper no. 10, Centre for the Study of Regulated Industries, London.

Bishop, M., and J. Kay. 1988. *Does Privatization Work? Lessons from the UK*. London: London Business School, Centre for Business Strategy.

Bishop, M., and J. Kay. 1989. "Privatization in the United Kingdom: Lessons from Experience." *World Development* 17, no. 5:643–657.

Bishop, M., J. Kay, and C. Mayer. 1994. "Introduction: Privatisation in Performance." In *Privatisation and Economic Performance*, ed. M. Bishop, J. Kay, and C. Mayer, 1–14. Oxford: Oxford University Press.

Bishop, M., and D. J. Thompson. 1992a. "Privatisation in the UK: Internal Organisation and Productive Efficiency." *Annals of Public and Cooperative Economics* 63, no. 2:171–188.

Bishop, M., and D. J. Thompson. 1992b. "Regulatory Reform and Productivity Growth in the UK's Public Utilities." *Applied Economics* 24, no. 11:1181–1190.

Bishop, M., and D. J. Thompson. 1993. "Privatisation in the UK: Deregulatory Reform and Public Enterprise Performance." In *Privatization: A Global Perspective*, ed. V. V. Ramanadham. London: Routledge, 1–28.

Boardman, T., and N. Ridley. 1979. *The Future of Nationalized Industries: Two Essays*. London: Aims for Freedom and Enterprise.

Boiteux, M. 1956. "Sur la gestion del monopoles publics astreints à l'équilibre budgetaire." *Econometrica* 24, no. 1:22–40.

Bös, D. 1991. *Privatization: A Theoretical Treatment*. Oxford: Oxford University Press.

Bös, D. 1993. "Privatisation in Europe, a Comparison of Approaches." *Oxford Review of Economic Policies* 9, no. 1:95–111.

Bös, D. 1994. *Pricing and Price Regulation: An Economic Theory for Public Enterprises and Public Utilities*. Amsterdam: North-Holland.

Bös, D. 1997. "An Alternative to Privatization: Coping with Managerial Slack in Public Firms." In *Privatization at the End of the Century*, ed. H. Giersch, 53–67. Heidelberg: Springer.

Bös, D. 1999. "Privatization and Restructuring: An Incomplete-Contract Approach." *Journal of Institutional and Theoretical Economics* 1, no. 3:337–354.

Bös, D., and W. Peters. 1991. "Privatization of Public Enterprises: A Principal-Agent Approach Comparing Efficiency in Private and Public Sectors." *Empirica* 18:5–16.

Boussofiane, A., S. Martin, and D. Parker. 1997. "The Impact on Technical Efficiency of the UK Privatization Programme." *Applied Economics* 29, no. 3:297–310.

Boycko, M., A. Schleifer, and R. Vishny. 1996. "A Theory of Privatisation." *Economic Journal* 106, no. 435:309–319.

Boyfield, K. 1997. *Privatization: A Prize Worth Pursuing*. London: European Policy Forum.

Boylaud, O., and G. Nicoletti. 2000. "Regulation, Market Structure and Performance in Telecommunications." Working paper no. 237, Economics Department, Organisation for Economic Cooperation and Development, Paris.

Braddon, D., and D. Foster. 1996. *Privatization: Social Science Themes and Perspectives.* Hampshire, U.K.: Ashgate.

Bradshaw, W. 1996. "Ten Turbulent Years—The Effects on the Bus Industry of Deregulation and Privatisation." *Policy Studies* 17, no. 2:125–136.

Bradshaw, W. 1997. "Competition in the Rail Industry." *Oxford Review of Economic Policy* 13, no. 1:93–103.

Bradshaw, W., and H. Lawton-Smith. 2000. *Privatisation and Deregulation of Transport.* Basingstoke, U.K.: Macmillan.

Brau, R., and M. Florio. 2002. "Privatisations as Price Reforms: Evaluating Consumers' Welfare Changes in the UK." Nota di lavoro 67, Fondazione Eni Enrico Mattei, Milan. Forthcoming in *Annals of Economics and Statistics.*

Brower, M. C. 1997. "The British Restructuring Experience: History and Lessons for the United States." Report to the National Council on Competition and the Electric Industry, Andover, MA.

Brown, W., S. Deakin, and P. Ryan. 1997. "The Effects of British Industrial Relations Legislation, 1979–97." *National Institute Economic Review* 161:69–83.

Browning, A. 1994. *Privatisation 1979–1994: Everyone's A winner.* London: Conservative Political Centre.

BT (British Telecom). 1983. *Statistics, 1982.* London.

BT (British Telecom). 1990. *Reports and Accounts, 1982–1989.* London.

BT (British Telecom). 1994. *Directors' Reports and Financial Statements, 1990–1993.* London.

BT (British Telecom). 1999. *Annual Report and Accounts, 1994–98.* London.

Buchanan, J., and R. Musgrave. 1999. *Public Finance and Public Choice: Two Contrasting Visions of the State.* CESifo Book Series. Cambridge: MIT Press.

Buiter, W. H. 1985. "A Guide to Public Sector Debt and Deficits." *Economic Policy* 1 (November): 13–79.

Buiter, W. H. 1990. "Can Public Spending Cuts Be Inflationary?" In W. H. Buiter, *Principles of Budgetary and Financial Policy.* Cambridge: MIT Press.

Buller, H. 1996. "Privatization and Europeization: The Changing Context of Water Supply in Britain and France." *Journal of Environmental Planning and Management* 39, no. 4:461–482.

Bunn, D., and K. Vlahos. 1989. "Evaluation of the Long-Term Effects on UK Electricity Prices Following Privatisation." *Fiscal Studies* 10, no. 4:104–116.

Burk, K. 1988. *The First Denationalisation: The Politicians, the City, and the Denationalisation of Steel.* London: Historians' Press.

Burniaux, P., T. Dang, D. Fore, M. Forster, M. Mira d'Ercole, and H. Oxley. 1998. "Income Distribution and Poverty in Selected OECD Countries." Working paper no. 189, Economics Department, Organisation for Economic Cooperation and Development, Paris.

Burns, P. 1994. *Discriminatory Pricing and Accounting Method in the UK Regulated Industry.* London: Centre for the Study of Regulated Industries.

Burns, P., and T. G. Weyman-Jones. 1994a. "Regulatory Incentives, Privatisation and Productivity Growth in UK Electricity Distribution." Centre for the Study of Regulated Industries Technical Paper no. 1. London: Chartered Institute of Public Finance and Accountancy.

Burns, P., and T. G. Weyman-Jones. 1994b. "Cost Drivers and Cost Efficiency in Electricity Distribution: A Stochastic Frontier Approach." Centre for the Study of Regulated Industries Technical Paper no. 2. London: Chartered Institute of Public Finance and Accountancy.

Burns, P., and T. G. Weyman-Jones. 1994c. "Productive Efficiency and the Regulatory Review of Regional Electricity Companies in the UK." Regulatory Policy Research Centre Discussion Paper no. 1, Hertford College, Oxford.

Button, K., and T. G. Weyman-Jones. 1993. "X-Inefficiency and Regulatory Regime Shift in the UK." *Journal of Evolutionary Economics* 3, no. 4:269–284.

Button, K., and T. G. Weyman-Jones. 1994. "Impacts of Privatisation Policy in Europe." *Contemporary Economic Policy* 12, no. 3:23–33.

Cave, M. 1993. "An Economist's Perspective on Regulating Quality Standards and Levels of Service." In *Utilities and Their Customers: Whose Quality of Service Is It*, ed. C. Hicks. London: Centre for the Study of Regulated Industries and Chartered Institute of Public Finance and Accountancy.

Cave, M. 2002. "Privatisation, Returns and the Stock Market." Paper presented at the First Milan European Economy Workshop, University of Milan, Milan, June.

Caves, R. 1990. "Lessons from Privatization in Britain, State Enterprise Behavior, Public Choice, and Corporate Governance." *Journal of Economic Behavior and Organization* 13, no. 2:145–169.

Cawthron, I. 1999. "Regulated Industries: Returns to Private Investors to May 1998." Occasional paper no. 11, Centre for the Study of Regulated Industries, London.

CEGB (Central Electricity Generating Board). Various years. *Annual Report*. London.

Chapman, C. 1990. *Selling the Family Silver*. London: Hutchison Random.

Checkland, S. G. 1989. "British Public Policy 1776–1939: An Economic, Social and Political Perspective." In *The Cambridge Economic History of Europe*, ed. P. Mathias and S. Pollard, vol. 8. Cambridge: Cambridge University Press.

Chennells, L. 1997. "The Windfall Tax." *Fiscal Studies* 18, no. 3:279–291.

Chester, M. 1975. *The Nationalisation of British Industry 1945–51*. London: HMSO.

Chisari, O., A. Estache, and C. Romero. 1999. "Winners and Losers from Utility Privatization in Argentina: Lessons from a General Equilibrium Model." *World Bank Economic Review* 13, no. 2:357–378.

Chong, A., and F. Lopez-de-Silanes. 2002. "Privatization and Labor Force Restructuring around the World." World Bank Working Papers—Labor & Employment, Labor Market Policies and Institutions, no. 2884, World Bank, Washington, DC.

Clarke, T., and C. Pitelis. 1993. "Introduction: The Political Economy of Privatization." In *The Political Economy of Privatization*, ed. T. Clarke and C. Pitelis, 1–28. London: Routledge.

Coady, D., and J. Drèze. 2002. "Commodity Taxation and Social Welfare: The Generalized Ramsey Rule." *International Tax and Public Finance* 9:295–316.

Coase, R. H. 1937. "The Nature of the Firm." *Economica*, n.s., 4:386–405.

Coates, D. 1996. *Industrial Policy in Great Britain*. London: Macmillan.

Coffee, Jr., J. C. 1999. "Privatisation and Corporate Governance: The Lessons from Securities Market Failure." Columbia Law and Economics Working Paper no. 158. New York: Columbia Law School.

Coffee, Jr., J. C. 2000. "Convergence and Its Critics: What Are the Preconditions to the Separation of Ownership and Control?" Columbia Law and Economics Working Paper no. 179. New York: Columbia Law School.

Collier, U. 1995. *Electricity Privatisation and Environmental Policy in the UK: Some Lessons for the Rest of Europe*. San Domenico, Italy: Economics Department, European University Institute.

Connolly, S., and A. Munro. 1999. *Economics of the Public Sector*. Prentice Hall Europe. London: Pearson Education.

Conservative Party (Great Britain). 1983. *The Conservative Manifesto*. London: Conservative Central Office.

Conservative and Unionist Party. 1979. *The Conservative Manifesto*. London.

Conyon, M. J., and K. J. Murphy. 2000. "The Prince and the Pauper? CEO Pay in the United States and United Kingdom." *Economic Journal* 110, no. 467:F640–671.

Crafts, N. F. R. 1998. "The Conservative Government's Economic Record: An End of Term Report." Occasional paper no. 104, Institute of Economic Affairs, London.

Cragg, M., and I. J. Dyck. 1999a. "Executive Pay and UK Privatisation: The Demise of 'One Country, Two Systems.'" *Journal of Business Research 2000* 47, no. 1:3–18.

Cragg, M., and I. J. Dyck. 1999b. "Management Control and Privatization in the UK." *RAND Journal of Economics* 30, no. 3:475–497.

Crosland, A. 1956. *The Future of Socialism*. London: Cape.

Cruickshank, D. 1998. "Telecoms: Ringing the Changes." *Consumer Policy Review* 8, no. 2:42–44.

Cubbin, J., S. Domberger, and S. Meadowcroft. 1987. "Competitive Tendering and Refuse Collection: Identifying the Sources of Efficiency Gains." *Fiscal Studies* 8, no. 3 (August): 49–58.

Curwen, P. 1997. *Restructuring Telecommunications: A Study of Europe in a Global Context*. London: Macmillan.

Curwen, P., and K. Hartley. 1997. "Privatisation." In *Understanding the UK Economy*, 4th ed., ed. P. Curwen. Basingstoke, U.K.: Macmillan.

Dahrendorf, R. G. 1995. *LSE: A History of the London School of Economics and Political Science, 1895–1995*. Oxford: Oxford University Press.

Datastream. n.d. Financial Times Stock Exchange 100 Index, 1978–2003, online database; available at ⟨www.datastream.com⟩.

De Alessi, L. 1969. "Implications of Property Rights for Government Investment Choices." *American Economic Review* 59:13–24.

De Alessi, L. 1974. "Managerial Tenure under Private and Government Ownership in the Electric Power Industry." *Journal of Political Economy* 82, no. 3:645–653.

De Alessi, L. 1980. "The Economics of Property Rights: A Review of the Evidence." *Research in Law and Economics* 2:1–47.

Dean, A., Y. Carlisle, and C. Baden-Fuller. 1999. "Punctuated and Continuous Change: The UK Water Industry." *British Journal of Management*, no. 11:3–16.

Demsetz, H. 1988. *Ownership, Control and the Firm*. London: Basil Blackwell.

Dessy, O., and M. Florio. 2003. "Workers' Earnings in the UK before and after Privatisation: A Study of Five Industries." Paper presented at Fifteenth SIEP Conference, University of Pavia, October.

DETRA (Department of Environment, Transport and the Regions). 1992. *Motorway Service Areas: Government Proposals to Deregulate the Provision of Motorway Service Areas*. Edinburgh: Scottish Office.

DETRA (Department of Environment, Transport and the Regions). 1993a. *Gaining Access to the Railway Network: The Government Proposals*. London.

DETRA (Department of Environment, Transport and the Regions). 1993b. *Rail Freight Privatisation: The Government Proposals*. London.

DETRA (Department of Environment, Transport and the Regions). 1994. "Review of the Economic Regulation of the Airport System." Consultation paper, London.

DETRA (Department of Environment, Transport, and the Regions). 1996, 1997. *Transport Statistics: Great Britain*. London.

DETRA (Department of Environment, Transport and the Regions). 1998a. *A New Strategic Rail Authority*. London.

DETRA (Department of Environment, Transport and the Regions). 1998b. "Water Charging in England and Wales." Consultation paper, London.

DETRA (Department of Environment, Transport and the Regions). 1999. *Housing: Key Background Figures*. London.

DETRA (Department of the Environment, Transport and the Regions). 1998c. "Prescott Unveils New Approach to Water Charging." Press release. Available at ⟨http://www.newsrelease-archive.net/coi/depts/GTE/coi9891d.ok⟩.

DETRA (Department of Environment, Transport and the Regions). 1992. "The Franchising of Passenger Rail Service." Consultation document, London.

Diamond, P., and J. A. Mirrlees. 1971a. "Optimal Taxation and Public Production, I: Production Efficiency." *American Economic Review* 61:8–27.

Diamond, P., and J. A. Mirrlees. 1971b. "Optimal Taxation and Public Production, II: Tax Rules." *American Economic Review* 61:261–278.

Diamond, P., and J. A. Mirrlees. 1976. "Private Constant Returns and Public Shadow Prices." *Review of Economic Studies* 43:41–48.

Dicey, A. J. 1907. *Lectures on the Relation between Law and the Public Opinion in England during the Nineteenth Century.* 2nd ed., London: Macmillan, 1962.

Dobek, M. M. 1993. *The Political Logic of Privatization: Lessons from Great Britain and Poland.* London: Praeger.

Domah, P. D., and M. G. Pollitt. 2001. "The Restructuring and Privatisation of the Regional Electricity Companies in England and Wales: A Social Cost-Benefit Analysis." *Fiscal Studies* 22, no. 1:107–146.

DOT (Department of Transportation), Civil Aviation Division. 1994. *Privatisation of the National Air Traffic Services (NATS).* London.

Doyle, C. 1997. "Promoting Efficient Competition in Telecommunications." *National Institute Economic Review* no. 159:82–91.

Drèze, J., and N. Stern. 1987. "The Theory of Cost-Benefit Analysis." In *Handbook of Public Economics,* ed. A. J. Auerbach and M. S. Feldestein, 2:909–989. Amsterdam: North-Holland.

Drèze, J., and N. Stern. 1990. "Policy Reform, Shadow Prices, and Market Prices." *Journal of Public Economics* 42:1–46.

DTI (Department of Trade and Industry). 1998. *A Fair Deal for Consumers: Modernising the Framework for Utility Regulation.* London: The Stationery Office Ltd.

DTI (Department of Trade and Industry). 1999. *UK Energy Sector Indicators.* London.

Dunleavy, P. 1986. "Explaining the Privatization Boom." *Public Administration* 69 (Spring): 13–34.

Durant, R. F., J. S. Legge, and A. Moussios. 1998. "People, Profits and Service Delivery: Lessons from the Privatization of British Telecom." *American Journal of Political Science* 42, no. 1 (January): 117–140.

Eckel, C., D. Eckel, and V. Singal. 1997. "Privatization and Efficiency: Industry Effects of the Sale of British Airways." *Journal of Financial Economics* 43, no. 2:275–298.

Economist. 1995. "How to Privatise: What the Rest of the World Can Learn from the Unpopularity of Privatisation in Britain." March 11.

Economist. 1999. "The Rail Billionaires." July 3.

Else, P. K., and T. J. James. 1994. "Will the Fare Be Fair? An Examination of the Pricing Effects of the Privatization of Rail Services." *International Review of Applied Economics* 8, no. 3:291–302.

Engle, R. F., and C. W. J. Granger. 1987. "Co-integration and Error Correction: Representation, Estimation, and Testing." *Econometrica* 55, no. 2:251–276.

Ernst, J. 1994. *Whose Utility? The Social Impact of Public Utility Privatisation and Regulation in Britain.* Buckingham: Open University Press.

Estrin, S., and C. Whitehead. 1987. "Privatisation and the Nationalized Industries." Paper presented at seminar at Suntory and Toyota International Centres for Economics and Related Disciplines (STICERD), London School of Economics, December 15.

Eurostat. 1997. *Panorama of EU Industry.* Luxembourg.

Farrell, M. J. 1957. "The Measurement of Productive Efficiency." *Journal of the Royal Statistical Society*, Series A, vol. 120, part 3:253–281.

Favero, C. 1988. "Privatisation: The Macroeconomic Impact. An Analysis of UK Experience and the Prospects for Italy." *European Economic Review* 32, nos. 2–3:482–490.

Fells, I. 1991. *UK Energy Policy Post-Privatisation*. Edinburgh: Scottish Nuclear.

Ferguson, P. 1988. *Industrial Economics: Issues and Perspectives*. Houndmills, U.K., and London: Macmillan.

Flemming, J., ed. 1996. *The Report of the Commission on the Regulation of Privatised Utilities, The European Policy Forum*. London: Hansard Society.

Florio, M. 1990a. "Cost-Benefit Analysis and the Control of Public Expenditure: An Assessment of the British Experience." *Journal of Public Policy* 10, no. 2:103–131.

Florio, M. 1990b. "Analyse coûts-avantages et objectives macro-économiques. Leçons tirées de l'experience italienne." *Annales de l'économie publique sociale et coopérative* 61, no. 1:63–90.

Florio, M. 2001. "On Cross-Country Comparability of Government Statistics: Public Expenditure Trends in OECD National Accounts." *International Review of Applied Economics* 5, no. 2:181–198.

Florio, M. 2002. "Economists, Privatisations in Russia and the Waning of the Washington Consensus: A Case History." *Review of International Political Economy* 9, no. 2:359–400.

Florio, M. 2003a. "Electricity Prices as Signals for the Evaluation of Reforms: An Empirical Analysis of Four European Countries." Working paper no. 14/2003, University of Milan, Department of Economics.

Florio, M. 2003b. "Does Privatization Matter? The Long-Term Performance of British Telecom over 40 years." *Fiscal Studies* 24, no. 2:197–234.

Florio, M., and S. Colantti. "A Logistic Growth Theory of Public Expenditures: A Study of Five Countries over 100 Years." Forthcoming in *Public Choice*.

Florio, M., and M. Grasseni. 2003. "The Missing Shock: The Macroeconomic Impact of British Privatisation." Working paper no. 21/2003, University of Milan, Department of Economics.

Florio, M., and K. Manzoni. 2004. "Abnormal Returns of UK Privatizations: From Underpricing to Outperformance." *Applied Economics* 36, no. 2:119–136.

Floud, Roderick, and Donald McCloskey, eds. 1994. *The Economic History of Britain since 1700*. 3 vols. 2nd ed. Cambridge: Cambridge University Press.

Foreman-Peck, J. 1989. "Ownership, Competition and Productivity Growth: The Impact of Liberalisation and Privatisation upon British Telecom." Warwick Economic Research Papers no. 338, University of Warwick.

Foreman-Peck, J., and D. Manning. 1988. "How Well Is BT Performing? An International Comparison of Telecommunications Total Factor Productivity." *Fiscal Studies* 9, no. 3:54–67.

Foreman-Peck, J., and R. Millward. 1994. *Public and Private Ownership of British Industry 1820–1990*. Oxford: Clarendon.

Foreman-Peck, J., and M. Waterson. 1984. "The Comparative Efficiency of Public and Private Enterprise in Britain: Electricity Generation between the World Wars." *Economic Journal*, 95 (Suppl.): 83–95.

Foster, C. D. 1992. *Privatisation, Public Ownership and the Regulation of Natural Monopoly*. Oxford: Blackwell.

Franks, J., and C. Mayer. 1997. "Corporate Ownership Structure in the UK, France, and Germany." In *Studies in International Corporate Finance and Governance Systems*, ed. D. Chew. Oxford: Oxford University Press.

Furubotn, E. G., and S. Pejovich. 1972. "Property Rights and Economic Theory: A Survey of the Recent Literature." *Journal of Economic Literature* 10:1137–1162.

Galal, A., L. Jones, P. Tandon, and I. Vogelsang. 1994. *Welfare Consequences of Selling Public Enterprises: An Empirical Analysis*. New York: Oxford University Press for the World Bank.

Gallup. 1997. *Political and Economic Index*. London.

Gallup. 1998. "Gallup Political and Economic Index: Report." London.

Gaved, M., and M. Goodman. 1992. "Deeper Share Ownership." Paper no. 12, Social Market Foundation, London.

Gibb, R., J. Shaw, and C. Charlton. 1998. "Competition, Regulation, and the Privatisation of British Rail." *Environment and Planning: Government and Policy* 16, no. 6:757–768.

Girard, L. 1989. "Transports." In *The Cambridge Economic History of Europe*, ed. H. J. Habakkuk and M. M. Postan, vol. 6. Cambridge: Cambridge University Press.

Glaister, S. 1996. "Incentives in Natural Monopoly: The Case of Water." In *Regulating Utilities: A Time for Change?* ed. M. Beesley. London: Institute of Economic Affairs.

Glennerster, H. 2000. *British Social Policy since 1945*. London: Blackwell.

Gootshalk, P., and P. Smeedling. 1997. "Cross-National Comparisons of Earnings and Income Inequality." *Journal of Economic Literature* 35:633–687.

Gourvish, T., and A. O'Day, eds. 1991. *Britain since 1945*. Basingstoke, England: Macmillan.

Graham, C., and T. Prosser. 1991. *Privatising Public Enterprises: Constitutions, The State and Regulation in Comparative Perspective*. Oxford: Clarendon.

Green, R., and J. Haskel. 2001. "Seeking a Premier League Economy: The Role of Privatisation." In *Seeking a Premier League Economy*, ed. R. Blundell, D. Card, and R. B. Freeman. Chicago: University of Chicago Press.

Gregg, P., ed. 1997. *Jobs, Wages and Poverty: Patterns of Persistence and Mobility in the Flexible Labour Market*. London: Centre for Economic Performance.

Gregg, P., S. Machin, and S. Szymanski. 1993. "The Disappearing Relationship between Pay and Corporate Performance." *British Journal of Industrial Relations* 31:1–10.

Gregg, P., and J. Wadsworth, eds. 1999. *The State of Working Britain*. Manchester: Manchester University Press.

Gregory, M. 1997. "Labour Market Deregulation: The UK Experience." Discussion paper no. 376, The Australian National University, Centre for Economic Policy Research.

Grossman, S., and O. Hart. 1980. "Takeover Bids, the Free Rider Problem and the Theory of the Corporation." *Bell Journal of Economics* 11:42–64.

Grout, P. A. 1988. "Employee Share Ownership and Privatisation: Some Theoretical Issues." *Economic Journal* 98, no. 390 (Suppl.): 97–104.

Grout, P. A. 1994. "Popular Capitalism." In *Privatisation and Economic Performance*, ed. M. Bishop, J. Kay, and C. Mayer. Oxford: Oxford University Press.

Gylfason, T. 1998. *Privatization, Efficiency and Economic Growth*. CEPR Discussion Paper Series no. 1844, Centre for Economic Policy Research, London.

Hamilton, N. M. 1971. *Pricking Pryke: The Facts on State Industry*. London: Aims of Industry.

Hammond, C. J. 1992. "Privatisation and the Efficiency of Decentralised Electricity Generation: Some Evidence from Inter-War Britain." *Economic Journal* 102, no. 412:538–553.

Hammond, E. M., D. R. Helm, and D. J. Thompson. 1985. "British Gas: Options for Privatisation." *Fiscal Studies* 6, no. 4:1–20.

Hancock, R., and C. Waddams Price. 1998. "Distributional Effects of Liberalising UK Residential Utlity Markets." *Fiscal Studies* 19, no. 3:295–319.

Hannah, L. 1994. "The Economic Consequences of the State Ownership of Industry 1945–1990." In *The Economic History of Britain since 1700*, ed. R. Floud and D. McCloskey, vol. 3:1939–1992, 168–194. Cambridge: Cambridge University Press.

Hare, P., and L. Simpson. 1996. "Privatisation." In *An Introduction to the UK Economy: Performance and Policy*, ed. P. Hare and L. Simpson, 49–65. Harvester Wheatsheaf/ Prentice Hall.

Harper, J. M. 1997. *Monopoly and Competition in British Telecommunication: The Past, the Present and the Future*. London: Pinter.

Harris, A. L. 1959. "J.S. Mill on Monopoly and Socialism: A Note." *Journal of Political Economy* 67, no. 6:604–611.

Harris, L., D. Parker, and A. Cox. 1998. "UK Privatization: Its Impact on Procurement." Special issue, *British Journal of Management* 9 (September).

Hart, O., and J. Moore. 1988. *Property Rights and the Nature of the Firm*. London: Suntory Toyota International Centre for Economics and Related Disciplines.

Hart, O., A. Shleifer, and R. Vishny. 1997. "The Proper Scope of Government: Theory and an Application to Prisons." *Quarterly Journal of Economics* 112, no. 4:1127–1161.

Hartley, K. 1990. "Contracting-Out in Britain: Achievements and Problems." In *Privatisation and Deregulation in Canada and Britain*, ed. J. J. Richardson, 177–198. Aldershot, U.K.: Institute for Research on Public Policy.

Hartley, K., and N. Hooper. 1990. "Industry and Policy." In *Understanding the UK Economy*, ed. P. Curwen, 266–305. New York: St. Martin's.

Hartley, K., D. Parker, and S. Martin. 1991. "Organisational Status, Ownership and Productivity." *Fiscal Studies* 12, no. 2:46–60.

Haskel, J. 1992. "UK Privatization: Process and Outcomes." Discussion paper no. 273, Department of Economics, Queen Mary and Westfield College, London.

Haskel, J., and S. Szymanski. 1991. "Privatization, Jobs and Wages." *Employment Policy Institute Economic Report* 7, no. 6.

Haskel, J., and S. Szymanski. 1992a. "A Bargaining Theory of Privatisation." *Annals of Public and Cooperative Economics* 63:207–227.

Haskel, J., and S. Szymanski. 1992b. "Privatisation and the Labour Market: Facts, Theory and Evidence." In *Privatisation and Regulation: The UK Experience*, ed. M. Bishop, J. A. Kay, C. P. Mayer, and D. J. Thompson, 336–351. Oxford: Oxford University Press.

Haskel, J., and S. Szymanski. 1993a. "Privatisation, Liberalisation, Wages and Employment: Theory and Evidence for the UK." *Economica* 60:161–182.

Haskel, J., and S. Szymanski. 1993b. "The Effect of Privatisation, Restructuring and Competition on Productivity Growth in UK Public Corporations." Discussion paper no. 286, Department of Economics, Queen Mary and Westfield College, London.

Hayri, A., and K. Yilmaz. 1997. "Privatisation and Stock Market Efficiency: The British Experience." *Scottish Journal of Political Economy* 44, no. 2:113–133.

Helm, D. 1994. "British Utility Regulation: Theory, Practice and Reform." *Oxford Review of Economic Policy* 10, no. 3:17–39.

Helm, D. 1995. *British Utility Regulation: Principles, Experience and Reform.* Oxford: Oxera.

Helm, D., and T. Jenkinson. 1998. *Competition in Regulated Industries.* Oxford: Oxford University Press.

Hicks, C., ed. 1993. *Utilities and Their Customers: Whose Quality of Service Is It?* London: Centre for the Study of Regulated Industries and Chartered Institute of Public Finance and Accountancy.

Hicks, J. R. 1946. *Value and Capital: An Inquiry into Some Fundamental Principles of Economic Theory.* 2nd ed. Oxford: Oxford University Press.

Hield, C. 1992. "British Rail: Whose Future." Research paper, HCL (House of Commons Library), London.

Hills, J. 1989. "Counting the Family Silver: The Public Sector's Balance Sheet 1957 to 1987." *Fiscal Studies* 10, no. 2:66–85.

Hills, J. 1998. *Thatcherism: New Labour and the Welfare State.* CASE Paper no. 13, CASE/London School of Economics, London.

H.M. Treasury. 1961. *The Financial and Economic Obligations of the Nationalised Industries.* Cmnd. 1337. London: HMSO.

H.M. Treasury. 1967. *Nationalised Industries: A Review of Economic and Financial Objectives.* Cmnd. 3437. London: HMSO.

H.M. Treasury. 1978. *The Nationalised Industries.* Cmnd. 7131. London: HMSO.

H.M. Treasury. 1989. *Privatisation in the United Kingdom.* London.

H.M. Treasury. 1993, 1995. *Guide to the UK Privatisation Programme*. London.

H.M. Treasury. 1997a. *The Public Sector Balance Sheet*. Prebudget Report Publications. London.

H.M. Treasury. 1997b. *Appraisal and Evaluation in Central Government: The Green Book*. London: HMSO.

H.M. Treasury. 1997c. *Public Expenditure: Statistical Analyses*. London: HMSO.

H.M. Treasury. 1998a. *New Ambitions for Britain: Financial Statement and Budget Report, March 1998*. London: The Stationery Office Ltd.

H.M. Treasury. 1998b. *The Public Sector Balance Sheet*. London: The Stationery Office Ltd.

H.M. Treasury. 1999a. *Budget Report 2000*. London: The Stationery Office Ltd.

H.M. Treasury. 1999b. *Stability and Steady Growth for Britain: Pre-Budget Report*. Cmnd. 4479. London: The Stationery Office Ltd.

Holtham, G. 1996. "Water: Our Mutual Friend." *New Economy* 3, no. 4:251–254.

Hood, C. 1994. *Explaining Economic Policy Reversals*. Buckingham, U.K.: Open University Press.

Hoopes, S. 1994. "The Privatization of UK Oil Assets, 1977–1987: Rational Policy-Making, International Changes and Domestic Constraints." PhD diss., London School of Economics.

Huang, Q., and R. M. Levich. 1999. "Underpricing of New Equity Offering by Privatised Firms: An International Test." Salomon Center Working Paper no. S/99/05, New York University.

Hulsink, W. 1999. *Privatisation and Liberalisation in European Telecommunications: Comparing Britain, Netherlands and France*. London: Routledge.

Hunt, L., and E. Lynk. 1995. "Privatisation and Efficiency in the UK Water Industry: An Empirical Analysis." *Oxford Bulletin of Economics and Statistics* 57, no. 3:371–388.

Hutchinson, G. 1991. "Efficiency Gains through Privatisations of UK Industries." In *Privatization and Economic Efficiency*, ed. K. Hartley and A. Ott, 87–107. Aldershot, U.K.: Elgar.

ITU (International Telecommunications Union). Various years. *Yearbook of Statistics*. Geneva.

Jackson, P. M., and C. Price, eds. 1994. *Privatisation and Regulation: A Review of the Issues*. Harlow, U.K.: Longman.

Jamasb, T., and M. Pollitt. 2001. *Benchmarking and Regulation of Electricity Transmission and Distribution Utilities: Lessons from International Experience*, DAE Working Paper, Department of Applied Economics, University of Cambridge.

Jenkin, S. 1995. *Accounting to None: The Tory Nationalisation of Great Britain*. London: Hamilton.

Jensen, M. C., and E. F. Fama. 2000. *A Theory of the Firm: Governance, Residual Claims and Organizational Forms*. Cambridge: Harvard University Press.

Jensen, M. C., and R. Ruback. 1983. "The Market for Corporate Control: The Scientific Evidence." *Journal of Financial Economics* 11:5–50.

Johnson, C. 1991. *The Economy under Mrs. Thatcher 1979–1990.* London: Penguin.

Jones, I., and S. Jones. 1993. "The Economics of Airport Slots." NERA topic no. 10. National Economics Research Associates, London.

Jones, L. P., P. Tandon, and I. Vogelsang. 1990. *Selling Public Enterprises: A Cost-Benefit Methodology.* Cambridge, MA: MIT Press.

Jones, L. P., P. Tandon, and I. Vogelsang. 1991. "Selling State-Owned Enterprises: A Cost-Benefit Approach." In *Privatization and Control of State-Owned Enterprises,* ed. R. Ramamurti and R. Vernon, chap. 2, 29–53. Washington, D.C.: World Bank.

Kahn, A. 1989. *The Economics of Regulation,* vol. 2. Cambridge, MA: MIT Press.

Kamerma, H., and A. Kahn. 1989. *Privatization and the Welfare State.* Princeton: Princeton University Press.

Kamps, C. 2003. "New Estimates of Government Net Capital Stocks for 22 OECD Countries 1960–2002." Paper presented at the 59th IIPF Congress, Prague, August.

Kay, J. 1987. *The State and the MKT: The UK Experience of Privatization.* New York: Group of Thirty.

Kay, J., M. Bishop, and C. Mayer. 1994. *Privatization and Economic Performance.* Oxford: Oxford University Press.

Kay, J., C. Mayer, and D. Thompson, eds. 1986. *Privatisation and Regulation: The UK Experience.* Oxford: Clarendon.

Kennedy, D., S. Glaister, and T. Travers. 1995. *London Bus Tendering.* London: Greater London Group, London School of Economics.

Kernot, C. 1993. *British Coal: Prospects for Privatization.* Cambridge, U.K.: Woodhead.

Keynes, J. M. [1926] 1989. *The End of Laissez-Faire.* In *Essays in Persuasion: The Collected Writings of John Maynard Keynes,* vol. 9. Cambridge: Macmillan and Cambridge University Press.

Keynes, J. M. 1936. *The General Theory of Employment, Interest and Money.* London: Macmillan and Cambridge: Cambridge University Press for Royal Economic Society.

Kikeri, S. 1998. "Privatization and Labor: What Happens to Workers When Governments Divest?" Technical paper no. 396, World Bank, Washington, DC.

Kleinwort Benson Ltd. 1984. *Offer for Sale of Ordinary Shares British Telecom.* London.

Kleinwort Benson Ltd. 1990a. *The Regional Electricity Companies Share Offers.* London.

Kleinwort Benson Ltd. 1990b. *The Regional Electric Companies Offer for Sale.* London.

Kornai, J. 1980. *Economics of Shortage.* Amsterdam and Oxford: North-Holland.

Kumbhakar, S., and L. Hjalmarsson. 1998. "Relative Performance of Public and Private Ownership under Yardstick Competition: Electricity Retail Distribution." *European Economic Review* 42, no. 1:97–122.

Kwoka, J. E. 1993. "The Effects of Divestitures, Privatisation and Competition on Productivity in US and UK Telecommunications." *Review of Industrial Organisation* 8:49–61.

Laffont, J. J., and J. Tirole. 1993. *A Theory of Incentives in Procurement and Regulation.* Cambridge, MA: MIT Press.

Laffont, J. J., and J. Tirole. 2000a. *Competition in Telecommunications.* Cambridge, MA: MIT Press.

Laffont, J. J., and J. Tirole. 2000b. "Privatisation and Incentives." *Journal of Law, Economics and Organisation* 7:84–105.

Landes, D. S. 1965. "The Unbound Prometheus: Technological Change and Industrial Development in Western Europe from 1750 to the Present." In *The Cambridge Economic History of Europe*, ed. H. J. Habakkuk and M. Postan, vol. 6, part 1. Cambridge: Cambridge University Press.

Leape, J. 1993. "Tax Policies in the 1980s and 1990s: The Case of the United Kingdom." In *Taxation in the United States and Europe: Theory and Practice*, ed. A. Knoester, 276–311. London: Macmillan.

Leape, J. 2002. "Conceptual Issues in Assessing the Welfare Impact of the British Privatisation Programme." Paper presented at the First Milan European Economy Workshop, University of Milan, Milan, June.

Le Grand, J. 1984. *Privatisation and the Welfare State.* London: Allen and Unwin.

Levis, M. 1993. "The Long Run Performance of Initial Public Offerings: The UK Experience 1980–88." *Financial Management* 22, no. 1 (Spring): 28–41.

Liesner, T. 1989. *One Hundred Years of Economic Statistics: United Kingdom, United States of America, Australia, Canada, France, Germany, Italy, Japan, Sweden.* London: Economist.

Liu, Z. 1995. "The Comparative Performance of Public and Private Enterprises: The Case of British Ports." *Journal of Transport Economics and Policy* 29, no. 3:263–274.

London Economics. 1994. *The Future of Postal Services: A Critique of Government's Green Paper.* London.

Lopez-de-Silanes, F. 1997. "Determinants of Privatization Prices." *Quarterly Journal of Economics* 112, no. 4:965–1025.

Lowe, P. 1998. "The Reform of Utility Regulation in Britain: Some Current Issues in Historical Perspective." *Journal of Economic Issues* 32, no. 1:171–190.

Lynk, E. L. 1993. "Privatisation, Joint Production and the Comparative Efficiencies of Private and Public Ownership: The UK Water Industry Case." *Fiscal Studies* 14, no. 2:98–116.

Mac Avoy, P., R. Zeckhauser, G. Yarrow, and W. Stanbury. 1989. *Privatisation and State Owned Enterprise: Lessons from the United States, Great Britain and Canada.* Dordrecht, the Netherlands: Kluwer.

Mackenzie, G. A. 1998. "The Macroeconomic Impact of Privatisation." *International Monetary Fund Staff Papers* 45, no. 2:363–373.

MacKinnon, J. G. 1991. "Critical Values for Cointegration Tests." In *Long-Run Economic Relationships: Readings in Cointegration*, ed. R. F. Engle and C. W. J. Granger, chap. 13. Oxford: Oxford University Press.

Maddison, A. 2001. *The World Economy: A Millennial Perspective*. Paris: Organisation for Economic Co-operation and Development.

Markou, E., and C. Waddams Price. 1999. "UK Utilities: Past Reform and Current Proposals." *Annals of Public and Cooperative Economics* 70, no. 3:371–416.

Marris, R. 1964. *The Economic Theory of "Managerial" Capitalism*. London: Macmillan.

Martin, S., and D. Parker. 1997. *The Impact of Privatisation: Ownership and Corporate Performance in the UK*. London: Routledge.

Marvin, S., S. Graham, and S. Guy. 1996. "Privatized Utilities and Regional Governance: The New Regional Managers?" *Regional Studies* 30, no. 8:733–739.

Mayer, C., and S. Meadowcraft. 1986. "Selling Public Assets: Technical and Financial Implications." In *Privatisation and Regulation: The UK Experience*, ed. J. Kay, C. Mayer, and D. Thompson. Oxford: Clarendon.

McDonald, O. 1989. *Own Your Own: Social Ownership Re-examined*. The Fabian Series. London: Unwin.

Megginson, W. L., and J. M. Netter. 2001. "From State to Market: A Survey of Empirical Studies on Privatization." *Journal of Economic Literature* 39, no. 3:321–389.

Middleton, R. 1996. *Government versus the Market: The Growth of the Public Sector, Economic Management and British Economic Performance, c. 1890–1979*. Aldershot, England: Edward Elgar.

Midttun, A., and S. Thomas. 1998. "Theoretical Ambiguity and the Weight of Historical Heritage: A Comparative Study of the British and Norwegian Electricity Liberalisation." *Energy Policy* 26, no. 3:179–197.

Miller, A. 1995. "British Privatization: Evaluating the Results." *Columbia Journal of World Business* 30, no. 4 (Winter): 83–98.

Miller, A. 1997. "Ideological Motivations of Privatization in Great Britain versus Developing Countries." *Journal of International Affairs* 50, no. 2:391–407.

Millward, R. 1990. "Productivity in the UK Service Sector: Historical Trends 1956–1985 and Comparisons with the USA 1950–1985." *Oxford Bulletin of Economics and Statistics* 52, no. 4:423–435.

Millward, R. 1991. "The Causes of the 1940s Nationalisations in Britain: A Survey." Working Paper in Economic and Social History no. 10, University of Manchester.

Millward, R. 2000. "State Enterprise in Britain in the Twentieth Century." In *The Rise and Fall of State-Owned Enterprises in the Western World*, ed. P. Toninelli. Cambridge: Cambridge University Press.

Millward, R. 2002. "The British Privatisation Programme: A Long Term Perspective." Paper presented at the First Milan European Economy Workshop, University of Milan, Milan, June.

Millward, R., and D. K. Benson. 1998. "United Kingdom: PFI Evolution Continues." In *Privatisation International Yearbook*. London: Privatisation International.

Millward, R., and D. Parker. 1983. "Public and Private Enterprise: Comparative Behaviour and Relative Efficiency." In *Public Sector Economics*, ed. R. Millward, D. Parker, L. Rosenthal, M. Sumer, and N. Topham. New York: Longman.

Millward, R., and J. Singleton, eds. 1995. *The Political Economy of Nationalisation in Britain, 1920–1959.* Cambridge: Cambridge University Press.

Millward, R., and R. Ward. 1987. "The Costs of Public and Private Gas Enterprises in Late 19th Century Britain." *Oxford Economic Papers* 39:719–737.

Mitchell, B. R. 1988. *British Historical Statistics.* Cambridge: Cambridge University Press.

Mitchell, B. R. 1998. *International Historical Statistics—Europe.* New York: Groves Dictionaries.

MMC (Monopoly and Mergers Commission). 1997. *BG plc: A Report under the Gas Act 1986 on the Restriction of Prices for Gas Transportation and Storage Service.* London: HMSO.

Moggridge, D. E. 1989. "The Gold Standard and National Financial Policies, 1919–1939." In *The Cambridge Economic History of Europe*, ed. P. Mathias and S. Pollard, 8:250–314. Cambridge: Cambridge University Press.

Molyneux, R., and D. Thompson. 1987. "Nationalised Industry Performance: Still Third-Rate?" *Fiscal Studies* 8, no. 1:48–82.

Moon, J., J. Richardson, and P. Smart. 1986. "The Privatisation of British Telecom: A Case-Study of the Extended Process of Legislation." *European Journal of Political Research* 14, no. 3:339–355.

Morgan, P., ed. 1995. *Privatisation and the Welfare State: Indications for Consumers and the Workforce.* Dartmouth, U.K.: Aldenshot.

MORI (Market and Opinion Research International). 1995. "The Changing Dynamics of Successful Privatizations: Attitudinal Factors." Report of system results. London.

MORI (Market and Opinion Research International). 1998a. *Gas Competition Review: December 1997.* London: OfGas–National Audit Office.

MORI (Market and Opinion Research International). 1998b. *Gas Competition Review: August 1998.* London: OfGas–National Audit Office.

Morrison, H. 1933. *Socialisation and Transport: The Organisation of Socialised Industries with Particular Reference to the London Passenger Transport Bill.* London: Constable.

Mueller, D. C. 2003. *Public Choice III.* Cambridge: Cambridge University Press.

Murray, A. 2001. *Off the Rails: Britain's Great Railway Crisis.* London: Verso.

Myners Committee. 1995. *Developing a Winning Partnership: How Companies and Institutional Investors Are Working Together.* London: Department of Trade and Industry.

Nash, C. 1993. "Developments in Transport Policy—Rail Privatisation in Britain." *Journal of Transport Economics and Policy* 27, no. 3:317–322.

National Audit Office. Various years. Press releases. Available at ⟨http://www.nao.gov.uk⟩.

NCC (National Consumer Council). 1992. *British Rail Privatisation: Response to the White Paper.* London.

NCC (National Consumer Council). 1993. *Paying the Price: A Consumer View of Water, Gas, Electricity and Telephone Regulation.* London: HMSO.

NCC (National Consumer Council). 1994. *Privatising Postal Services: The Consumer View.* London.

NEDO (National Economic Development Office). 1976. *A Study of UK Nationalised Industries: Their Role in the Economy and Control in the Future.* Background paper 1: "Financial Analysis"; Background paper 2: "Relationships of Governement and Public Enterprises in France, West Germany and Sweden"; Background paper 3: "Output, Investment and Productivity"; Background paper 4: "Manpower and Pay Trends"; Background paper 5: "Price Behaviour"; Background paper 6: "Relationships with Other Sectors of the Economy: The Evidence of Input-Output Analysis"; Background paper 7: "Exports and Imports"; Appendix volume. London.

Nejad, A. 1987. "Employee Ownership in Privatisation." PhD diss., London School of Economics.

NERA (National Economics Research Associates). 1995. *BT Comparative Efficiency Study.* London: Office of Telecommunications.

NERA (National Economics Research Associates). 1996. "The Performance of Privatised Industries." Report by NERA for the Centre for Policy Studies, London.

NERA (National Economics Research Associates). 2000. *The Competitive Efficiency of BT.* London: Office of Telecommunications.

Neuberger, J., ed. 1987. *Privatisation . . . Fair Shares for All or Selling the Family Silver?* London: Macmillan.

Newbery, D. M. 1995. "The Distributional Impact of Price Changes in Hungary and the United Kingdom." *Economic Journal* 105 (July): 847–863.

Newbery, D. M. 2000. *Privatization, Restructuring and Regulation of Network Utilities.* Cambridge, MA: MIT Press.

Newbery, D. M. 2002. "What Europe Can Learn from British Privatisations." Paper presented at the First Milan European Economy Workshop, University of Milan, Milan, June.

Newbery, D. M., and M. G. Pollitt. 1997. "The Restructuring and Privatisation of Britain's CEGB—Was It Worth It?" *Journal of Industrial Economics* 45, no. 3 (September): 269–303.

Newbery, D. M., and G. Santos. 1999. "Road Taxes, Road User Charges and Earmarking." *Fiscal Studies* 20, no. 2:103–132.

Newbery, D. M., and N. Stern. 1987. *The Theory of Taxation for Developing Countries.* Oxford: Oxford University Press for the World Bank.

Newman. K. 1986. *The Selling of British Telecom.* New York: Holt, Rinehart, Winston.

Niskanen, W. A. Jr. 1971. *Bureaucracy and Representative Government.* Chicago: Aldine-Atherton.

O'Connell Davidson, J. 1993. *Privatization and Employment Relations: The Case of Water Industry.* London: Mansill.

Odling-Smee, J., and C. Riley. 1985. "Approaches to PSBR." *National Institute Economic Review* 113 (August): 65–80.

OECD (Organization for Economic Cooperation and Development). 1997. "Corporate Governance, State-Owned Enterprises and Privatisation." OECD Proceedings, OECD, Paris.

OECD (Organization for Economic Cooperation and Development). 1998. *Economic Surveys, 1997–98 United Kingdom.* Paris.

OECD (Organization for Economic Cooperation and Development). 2000. *Economic Surveys, 1999–2000 United Kingdom.* Paris.

OECD (Organization for Economic Cooperation and Development). n.d. Online database. Available at ⟨http://www.oecd.org⟩.

OECD (Organization for Economic Cooperation and Development). Statistics Directorate. n.d. "Labour Force: GBR Unemployed percent Total Labour Force: Percent of Total Labour, 1979–1999." Quarterly Labour Force Statistics online database; available at ⟨http://www.oecd.org⟩.

OFFER (Office of the Electricity Regulator). 1995. *The Competitive Electricity Market from 1998.* London.

OFFER (Office of the Electricity Regulator). 1998. "Energy Efficiency: New Standards of Preference." Consultation paper. London.

OFFER (Office of the Electricity Regulator). 1999. "Social Action Plan Discussion Document." London: OfGas.

OFGAS (Office of the Gas Regulator). 1998. *The Utility Industry Achievement Awards 1998.* London: The OfGas Campaign, Marketing Initiative of the Year.

OFGEM (Office of Gas and Electricity Markets). 1999. *All You Need to Know about Gas Competition.* London.

OFGEM (Office of Gas and Electricity Markets). 2000. "Gas and Electricity: The Customers Save Almost £2 Billion." London.

OFTEL (Office of the Telecommunications Regulator). 1995. *British Telecom Comparative Efficency Study.* London.

OFTEL (Office of the Telecommunications Regulator). 2000. *The UK Telecommunications Industry: Market Information 1994–95 to 1998–99.* London.

OFWAT (Office of Water Services). 1991. *Cost of Capital: A Consultation Paper,* vol. 2. Birmingham, U.K.

OFWAT (Office of Water Services). 1992. "1991/1992 Report on Capital Investment of the Water Companies in England and Wales." Birmingham.

OFWAT (Office of Water Services). 1999. "1998–1999 Report on the Financial Performance and Expenditures of Water Companies in England and Wales." Available at ⟨http://www.ofwat.gov.uk/aptrix/ofwat/publish.nsf/Content/1998-99financialperformance⟩.

Ogden, S. 1994. "The Reconstruction of Industrial Relations in the Privatized Water Industry." *British Journal of Industrial Relations* 32, no. 1:67–84.

Ogden, S., and F. Anderson. 1995. "Representing Customers' Interests: The Case of the Privatized Water Industry in England and Wales." *Public Administration* 73 (Winter): 535–559.

Ogden, S., and R. Watson. 1999. "Corporate Performance and Stake-Holder Management: Balancing Stake-Holder and Customer Interests." *U.K. Privatised Water Industry* 42 (October): 526–538.

O'Mahony, M. 1999. *Britain's Productivity Performance 1950–1996: An International Perspective.* London: National Institute of Economics and Social Research.

O'Mahony, M., and N. Oulton. 1994. "Productivity and Growth: A Study of British Industry 1954–86." Occasional paper, National Institute of Economic and Social Research, London.

O'Neill, D. 1996. "Regulated Industries: The UK Gas Industry." Regulatory brief no. 10, Centre for the Study of Regulated Industries and Chartered Institute of Public Finance and Accountancy, London.

ONS (Office for National Statistics). 1999. *Share Ownership 1999.* London: The Stationery Office Ltd.

ONS (Office for National Statistics). 2000a. *Social Inequalities 2000.* London: The Stationery Office Ltd.

ONS (Office for National Statistics). 2000b. *Social Trends 30.* London: The Stationery Office Ltd.

ONS (Office for National Statistics). 2000c. *Financial Statistics Explanatory Handbook.* 2000 ed. London: The Stationery Office Ltd.

ONS (Office for National Statistics). Various years. "New Industry Survey (NES): Analysis by Industry. Part C, ONS." London.

ONS (Office for National Statistics). n.d.-a. General Government Data/Blue Book. Available at ⟨http://www.statistics.gov.uk/StatBase⟩.

ONS (Office for National Statistics). n.d.-b. Statistics Online. Available at ⟨http://www.statistics.gov.uk/StatBase⟩.

OPRAF (Office of Passenger Rail Franchising). 2000. *Annual Report 1998–1999.* London.

Orietta, D., and M. Florio. 2003. "Workers' Earnings in the UK Before and After Privatisation: A Study of Five Industries." Paper presented at Fifteenth SIEP Conference, University of Pavia, October.

ORR (Office of the Rail Regulator). 1994. "Competition for Railway Passenger Services." Consultation document. London.

ORR (Office of the Rail Regulator). 1995. "Railtrack's Access Charges for Franchised Passenger Services: A Policy Statement." London.

ORR (Office of the Rail Regulator). 1997. *Railtrack's Investment Programme: Increasing Public Accountability.* London.

ORR (Office of the Rail Regulator). 1998. "Rail Complaints." *Rail Complaints Bulletin,* Report no. 1, 1997/1998. London.

ORR (Office of the Rail Regulator). 1999a. "Rail Complaints." *Rail Complaints Bulletin,* Report no. 2, 1998/1999. London.

ORR (Office of the Rail Regulator). 1999b. *The Periodic Review of Railtrack's Access Charges: Provisional Conclusions on Revenue Requirements.* London.

Oswald, C. 1999. *Patterns of Labour Market Exit in Germany and the UK.* Working paper, Universitaet Bremen, Bremen, Germany.

Otero, J., and C. Waddams Price. 2001a. "Price Discrimination, Regulation and Entry in the UK Residential Electricity Market." *Bulletin of Economic Research* 53, no. 3:161–175.

Otero, J., and C. Waddams Price. 2001b. "Incumbent and Entrant Response to Regulated Competition: Signaling with Accounting Costs and Market Prices." *Journal of Economics and Business* 53:209–223.

Oulton, N. 1995. "Supply Side Reform and UK Economic Growth: What Happened to the Miracle?" *National Institute Economic Review* 154:53–70.

Parker, D. 1994. "A Decade of Privatisation: The Effect of Ownership Change and Competition on British Telecom." *British Review of Economic Issues* 16, no. 40:87–113.

Parker, D. 1997a. "Caveat Emptor at Privatisation? Reflections on the Regulatory Contract in the UK." Occasional paper no. 9, Centre for the Study of Regulated Industries, London.

Parker, D. 1997b. *Privatisation and Regulation: Some Comments on the UK Experience.* London: Centre for the Study of Regulated Industries.

Parker, D., and S. Martin. 1995. "The Impact of UK Privatisation on Labour and Total Factor Productivity." *Scottish Journal of Political Economy* 42, no. 2:201–220.

Parker, D., Martin, S., and A. Boussofiane. 1997. "The Impact on Technical Efficiency of the UK Privatization Programme." *Applied Economics* 29:297–310.

Parker, D., and D. Saal. 2001. "Productivity and Price Performance in the Privatised Water and Sewerage Companies in England and Wales." *Journal of Regulatory Economics* 20, no. 1:61–69.

Parry, D., D. Waddington, and C. Critcher. 1997. "Industrial Relations in the Privatized Mining Industry." *British Journal of Industrial Relation* 35, no. 2:173–196.

Payne, P. L. 1978. "British Entrepreneurship in the Nineteenth Century." In *The Cambridge Economic History of Europe*, ed. M. M. Postan and P. Mathias, vol. 7. Cambridge: Cambridge University Press.

Peacock, A. T., and J. Wiseman. 1960. *The Growth of Public Expenditure in the United Kingdom.* Princeton: Princeton University Press and London: Oxford University Press.

Pejovich, S. 1990. *The Economics of Property Rights: Towards a Theory.* Dordrecht, the Netherlands: Kluwer.

Pendleton, A. 1999. "Ownership or Competition? An Evaluation of the Effects of Privatisation on Industrial Relations Institutions, Process and Outcomes." *Public Administration* 77, no. 4:769–791.

Pendleton, A., and J. Winterton, eds. 1993. *Public Enterprise in Transition: Industrial Relations in State and Private Corporations.* London: Routledge.

Penn, R. 1988. "Skilled Maintenance Work at British Telecom: Findings from the Social Change and Economic Life Research Initiative. New Technology, Work and Employment." *Industrial Relations Journal* 29:135–144.

Peoples, J., ed. 1990. *Regulatory Reform and Labor Markets.* Boston: Kluwer.

Perotti, E. C., and S. E. Guney. 1993. "The Structure of Privatisation Plans." *Financial Management* 22:84–98.

Piachaud, D., and H. Sutherland. 2000. "How Effective is the British Government's Attempt to Reduce Child Poverty?" London: Centre for Analysis of Social Exclusion.

Pirie, M. 1988. *Privatization: Theory, Practice and Choice.* Aldershot, U.K.: Wildwood House.

Pitt, D. C. 1990. "An Essentially Contestable Organisation: British Telecom and the Privatisation Debate." In *Privatisation and Deregulation in Canada and Britain,* ed. J. J. Richardson, 55–76. Aldershot, U.K.: Institute for Research on Public Policy.

Polanyi, G. 1968. *Comparative Returns from Investment in Nationalised Industries.* London: Institute of Economic Affairs.

Polanyi, G., and P. Polanyi. 1972. "The Efficiency of Nationalised Industries." *Moorgate and Wall Street Review* (Spring): 17–49.

Polanyi, G., and P. Polanyi. 1974. *Failing the Nation: The Record of the Nationalised Industries.* London: Fraser Ansbacher.

Polanyi, K. [1944] 2001. *The Great Transformation: The Political and Economic Origins of Our Time.* 2nd ed. Boston: Beacon.

Pollard, S. 1978. "Labour in Great Britain." In *Cambridge Economic History of Europe,* ed. M. M. Postan and P. Mathias, vol. 7. Cambridge: Cambridge University Press.

Pollitt, M. G. 1995. *Ownership and Performance in Electric Utilities: The International Evidence on Privatization and Efficiency.* Oxford: Oxford University Press.

Pollitt, M. G. 1997. "The Restructuring and Privatisation of Electricity in Northern Ireland—Will It Be Worth It?" Discussion paper no. 97/01, University of Cambridge, Department of Applied Economics.

Pollitt, M. G. 1999. "A Survey of the Liberalisation of Public Enterprises in the UK since 1979." Working paper, University of Cambridge.

Pollitt, M. G. 2000. "The Declining Role of the State in Infrastucture Investments in the UK." Working paper, University of Cambridge.

Pollitt, M. G., and A. S. J. Smith. 2001. "The Restructuring and Privatisation of British Rail: Was It Really That Bad?" Working paper no. 01/18, University of Cambridge, Department of Applied Economics.

Prais, S. J. 1974. "A New Look to the Growth of Industrial Concentration." *Oxford Economic Papers* 26, no. 2:273–288.

Price Waterhouse. 1989a. *Privatization: Learning the Lessons from the UK Experience.* London.

Price Waterhouse. 1989b. *Privatization: The Facts.* London.

Pryke, R. 1971. *Public Enterprise in Practice.* London: MacGibbon & Kee.

Pryke, R. 1981. *The Nationalized Industries: Policies and Performance since 1968.* Oxford: Robertson.

Pryke, R. 1982. "The Comparative Performance of Public and Private Enterprise." *Fiscal Studies* 3, no. 2:68–81.

Privatisation International. 1994, 1999, 2000. *Privatisation Yearbook*. London.

Prosser, T. 1997. *Law and the Regulators*. Oxford: Clarendon.

Puxty, A. 1997. "Accounting Choice and a Theory of Crisis: The Cases of Post-Privatisation British Telecom and British Gas." *Accounting, Organisations and Society* 22, no. 7:713–735.

Ramanadhan, V. V., ed. 1988. *Privatisation in the UK*. London: Routledge.

Redwood, J. 1998. *Popular Capitalism*. London: Routledge.

Rees, J. 1989. *Water Privatisation and the Environment: An Overview of the Issues*. London: Friends of the Earth.

Ritter, J. R. 1991. "The Long-Run Performance of Initial Public Offerings." *Journal of Finance* 46:3–27.

Robinson, C. 1992. "Privatising the British Energy Industries: The Lesson to Be Learned." *Metroeconomica* 43, nos. 1–2:103–129.

Rock, K. 1986. "Why New Issues Are Underpriced." *Journal of Financial Economics* 15:187–212.

Rovizzi, L., and D. Thompson. 1992. "The Regulation of Product Quality in the Public Utilities and the Citizen's Charter." *Fiscal Studies* 13, no. 3:74–95.

Rowley, C. K., and G. K. Yarrow. 1981. "Property Rights, Regulation and Public Enterprise: The Case of the British Steel Industry 1957–1975." *International Review of Law and Economics* 1:63–96.

Salama, A. 1995. *Privatization: Implications for Cultural Change*. Aldershot, U.K.: Avebury.

Salveson, P. 1989. *British Rail: The Radical Alternative to Privatisation*. Manchester: Centre for Social Economic Strategies.

Sanchis, A. 1997. "Does Privatisation Remove Restrictive Working Practices? Evidence from UK Establishments." *Applied Economics* 32, no. 14:1793–1800.

Sappington, D., and J. Stiglitz. 1987. "Privatization, Information and Incentives." *Journal of Policy Analysis and Management* 6:567–582.

Sargant Florence, P. 1957. *Industry and the State*. London: Hutchison.

Sassoon, D. 1996. *One Hundred Years of Socialism*. London: Tauris.

Saunders, P., and C. Harris. 1994. *Privatization and Popular Capitalism*. Buckingham: Open University Press.

Savage, I. 1993. "Deregulation and Privatization of Britain's Local Bus Industry." *Journal of Regulatory Economics* 5:143–158.

Sawyer, M. 2003. "The Private Finance Initiative: A Critical Assessment." In *Industrial and Labour Market Policy and Performance*, ed. D. Coffey, chap. 11, 171–189. London: Routledge.

Sawyer, M., and K. O'Donnell. 1999. *A Future for Public Ownership*. London: Lawrence and Wishart.

Schipke, A. 2001. *Why Do Governments Divest? The Macroeconomics of Privatisation*. Heidelberg: Springer Verlag.

Shleifer, A. 1998. "Status versus Private Ownership." *Journal of Economic Perspectives* 12, no. 4:133–150.

Shleifer, A., and R. W. Vishny. 1997. "A Survey of Corporate Governance." *Journal of Finance* 52:737–783.

Schmidt, K. M. 1996. "The Costs and Benefits of Privatization: An Incomplete Contracts Approach." *Journal of Law, Economics and Organization* 12, no. 1:1–24.

Schremmer, D. E. 1989. "Taxation and Public Finance: Britain, France, and Germany." In *The Cambridge Economic History of Europe*, ed. P. Mathias and S. Pollard, 8:315–494. Cambridge: Cambridge University Press.

Seldon, A., and D. Collings. 2000. *Britain under Thatcher*. London: Longman.

Shaoul, J. 1997. "A Critical Financial Analysis of the Performance of Privatised Industries: The Case of the Water Industry in England and Wales." *Critical Perspectives on Accounting*, no. 8:479–505.

Shapiro, C., and R. Willig. 1990. "Economic Rationales for the Scope of Privatization." In *The Political Economy of Public Sector Reform and Privatization*, ed. E. Suleiman and J. Waterbury, 55–87. Oxford: Westview.

Shirley, M., and P. Walsh. 2000. "Public versus Private Ownership: The Current State of the Debate." World Bank Working Papers—Private Sector Development: Investment Behavior of Firms no. 2420, World Bank, Washington, DC.

Simpson, R. 2000. "The Experience of Consumer Participation in the Other Countries." In *The Experience of the National Consumer Council Regarding Public Services in the U.K.* London: National Consumer Council.

Simpson, R. 2002. "Much Ado about Nothing? The Consumers' Associations Perspective." Paper presented at the First Milan European Economy Workshop, University of Milan, Milan, June.

Spence, A. M. 1975. "Monopoly, Quality and Regulation." *Bell Journal of Economics* 16:417–429.

SSRA (Shadow Strategic Rail Authority). 2000a. *Building a Better Railway—The New Franchising Map*. London.

SSRA (Shadow Strategic Rail Authority). 2000b. *On Track ... Rail Performance Trends 17 October 1999 to 31 March 2000*. London.

Starrett, D. A. 1988. *Foundations of Public Economics*. Cambridge: Cambridge University Press.

Steiner, F. 2000. *Regulation, Industry Structure and Performance in the Electricity Supply Industry*. Working paper no. 238, Economic Department, Organisation for Economic Cooperation and Development, Paris.

Stern, J. 1997. "The British Gas Market 10 Years after Privatisation: A Model or a Warning for the Rest of Europe?" *Energy Policy* 25, no. 4:387–392.

Stewart, M. 1990. "Union Wage Differentials, Product Market Influences and the Division of Rents." *Economic Journal* 100, no. 43:1122–1137.

Surrey, J., ed. 1996. *The British Electricity Experiment. Privatization: The Record, the Issues, the Lessons*. London: Earthscan.

Talley, W. K. 1998. "The Indirect Cost-Saving Hypothesis of Privatisation: A Public Transport Labour Earnings Test." *Journal of Transport Economics and Policy* 32, no. 3:351–364.

Tanzi, V., and L. Schucknecht. 1995. "The Growth of Government and the Role of the State in Industrialized Countries." Working paper no. 95/130, International Monetary Fund, Washington, DC. Reprinted in *Social Inequality, the State and Values*, ed. A. Solimano. Ann Arbor: University of Michigan Press, 1998.

Thatcher, M. 1993. *The Downing Street Years*. London: HarperCollins.

Thatcher, M. 1997. *The Collected Speeches of Margaret Thatcher*, ed. Robin Harris. New York and London: HarperCollins.

Thomas, S. 2000. *Has Privatisation Reduced the Price of Power in Britain?* London: UNISON.

Thompson, C. D. 1925. *Public Ownership, A Survey of Public Enterprises, Municipal, State and Federal in the United States and Elsewhere*. New York: Cromwell.

Thompson, D. J. 1987. "Privatisation in the U.K.: De-regulation and the Advantage of Incumbency." *European Economic Review* 31, no. 1–2:368–374.

Thompson, R., ed. 2000. *A New Framework for Railways*. London: Shadow Strategic Rail Authority.

Tirole, J. 2001. "Corporate Governance." *Econometrica* 69, no. 1:1–35.

Tittenbrun, J. 1996. *Private versus Public Enterprise—In Search of the Economic Rationale for Privatisation*. London: Janus.

Tomlinson, J. 1994. *Government and Enterprises since 1900: The Changing Problem of Efficiency*. Oxford: Clarendon.

Toninelli, P., ed. 2000. *The Rise and Fall of State-Owned Enterprises in the Western World*. Cambridge: Cambridge University Press.

Trevelyan, G. M. [1942] 1959. *A Shortened History of England*. Middlesex, England: Penguin.

Turk, J. 2002. "British Telecommunications PLC: Privatisation and the Dynamics of Corporate and Industrial Culture." Paper presented at the First Milan European Economy Workshop, University of Milan, Milan, June.

UIC Statistics Centre (Union International of Railways). 1999. *Railway Statistics Synopsis*. Paris: UIC.

Vass, P., ed. 1997. *Regulatory Review 1997*. London: Chartered Institute of Public Finance and Accountancy/Centre for the Study of Regulated Industries.

Veljanovski, C. 1987. *Selling the State: Privatization in Britain*. London: Wedenfeld and Nicolson.

Veljanovski, C. 1991. *Regulators and the Market: An Assessment of the Growth of Regulation in the UK*. London: Institute of Economic Affairs.

Veljanovski, C. 1993. *The Future of Industry Regulation in the UK: A Report of an Independent Inquiry*. London: European Policy Forum.

Vickers, J., and G. Yarrow. 1988a. *Privatization: An Economic Analysis*. Cambridge, MA: MIT Press.

Vickers, J., and G. Yarrow. 1988b. "Regulation of Privatised Firms in Britain, Privatisation and Regulation." *European Economic Review* 32, nos. 2–3:465–472.

Vickers, J., and G. Yarrow. 1990. "Regulation of Privatised Firms in Britain." In *Privatisation and Deregulation in Canada and Britain*, ed. J. J. Richardson, 221–228. Aldershot, U.K.: Institute for Research on Public Policy.

Villalonga, B. 2000. "Privatization and Efficiency: Differentiating Ownership Effects from Political, Organizational, and Dynamic Effects." *Journal of Economic Behavior & Organization* 42:43–74.

Vogelsang, I., P. L. Jones, and P. Tandon (with M. Abdala and C. Doyle). 1994. "British Telecom." In A. Galal, L. Jones, P. Tandon, and I. Vogelsang, *Welfare Consequences of Selling Public Enterprises: An Empirical Analysis*, 51–106. New York: Oxford University Press.

Waddams Price, C. 1997. Undue Discrimination and Cross-Subsidies: Price Structures in UK Utilities. *Utility Law Review* 8, no. 5 (September–October): 91–200.

Waddams Price, C. 2002. "The Impact of Competition on British Consumers." Paper presented at the First Milan European Economy Workshop, University of Milan, Milan, June.

Waddams Price, C., and T. Weyman-Jones. 1993. "Malmquist Indices of Productivity Change in the UK Gas Industry before and after Privatisation." *Applied Economics* 28, no. 1:29–39.

Waldron, J. 1990. *The Right to Private Property*. Oxford: Oxford University Press.

Wallis, K. F. 1987. *Models of UK Economy: A Fourth Review by the ESRC Macroeconomic Modelling Bureau*. Oxford: Oxford University Press.

Walters, A. 1989. "Privatization in Britain: Comment." In *Privatization and State-Owned Enterprises: Lessons from the United States, Great Britain and Canada*, ed. P. MacAvoy et al. Dordrecht: Kluwer.

Waterson, M. 1992. "Privatization and the British Post Office." *International Review of Applied Economics* 6, no. 2:152–165.

Welsby, J., and A. Nichols. 1999. "The Privatization of Britain's Railways: An Inside View." *Journal of Transport Economics and Policy* 33, no. 1:55–76.

White, P. 1990. "Bus Deregulation: A Welfare Balance Sheet." *Journal of Transport of Economics and Policy* 24:311–332.

Worcester, R. 1994. "Public Opinion and Privatisation: Lessons from the British Experience." *European Business Journal* 6, no. 1:39–44.

Wright, M., R. S. Thompson, and K. Robbie. 1989. "Privatisation via Management and Employee Buyouts: Analysis and U.K. Experience." *Annals of Public and Co-operative Economy* 60, no. 4:399–429.

Wright, M., R. S. Thompson, and K. Robbie. 1994. "Management Buy-Outs and Privatisation." In *Privatisation and Economic Performance*, ed. M. Bishop, J. Kay, and C. Mayer. Oxford: Oxford University Press.

Yarrow, G. 1986. "Privatization in Theory and Practice." *Economic Policy* 2:324–377.

Yarrow, G. 1989. "Privatization and Economic Performance in Britain." *Carnegie-Rochester Conference Series on Public Policy* 31:303–344.

Yarrow, G. 1992. *British Electricity Prices since Privatisation*. Oxford: Regulatory Policy Institute.

Yarrow, G. 1993. "Privatization in the UK." In *Constraints and Impacts of Privatization*, ed. V. V. Ramanadham, 64–80. London: Routledge.

Yarrow, G., and P. Jasinsk, eds. 1999. *Privatization. Critical Perspectives on the World Economy*. 4 vols. London: Routledge.

Yergin, D., and J. Stanislaw. 1998. *The Commanding Heights: The Battle between Government and the Marketplace That Is Remaking the Modern World*. New York: Simon & Schuster.

Index